The Unified Modeling Language Reference Manual

The Addison-Wesley Object Technology Series

Grady Booch, Ivar Jacobson, and James Rumbaugh, Series Editors

For more information check out the series web site [http://www.awl.com /cseng/otseries/] as well as the pages on each book [http://www.awl.com/cseng/I-S-B-N/] (I-S-B-N represents the actual ISBN, including dashes).

David Bellin and Susan Suchman Simone, *The CRC Card Book*, ISBN 0-201-89535-8

Robert V. Binder, *Testing Object-Oriented Systems: Models, Patterns, and Tools*, ISBN 0-201-80938-9

Bob Blakley, *CORBA Security: An Introduction to Safe Computing with Objects*, ISBN 0-201-32565-9

Grady Booch, *Object Solutions: Managing the Object-Oriented Project*, ISBN 0-8053-0594-7

Grady Booch, *Object-Oriented Analysis and Design with Applications, Second Edition*, ISBN 0-8053-5340-2

Grady Booch, James Rumbaugh, and Ivar Jacobson, *The Unified Modeling Language User Guide*, ISBN 0-201-57168-4

Don Box, *Essential COM*, ISBN 0-201-63446-5

Don Box, Keith Brown, Tim Ewald, and Chris Sells, *Effective COM: 50 Ways to Improve Your COM and MTS-based Applications*, ISBN 0-201-37968-6

Alistair Cockburn, *Surviving Object-Oriented Projects: A Manager's Guide*, ISBN 0-201-49834-0

Dave Collins, *Designing Object-Oriented User Interfaces*, ISBN 0-8053-5350-X

Jim Conallen, *Building Web Applications with UML*, ISBN 0-201-61577-0

Bruce Powel Douglass, *Doing Hard Time: Designing and Implementing Embedded Systems with UML*, ISBN 0-201-49837-5

Bruce Powel Douglass, *Real-Time UML, Second Edition: Developing Efficient Objects for Embedded Systems*, ISBN 0-201-65784-8

Desmond F. D'Souza and Alan Cameron Wills, *Objects, Components, and Frameworks with UML: The Catalysis Approach*, ISBN 0-201-31012-0

Martin Fowler, *Analysis Patterns: Reusable Object Models*, ISBN 0-201-89542-0

Martin Fowler, *Refactoring: Improving the Design of Existing Code*, ISBN 0-201-48567-2

Martin Fowler with Kendall Scott, *UML Distilled, Second Edition: Applying the Standard Object Modeling Language*, ISBN 0-201-65783-X

Peter Heinckiens, *Building Scalable Database Applications: Object-Oriented Design, Architectures, and Implementations*, ISBN 0-201-31013-9

Christine Hofmeister, Robert Nord, Soni Dilip, *Applied Software Architecture*, ISBN 0-201-32571-3

Ivar Jacobson, Grady Booch, and James Rumbaugh, *The Unified Software Development Process*, ISBN 0-201-57169-2

Ivar Jacobson, Magnus Christerson, Patrik Jonsson, and Gunnar Overgaard, *Object-Oriented Software Engineering: A Use Case Driven Approach*, ISBN 0-201-54435-0

Ivar Jacobson, Maria Ericsson, and Agneta Jacobson, *The Object Advantage: Business Process Reengineering with Object Technology,* ISBN 0-201-42289-1

Ivar Jacobson, Martin Griss, and Patrik Jonsson, *Software Reuse: Architecture, Process and Organization for Business Success,* ISBN 0-201-92476-5

David Jordan, *C++ Object Databases: Programming with the ODMG Standard*, ISBN 0-201-63488-0

Philippe Kruchten, *The Rational Unified Process: An Introduction,* ISBN 0-201-60459-0

Wilf LaLonde, *Discovering Smalltalk*, ISBN 0-8053-2720-7

Dean Leffingwell and Don Widrig, *Managing Software Requirements: A Unified Approach*, ISBN 0-201-61593-2

Chris Marshall, *Enterprise Modeling with UML: Designing Successful Software through Business Analysis*, ISBN 0-201-43313-3

Lockheed Martin Advanced Concepts Center and Rational Software Corporation, *Succeeding with the Booch and OMT Methods: A Practical Approach*, ISBN 0-8053-2279-5

Thomas Mowbray and William Ruh, *Inside CORBA: Distributed Object Standards and Applications*, ISBN 0-201-89540-4

Bernd Oestereich, *Developing Software with UML: Object-Oriented Analysis and Design in Practice*, ISBN 0-201-39826-5

Meilir Page-Jones, *Fundamentals of Object-Oriented Design in UML*, ISBN 0-201-69946-X

Ira Pohl, *Object-Oriented Programming Using C++, Second Edition,* ISBN 0-201-89550-1

Rob Pooley and Perdita Stevens, *Using UML: Software Engineering with Objects and Components*, ISBN 0-201-36067-5

Terry Quatrani, *Visual Modeling with Rational Rose 2000 and UML,* ISBN 0-201-69961-3

Brent E. Rector and Chris Sells, *ATL Internals*, ISBN 0-201-69589-8

Paul R. Reed, Jr., *Developing Applications with Visual Basic and UML*, ISBN 0-201-61579-7

Doug Rosenberg with Kendall Scott, *Use Case Driven Object Modeling with UML: A Practical Approach*, ISBN 0-201-43289-7

Walker Royce, *Software Project Management: A Unified Framework,* ISBN 0-201-30958-0

William Ruh, Thomas Herron, and Paul Klinker, *IIOP Complete: Middleware Interoperability and Distributed Object Standards*, ISBN 0-201-37925-2

James Rumbaugh, Ivar Jacobson, and Grady Booch, *The Unified Modeling Language Reference Manual*, ISBN 0-201-30998-X

Geri Schneider and Jason P. Winters, *Applying Use Cases: A Practical Guide*, ISBN 0-201-30981-5

Yen-Ping Shan and Ralph H. Earle, *Enterprise Computing with Objects: From Client/Server Environments to the Internet*, ISBN 0-201-32566-7

David N. Smith, *IBM Smalltalk: The Language*, ISBN 0-8053-0908-X

Daniel Tkach, Walter Fang, and Andrew So, *Visual Modeling Technique: Object Technology Using Visual Programming*, ISBN 0-8053-2574-3

Daniel Tkach and Richard Puttick, *Object Technology in Application Development, Second Edition*, ISBN 0-201-49833-2

Jos Warmer and Anneke Kleppe, *The Object Constraint Language: Precise Modeling with UML*, ISBN 0-201-37940-6

The Unified Modeling Language Reference Manual

James Rumbaugh
Ivar Jacobson
Grady Booch

ADDISON-WESLEY

An imprint of Addison Wesley Longman, Inc.

Reading, Massachusetts • Harlow, England • Menlo Park, California
Berkeley, California • Don Mills, Ontario • Sydney
Bonn • Amsterdam • Tokyo • Mexico City

Many of the designations used by manufacturers and sellers to distinguish their products are claimed as trademarks. Where those designations appear in this book and Addison-Wesley was aware of a trademark claim, the designations have been printed in initial caps or all caps.

Unified Modeling Language, UML, and the UML cube logo are trademarks of the Object Management Group. Some material in this book is derived from the Object Management Group UML Specification documentation. Used by permission of the Object Management Group.

The authors and publisher have taken care in the preparation of this book but make no expressed or implied warranty of any kind and assume no responsibility for errors or omissions. No liability is assumed for incidental or consequential damages in connection with or arising out of the use of the information or programs contained herein.

The publisher offers discounts on this book when ordered in quantity for special sales. For more information, please contact:
> AWL Direct Sales
> Addison Wesley Longman, Inc.
> One Jacob Way
> Reading, Massachusetts 01867
> (781) 944-3700
Visit AW on the Web: www.awl.com/cseng/

Library of Congress Cataloging-in-Publication Data
Rumbaugh, James.
    The unified modeling language reference manual / James Rumbaugh, Ivar Jacobson, Grady Booch.
        p. cm. — (The Addison-Wesley object technology series)
    Includes bibliographical references and index.
    ISBN 0-201-30998-X
    1. Computer software—Development. 2. UML (Computer science) I. Jacobson, Ivar. II. Booch, Grady.
III. Title. IV. Series.
QA76.76.D47R86 1999
005.1—dc21   98-33392
                                                                                   CIP

Executive Editor: J. Carter Shanklin   Project Editor: Krysia Bebick
Editorial Assistant: Kristin Erickson   Production Manager: Jacquelyn Young
Copy Editor: Arlene Richman   Compositor: James Rumbaugh
Cover Designer: Simone R. Payment

Text printed on recycled and acid-free paper.

ISBN 0-13-087014-5
Text printed on recycled and acid-free paper.
1 2 3 4 5 MA 02 01 00
First Printing February 2000

For Madeline, Nick and Alex

—Jim

Contents

Part 2: UML Concepts

Part 4: Appendices

Preface

Goals

This book is intended to be a complete and useful reference to the Unified Modeling Language (UML) for the developer, architect, project manager, system engineer, programmer, analyst, contracting officer, customer, and anyone else who needs to specify, design, build, or understand complex software systems. It provides a full reference to the concepts and constructs of UML, including their semantics, syntax, notation, and purpose. It is organized to be a convenient but thorough reference for the working professional developer. It also attempts to provide additional detail about issues that may not be clear from the standards documents and to provide a rationale for many decisions that went into the UML.

This book is not intended as a guide to the UML standards documents or to the internal structure of the metamodel contained in them. The details of the metamodel are of interest to methodologists and UML tool builders, but most other developers have little need for the arcane details of the Object Management Group (OMG) documents. This book provides all the details of UML that most developers need; in many cases, it makes information explicit that must otherwise be sought between the lines of the original documents. For those who do wish to consult the source documents, they are included on the accompanying CD.

This book is intended as a reference for those who already have some understanding of object-oriented technology. For beginners, the original books by us and by other authors are listed in the bibliography; although some of the notation has changed, books such as [Rumbaugh-91], [Booch-94], [Jacobson-92], and [Meyer-88] provide an introduction to object-oriented concepts that is still valid and therefore unnecessary to duplicate here. For a tutorial introduction to UML that shows how to model a number of common problems, see *The Unified Modeling Language User Guide* [Booch-99]. Those who already know an object-oriented method, such as OMT, Booch, Objectory, Coad-Yourdon, or Fusion, should be able to read the *Reference Manual* and use it to understand UML notation and semantics; to learn UML quickly, they may nevertheless find it useful to read the *User Guide*.

UML does not require a particular development process, and this book does not describe one. Although UML may be used with a variety of development processes, it was designed to support an iterative, incremental, use-case–driven process with a strong architectural focus—the kind we feel is most suitable for the development of modern, complex systems. *The Unified Software Development Process* [Jacobson-99] describes the kind of process we believe complements the UML and best supports software development.

Outline of the Book

The UML Reference Manual is organized into three parts: an overview of UML history and of modeling, a survey of UML concepts, and an alphabetical encyclopedia of UML terms and concepts.

The first part is a survey of UML—its history, purposes, and uses—to help you understand the origin of UML and the need it tries to fill.

The second part is a brief survey of UML views so that you can put all the concepts into perspective. The survey provides a brief overview of the views UML supports and shows how the various constructs work together. This part begins with an example that walks through various UML views and then contains one chapter for each kind of UML view. This survey is not intended as a full tutorial or as a comprehensive description of concepts. It serves mainly to summarize and relate the various UML concepts and provides starting points for detailed readings in the encyclopedia.

The third part contains the reference material organized for easy access to each topic. The bulk of the book is an alphabetical encyclopedia of all of the concepts and constructs in UML. Each UML term of any importance has its own entry in the encyclopedia. The encyclopedia is meant to be complete; therefore, everything in the concept overview in Part 2 is repeated in more detail in the encyclopedia. The same or similar information has sometimes been included in multiple encyclopedia articles so that the reader can conveniently find it.

The reference part also contains an alphabetic list of UML standard elements. A standard element is a feature predefined using the UML extensibility mechanisms. The standard elements are extensions that are felt to be widely useful.

Appendices show the UML metamodel, a summary of UML notation, and some standard sets of extensions for particular domains. There is a brief bibliography of major object-oriented books, but no attempt has been made to include a comprehensive citation of sources of ideas for UML or other approaches. Many of the books in the bibliography contain excellent lists of references to books and journal articles for those interested in tracking the development of the ideas.

Encyclopedia Article Formatting Conventions

The encyclopedia part of the book is organized as an alphabetical list of entries, each describing one concept in some detail. The articles represent a flat list of UML concepts at various conceptual levels. A high-level concept typically contains a summary of its subordinate concepts, each of which is fully described in a separate article. The articles are highly cross-referenced. This flat encyclopedia organization permits the description of each concept to be presented at a fairly uniform level of detail, without constant shifts in level for the nested descriptions that would be necessary for a sequential presentation. The hypertext format of the document should also make it convenient for reference. It should not be necessary to use the index much; instead go directly to the main article in the encyclopedia for any term of interest and follow cross-references. This format is not necessarily ideal for learning the language; beginners are advised to read the overview description of UML found in Part 2 or to read introductory books on UML, such as the *UML User Guide* [Booch-99].

Encyclopedic articles have the following divisions, although not all divisions appear in all articles.

Brief definition

The name of the concept appears in boldface, set to the left of the body of the article. A brief definition follows in normal type. This definition is intended to capture the main idea of the concept, but it may simplify the concept for concise presentation. Refer to the main article for precise semantics.

Semantics

This section contains a detailed description of the meaning of the concept, including constraints on its uses and its execution consequences. Notation is not covered in this section, although examples use the appropriate notation. General semantics are given first. For concepts with subordinate structural properties, a list of the properties follows the general semantics, often under the subheading *Structure*. In most cases, the properties appear as a table in alphabetical order by property name, with the description of each property on the right. If a property has a brief enumerated list of choices, they may be given as an indented sublist. In more complicated cases, the property is given its own article to avoid excessive nesting. When properties require more explanation than permitted by a table, they are described in normal text with run-in headers in boldface italics. In certain cases, the main concept is best described under several logical subdivisions rather than one list. In such cases, additional sections follow or replace the *Structure* subsection. Although several organizational mechanisms have been used, their structure should be obvious to the reader.

Notation

This section contains a detailed description of the notation for the concept. Usually, the notation section has a form that parallels the preceding semantics section, which it references, and it often has the same divisions. The notation section usually includes one or more diagrams to illustrate the concept. The actual notation is printed in black ink. To help the reader understand the notation, many diagrams contain annotations in blue ink. Any material in blue is commentary and is not part of the actual notation.

Example

This subsection contains examples of notation or illustrations of the use of the concept. Frequently, the examples also treat complicated or potentially confusing situations.

Discussion

This section describes subtle issues, clarifies tricky and frequently confused points, and contains other details that would otherwise digress from the more descriptive semantics section. A minority of articles have a discussion section.

This section also explains certain design decisions that were made in the development of the UML, particularly those that may appear counterintuitive or that have provoked strong controversy. Only a fraction of articles have this section. Simple differences in taste are generally not covered.

Standard elements

This section lists standard constraints, tags, stereotypes, and other conventions that are predefined for the concept in the article. This section is fairly rare.

Syntax Conventions

Syntax expressions. Syntax expressions are given in a modified BNF format in a sans serif font. To avoid confusing literal values and syntax productions, literal values that appear in the target sentence are printed in black ink, and the names of syntax variables and special syntax operators are printed in blue ink.

Text printed in black ink appears in that form in the target string.

Punctuation marks (they are always printed in black) appear in the target string.

Any word printed in blue ink represents a variable that must be replaced by another string or another syntax production in the target string. Words may contain letters and hyphens. If a blue word is italicized or underlined, the actual replacement string must be italicized or underlined.

In code examples, comments are printed in blue ink to the right of the code text. Subscripts and overbars are used as syntax operators as follows:

$expression_{opt}$	The expression is optional.
$expression_{list,}$	A comma-separated list of the expression may appear. If there is zero or one repetition, there is no separator. Each repetition may have a separate substitution. If a different punctuation mark than a comma appears in the subscript, then it is the separator.
$\overline{= expression}_{opt}$	An overbar ties together two or more terms that are considered a unit for optional or repeated occurrences. In this example, the equal sign and the expression form one unit that may be omitted or included. The overbar is unnecessary if there is only one term.

Two-level nesting is avoided.

Literal strings. In running text, language keywords, names of model elements, and sample strings from models are shown in a sans serif font.

Diagrams. In diagrams, blue text and arrows are annotations, that is, explanations of the diagram notation that do not appear in an actual diagram. Any text and symbols in black ink are actual diagram notation.

CD

This book is accompanied by a CD containing the full text of the book in Adobe Reader (PDF) format. Using Adobe Reader, the viewer can easily search the book for a word or phrase. The CD version also contains a clickable table of contents, index, Adobe Reader thumbnails, and extensive hot links in the body of the articles. Simply click on one of the links to jump to the encyclopedia article for the word or phrase.

The CD also contains the full text of the OMG UML specifications, included by the permission of the Object Management Group.

We feel that this CD will be a useful on-line reference to UML for advanced users.

For More Information

Additional source files and up-to-date information on further work on UML and related topics can be found on the World Wide Web sites www.rational.com and www.omg.org.

Acknowledgments

We want to thank many people who made the UML possible. First, we must thank Rational Software Corporation, especially Mike Devlin and Paul Levy, who had the vision to bring us together, start the unification work, and stay the course during the four years that were required to bring the work to successful completion. We also thank the Object Management Group for providing the framework that brought together many diverse viewpoints and merged them together into a broad consensus that was much greater than any one contribution.

We particularly want to thank Cris Kobryn, who led the technical team that prepared the UML standard and who managed to achieve a consensus among an extremely strong-willed group of persons (and the three of us were not the least of his problems). His diplomatic skills and technical balance kept the UML effort from foundering amid many differences of opinion. Cris also reviewed the book and provided countless useful suggestions.

We would like to thank Gunnar Övergaard for reviewing the book thoroughly, as well as for his perseverance in completing many sections of the UML documents that were not fun to write but were necessary to its formal correctness.

We want to thank Karin Palmkvist for an exceedingly thorough review that uncovered many bugs in technical content, as well as many flaws in grammar, phrasing, and presentation.

We would also like to thank Mike Blaha, Conrad Bock, Perry Cole, Bruce Douglass, Martin Fowler, Eran Gery, Pete McBreen, Guus Ramackers, Tom Schultz, Ed Seidewitz, and Bran Selic for their helpful reviews.

Most of all, we want to thank the scores or even hundreds of persons who contributed to the community of ideas from which UML was drawn—ideas in object-oriented technology, software methodology, programming languages, user interfaces, visual programming, and numerous other areas of computer science. It is impossible to list them all, or indeed to track even the major chains of influence, without a major scholarly effort, and this is an engineering book, not a historical review. Many are well known, but many good ideas came from those who did not have the good fortune to be widely recognized.

On a more personal note, I wish to thank Professor Jack Dennis, who inspired my work in modeling and the work of many other students, more than twenty-five years ago. The ideas from his Computations Structures Group at MIT have borne much fruit, and they are not the least of the sources of UML. I must also thank Mary Loomis and Ashwin Shah, with whom I developed the original ideas of OMT, and my former colleagues at GE R&D Center, Mike Blaha, Bill Premerlani, Fred Eddy, and Bill Lorensen, with whom I wrote the OMT book.

Finally, without the patience of my wife, Madeline, and my sons, Nick and Alex, there would have been no UML and no book about it.

James Rumbaugh
Cupertino, California
November 1998

Part 1: Background

This part describes general principles underlying UML, including the nature and purpose of modeling and those aspects of the UML that pervade all functional areas.

UML Overview

This chapter is a quick overview of UML and what it is good for.

Brief Summary of UML

The Unified Modeling Language (UML) is a general-purpose visual modeling language that is used to specify, visualize, construct, and document the artifacts of a software system. It captures decisions and understanding about systems that must be constructed. It is used to understand, design, browse, configure, maintain, and control information about such systems. It is intended for use with all development methods, lifecycle stages, application domains, and media. The modeling language is intended to unify past experience about modeling techniques and to incorporate current software best practices into a standard approach. UML includes semantic concepts, notation, and guidelines. It has static, dynamic, environmental, and organizational parts. It is intended to be supported by interactive visual modeling tools that have code generators and report writers. The UML specification does not define a standard process but is intended to be useful with an iterative development process. It is intended to support most existing object-oriented development processes.

The UML captures information about the static structure and dynamic behavior of a system. A system is modeled as a collection of discrete objects that interact to perform work that ultimately benefits an outside user. The static structure defines the kinds of objects important to a system and to its implementation, as well as the relationships among the objects. The dynamic behavior defines the history of objects over time and the communications among objects to accomplish goals. Modeling a system from several separate but related viewpoints permits it to be understood for different purposes.

The UML also contains organizational constructs for arranging models into packages that permit software teams to partition large systems into workable pieces, to understand and control dependencies among the packages, and to manage the versioning of model units in a complex development environment. It contains constructs for representing implementation decisions and for organizing run-time elements into components.

UML is not a programming language. Tools can provide code generators from UML into a variety of programming languages, as well as construct reverse-engineered models from existing programs. The UML is not a highly formal language intended for theorem proving. There are a number of such languages, but they are not easy to understand or to use for most purposes. The UML is a general-purpose modeling language. For specialized domains, such as GUI layout, VLSI circuit design, or rule-based artificial intelligence, a more specialized tool with a special language might be appropriate. UML is a discrete modeling language. It is not intended to model continuous systems such as those found in engineering and physics. UML is intended to be a universal general-purpose modeling language for discrete systems such as those made of software, firmware, or digital logic.

UML History

UML was developed in an effort to simplify and consolidate the large number of object-oriented development methods that had emerged.

Object-oriented development methods

Development methods for traditional programming languages, such as Cobol and Fortran, emerged in the 1970s and became widespread in the 1980s. Foremost among them was Structured Analysis and Structured Design [Yourdon-79] and its variants, such as Real-Time Structured Design [Ward-85] and others. These methods, originally developed by Constantine, DeMarco, Mellor, Ward, Yourdon, and others, achieved some penetration into the large system area, especially for government-contracted systems in the aerospace and defense fields, in which contracting officers insisted on an organized development process and ample documentation of the system design and implementation. The results were not always as good as hoped for—many computer-aided software engineering (CASE) systems were little more than report generators that extracted designs after the implementation was complete—but the methods included good ideas that were occasionally used effectively in the construction of large systems. Commercial applications were more reluctant to adopt large CASE systems and development methods. Most businesses developed software internally for their own needs, without the adversarial relationship between customer and contractors that characterized large government projects. Commercial systems were perceived to be simpler, whether or not this was actually true, and there was less need for review by outside organizations.

The first object-oriented language is generally acknowledged to be Simula-67, developed in 1967. This language never had a significant following, although it greatly influenced the developers of several of the later object-oriented languages. The object-oriented movement became active with the widespread availability of Smalltalk in the early 1980s, followed by other object-oriented languages, such as Objective C, C++, Eiffel, and CLOS. The actual usage of object-oriented languages was limited at first, but object-orientation attracted a lot of attention. About five years after Smalltalk became widely known, the first object-oriented development methods were published by Shlaer/Mellor [Shlaer-88] and Coad/Yourdon [Coad-91], followed closely by books by Booch [Booch-91], Rumbaugh/Blaha/ Premerlani/Eddy/Lorensen [Rumbaugh-91], and Wirfs-Brock/Wilkerson/Wiener [Wirfs-Brock-90] (note that copyright years often begin in July of the previous calendar year). These books, added to earlier programming-language design books by Goldberg/Robson [Goldberg-83], Cox [Cox-86], and Meyer [Meyer-88], started the field of object-oriented methodology. The first phase was complete by the end of 1990. The Objectory book [Jacobson-92] was published slightly later, based on work that had appeared in earlier papers. This book took a somewhat different approach, with its focus on use cases and the development process.

Over the next five years, a plethora of books on object-oriented methodology appeared, each with its own set of concepts, definitions, notation, terminology, and process. Some added useful new concepts, but overall there was a great similarity among the concepts proposed by different authors. Many of the newer books started from one or more of the existing methods and made extensions or minor changes. The original authors were not idle either; most of them updated their original work, often incorporating good ideas from other authors. In general, there emerged a pool of common core concepts, together with a wide variety of concepts embraced by one or two authors but not widely used. Even in the core concepts, there were minor discrepancies among methods that made detailed comparison somewhat treacherous, especially for the casual reader.

Unification effort

There were some early attempts to unify concepts among methods. A notable example was Fusion by Coleman and his colleagues [Coleman-94], which included concepts from OMT [Rumbaugh-91], Booch [Booch-91], and CRC [Wirfs-Brock-90]. As it did not involve the original authors, it must be regarded as another new method rather than as a replacement of several existing methods. The first successful attempt to combine and replace existing approaches came when Rumbaugh joined Booch at Rational Software Corporation in 1994. They began combining the concepts from the OMT and Booch methods, resulting in a first proposal in

1995. At that time, Jacobson also joined Rational and began working with Booch and Rumbaugh. Their joint work was called the Unified Modeling Language (UML). The momentum gained by having the authors of three of the top methods working together to unify their approaches shifted the balance in the object-oriented methodology field, where there had previously been little incentive (or at least little willingness) for methodologists to abandon some of their own concepts to achieve harmony.

In 1996, the Object Management Group (OMG) issued a request for proposals for a standard approach to object-oriented modeling. UML authors Booch, Jacobson, and Rumbaugh began working with methodologists and developers from other companies to produce a proposal attractive to the membership of OMG, as well as a modeling language that would be widely accepted by tool makers, methodologists, and developers who would be the eventual users. Several competing efforts also were started. Eventually, all the proposals coalesced in the final UML proposal that was submitted to the OMG in September 1997. The final product is a collaboration among many people. We began the UML effort and contributed a few good ideas, but the ideas in it are the product of many minds.

Standardization

The Unified Modeling Language was adopted unanimously by the membership of the OMG as a standard in November 1997 [UML-98]. The OMG assumed responsibility for the further development of the UML standard. Even before final adoption, a number of books were published outlining the highlights of the UML. Many tool vendors announced support or planned support for the UML, and several methodologists announced that they would use UML notation for further work. The emergence of the UML appears to be attractive to the general computing public because it consolidates the experiences of many authors with an official status that will reduce gratuitous divergence among tools. We hope that standardization will encourage both widespread use of object-oriented modeling among developers and a robust market in support tools and training, now that neither users nor vendors have to guess which approaches to use and support.

Core team

The following persons were the core development team of the UML proposal or served on the Revision Task Force:

Data Access Corporation: Tom Digre
DHR Technologies: Ed Seidewitz
HP: Martin Griss
IBM: Steve Brodsky, Steve Cook, Jos Warmer

I-Logix: Eran Gery, David Harel

ICON Computing: Desmond D'Souza

IntelliCorp and James Martin & Co.: Conrad Bock, James Odell

MCI Systemhouse: Cris Kobryn, Joaquin Miller

ObjecTime: John Hogg, Bran Selic

Oracle: Guus Ramackers

Platinum Technology: Dilhar DeSilva

Rational Software: Grady Booch, Ed Eykholt, Ivar Jacobson,
　　　Gunnar Övergaard, Karin Palmkvist, James Rumbaugh

SAP: Oliver Wiegert

SOFTEAM: Philippe Desfray

Sterling Software: John Cheesman, Keith Short

Taskon: Trygve Reenskaug

Unisys: Sridhar Iyengar, GK Khalsa

What does *unified* mean?

The word *unified* has the following relevant meanings for UML.

Across historical methods and notations. The UML combines the commonly accepted concepts from many object-oriented methods, selecting a clear definition for each concept, as well as a notation and terminology. The UML can represent most existing models as well as or better than the original methods can.

Across the development lifecycle. The UML is seamless from requirements to deployment. The same set of concepts and notation can be used in different stages of development and even mixed within a single model. It is unnecessary to translate from one stage to another. This seamlessness is critical for iterative, incremental development.

Across application domains. The UML is intended to model most application domains, including those involving systems that are large, complex, real-time, distributed, data or computation intensive, among other properties. There may be specialized areas in which a special-purpose language is more useful, but UML is intended to be as good as or better than any other general-purpose modeling language for most application areas.

Across implementation languages and platforms. The UML is intended to be usable for systems implemented in various implementation languages and platforms, including programming languages, databases, 4GLs, organization documents, firmware, and so on. The front-end work should be identical or similar in all cases, while the back-end work will differ somewhat for each medium.

Across development processes. The UML is a modeling language, not a description of a detailed development process. It is intended to be usable as the modeling language underlying most existing or new development processes, just as a general-purpose programming language can be used in many styles of programming. It is particularly intended to support the iterative, incremental style of development that we recommend.

Across internal concepts. In constructing the UML metamodel, we made a deliberate effort to discover and represent underlying relationships among various concepts, trying to capture modeling concepts in a broad way applicable to many known and unknown situations. This process led to a better understanding of the concepts and a more general applicability of them. This was not the original purpose of the unification work, but it was one of the most important results.

Goals of UML

There were a number of goals behind the development of the UML. First and most important, UML is a general-purpose modeling language that all modelers can use. It is nonproprietary and based on common agreement by much of the computing community. It is meant to include the concepts of the leading methods so that it can be used as their modeling language. At the very least, it was intended to supersede the models of OMT, Booch, and Objectory, as well as those of other participants of the proposal. It was intended to be as familiar as possible; whenever possible, we used notation from OMT, Booch, Objectory, and other leading methods. It is meant to support good practices for design, such as encapsulation, separation of concerns, and capture of the intent of a model construct. It is intended to address current software development issues, such as large scale, distribution, concurrency, patterns, and team development.

UML is not intended to be a complete development method. It does not include a step-by-step development process. We believe that a good development process is crucial to the success of a software development effort, and we propose one in a companion book [Jacobson-99]. It is important to realize that UML and a process for using UML are two separate things. UML is intended to support all, or at least most, of the existing development processes. UML includes all the concepts that we believe are necessary to support a modern iterative process based on building a strong architecture to solve user-case–driven requirements.

A final goal of UML was to be as simple as possible while still being capable of modeling the full range of practical systems that need to be built. UML needs to be expressive enough to handle all the concepts that arise in a modern system, such as concurrency and distribution, as well as software engineering mechanisms, such as encapsulation and components. It must be a universal language, like any general-purpose programming language. Unfortunately, that means that it cannot be small if we want it to handle things other than toy systems. Modern languages and modern operating systems are more complicated than those of 40 years ago because we expect much more of them. UML has several kinds of models; it is not something you can master in one day. It is more complicated than some of its antecedents because it is intended to be more comprehensive. But you don't have to learn it all at once, any more than you would a programming language, an operating system, or a complex user application.

UML Concept Areas

UML concepts and models can be grouped into the following concept areas.

Static structure. Any precise model must first define the universe of discourse, that is, the key concepts from the application, their internal properties, and their relationships to each other. This set of constructs is the static view. The application concepts are modeled as classes, each of which describes a set of discrete objects that hold information and communicate to implement behavior. The information they hold is modeled as attributes; the behavior they perform is modeled as operations. Several classes can share their common structure using generalization. A child class adds incremental structure and behavior to the structure and behavior that it obtains by inheritance from the common parent class. Objects also have run-time connections to other individual objects. Such object-to-object relationships are modeled as associations among classes. Some relationships among elements are grouped together as dependency relationships, including relationships for modeling shifts in levels of abstraction, binding of template parameters, granting of permission, and usage of one element by another. Other relationships include combination of use cases and flow of values. The static view is notated using class diagrams. The static view can be used to generate most data structure declarations in a program. There are several other kinds of elements in UML diagrams, such as interfaces, data types, use cases, and signals. Collectively, these are called classifiers, and they behave much like classes with certain restrictions on each kind of classifier.

Dynamic behavior. There are two ways to model behavior. One is the life history of one object as it interacts with the rest of the world; the other is the communication patterns of a set of connected objects as they interact to implement behavior. The view of an object in isolation is a state machine—a view of an object as it responds to events based on its current state, performs actions as part of its response, and transitions to a new state. State machines are displayed in statechart diagrams.

The view of a system of interacting objects is a collaboration, a context-dependent view of objects and their links to each other, together with the flow of messages between objects across data links. This viewpoint unifies data structure, control flow, and data flow in a single view. Collaborations and interactions are shown in sequence diagrams and collaboration diagrams. Guiding all the behavior views is a set of use cases, each a description of a slice of system functionality as visible to an actor, an external user of the system.

Implementation constructs. UML models are meant for both logical analysis and physical implementation. Certain constructs represent implementation items. A component is a physical, replaceable part of a system that conforms to and provides the realization of a set of interfaces. It is intended to be easily substitutable for other components that meet the same specification. A node is a run-time computing resource that defines a location. It can hold components and objects. The deployment view describes the configuration of nodes in a running system and the arrangement of components and objects on them, including possible migration of contents among nodes.

Model organization. Computers can deal with large flat models, but humans cannot. In a large system, the modeling information must be divided into coherent pieces so that teams can work on different parts concurrently. Even on a smaller system, human understanding requires the organization of model content into packages of modest size. Packages are general-purpose hierarchical organizational units of UML models. They can be used for storage, access control, configuration management, and constructing libraries that contain reusable model fragments. A dependency between packages summarizes the dependencies among the package contents. A dependency among packages can be imposed by the overall system architecture. Then the contents of the packages must conform to the package dependencies and to the imposed system architecture.

Extensibility mechanisms. No matter how complete the facilities in a language, people will want to make extensions. We have provided a limited extensibility capability within UML that we believe will accommodate most of the day-to-day needs for extensions, without requiring a change to the basic language. A stereotype is a new kind of model element with the same structure as an existing element, but with additional constraints, a different interpretation and icon, and different treatment by code generators and other back-end tools. A tagged value is an arbitrary tag-value pair of strings that can be attached to any kind of model element to hold arbitrary information, such as project management information, code generator guidance, and required values for stereotypes. The tag and the value are represented as strings. A constraint is a well-formedness condition expressed as a text string in some constraint language, such as a programming language, special constraint language, or natural language. UML includes a constraint language called OCL. As with any extensibility mechanism, these mechanisms must be used with care because of the risk of producing a private dialect unintelligible to others. But they can avoid the need for more radical changes.

Syntax of Expressions and Diagrams

This book contains expressions and diagrams that show examples of actual models, as well as syntax of expressions and annotations explaining the diagrams. To reduce the danger of confusing the explanations with the examples, certain formatting conventions have been used.

Within diagrams and text expressions, diagram fragments or literal text that would appear in the actual notation are shown in black in a sans serif typeface (Myriad). For example, a class name in black is a legal name that could appear in a model. A parenthesis in a syntax expression is a literal parenthesis that would appear in an actual expression; it is not part of the syntax machinery. For example:

Order . create (customer, amount)

Within running text, literal keywords from a model and the names of model elements are also shown in the Myriad font, such as **Order** or **customer**.

In a syntax expression, the names of syntactical units that are meant to be replaced by actual text expansions are shown in blue Myriad font, such as name. The appearance of black text in an expression represents a literal value that appears in the target notation. The use of italics or underlining means that the replacement text has the given property. For example:

name .operation (argument ,...)

object-name :class

In a syntax expression, a blue subscript and a blue overbar are used to denote certain syntactic properties.

expression$_{opt}$ The expression is optional.

expression$_{list,}$ A comma-separated list of the expression may appear. If there is zero or one repetition, there is no separator. Each repetition may have a separate substitution. If a different punctuation mark than a comma appears in the subscript, it is the separator.

$\overline{= \text{expression}}_{opt}$ An overbar ties together two or more terms that are considered a unit for optional or repeated occurrences. In this example, the equal sign and the expression form one unit that may be omitted or included. The overbar is unnecessary if there is only one term.

In a diagram, text and arrows in blue are annotations. They are not part of the actual notation but are intended as explanations. The symbols and text in black are part of the target notation.

2
The Nature and Purpose of Models

This chapter explains what models are, what they are good for, and how they are used. It also explains the various grades of models: ideal, partial, and tool-based.

What Is a Model?

A model is a representation in a certain medium of something in the same or another medium. The model captures the important aspects of the thing being modeled from a certain point of view and simplifies or omits the rest. Engineering, architecture, and many other creative fields use models.

A model is expressed in a medium that is convenient for working. Models of buildings may be drawings on paper, 3-D figures made of cardboard and papier-mâché, or finite-element equations in a computer. A construction model of a building shows the appearance of the building but can also be used to make engineering and cost calculations.

A model of a software system is made in a modeling language, such as UML. The model has both semantics and notation and can take various forms that include both pictures and text. The model is intended to be easier to use for certain purposes than the final system.

What Are Models For?

Models are used for several purposes.

To capture and precisely state requirements and domain knowledge so that all stakeholders may understand and agree on them. Various models of a building capture requirements about the appearance, traffic patterns, various kinds of utility services, strength against wind and earthquakes, cost, and many other things. Stakeholders include the architect, structural engineer, general contractor, various subcontractors, owner, renters, and the city.

Different models of a software system may capture requirements about its application domain, the ways users will use it, its breakdown into modules, common patterns used in its construction, and other things. Stakeholders include the architect, analysts, programmers, project manager, customers, funders, end users, and operators. Various kinds of UML models are used.

To think about the design of a system. An architect uses models on paper, on a computer, or as 3-D constructs to visualize and experiment with possible designs. The simplicity of creating and modifying small models permits creative thought and innovation at little cost.

A model of a software system helps developers explore several architectures and design solutions easily before writing code. A good modeling language allows the designer to get the overall architecture right before detailed design begins.

To capture design decisions in a mutable form separate from the requirements. One model of a building shows the external appearance agreed to with the customer. Another model shows the internal routing of wires, pipes, and ventilation ducts. There are many ways to implement these services. The final model shows a design that the architect believes is a good one. The customer may verify this information, but often customers are not concerned about the details, as long as they work.

One model of a software system can capture the external behavior of a system and the real-world domain information represented by the system. Another model shows the internal classes and operations that implement the external behavior. There are many ways to implement the behavior; the final design model shows one approach that the designer believes is a good one.

To generate usable work products. A model of a building can be used to generate various kinds of products. These include a bill of materials, a simulated animated walkthrough, a table of deflections at various wind speeds, and a visualization of strain at various points in the frame.

A model of a software system can be used to generate class declarations, procedure bodies, user interfaces, databases, scenarios of legal use, configuration scripts, and lists of race conditions.

To organize, find, filter, retrieve, examine, and edit information about large systems. A model of a building organizes information by service: structural, electrical, plumbing, ventilation, decoration, and so on. Unless the model is on a computer, however, finding things and modifying them are not so easy. If it is on a computer, changes can be made and recalled easily, and multiple designs can be easily explored while sharing some common elements.

A model of a software system organizes information into several views: static structure, state machines, interactions, requirements, and so on. Each view is a projection of the information in the complete model as selected for a purpose. Keeping a model of any size accurate is impossible without having an editing tool that manages the model. An interactive graphical model editor can present information in different formats, hide information that is unnecessary for a given purpose and show it again later, group related operations together, make changes to individual elements, as well as change groups of elements with one command, and so on.

To explore multiple solutions economically. The advantages and risks of different design methods for buildings may not be clear at first. For example, different substructures may interact in complicated ways that cannot be evaluated in an engineer's head. Models can explore the various designs and permit calculations of costs and risks before the actual building is constructed.

Models of a large software system permit several designs to be proposed and compared. The models are not constructed in full detail, of course, but even a rough model can expose many issues the final design must deal with. Modeling permits several designs to be considered, at a small cost of implementing any one design.

To master complex systems. An engineering model of a tornado approaching a building provides understanding that is not possible from a real-world building. A real tornado cannot be produced on demand, and it would destroy the measuring instruments, anyway. Many fast, small, or violent physical processes can now be understood using physical models.

A model of a large software system permits dealing with complexity that is too difficult to deal with directly. A model can abstract to a level that is comprehensible to humans, without getting lost in details. A computer can perform complicated analyses on a model in an effort to find possible trouble spots, such as timing errors and resource overruns. A model can determine the potential impact of a change before it is made, by exploring dependencies in the system. A model can also show how to restructure a system to reduce such effects.

Levels of Models

Models take on different forms for various purposes and appear at different levels of abstraction. The amount of detail in the model must be adapted to one of the following purposes.

Guides to the thought process. High-level models built early in a project serve to focus the thought process of the stakeholders and highlight options. They capture requirements and represent a starting point toward a system design. The early models help the originators explore possible options before converging on a system concept. As design progresses, the early models are replaced by more accurate models. There is no need to preserve every twist and turn of the early exploratory process. Its purpose is to produce ideas. The final "thinking models" should be preserved even after the focus shifts to design issues, however. Early models do not require the detail or precision of an implementation model, and they do not require a full range of implementation concepts. Such models use a subset of UML constructs, a more limited subset than later design models.

When an early model is a complete view of a system at a given precision—for example, an analysis model of what must be done—then it should be preserved when development shifts to the next stage. There is an important difference between adding detail (in which case, the chain of reasoning should be preserved) and the normal random-walk process of exploring many dead ends before arriving at the right solution. In the latter case, it is usually overwhelming and unnecessary to save the entire history except in extraordinary situations in which complete traceability is required.

Abstract specifications of the essential structure of a system. Models in the analysis or preliminary design stages focus on the key concepts and mechanisms of the eventual system. They correspond in certain ways with the final system. But details are missing from the model, which must be added explicitly during the design process. The purpose of the abstract models is to get the high-level pervasive issues correct before tackling the more localized details. These models are intended to be evolved into the final models by a careful process that guarantees that the final system correctly implements the intent of the earlier models. There must be traceability from these essential models to the full models; otherwise, there is no assurance that the final system correctly incorporates the key properties that the essential model sought to show. Essential models focus on semantic intent. They do not need the full range of implementation options. Indeed, low-level performance distinctions often obscure the logical semantics. The path from an essential model to a complete implementation model must be clear and straightforward, however, whether it is generated automatically by a code generator or evolved manually by a designer.

Full specifications of a final system. An implementation model includes enough information to build the system. It must include not only the logical semantics of the system and the algorithms, data structures, and mechanisms that ensure proper performance, but also organizational decisions about the system artifacts that are necessary for cooperative work by humans and processing by tools. This kind of model must include constructs for packaging the model for human understanding and for computer convenience. These are not properties of the target application itself. Rather, they are properties of the construction process.

Exemplars of typical or possible systems. Well-chosen examples can give insight to humans and can validate system specifications and implementations. Even a large collection of examples, however, necessarily falls short of a definitive description. Ultimately, we need models that specify the general case; that is what a program is, after all. Examples of typical data structures, interaction sequences, or object histories can help a human trying to understand a complicated situation, however. Examples must be used with some care. It is logically impossible to induce the general case from a set of examples, but well-chosen prototypes are the way most people think. An example model includes instances rather than general descriptors. It therefore tends to have a different feel than a generic descriptive model. Example models usually use only a subset of the UML constructs, those that deal with instances. Both descriptive models and exemplar models are useful in modeling a system.

Complete or partial descriptions of systems. A model can be a complete description of a single system with no outside references. More often, it is organized as a set of distinct, discrete units, each of which may be stored and manipulated separately as a part of the entire description. Such models have "loose ends" that must be bound to other models in a complete system. Because the pieces have coherence and meaning, they can be combined with other pieces in various ways to produce many different systems. Achieving reuse is an important goal of good modeling.

Models evolve over time. Models with greater degrees of detail are derived from more abstract models, and more concrete models are derived from more logical models. For example, a model might start as a high-level view of the entire system, with a few key services in brief detail and no embellishments. Over time, much more detail is added and variations are introduced. Also over time, the focus shifts from a front-end, user-centered logical view to a back-end, implementation-centered physical view. As the developers work with a system and understand it better, the model must be iterated at all levels to capture that understanding; it is impossible to understand a large system in a single, linear pass. There is no one "right" form for a model.

What Is in a Model?

Semantics and presentation. Models have two major aspects: semantic information (semantics) and visual presentation (notation).

The semantic aspect captures the meaning of an application as a network of logical constructs, such as classes, associations, states, use cases, and messages. Semantic model elements carry the meaning of the model—that is, they convey the semantics. The semantic modeling elements are used for code generation, validity checking, complexity metrics, and so on. The visual appearance is irrelevant to most tools that process models. The semantic information is often called *the model*. A semantic model has a syntactic structure, well-formedness rules, and execution dynamics. These aspects are often described separately (as in the UML definition documents), but they are tightly interrelated and part of a single coherent model.

The visual presentation shows semantic information in a form that can be seen, browsed, and edited by humans. Presentation elements carry the visual presentation of the model—that is, they show it in a form directly apprehensible by humans. They do not add meaning, but they do organize the presentation to emphasize the arrangement of the model in a usable way. They therefore guide human understanding of a model. Presentation elements derive their semantics from semantic model elements. But inasmuch as the layout of the diagrams is supplied by humans, presentation elements are not completely derivable from logical elements. The arrangement of presentation elements may convey connotations about semantic relationships that are too weak or ambiguous to formalize in the semantic model but are nevertheless suggestive to humans.

Context. Models are themselves artifacts in a computer system, and they are used within a larger context that gives them their full meaning. This context includes the internal organization of the model, annotations about the use of each model in the overall development process, a set of defaults and assumptions for element creation and manipulation, and a relationship to the environment in which they are used.

Models require an internal organization that permits simultaneous use by multiple work groups without undue interference. This decomposition is not needed for semantic reasons—a large monolithic model would be as precise as a set of models organized into coherent packages, maybe even more precise because the organizational boundaries complicate the job of defining precise semantics. But teams of workers could not work effectively on a large monolithic model without constantly getting in each other's way. Moreover, a monolithic model has no pieces that can be reused in other situations. Finally, changes to a large model have consequences that are difficult to determine. Changes to a small, isolated piece of a large model can be tractable if the model is properly structured into subsystems with well-defined interfaces. In any case, dividing large systems into a hierarchy of well-chosen pieces is the most reliable way to design large systems that humans have invented over thousands of years.

Models capture semantic information about an application system, but they also need to record many kinds of information about the development process itself, such as the author of a class, the debug status of a procedure, and the human access permission of a diagram. Such information is, at best, peripheral to the semantics of the system, but it is important to the development process. A model of a system therefore needs to include both viewpoints. This is most easily achieved by regarding the project management information as annotations to the semantic model—that is, arbitrary descriptions attached to model elements but whose meaning is outside the modeling language. In UML these annotations are implemented as text strings.

The commands used to create and modify a model are not part of the semantics of the modeling language any more than the commands of a text editor or browser are part of the semantics of a programming language. Model element properties do not have *default* values; in a particular model, they simply have *values*. For practical development, however, humans need to build and modify models without having to specify everything in full detail. Default values exist in the boundary between the modeling language and the editing tool that supports it. They are really defaults on the tool commands that create a model, although they may transcend an individual tool and become user expectations about the implementation of the language by tools in general.

Models are not built and used in isolation. They are part of a larger environment that includes modeling tools, languages and compilers, operating systems, networks of computers, implementation constraints, and so on. The information about a system includes information about all parts of the environment. Some of it will be stored in a model even though it is not semantic information. Examples include project management annotations (discussed above), code generation hints and directives, model packaging, and default command settings for an editor tool. Other information may be stored separately. Examples include program source code and operating system configuration commands. Even if some information is part of a model, the responsibility for interpreting it may lie in various places, including the modeling language, the modeling tool, the code generator, the compiler, a command language, and so on. This book describes the interpretation of models by the UML itself. But when operating in a physical development environment, other sources may add additional interpretations to information that is opaque to UML.

What Does a Model Mean?

A model is a *generator* of potential configurations of systems; the possible systems are its *extent*, or values. Ideally, all configurations consistent with the model should be possible. Sometimes, however, it is not possible to represent all constraints within a model. A model is also a description of the generic structure and meaning of a system. The descriptions are its *intent*, or meaning. A model is always an abstraction at some level. It captures the *essential* aspects of a system and ignores some of the details. There are the following aspects to consider for models.

Abstraction versus detail. A model captures the essential aspects of a system and ignores others. Which ones are essential is a matter of judgment that depends on the purpose of the model. This is not a dichotomy; there may be a spectrum of models of increasing precision. A modeling language is not a programming language. A modeling language may be less precise on purpose because additional detail is irrelevant for the purpose at hand. Models at different levels of precision can be used across the life of a project. A model intended for code generation requires at least some programming language issues to be addressed. Typically, models have low precision during early analysis. They gain detail as the development cycle progresses, so the final models have considerable detail and precision.

Specification versus implementation. A model can tell *what* something does (*specification*), as well as *how* the function is accomplished (*implementation*). These aspects should be separated in modeling. It is important to get the *what* correct before investing much time in the *how*. Abstracting away from implementation is an important facet of modeling. There may be a chain of several specification-implementation relationships, in which each implementation defines the specifications for the next layer.

Description versus instance. Models are mostly description. The things they describe are instances, which usually appear in models only as examples. Most instances exist only as part of the run-time execution. Sometimes, however, run-time instances are themselves descriptions of other things. We call these hybrid objects *metadata*. Looked at more deeply, it is unrealistic to insist that everything is either an instance or a description. Something is an instance or a description not in isolation but only in relation to something else, and most things can be approached from multiple viewpoints.

Variations in interpretation. There are many possible interpretations of models in a modeling language. One can define certain *semantic variation points*—places at which different interpretations are possible—and assign each interpretation a name as a *semantic variation* so that one can state which variation is being used. For example, users of Smalltalk might wish to avoid multiple inheritance in an implementation model because it is not supported by the programming language. Users of other programming languages would need it. Semantic variation points permit different execution models to be supported.

Part 2: UML Concepts ————

This part contains an overview of UML concepts to show how they fit together in modeling a system. This part is not meant to describe concepts in full detail. For full details about a UML concept, see the encyclopedia section of this book.

3

UML Walkthrough

This chapter presents a brief walkthrough of UML concepts and diagrams using a simple example. The purpose of the chapter is to organize the high-level UML concepts into a small set of views and diagrams that present the concepts visually. It shows how the various concepts are used to describe a system and how the views fit together. This summary is not intended to be comprehensive; many concepts are omitted. For more details, see the subsequent chapters that outline the UML semantic views, as well as the detailed reference material in the encyclopedia chapter.

The example used here is a theater box office that has computerized its operations. This is a contrived example, the purpose of which is to highlight various UML constructs in a brief space. It is deliberately simplified and is not presented in full detail. Presentation of a full model from an implemented system would neither fit in a small space nor highlight a sufficient range of constructs without excessive repetition.

UML Views

There is no sharp line between the various concepts and constructs in UML, but, for convenience, we divide them into several views. A view is simply a subset of UML modeling constructs that represents one aspect of a system. The division into different views is somewhat arbitrary, but we hope it is intuitive. One or two kinds of diagrams provide a visual notation for the concepts in each view.

At the top level, views can be divided into three areas: structural classification, dynamic behavior, and model management.

Structural classification describes the things in the system and their relationships to other things. Classifiers include classes, use cases, components, and nodes. Classifiers provide the basis on top of which dynamic behavior is built. Classification views include the static view, use case view, and implementation view.

Table 3-1: *UML Views and Diagrams*

Major Area	View	Diagrams	Main Concepts
structural	static view	class diagram	class, association, generalization, dependency, realization, interface
	use case view	use case diagram	use case, actor, association, extend, include, use case generalization
	implementation view	component diagram	component, interface, dependency, realization
	deployment view	deployment diagram	node, component, dependency, location
dynamic	state machine view	statechart diagram	state, event, transition, action
	activity view	activity diagram	state, activity, completion transition, fork, join
	interaction view	sequence diagram	interaction, object, message, activation
		collaboration diagram	collaboration, interaction, collaboration role, message
model management	model management view	class diagram	package, subsystem, model
extensibility	all	all	constraint, stereotype, tagged values

Dynamic behavior describes the behavior of a system over time. Behavior can be described as a series of changes to snapshots of the system drawn from the static view. Dynamic behavior views include the state machine view, activity view, and interaction view.

Model management describes the organization of the models themselves into hierarchical units. The package is the generic organizational unit for models. Special packages include models and subsystems. The model management view crosses the other views and organizes them for development work and configuration control.

UML also contains several constructs intended to provide a limited but useful extensibility capability. These constructs include constraints, stereotypes, and tagged values. These constructs are applicable to elements of all views.

Table 3-1 shows the UML views and the diagrams that display them, as well as the main concepts relevant to each view. This table should not be taken as a rigid set of rules but merely as a guide to normal usage, as mixing of views is permitted.

Static View

The static view models concepts in the application domain, as well as internal concepts invented as part of the implementation of an application. This view is static because it does not describe the time-dependent behavior of the system, which is described in other views. The main constituents of the static view are classes and their relationships: association, generalization, and various kinds of dependency, such as realization and usage. A class is the description of a concept from the application domain or the application solution. Classes are the center around which the class view is organized; other elements are owned by or attached to classes. The static view is displayed in class diagrams, so called because their main focus is the description of classes.

Classes are drawn as rectangles. Lists of attributes and operations are shown in separate compartments. The compartments can be suppressed when full detail is not needed. A class may appear on several diagrams. Its attributes and operations are often suppressed on all but one diagram.

Relationships among classes are drawn as paths connecting class rectangles. The different kinds of relationships are distinguished by line texture and by adornments on the paths or their ends.

Figure 3-1 shows a class diagram from the box office application. This diagram contains part of a ticket-selling domain model. It shows several important classes, such as **Customer, Reservation, Ticket,** and **Performance.** Customers may have many reservations, but each reservation is made by one customer. Reservations are of two kinds: subscription series and individual reservations. Both reserve tickets: in one case, only one ticket; in the other case, several tickets. Every ticket is part of a subscription series or an individual reservation, but not both. Every performance has many tickets available, each with a unique seat number. A performance can be identified by a show, date, and time.

Classes can be described at various levels of precision and concreteness. In the early stages of design, the model captures the more logical aspects of the problem. In the later stages, the model also captures design decisions and implementation details. Most of the views have a similar evolutionary quality.

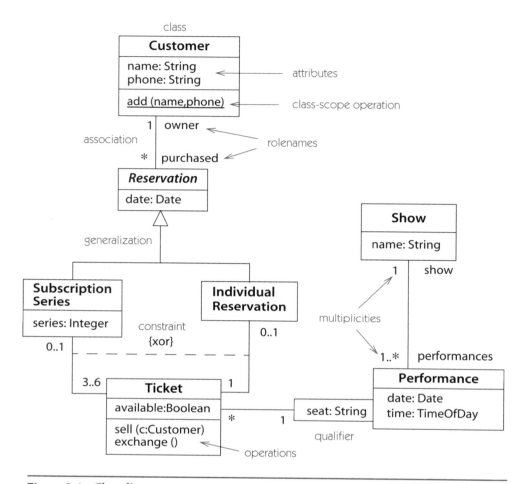

Figure 3-1. *Class diagram*

Use Case View

The use case view models the functionality of the system as perceived by outside users, called actors. A use case is a coherent unit of functionality expressed as a transaction among actors and the system. The purpose of the use case view is to list the actors and use cases and show which actors participate in each use case.

Figure 3-2 shows a use case diagram for the box office example. Actors include the clerk, supervisor, and kiosk. The kiosk is another system that accepts orders from a customer. The customer is not an actor in the box office application because the customer is not directly connected to the application. Use cases include buying tickets through the kiosk or the clerk, buying subscriptions (only through the clerk), and surveying total sales (at the request of the supervisor). Buying tick-

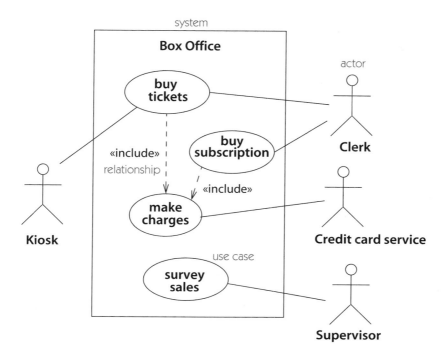

Figure 3-2. *Use case diagram*

ets and buying subscriptions include a common fragment—that is, making charges to the credit card service. (A complete description of a box office system would involve a number of other use cases, such as exchanging tickets and checking availability.)

Use cases can also be described at various levels of detail. They can be factored and described in terms of other, simpler use cases. A use case is implemented as a collaboration in the interaction view.

Interaction View

The interaction view describes sequences of message exchanges among roles that implement behavior of a system. A classifier role is the description of an object that plays a particular part within an interaction, as distinguished from other objects of the same class. This view provides a holistic view of behavior in a system—that is, it shows the flow of control across many objects. The interaction view is displayed in two diagrams focused on different aspects: sequence diagrams and collaboration diagrams.

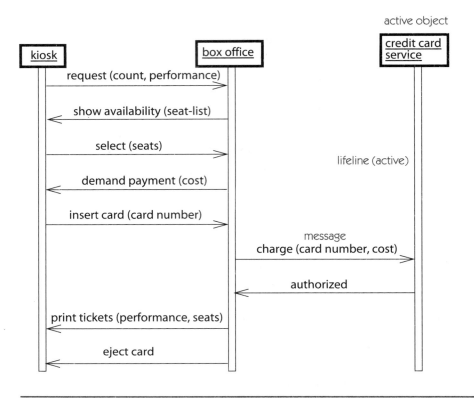

Figure 3-3. *Sequence diagram*

Sequence diagram

A sequence diagram shows a set of messages arranged in time sequence. Each classifier role is shown as a lifeline—that is, a vertical line that represents the role over time through the entire interaction. Messages are shown as arrows between lifelines. A sequence diagram can show a scenario—that is, an individual history of a transaction.

One use of a sequence diagram is to show the behavior sequence of a use case. When the behavior is implemented, each message on a sequence diagram corresponds to an operation on a class or an event trigger on a transition in a state machine.

Figure 3-3 shows a sequence diagram for the **buy tickets** use case. This use case is initiated by the customer at the kiosk communicating with the box office. The steps for the **make charges** use case are included within the sequence, which involves communication with both the kiosk and the credit card service. This sequence diagram is at an early stage of development and does not show the full details of the user interface. For example, the exact form of the seat list and the mechanism of specifying seats must still be determined, but the essential communication of the interaction has been specified by the use case.

Collaboration diagram

A collaboration models the objects and links that are meaningful within an interaction. The objects and links are meaningful only in the context provided by the interaction. A classifier role describes an object and an association role describes a link within a collaboration. A collaboration diagram shows the roles in the interaction as a geometric arrangement (Figure 3-4). The messages are shown as arrows attached to the relationship lines connecting classifier roles. The sequence of messages is indicated by sequence numbers prepended to message descriptions.

One use of a collaboration diagram is to show the implementation of an operation. The collaboration shows the parameters and local variables of the operation,

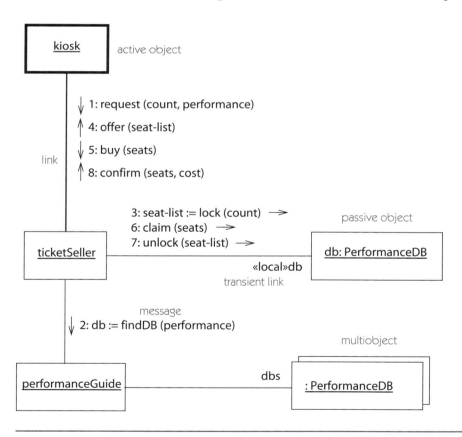

Figure 3-4. *Collaboration diagram*

as well as more permanent associations. When the behavior is implemented, the message sequencing corresponds to the nested calling structure and signal passing of the program.

Figure 3-4 shows a collaboration diagram for the reserve tickets interaction at a later stage of development. The collaboration shows the interaction among internal objects in the application to reserve tickets. The request arrives from the kiosk and is used to find the database for the particular performance from the set of all performances. The pointer **db** that is returned to the **ticketSeller** object represents a local transient link to a performance database that is maintained during the interaction and then discarded. The ticket seller requests a number of seats to the performance; a selection of seats in various price ranges is found, temporarily locked, and returned to the kiosk for the customer's selection. When the customer makes a selection from the list of seats, the selected seats are claimed and the rest are unlocked.

Both sequence diagrams and collaboration diagrams show interactions, but they emphasize different aspects. A sequence diagram shows time sequence as a geometric dimension, but the relationships among roles are implicit. A collaboration diagram shows the relationships among roles geometrically and relates messages to the relationships, but time sequences are less clear because they are implied by the sequence numbers. Each diagram should be used when its main aspect is the focus of attention.

State Machine View

A state machine models the possible life histories of an object of a class. A state machine contains states connected by transitions. Each state models a period of time during the life of an object during which it satisfies certain conditions. When an event occurs, it may cause the firing of a transition that takes the object to a new state. When a transition fires, an action attached to the transition may be executed. State machines are shown as statechart diagrams.

Figure 3-5 shows a statechart diagram for the history of a ticket to a performance. The initial state of a ticket (shown by the black dot) is the **Available** state. Before the season starts, seats for season subscribers are assigned. Individual tickets purchased interactively are first locked while the customer makes a selection. After that, they are either sold or unlocked if they are not chosen. If the customer takes too long to make a selection, the transaction times out and the seat is released. Seats sold to season subscribers may be exchanged for other performances, in which case they become available again.

State machines may be used to describe user interfaces, device controllers, and other reactive subsystems. They may also be used to describe passive objects that go through several qualitatively distinct phases during their lifetime, each of which has its own special behavior.

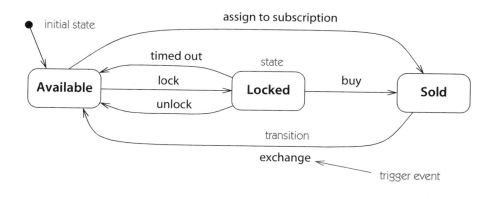

Figure 3-5. *Statechart diagram*

Activity View

An activity graph is a variant of a state machine that shows the computational activities involved in performing a calculation. An activity state represents an activity: a workflow step or the execution of an operation. An activity graph describes both sequential and concurrent groups of activities. Activity graphs are shown on activity diagrams.

Figure 3-6 shows an activity diagram for the box office. This diagram shows the activities involved in mounting a show. (Don't take this example too seriously if you have theater experience!) Arrows show sequential dependencies—for example, shows must be picked before they are scheduled. Heavy bars show forks or joins of control. For example, after the show is scheduled, the theater can begin to publicize it, buy scripts, hire artists, build sets, design lighting, and make costumes, all concurrently. Before rehearsal can begin, however, the scripts must be ordered and the artist must be hired.

This example shows an activity diagram the purpose of which is to model the real-world workflows of a human organization. Such business modeling is a major purpose of activity diagrams, but activity diagrams can also be used for modeling software activities. An activity diagram is helpful in understanding the high-level execution behavior of a system, without getting involved in the internal details of message passing required by a collaboration diagram.

The input and output parameters of an action can be shown using flow relationships connecting the action and an object flow state.

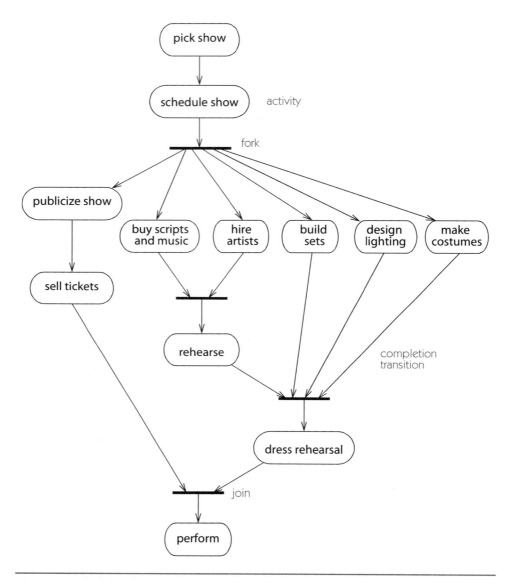

Figure 3-6. *Activity diagram*

Physical Views

The previous views model the concepts in the application from a logical view-point. The physical views model the implementation structure of the application itself, such as its organization into components and its deployment onto run-time nodes. These views provide an opportunity to map classes onto implementation components and nodes. There are two physical views: the implementation view and the deployment view.

The implementation view models the components in a system—that is, the software units from which the application is constructed—as well as the dependencies among components so that the impact of a proposed change can be assessed. It also models the assignment of classes and other model elements to components.

The implementation view is displayed on component diagrams. Figure 3-7 shows a component diagram for the box office system. There are three user

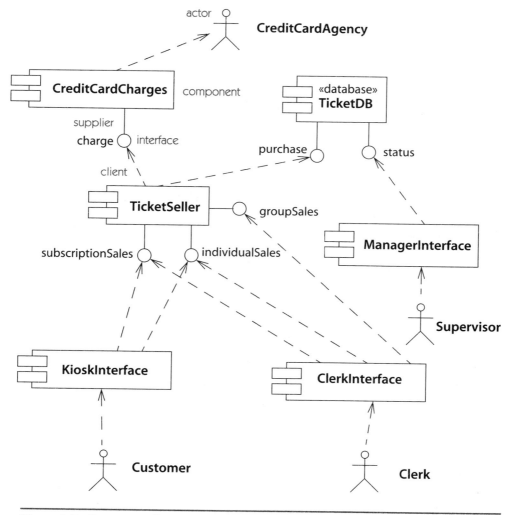

Figure 3-7. *Component diagram*

interfaces: one each for customers using a kiosk, clerks using the on-line reservation system, and supervisors making queries about ticket sales. There is a ticket seller component that sequentializes requests from both kiosks and clerks; a component that processes credit card charges; and the database containing the ticket information. The component diagram shows the kinds of components in the system; a particular configuration of the application may have more than one copy of a component.

A small circle with a name is an interface—a coherent set of services. A solid line from a component to an interface indicates that the component provides the ser-

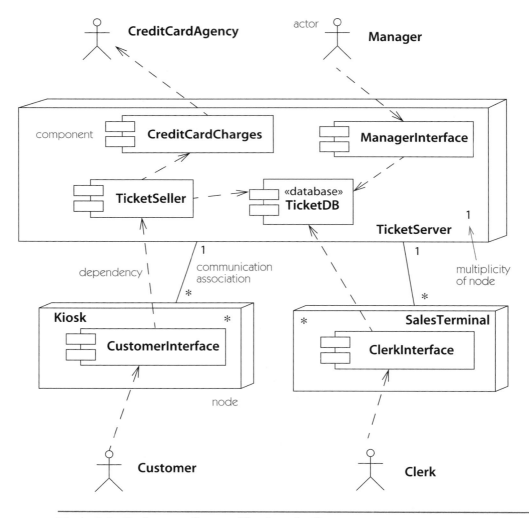

Figure 3-8. *Deployment diagram (descriptor level)*

vices listed in the interface. A dashed arrow from a component to an interface indicates that the component requires the services provided by the interface. For example, subscription sales and group sales are both provided by the ticket seller component; subscription sales are accessible from both kiosks and clerks, but group sales are only accessible from a clerk.

The deployment view represents the arrangement of run-time component instances on node instances. A node is a run-time resource, such as a computer, device, or memory. This view permits the consequences of distribution and resource allocation to be assessed.

The deployment view is displayed on deployment diagrams. Figure 3-8 shows a descriptor-level deployment diagram for the box office system. This diagram shows the kinds of nodes in the system and the kinds of components they hold. A node is shown as a cube symbol.

Figure 3-9 shows an instance-level deployment diagram for the box office system. The diagram shows the individual nodes and their links in a particular version of the system. The information in this model is consistent with the descriptor-level information in Figure 3-8.

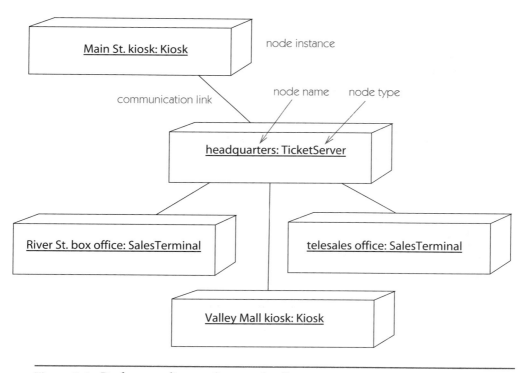

Figure 3-9. *Deployment diagram (instance level)*

Model Management View

The model management view models the organization of the model itself. A model comprises a set of packages that hold model elements, such as classes, state machines, and use cases. Packages may contain other packages: therefore, a model designates a root package that indirectly contains all the contents of the model. Packages are units for manipulating the contents of a model, as well as units for access control and configuration control. Every model element is owned by one package or one other element.

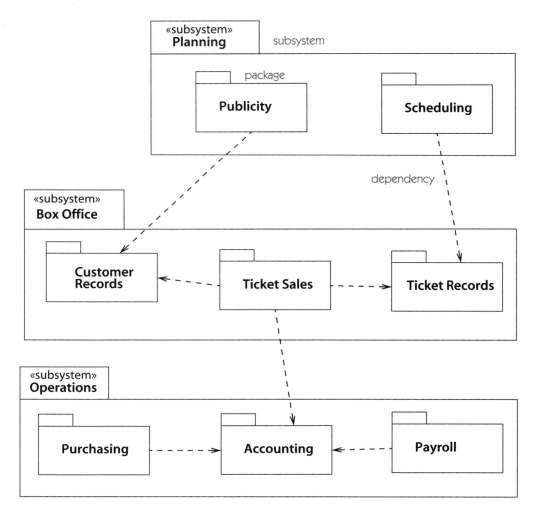

Figure 3-10. *Packages*

A model is a complete description of a system at a given precision from one viewpoint. There may be several models of a system from various viewpoints—for example, an analysis model as well as a design model. A model is shown as a special kind of package.

A subsystem is another special package. It represents a portion of a system, with a crisp interface that can be implemented as a distinct component.

Model management information is usually shown on class diagrams.

Figure 3-10 shows the breakdown of the entire theater system into packages and their dependency relationships. The box office subsystem includes the previous examples in this chapter; the full system also includes theater operations and planning subsystems. Each subsystem consists of several packages.

Extensibility Constructs

UML includes three main extensibility constructs: constraints, stereotypes, and tagged values. A constraint is a textual statement of a semantic relationship expressed in some formal language or in natural language. A stereotype is a new kind of model element devised by the modeler and based on an existing kind of model element. A tagged value is a named piece of information attached to any model element.

These constructs permit many kinds of extensions to UML without requiring changes to the basic UML metamodel itself. They may be used to create tailored versions of the UML for an application area.

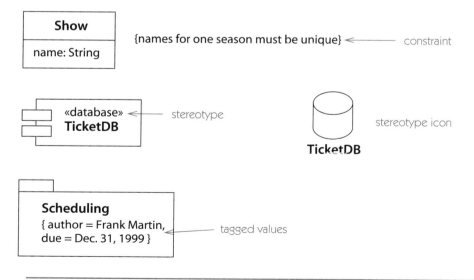

Figure 3-11. *Extensibility constructs*

Figure 3-11 shows examples of constraints, stereotypes, and tagged values. The constraint on class **Show** ensures that the names of shows are unique. Figure 3-1 shows an **xor** constraint on two associations; an object can have a link from one of them at a time. Constraints are useful for making statements that can be expressed in a text language but which are not directly supported by UML constructs.

The stereotype on component **TicketDB** indicates that the component is a database, which permits the interfaces supported by the component to be omitted as they are the interfaces supported by all databases. Modelers can add new stereotypes to represent special elements. A set of implied constraints, tagged values, or code generation properties can be attached to a stereotype. A modeler can define an icon for a given stereotype name as a visual aid, as shown in the diagram. The textual form may always be used, however.

The tagged values on package **Scheduling** show that Frank Martin is responsible for finishing it before the end of the millennium. Any arbitrary piece of information can be attached to a model element as a tagged value under a name chosen by the modeler. Text values are especially useful for project management information and for code generation parameters. Most tagged values would be stored as pop-up information within an editing tool and would not usually be displayed on printed pictures.

Connections Among Views

The various views coexist within a single model and their elements have many connections, some of which are shown in Table 3-2. This table is not meant to be complete, but it shows some of the major relationships among elements from different views.

Table 3-2: *Some Relationships Among Elements in Different Views*

Element	Element	Relationship
class	state machine	ownership
operation	interaction	realization
use case	collaboration	realization
use case	interaction instance	sample scenario
component instance	node instance	location
action	operation	call
action	signal	send
activity	operation	call
message	action	invocation
package	class	ownership
role	class	classification

Overview

The static view is the foundation of UML. The elements of the static view of a model are the concepts that are meaningful in an application, including real-world concepts, abstract concepts, implementation concepts, computer concepts—all kinds of concepts found in systems. For example, a ticket system for a theater has concepts such as tickets, reservations, subscription plans, seat assignment algorithms, interactive web pages for ordering, and archival data for redundancy.

The static view captures object structure. An object-oriented system unifies data structure and behavioral features into a single object structure. The static view includes all the traditional data structure concerns, as well as the organization of the operations on the data. Both data and operations are quantized into classes. In the object-oriented perspective, data and behavior are closely related. For example, a **Ticket** object carries data, such as its price, date of performance, and seat number, as well as operations on it, such as reserving itself or computing its price with a special discount.

The static view describes behavioral entities as discrete modeling elements, but it does not contain the details of their dynamic behavior. It treats them as things to be named, owned by classes, and invoked. Their dynamic execution is described by other views that describe the internal details of their dynamics. These other views include the interaction view and the state machine view. Dynamic views require the static view to describe the things that interact dynamically—you can't say *how* something interacts without first saying *what* is interacting. The static view is the foundation on which the other views are built.

The key elements in the static view are classifiers and their relationships. A classifier is a modeling element that describes things. There are several kinds of classifiers, including classes, interfaces, and data types. Behavioral things are reified by other classifiers, including use cases and signals. Implementation purposes are behind several kinds of classifiers, such as subsystems, components, and nodes.

Large models must be organized into smaller units for human understanding and reusability. A package is a general-purpose organizational unit for owning and managing the contents of a model. Every element is owned by some package. A model is a package that describes a complete view of a system and can be used more or less independently of other models; it is a root for the ownership of the more detailed packages that describe the system.

An object is a discrete unit out from which the modeler understands and constructs a system. It is an instance of a class—that is, an individual with identity whose structure and behavior are described by the class. An object is an identifiable piece of state with well-defined behavior that can be invoked.

Relationships among classifiers are association, generalization, and various kinds of dependency, including realization and usage.

Classifiers

A classifier is a discrete concept in the model, having identity, state, behavior, and relationships. Kinds of classifiers include class, interface, and data type. Other kinds of classifiers are reifications of behavioral concepts, things in the environment, or implementation structures. These classifiers include use case, actor, component, node, and subsystem. Table 4-1 lists the various kinds of classifiers and their functions. The metamodel term classifier includes all these concepts, but as class is the most familiar term, we will discuss it first and define the other concepts by difference from it.

Class. A class represents a discrete concept within the application being modeled—a physical thing (such as an airplane), a business thing (such as an order), a logical thing (such as a broadcasting schedule), an application thing (such as a cancel button), a computer thing (such as a hash table), or a behavioral thing (such as a task). A class is the descriptor for a set of objects with similar structure, behavior, and relationships. All attributes and operations are attached to classes or other classifiers. Classes are the foci around which object-oriented systems are organized.

An object is a discrete entity with identity, state, and invocable behavior. Objects are the individual pieces out of which a run-time system is constructed; classes are the individual concepts by which to understand and describe the multitude of individual objects.

A class defines a set of objects that have state and behavior. State is described by attributes and associations. Attributes are generally used for pure data values without identity, such as numbers and strings, and associations are used for connections among objects with identity. Individual pieces of invocable behavior are described by operations; a method is the implementation of an operation. The lifetime history of an object is described by a state machine attached to a class. The

Table 4-1: *Kinds of Classifiers*

Classifier	Function	Notation
actor	An outside user of a system	
class	A concept from the modeled system	Name
class-in-state	A class restricted to being in a given state	Name[S]
classifier role	A classifier restricted to a particular usage in a collaboration	role:Name
component	A physical piece of a system	
data type	A descriptor of a set of primitive values that lack identity	**Name**
interface	A named set of operations that characterize behavior	○ Iname
node	A computational resource	
signal	An asynchronous communication among objects	«signal»
subsystem	A package that is treated as a unit with a specification, implementation, and identity	«subsystem»
use case	A specification of the behavior of an entity in its interaction with outside agents	⬭

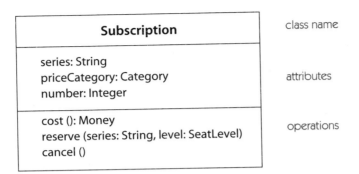

Figure 4-1. *Class notation*

notation for a class is a rectangle with compartments for the name of the class, attributes, and operations, as shown in Figure 4-1.

A set of classes may use the generalization relationship and the inheritance mechanism built on it to share common pieces of state and behavior description. Generalization relates more specific classes (subclasses) to more general classes (superclasses) that contain properties common to several subclasses. A class may have zero or more parents (superclasses) and zero or more children (subclasses). A class inherits state and behavior descriptions from its parents and other ancestors, and it defines state and behavior descriptions that its children and other descendants inherit.

A class has a unique name within its container, which is usually a package but is sometimes another class. The class has a visibility with respect to its container; the visibility specifies how it may be used by other classes outside the container. A class has a multiplicity that specifies how many instances of it may exist. Most often, this is many (zero or more, without explicit limit), but singleton classes occur for which a single instance exists during execution.

Interface. An interface is the description of behavior of objects without giving their implementation or state; an interface contains operations but not attributes, and it does not have outgoing associations that are visible to it. One or more classes or components may realize an interface, and each class implements the operations found in the interface.

Data type. A data type is the description of primitive values that lack identity (independent existence and the possibility of side effects). Data types include numbers, strings, and enumerated values. Data types are passed by value and are immutable entities. A data type has no attributes but may have operations. Operations do not modify data values, but they may return data values as results.

Levels of meaning. Classes can exist at several levels of meaning in a model, including the analysis, design, and implementation levels. When representing real-world concepts, it is important to capture the real-world state, relationships, and behavior. But implementation concepts, such as information hiding, efficiency, visibility, and methods, are not relevant real-world concepts (they *are* relevant design concepts). Many potential properties of a class are simply irrelevant at this level. An analysis-level class represents a logical concept in the application domain or in the application itself. The analysis model should be a minimal representation of the system being modeled, sufficient to capture the essential logic of the system without getting into issues of performance or construction.

When representing a high-level design, concepts such as localization of state to particular classes, efficiency of navigating among objects, separation of external behavior and internal implementation, and specification of the precise operations are relevant to a class. A design-level class represents the decision to package state information and the operations on it into a discrete unit. It captures the key design decision, the localization of information and functionality to objects. Design-level classes contain both real-world content and computer system content.

Finally, when representing programming-language code, the form of a class closely matches the chosen programming language, and some abilities of a general class may be forgone if they have no direct implementation in the language. An implementation-level class maps directly into programming-language code.

The same system can contain more than one level of class; implementation-oriented classes may realize the more logical classes in the model. An implementation class represents the declaration of a class as found in a particular programming language. It captures the exact form of a class, as needed by the language. In many cases, however, analysis, design, and implementation information can be nested into a single class.

Relationships

Relationships among classifiers are association, generalization, flow, and various kinds of dependency, including realization and usage (see Table 4-2).

The association relationship describes semantic connections among individual objects of given classes. Associations provide the connections with which objects of different classes can interact. The remaining relationships relate the descriptions of classifiers themselves, not their instances.

The generalization relationship relates general descriptions of parent classifiers (superclasses) to more specialized child classifiers (subclasses). Generalization facilitates the description of classifiers out of incremental declaration pieces, each of which adds to the description inherited from its ancestors. The inheritance mechanism constructs complete descriptions of classifiers from incremental descriptions using generalization relationships. Generalization and inheritance permit

Table 4-2: *Kinds of Relationships*

Relationship	Function	Notation
association	A description of a connection among instances of classes	————
dependency	A relationship between two model elements	- - - -≫
flow	A relationship between two versions of an object at successive times	- - - -≫
generalization	A relationship between a more general description and a more specific variety of the general thing, used for inheritance	———▷
realization	Relationship between a specification and its implementation	- - - -▷
usage	A situation in which one element requires another for its correct functioning	- - - -≫

different classifiers to share the attributes, operations, and relationships that they have in common, without repetition.

The realization relationship relates a specification to an implementation. An interface is a specification of behavior without implementation; a class includes implementation structure. One or more classes may realize an interface, and each class implements the operations found in the interface.

The flow relationship relates two versions of an object at successive times. It represents a transformation of the value, state, or location of an object. The flow relationship may connect classifier roles in an interaction. Varieties of flow are become (two versions of the same object) and copy (a new object created from an existing object).

The dependency relationship relates classes whose behavior or implementation affects other classes. There are several kinds of dependency in addition to realization, including trace (a loose connection among elements in different models), refinement (a mapping between two levels of meaning), usage (a requirement for the presence of another element within a single model), and binding (the assignment of values to template parameters). Usage dependency is frequently used to represent implementation relationships, such as code-level relationships. Dependency is particularly useful when summarized on model organization units, such as packages, on which it shows the architectural structure of a system. Compilation constraints can be shown by dependencies, for example.

Associations

An association describes discrete connections among objects or other instances in a system. An association relates an ordered list (tuple) of two or more classifiers, with repetitions permitted. The most common kind of association is a binary association between a pair of classifiers. An instance of an association is a link. A link comprises a tuple (an ordered list) of objects, each drawn from its corresponding class. A binary link comprises a pair of objects.

Associations carry information about relationships among objects in a system. As a system executes, links among objects are created and destroyed. Associations are the "glue" that ties a system together. Without associations, there are nothing but isolated classes that don't work together.

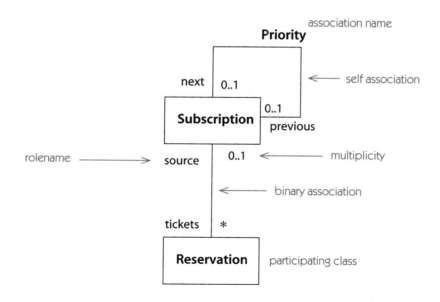

Figure 4-2. *Association notation*

A single object may be associated with itself if the same class appears more than once in an association. If the same class appears twice in an association, the two instances do not have to be the same object, and usually they are not.

Each connection of an association to a class is called an association end. Most information about an association is attached to one of its ends. Association ends can have names (rolenames) and visibility. The most important property they have is multiplicity—how many instances of one class can be related to one instance of the other class. Multiplicity is most useful for binary associations because its definition for *n*-ary associations is complicated.

The notation for a binary association is a line or path connecting the participating classes. The association name is placed along the line with the rolename and multiplicity at each end, as shown in Figure 4-2.

An association can also have attributes of its own, in which case it is both an association and a class—an association class (see Figure 4-3). If an association attribute is unique within a set of related objects, then it is a qualifier (see Figure 4-4). A qualifier is a value that selects a unique object from the set of related objects across an association. Lookup tables and arrays may be modeled as qualified associations. Qualifiers are important for modeling names and identification codes. Qualifiers also model indexes in a design model.

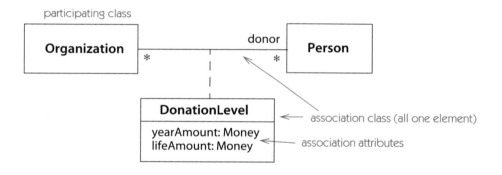

Figure 4-3. *Association class*

Figure 4-4. *Qualified association*

During analysis, associations represent logical relationships among objects. There is no great need to impose direction or to be concerned about how to implement them. Redundant associations should be avoided because they add no logical information. During design, associations capture design decisions about data structure, as well as separation of responsibilities among classes. Directionality of associations is important, and redundant associations may be included for efficiency of object access, as well as to localize information in a particular class. Nevertheless, at this stage of modeling, associations should not be equated with C++ pointers. A navigable association at the design stage represents state information available to a class, but it can be mapped into programming-language code in various ways. The implementation can be a pointer, a container class embedded in a class, or even a completely separate table object. Other kinds of design properties include visibility and changeability of links. Figure 4-5 shows some design properties of associations.

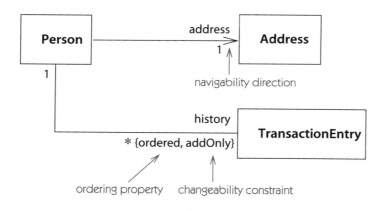

Figure 4-5. *Design properties of association*

Aggregation and composition. An aggregation is an association that represents a part-whole relationship. It is shown by a hollow-diamond adornment on the end of the path attached to the aggregate class. A composition is a stronger form of association in which the composite has sole responsibility for managing its parts—such as their allocation and deallocation. It is shown by a filled-diamond adornment on the composite end. There is a separate association between each class representing a part and the class representing the whole, but for convenience the paths attached to the whole may be joined together so that the entire set of associations is drawn as a tree. Figure 4-6 shows an aggregate and a composite.

Links. An instance of an association is a link. A link is an ordered list of object references, each of which must be an instance of the corresponding class in the

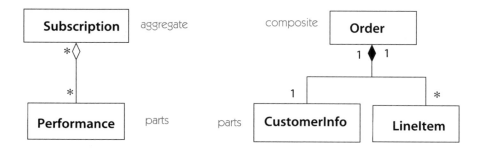

Figure 4-6. *Aggregation and composition*

association or an instance of a descendant of the class. The links in a system constitute part of the system state. Links do not exist independently of objects; they take their identity from the objects they relate (in database terms, the list of objects is the *key* for the link). Conceptually, an association is distinct from the classes that it relates. In practice, associations are often implemented using pointers in the participating classes, but they can be implemented as container objects separate from the classes they connect.

Bidirectionality. The different ends of an association are distinguishable, even if two of them involve the same class. This simply means that different objects of the same class can be related. Because the ends are distinguishable, an association is not symmetric (except in special cases); the ends cannot be interchanged. This is only common sense in ordinary discourse; the subject and the object of a verb are not interchangeable. An association is sometimes said to be bidirectional. This means that the logical relationships work both ways. This statement is frequently misunderstood, even by some methodologists. It does not mean that each class "knows" the other class, or that, in an implementation, it is possible to access each class from the other. It simply means that any logical relationship has an inverse, whether or not the inverse is easy to compute. To assert the ability to traverse an association in one direction but not the other as a design decision, associations can be marked with navigability.

Why is the basic model relational, rather than the pointer model prevalent in programming languages? The reason is that a model attempts to capture the intent behind an implementation. If a relationship between two classes is modeled as a pair of pointers, the pointers are nevertheless related. The association approach acknowledges that relationships are meaningful in both directions, regardless of how they are implemented. It is simple to convert an association into a pair of pointers for implementation, but very difficult to recognize that two pointers are inverses of each other unless this fact is part of the model.

Generalization

The generalization relationship is a taxonomic relationship between a more general description and a more specific description that builds on it and extends it. The more specific description is fully consistent with the more general one (it has all its properties, members, and relationships) and may contain additional information. For example, a mortgage is a more specific kind of loan. A mortgage keeps the basic characteristics of a loan but adds additional characteristics, such as a house as security for the loan. The more general description is called the parent; an element in the transitive closure is an ancestor. The more specific description is called the child; an element in the transitive closure is a descendant. In the example, **Loan** is the parent class and **Mortgage** is the child class. Generalization is used for classifiers (classes, interfaces, data types, use cases, actors, signals, and so on), packages, state machines, and other elements. For classes, the term superclass and subclass are used for parent and child.

A generalization is drawn as an arrow from the child to the parent, with a large hollow triangle on the end connected to the parent (Figure 4-7). Several generalization relationships can be drawn as a tree with one arrowhead branching into several lines to the children.

Purpose of generalization. Generalization has two purposes. The first is to define the conditions under which an instance of one class (or other element) can be used when a variable (such as a parameter or procedure variable) is declared as holding values of a given class. This is called the substitutability principle (from

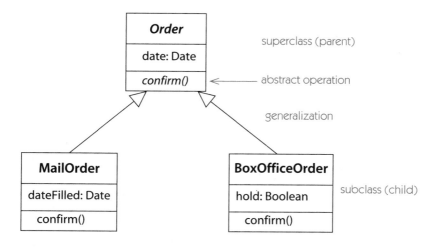

Figure 4-7. *Generalization notation*

Barbara Liskov). The rule is that an instance of a descendant may be used wherever the ancestor is declared. For example, if a variable is declared to hold loans, then a mortgage object is a legal value.

Generalization enables polymorphic operations—that is, operations whose implementation (method) is determined by the class of object they are applied to rather than being explicitly stated by the caller. This works because a parent class may have many possible children, each of which implements its own variation of an operation, which is defined across the entire set of classes. For example, computing interest would work differently for a mortgage and an automobile loan, but each of them is a variation on computing interest on the parent **Loan** class. A variable is declared to hold the parent class, and then an object of any child class can be used, any of which has its own particular operations. This is particularly useful because new classes can be added later, without the need to modify existing polymorphic calls. For example, a new kind of loan could be added later, and existing code that uses the **compute interest** operation would still work. A polymorphic operation can be declared without an implementation in a parent class with the intent that an implementation must be supplied by each descendant class. Such an incomplete operation is abstract (shown by italicizing its name).

The other purpose of generalization is to permit the incremental description of an element by sharing the descriptions of its ancestors. This is called inheritance. Inheritance is the mechanism by which a description of the objects of a class is assembled out of declaration fragments from the class and its ancestors. Inheritance permits shared parts of the description to be declared once and shared by many classes, rather than be repeated in each class that uses it. This sharing reduces the size of a model. More importantly, it reduces the number of changes that must be made on an update to the model and reduces the chance of accidental inconsistency. Inheritance works in a similar way for other kinds of elements, such as states, signals, and use cases.

Inheritance

Each kind of generalizable element has a set of inheritable properties. For any model element, these include constraints. For classifiers, they also include features (attributes, operations, and signal reception) and participation in associations. A child inherits all the inheritable properties of all its ancestors. Its complete set of properties is the set of inherited properties together with the properties that it declares directly.

For a classifier, no attribute with the same signature may be declared more than once (directly or inherited). Otherwise, there is a conflict, and the model is ill formed. In other words, an attribute declared in an ancestor may not be redeclared in a descendant. An operation may be declared in more than one classifier, provided the specifications are consistent (same parameters, constraints, and meaning). Additional declarations are simply redundant. A method may be declared by multiple classes in a hierarchy. A method attached to a descendant supersedes and replaces (overrides) a method with the same signature declared in any ancestor. If two or more distinct copies of a method are nevertheless inherited by a class (via multiple inheritance from different classes), then they conflict and the model is ill formed. (Some programming languages permit one of the methods to be explicitly chosen. We find it simpler and safer just to redefine the method in the child class.) Constraints on an element are the union of the constraints on the element itself and all its ancestors; if any of them is inconsistent, then the model is ill formed.

In a concrete class, each inherited or declared operation must have a method defined, either directly or by inheritance from an ancestor.

Multiple inheritance

If a classifier has more than one parent, it inherits from each one (Figure 4-8). Its features (attributes, operations, and signals) are the union of those of its parents. If the same class appears as an ancestor by more than one path, it nevertheless contributes only one copy of each of its members. If a feature with the same signature is declared by two classes that do not inherit it from a common ancestor (independent declarations), then the declarations conflict and the model is ill formed. UML does not provide a conflict resolution rule for this situation because experience has shown that the designer should explicitly resolve it. Some

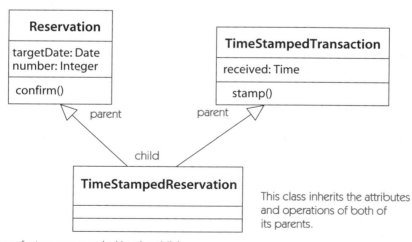

Figure 4-8. *Multiple inheritance*

languages, such as Eiffel, permit conflicts to be explicitly resolved by the programmer, which is much safer than implicit conflict resolution rules, which frequently lead to surprises for the developer.

Single and multiple classification

In the simplest formulation, an object has one direct class. Many object-oriented languages have that restriction. There is no logical necessity that an object have a single class—we typically look at real-world objects from many angles simultaneously. In the more general formulation of UML, an object may have one or more direct classes. The object behaves as if it belonged to an implicit class that was a child of each of the direct classes—effectively, multiple inheritance without the need to actually declare the new class.

Static and dynamic classification

In the simplest formulation, an object may not change its class after it is created. Again, there is no logical necessity for this restriction. It is primarily intended to make the implementation of object-oriented programming languages easier. In the more general formulation, an object may change its direct class dynamically. In doing so, it may lose or gain attributes or associations. If it loses them, the information in them is lost and cannot be recovered later, even if it changes back to the original class. If it gains attributes or associations, then they must be initialized at the time of the change, in a similar manner to the initialization of a new object.

When multiple classification is combined with dynamic classification, an object can gain and lose classes during its life. The dynamic classes are sometimes called roles or types. One common modeling pattern is to require that each object have a single static inherent class (one that cannot change during the life of the object) plus zero or more role classes that may be added or removed over the lifetime of the object. The inherent class describes its fundamental properties, and the role classes describe properties that are transient. Although many programming languages do not support multiple dynamic classification in the class declaration hierarchy, it is nevertheless a valuable modeling concept that can be mapped into associations.

Realization

The realization relationship connects a model element, such as a class, to another model element, such as an interface, that supplies its behavioral specification but not its structure or implementation. The client must support (by inheritance or by direct declaration) at least all the operations that the supplier has. Although realization is meant to be used with specification elements, such as interfaces, it can also be used with a concrete implementation element to indicate that its specification (but not its implementation) must be supported. This might be used to show the relationship of an optimized version of a class to a simpler but inefficient version, for example.

Both generalization and realization relate a more general description to more detailed versions of it. Generalization relates two elements at the same semantic level (at the same level of abstraction, for example), usually within the same model; realization relates two elements at different semantic levels (an analysis class and a design class, for example, or an interface and a class), often found in different models. There may be two or more entire class hierarchies at different stages of development whose elements are related by realization. The two hierarchies need not have the same form because the realizing classes may have implementation dependencies that are not relevant to the specifying classes.

Realization is displayed as a dashed arrow with a closed hollow arrowhead (Figure 4-9). It is similar to the generalization symbol with a dashed line, to indicate that it is similar to a kind of inheritance.

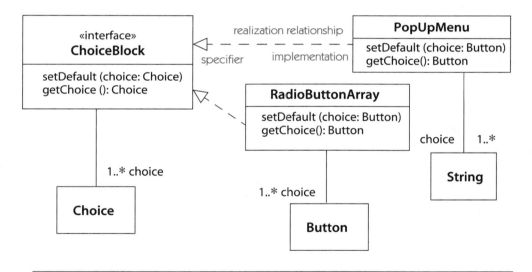

Figure 4-9. *Realization relationship*

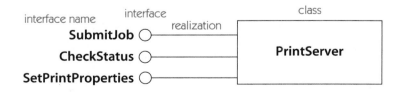

Figure 4-10. *Interface and realization icons*

There is a special collapsed notation to show interfaces (without their contents) and the classes or components that realize them. The interface is shown as a small circle attached to the classifier rectangle by a solid line (Figure 4-10).

Dependencies

A dependency indicates a semantic relationship between two or more model elements. It relates the model elements themselves and does not require a set of instances for its meaning. It indicates a situation in which a change to the supplier element may require a change to or indicate a change in meaning of the client element in the dependency.

The association and generalization relationships are dependencies by this definition, but they have specific semantics with important consequences. Therefore, they have their own names and detailed semantics. We normally use the word dependency for all the other relationships that don't fit the sharper categories. Table 4-3 lists the kinds of dependency found in the UML base model.

A trace is a conceptual connection among elements in different models, often models at different stages of development. It lacks detailed semantics. It is typically used to trace system requirements across models and to keep track of changes made to models that may affect other models.

A refinement is a relationship between two versions of a concept at different stages of development or at different levels of abstraction. The two concepts are not meant to coexist in the final detailed model. One of them is usually a less finished version of the other. In principle, there is a mapping from the less finished concept to the more finished concept. This does not mean that translation is automatic. Usually, the more detailed concept contains design decisions that have been made by the designer, decisions that might be made in many ways. In principle, changes to one model could be validated against the other, with deviations flagged. In practice, tools cannot do all this today, although some simpler mappings can be enforced. Therefore a refinement is mostly a reminder to the modeler that multiple models are related in a predictable way.

A derivation dependency indicates that one element can be computed from another element (but the derived element may be explicitly included in the system to avoid a costly recomputation). Derivation, realization, refinement, and trace are abstraction dependencies—they relate two versions of the same underlying thing.

A usage dependency is a statement that the behavior or implementation of one element affects the behavior or implementation of another element. Frequently, this comes from implementation concerns, such as compiler requirements that the definition of one class is needed to compile another class. Most usage dependencies can be derived from the code and do not need to be explicitly declared, unless they are part of a top-down design style that constrains the organization of the system (for example, by using predefined components and libraries). The specific

Table 4-3: *Kinds of Dependencies*

Dependency	Function	Keyword
access	Permission for a package to access the contents of another package	access
binding	Assignment of values to the parameters of a template to generate a new model element	bind
call	Statement that a method of one class calls an operation of another class	call
derivation	Statement that one instance can be computed from another instance	derive
friend	Permission for an element to access the contents of another element regardless of visibility	friend
import	Permission for a package to access the contents of another package and add aliases of their names to the importer's namespace	import
instantiation	Statement that a method of one class creates instances of another class	instantiate
parameter	Relationship between an operation and its parameters	parameter
realization	Mapping between a specification and an implementation of it	realize
refinement	Statement that a mapping exists between elements at two different semantic levels	refine
send	Relationship between the sender of a signal and the receiver of the signal	send
trace	Statement that some connection exists between elements in different models, but less precise than a mapping	trace
usage	Statement that one element requires the presence of another element for its correct functioning (includes call, instantiation, parameter, send, but open to other kinds)	use

kind of usage dependency can be specified, but this is often omitted because the purpose of the relationship is to highlight the dependency. The exact details can often be obtained from the implementation code. Stereotypes of usage include call and instantiation. The call dependency indicates that a method on one class calls an operation on another class; instantiation indicates that a method on one class creates an instance of another class.

Several varieties of usage dependency grant permission for elements to access other elements. The access dependency permits one package to see the contents of another package. The import dependency goes further and adds the names of the target package contents to the namespace of the importing package. The friend dependency is an access dependency that permits the client to see even the private contents of the supplier.

A binding is the assignment of values to the parameters of a template. It is a highly structured relationship with precise semantics obtained by substituting the arguments for the parameters in a copy of the template.

Usage and binding dependencies involve strong semantics among elements at the same semantic level. They must connect elements in the same level of model (both analysis or both design, and at the same level of abstraction). Trace and refinement dependencies are vaguer and can connect elements from different models or levels of abstraction.

The instance of relationship (a metarelationship, not strictly a dependency) indicates that one element (such as an object) is an instance of another element (such as a class).

A dependency is drawn as a dashed arrow from the client to the supplier, with a stereotype keyword to distinguish its kind, as shown in Figure 4-11.

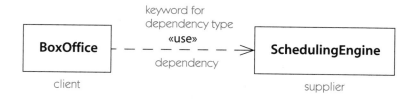

Figure 4-11. *Dependencies*

Constraint

UML supplies a set of concepts and relationships for modeling systems as graphs of modeling elements. Some things, however, are better expressed linguistically—that is, using the power of a textual language. A constraint is a Boolean expression represented as a string to be interpreted in a designated language. Natural language, set theoretic notation, constraint languages, or various programming languages may be used to express constraints. The UML includes the definition of a constraint language, called OCL, that is convenient for expressing UML constraints and is expected to be widely supported. See the entry for OCL and the book [Warmer-99] for more information on OCL.

Constraints can be used to state various nonlocal relationships, such as restrictions on paths of associations. In particular, constraints can be used to state existence properties (*there exists an X such that condition C is true*) and universal properties (*for all y in Y, condition D must be true*).

Some standard constraints are predefined as UML standard elements, including associations in an exclusive-or relationship and various constraints on the relationships of subclasses in generalization.

See Chapter 14, Standard Elements, for more information.

A constraint is shown as a text expression in braces. It may be written in a formal language or natural language. The text string may be placed in a note or attached to a dependency arrow. Figure 4-12 shows some constraints.

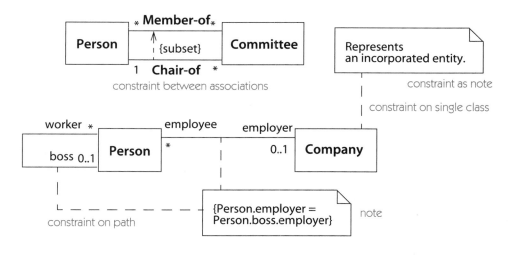

Figure 4-12. *Constraints*

Instances

An instance is a run-time entity with identity, that is, something that can be distinguished from other run-time entities. It has a value at any moment in time. Over time the value can change in response to operations on it.

One purpose of a model is to describe the possible states of a system and their behavior. A model is a statement of potentiality, of the possible collections of objects that might exist and the possible behavior history that the objects might undergo. The static view defines and constrains the possible configurations of values that an executing system may assume. The dynamic view defines the ways in which an executing system may pass from one configuration to another. Together, the static view and the various dynamic views based on it define the structure and behavior of a system.

A particular static configuration of a system at one instant is called a snapshot. A snapshot comprises objects and other instances, values, and links. An object is an instance of a class. Each object is a direct instance of the class that completely describes it and an indirect instance of the ancestors of that class. (If multiple classification is allowed, then an object may be the direct instance of more than one class.) Similarly, each link is an instance of an association, and each value is an instance of a data type.

An object has one data value for each attribute in its class. The value of each attribute must be consistent with the data type of the attribute. If the attribute has optional or multiple multiplicity, then the attribute may hold zero or multiple values. A link comprises a tuple of values, each of which is a reference to an object of a given class (or one of its descendants). Objects and links must obey any constraints on the classes or associations of which they are instances (including both explicit constraints and built-in constraints, such as multiplicity).

The state of a system is a *valid system instance* if every instance in it is an instance of some element in a well-formed system model and if all the constraints imposed by the model are satisfied by the instances.

The static view defines the set of objects, values, and links that can exist in a single snapshot. In principle, any combination of objects and links that is consistent with a static view is a possible configuration of the model. This does not mean that every possible snapshot can or will occur. Some snapshots may be legal statically but may not be dynamically reachable under the dynamic views in the system.

The behavioral parts of UML describe the valid sequences of snapshots that may occur as a result of both external and internal behavioral effects. The dynamic views define how the system moves from one snapshot to another.

Object diagram

A diagram of a snapshot is an image of a system at a point in time. Because it contains images of objects, it is called an object diagram. It can be useful as an example of the system, for example, to illustrate complicated data structures or to show behavior through a sequence of snapshots over time (Figure 4-13). Remember that all snapshots are examples of systems, not definitions of systems. The definition of system structure and behavior is found in the definitional views, and constructing the definitional views is the goal of modeling and design.

The static view describes the possible instances that can occur. Actual instances do not usually appear directly in models, except as examples.

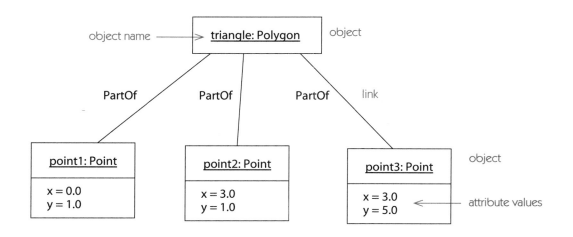

Figure 4-13. *Object diagram*

Overview

The use case view captures the behavior of a system, subsystem, or class as it appears to an outside user. It partitions the system functionality into transactions meaningful to actors—idealized users of a system. The pieces of interactive functionality are called use cases. A use case describes an interaction with actors as a sequence of messages between the system and one or more actors. The term *actor* includes humans, as well as other computer systems and processes. Figure 5-1 shows a use case diagram for a telephone catalog sales application. The model has been simplified as an example.

Actor

An actor is an idealization of an external person, process, or thing interacting with a system, subsystem, or class. An actor characterizes the interactions that outside users may have with the system. At run time, one physical user may be bound to multiple actors within the system. Different users may be bound to the same actor and therefore represent multiple instances of the same actor definition.

Each actor participates in one or more use cases. It interacts with the use case (and therefore with the system or class that owns the use case) by exchanging messages. The internal implementation of an actor is not relevant in the use case; an actor may be characterized sufficiently by a set of attributes that define its state.

Actors may be defined in generalization hierarchies, in which an abstract actor description is shared and augmented by one or more specific actor descriptions.

An actor may be a human, another computer system, or some executable process.

An actor is drawn as a small stick person with the name below it.

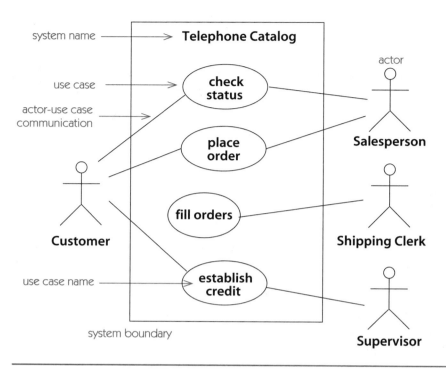

Figure 5-1. *Use case diagram*

Use Case

A use case is a coherent unit of externally visible functionality provided by a system unit and expressed by sequences of messages exchanged by the system unit and one or more actors of the system unit. The purpose of a use case is to define a piece of coherent behavior without revealing the internal structure of the system. The definition of a use case includes all the behavior it entails—the mainline sequences, different variations on normal behavior, and all the exceptional conditions that can occur with such behavior, together with the desired response. From the user's point of view, these may be abnormal situations. From the system's point of view, they are additional variations that must be described and handled.

In the model, the execution of each use case is independent of the others, although an implementation of the use cases may create implicit dependencies among them due to shared objects. Each use case represents an orthogonal piece of functionality whose execution can be mixed with the execution of other use cases.

The dynamics of a use case may be specified by UML interactions, shown as statechart diagrams, sequence diagrams, collaboration diagrams, or informal text descriptions. When use cases are implemented, they are realized by collaborations among classes in the system. One class may participate in multiple collaborations and therefore in multiple use cases.

At the system level, use cases represent external behavior of the entire system as visible to outside users. A use case is like a system operation, an operation invocable by an outside user. Unlike an operation, however, a use case can continue to receive input from its actors during its execution. Use cases can also be applied internally to smaller units of a system, such as subsystems and individual classes. An internal use case represents behavior that a part of the system presents to the rest of the system. For example, a use case for a class represents a coherent chunk of functionality that a class provides to other classes that play certain roles within the system. A class can have more than one use case.

A use case is a logical description of a slice of system functionality. It is not a manifest construct in the implementation of a system. Instead, each use case must be mapped onto the classes that implement a system. The behavior of the use case is mapped onto the transitions and operations of the classes. Inasmuch as a class can play multiple roles in the implementation of a system, it may therefore realize portions of multiple use cases. Part of the design task is to find implementation classes that cleanly combine the proper roles to implement all the use cases, without introducing unnecessary complications. The implementation of a use case can be modeled as a set of one or more collaborations. A collaboration is a realization of a use case.

A use case can participate in several relationships, in addition to association with actors (Table 5-1).

Table 5-1: *Kinds of Use Case Relationships*

Relationship	Function	Notation
association	The communication path between an actor and a use case that it participates in	———
extend	The insertion of additional behavior into a base use case that does not know about it	«extend» - - - ⇢
use case generalization	A relationship between a general use case and a more specific use case that inherits and adds features to it	———▷
include	The insertion of additional behavior into a base use case that explicitly describes the insertion	«include» - - - ⇢

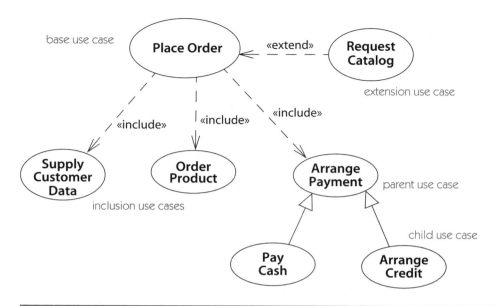

Figure 5-2. *Use case relationships*

A use case is drawn as an ellipse with its name inside or below it. It is connected by solid lines to actors that communicate with it.

Although each use case instance is independent, the description of a use case can be factored into other, simpler use cases. This is similar to the way the description of a class can be defined incrementally from the description of a superclass. A use case can simply incorporate the behavior of other use cases as fragments of its own behavior. This is called an include relationship. In this case, the new use case is not a special case of the original use case and cannot be substituted for it.

A use case can also be defined as an incremental extension to a base use case. This is called an extend relationship. There may be several extensions of the same base use case that may all be applied together. The extensions to a base use case add to its semantics; it is the base use case that is instantiated, not the extension use cases.

The include and extend relationships are drawn as dashed arrows with the keyword «include» or «extend». The include relationship points at the use case to be included; the extend relationship points at the use case to be extended.

A use case can also be specialized into one or more child use cases. This is use case generalization. Any child use case may be used in a situation in which the parent use case is expected.

Use case generalization is drawn the same as any generalization, as a line from the child use case to the parent use case with a large triangular arrowhead on the parent end. Figure 5-2 shows use case relationships in the catalog sales application.

6

State Machine View

Overview

The state machine view describes the dynamic behavior of objects over time by modeling the lifecycles of objects of each class. Each object is treated as an isolated entity that communicates with the rest of the world by detecting events and responding to them. Events represent the kinds of changes that an object can detect—the receipt of calls or explicit signals from one object to another, a change in certain values, or the passage of time. Anything that can affect an object can be characterized as an event. Real-world happenings are modeled as signals from the outside world to the system.

A state is a set of object values for a given class that have the same qualitative response to events that occur. In other words, all objects with the same state react in the same general way to an event, so all objects in a given state execute the same action when they receive the same event. Objects in different states, however, may react differently to the same event, by performing different actions. For example, an automatic teller machine reacts to the cancel button one way when it is processing a transaction and another way when it is idle.

State machines describe the behavior of classes, but they also describe the dynamic behavior of use cases, collaborations, and methods. For one of these objects, a state represents a step in its execution. We talk mostly in terms of classes and objects in describing state machines, but they can be applied to other elements in a straightforward way.

State Machine

A state machine is a graph of states and transitions. Usually a state machine is attached to a class and describes the response of an instance of the class to events that it receives. State machines may also be attached to operations, use cases, and collaborations to describe their execution.

A state machine is a model of all possible life histories of an object of a class. The object is examined in isolation. Any external influence from the rest of the world is summarized as an event. When the object detects an event, it responds in a way that depends on its current state. The response may include the execution of an action and a change to a new state. State machines can be structured to inherit transitions, and they can model concurrency.

A state machine is a localized view of an object, a view that separates it from the rest of the world and examines its behavior in isolation. It is a reductionist view of a system. This is a good way to specify behavior precisely, but often it is not a good way to understand the overall operation of a system. For a better idea of the system-wide effects of behavior, interaction views are often more useful. State machines are useful for understanding control mechanisms, however, such as user interfaces and device controllers.

Event

An event is a noteworthy occurrence that has a location in time and space. It occurs at a point in time; it does not have duration. Model something as an event if its occurrence has consequences. When we use the word *event* by itself, we usually mean an event descriptor—that is, a description of all the individual event occurrences that have the same general form, just as the word *class* means all the individual objects that have the same structure. A specific occurrence of an event is called an event instance. Events may have parameters that characterize each individual event instance, just as classes have attributes that characterize each object. As with classes, signals can be arranged in generalization hierarchies to share common structure. Events can be divided into various explicit and implicit kinds: signal events, call events, change events, and time events. Table 6-1 is a list of event types and their descriptions.

Table 6-1: *Kinds of Events*

Event Type	Description	Syntax
call event	Receipt of an explicit synchronous request among objects that waits for a response	op (a:T)
change event	A change in value of a Boolean expression	**when** (exp)
signal event	Receipt of an explicit, named, asynchronous communication among objects	sname (a:T)
time event	The arrival of an absolute time or the passage of a relative amount of time	**after** (time)

Signal event. A signal is a named entity that is explicitly intended as a communication vehicle between two objects; the reception of a signal is an event for the receiving object. The sending object explicitly creates and initializes a signal instance and sends it to one or a set of explicit objects. Signals embody asynchronous one-way communication, the most fundamental kind. The sender does not wait for the receiver to deal with the signal but continues with its own work independently. To model two-way communication, multiple signals can be used, at least one in each direction. The sender and the receiver can be the same object.

Signals may be declared in class diagrams as classifiers, using the keyword «signal»; the parameters of the signal are declared as attributes. As classifiers, signals can have generalization relationships. Signals may be children of other signals; they inherit the parameters of their parents, and they trigger transitions that depend on the parent signal (Figure 6-1).

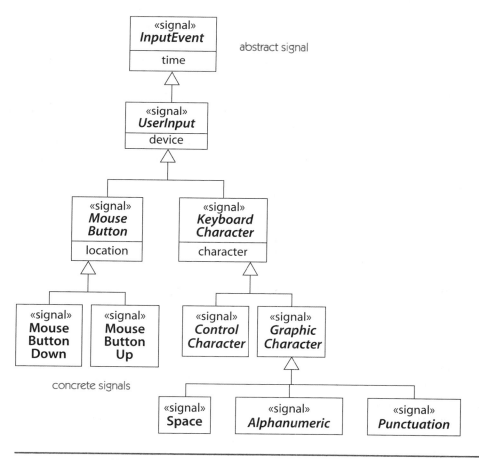

Figure 6-1. *Signal hierarchy*

Call event. A call event is the reception of a call by an object that chooses to implement an operation as a state machine transition rather than as a fixed procedure. To the caller, an ordinary call (implemented by a method) is indistinguishable from a call event. The receiver chooses whether an operation will be implemented as a method or a call event trigger in a state machine. The parameters of the operation are the parameters of the event. Once the receiving object processes the call event by taking a transition triggered by the event or failing to take any transition, control returns to the calling object. Unlike an ordinary call, however, the receiver of a call event may continue its own execution in parallel with the caller.

Change event. A change event is the satisfaction of a Boolean expression that depends on certain attribute values. This is a declarative way to wait until a condition is satisfied, but it must be used with care, because it represents a continuous and potentially nonlocal computation (action at a distance, because the value or values tested may be distant). This is both good and bad. It is good because it focuses the model on the true dependency—an effect that occurs when a given condition is satisfied—rather than on the mechanics of testing the condition. It is bad because it obscures the cause-and-effect relationship between the action that changes an underlying value and the eventual effect. The cost of testing a change event is potentially large, because in principle it is continuous. In practice, however, there are ways to avoid unnecessary computation. Change events should be used only when a more explicit form of communication is unnatural.

Note the difference between a guard condition and a change event. A guard condition is evaluated once when the trigger event on the transition occurs and the receiver handles the event. If it is false, the transition does not fire and the condition is not reevaluated. A change event is evaluated continuously until it becomes true, at which time the transition fires.

Time event. Time events represent the passage of time. A time event can be specified either in absolute mode (time of day) or relative mode (time elapsed since a given event). In a high-level model, time events can be thought of as events from the universe; in an implementation model, they are caused by signals from some specific object, either the operating system or an object in the application.

State

A state describes a period of time during the life of an object of a class. It can be characterized in three complementary ways: as a set of object values that are qualitatively similar in some respect; as a period of time during which an object waits for some event or events to occur; or as a period of time during which an object performs some ongoing activity. A state may have a name, although often it is anonymous and is described simply by its actions.

In a state machine, a set of states is connected by transitions. Although transitions connect two states (or more, if there is a fork or join of control), transitions are processed by the state that they leave. When an object is in a state, it is sensitive to the trigger events on transitions leaving the state.

A state is shown as a rectangle with rounded corners (Figure 6-2).

Confirm Credit

Figure 6-2. *State*

Transition

A transition leaving a state defines the response of an object in the state to the occurrence of an event. In general, a transition has an event trigger, a guard condition, an action, and a target state. Table 6-2 shows kinds of transitions and implicit actions invoked by transitions.

External transition. An *external transition* is a transition that changes the active state. This is the most common kind of transition. It is drawn as an arrow from the

Table 6-2: *Kinds of Transitions and Implicit Actions*

Transition Kind	Description	Syntax
entry action	An action that is executed when a state is entered	entry/ action
exit action	An action that is executed when a state is exited	exit/ action
external transition	A response to an event that causes a change of state or a self-transition, together with a specified action. It may also cause the execution of exit and/or entry actions for states that are exited or entered.	e(a:T)[exp]/action
internal transition	A response to an event that causes the execution of an action but does not cause a change of state or execution of exit or entry actions	e(a:T)[exp]/action

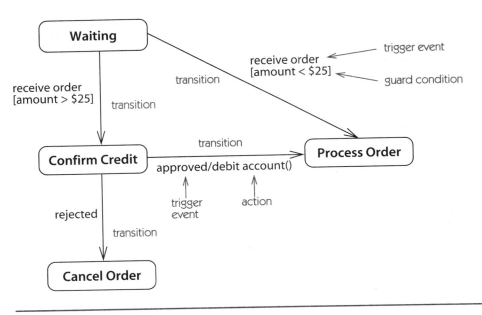

Figure 6-3. *External transitions*

source state to the target state, with other properties shown as a text string attached to the arrow (Figure 6-3).

Trigger event. The trigger is an event the occurrence of which enables the transition. The event may have parameters, which are available to an action on the transition. If a signal has descendants, any descendant of the signal enables the transition. For example, if a transition has **MouseButton** as a trigger (see Figure 6-1), then **MouseButtonDown** will trigger the transition.

An event is not a continuous thing; it occurs at a point in time. When an object receives an event, it saves the event if it is not free to handle the event. An object handles one event at a time. A transition must fire at the time the object handles the event; the event is not "remembered" until later (except in the special case of deferred events, which are saved until they trigger a transition or until the object is in a state where they are not deferred). If two events occur simultaneously, they are handled one at a time. An event that does not trigger any transition is simply ignored and lost. This is not an error. It is much easier to ignore unwanted events than to try to specify all of them.

Guard condition. A transition may have a guard condition, which is a Boolean expression. It may reference attributes of the object that owns the state machine, as well as parameters of the trigger event. The guard condition is evaluated when a trigger event occurs. If the expression evaluates as true, then the transitions fires—that is, its effects occur. If the expression evaluates as false, then the transition does not fire. The guard condition is evaluated only once, at the time the trigger event occurs. If the condition is false and later becomes true, it is too late to fire the transition.

The same event can be a trigger for more than one transition leaving a single state. Each transition with the same event must have a different guard condition. If the event occurs, a transition triggered by the event may fire if its condition is true. Often, the set of guard conditions covers all possibilities so that the occurrence of the event is guaranteed to fire some transition. If all possibilities are not covered and no transition is enabled, then an event is simply ignored. Only one transition may fire (within one thread of control) in response to one event occurrence. If an event enables more than one transition, only one of them fires. A transition on a nested state takes precedence over a transition on one of its enclosing states. If two conflicting transitions are enabled at the same time, one of them fires nondeterministically. The choice may be random or it may depend on implementation details, but the modeler should not count on a predicable result.

Completion transition. A transition that lacks an explicit trigger event is triggered by the completion of activity in the state that it leaves (this is a completion transition). A completion transition may have a guard condition, which is evaluated at the time the activity in the state completes (and not thereafter).

Action. When a transition fires, its action (if any) is executed. An action is an atomic and normally brief computation, often an assignment statement or simple arithmetic computation. Other actions include sending a signal to another object, calling an operation, setting return values, creating or destroying an object, and undefined control actions specified in an external language. An action may also be an action sequence—that is, a list of simpler actions. An action or action sequence cannot be terminated or affected by simultaneous actions. Conceptually, its duration is negligible compared to outside event timing; therefore, a second event cannot occur during its execution. In practice, however, actions take some time, and incoming events must be placed on a queue.

The overall system can perform multiple actions simultaneously. When we call actions atomic, we do not imply that the entire system is atomic. The system can process hardware interrupts and time share between several actions. An action is atomic within its own thread of control. Once started, it must complete and it must not interact with other simultaneously active actions. But actions should not be used as a long transaction mechanism. Their duration should be brief compared to the response time needed for external events. Otherwise, the system might be unable to respond in a timely manner.

An action may use parameters of the trigger event and attributes of the owning object as part of its expression.

Table 6-3 lists the kinds of actions and their descriptions.

Table 6-3: *Kinds of Actions*

Action Kind	Description	Syntax
assignment	Sets the value of a variable	target := expression
call	Calls an operation on a target object; waits for completion of the operation execution; may return a value	opname (arg, arg)
create	Creates a new object	**new** Cname (arg, arg)
destroy	Destroys an object	object **.destroy** ()
return	Specifies return values for the caller	**return** value
send	Creates a signal instance and sends it to a target object or set of objects	sname (arg, arg)
terminate	Self-destruction of the owning object	**terminate**
uninterpreted	Language-specific action, such as conditional or iteration	[language specific]

Change of state. When the execution of the action is complete, the target state of the transition becomes active. This may trigger exit actions or entry actions.

Nested states. States may be nested inside other composite states (see following entry). A transition leaving an outer state is applicable to all states nested within it. The transition is eligible to fire whenever any nested state is active. If it fires, the target state of the transition becomes active. Composite states are useful for expressing exception and error conditions, because transitions on them apply to all nested states without the need for each nested state to handle the exception explicitly.

Entry and exit actions. A transition across one or more levels of nesting may exit and enter states. A state may have actions that are performed whenever the state is entered or exited. Entering the target state executes an entry action attached to the state. If the transition leaves the original state, then its exit action is executed before the action on the transition and the entry action on the new state.

Entry actions are often used to perform setup needed within a state. Because an entry action cannot be evaded, any actions that occur inside the state can assume that the setup has occurred, regardless of how the state is entered. Similarly, an exit action is an action that occurs whenever the state is exited, an opportunity to perform clean up. It is particularly useful when there are high-level transitions that represent error conditions that abort nested states. The exit action can clean up such cases so that the state of the object remains consistent. Entry and exit actions could in principle be attached to incoming and outgoing transitions, but declaring them as special actions of the state permits the state to be defined independently of its transitions and therefore encapsulated.

Internal transition. An internal transition has a source state but no target state. The firing rules for an internal transition are the same as for a transition that changes state. An internal transition has no target state, so the active state does not change as a result of its firing. If an internal transition has an action, it is executed, but no change of state occurs, and therefore no exit or entry actions are executed. Internal transitions are useful for modeling interrupt actions that do not change the state (such as counting occurrences of an event or putting up a help screen).

Entry and exit actions use the same notation as internal transitions, except they use the reserved words **entry** and **exit** in place of the event trigger name, although these actions are triggered by external transitions that enter or leave the state.

A self-transition invokes exit and entry actions on its state (conceptually, it exits and then reenters the state); therefore, it is not equivalent to an internal transition. Figure 6-4 shows entry and exit actions as well as internal transitions.

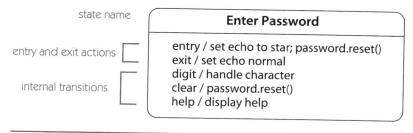

Figure 6-4. *Internal transitions, and entry and exit actions*

Composite States

A simple state has no substructure, just a set of transitions and possible entry and exit actions. A composite state is one that has been decomposed into sequential substates or concurrent substates. Table 6-4 lists the various kinds of states.

A decomposition into disjoint substates is a kind of specialization of a state. An outer state is refined into several inner states, each of which inherits the transitions of the outer state. Only one sequential substate can be active at one time. The outer state represents the condition of being in any one of the inner states.

Table 6-4: *Kinds of States*

State Kind	Description	Notation
simple state	A state with no substructure	
concurrent composite state	A state that is divided into two or more concurrent substates, all of which are concurrently active when the composite state is active	
sequential composite state	A state that contains one or more disjoint substates, exactly one of which is active at one time when the composite state is active	
initial state	A pseudostate that indicates the starting state when the enclosing state in invoked	
final state	A special state whose activation indicates the enclosing state has completed activity	
junction state	A pseudostate that chains transition segments into a single run-to-completion transition	
history state	A pseudostate whose activation restores the previously active state within a composite state	
submachine reference state	A state that references a submachine, which is implicitly inserted in place of the submachine reference state	include **S**
stub state	A pseudostate within a submachine reference state that identifies a state in the referenced state machine	

Transitions into or out of a composite state invoke the entry actions or exit actions of the state. If there are several composite states, a transition across several levels may invoke multiple entry actions (outermost first) or several exit actions (innermost first). If there is an action on the transition itself, the action is executed after any exit actions and before any entry actions are executed.

A composite state may also have an initial state within it. A transition to the composite state boundary is implicitly a transition to the initial state. A new object starts at its initial state of its outermost state. Similarly, a composite state can have a final state. A transition to the final state triggers a completion transition (trigger-less transition) on the composite state. If an object reaches the final state of its outermost state, it is destroyed. Initial states, final states, entry actions, and exit actions permit the definition of a state to be encapsulated independent of transitions to and from it.

Figure 6-5 shows a sequential decomposition of a state, including an initial state. This is the control for a ticket-selling machine.

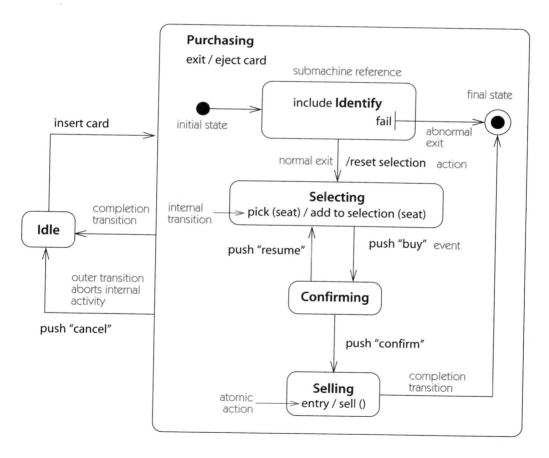

Figure 6-5. *State machine*

A decomposition into concurrent substates represents independent computation. When a concurrent superstate is entered, the number of control threads increases. When it is exited, the number of control threads decreases. Often, concurrency is implemented by a distinct object for each substate, but concurrent substates can also represent logical concurrency within a single object. Figure 6-6 shows the concurrent decomposition of taking a university class.

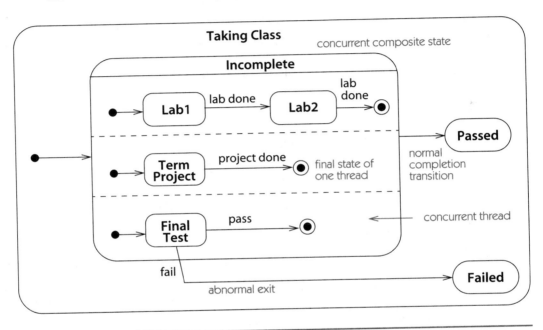

Figure 6-6. *State machine with concurrent composite state*

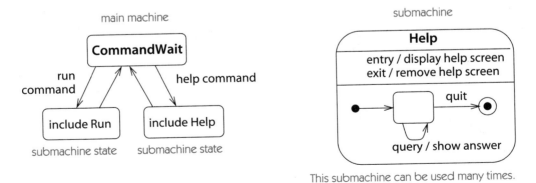

Figure 6-7. *Submachine state*

It is often convenient to reuse a fragment of a state machine in other state machines. A state machine can be given a name and referenced from a state of one or more other machines. The target state machine is a submachine, and the state referencing it is called a submachine reference state. It implies the (conceptual) substitution of a copy of the referenced state machine at the place of reference, a kind of state machine subroutine. Instead of a submachine, a state can contain an activity—that is, a computation or continuous occurrence that takes time to complete and that may be interrupted by events. Figure 6-7 shows a submachine reference.

A transition to a submachine reference state causes activation of the initial state of the target submachine. To enter a submachine at other states, place one or more stub states in the submachine reference state. A stub state identifies a state in the submachine.

7

Activity View

Overview

An activity graph is a special form of state machine intended to model computations and workflows. The states of the activity graph represent the states of executing the computation, not the states of an ordinary object. Normally, an activity graph assumes that computations proceed without external event-based interruptions (otherwise, an ordinary state machine may be preferable).

An activity graph contains activity states. An activity state represents the execution of a statement in a procedure or the performance of an activity in a workflow. Instead of waiting for an event, as in a normal wait state, an activity state waits for the completion of its computation. When the activity completes, then execution proceeds to the next activity state within the graph. A completion transition in an activity diagram fires when the preceding activity is complete. Activity states usually do not have transitions with explicit events, but they may be aborted by transitions on enclosing states.

An activity graph may also contain action states, which are similar to activity states, except that they are atomic and do not permit transitions while they are active. Action states should usually be used for short bookkeeping operations.

An activity diagram may contain branches, as well as forking of control into concurrent threads. Concurrent threads represent activities that can be performed concurrently by different objects or persons in an organization. Frequently concurrency arises from aggregation, in which each object has its own concurrent thread. Concurrent activities can be performed simultaneously or in any order. An activity graph is like a traditional flow chart except it permits concurrent control in addition to sequential control—a big difference.

Activity Diagram

An activity diagram is the notation for an activity graph (Figure 7-1). It includes some special shorthand symbols for convenience. These symbols can actually be

BoxOffice::ProcessOrder

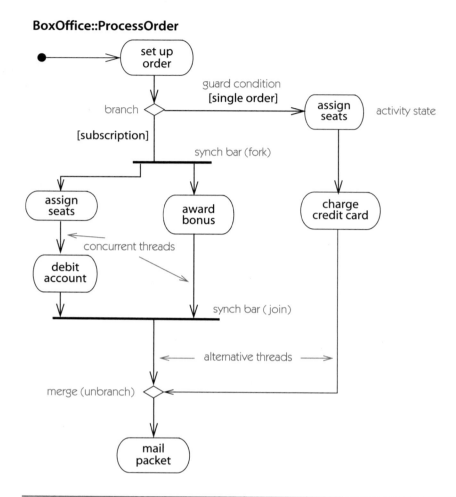

Figure 7-1. *Activity diagram*

used on any statechart diagram, although mixing notation may be ugly much of the time.

An activity state is shown as a box with rounded ends containing a description of the activity. (Normal state boxes have straight sides and rounded corners.) Simple completion transitions are shown as arrows. Branches are shown as guard conditions on transitions or as diamonds with multiple labeled exit arrows. A fork or join of control is shown the same way as on a statechart, by multiple arrows entering or leaving a heavy synchronization bar. Figure 7-1 shows an activity diagram for processing an order by the box office.

For those situations in which external events must be included, the receipt of an event can be shown as a trigger on a transition or as a special inline symbol that denotes waiting for a signal. A similar notation shows sending a signal. If there are many event-driven transitions, however, an ordinary statechart diagram is probably preferable.

Swimlanes. It is often useful to organize the activities in a model according to responsibility—for example, by grouping together all the activities handled by one business organization. This kind of assignment can be shown by organizing the activities into distinct regions separated by lines in the diagram. Because of their appearance, each region is called a swimlane. Figure 7-2 shows swimlanes.

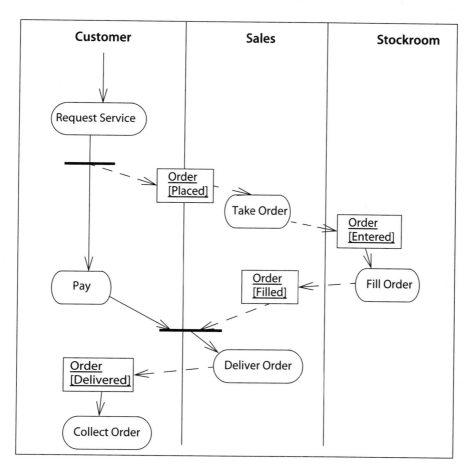

Figure 7-2. *Swimlanes and object flows*

Object flows. An activity diagram can show the flow of object values, as well as the flow of control. An object flow state represents an object that is the input or output of an activity. For an output value, a dashed arrow is drawn from an activity to an object flow state. For an input value, a dashed arrow is drawn from an object flow state to an activity. If an activity has more than one output value or successor control flow, the arrows are drawn from a fork symbol. Similarly, multiple inputs are drawn to a join symbol.

Figure 7-2 shows an activity diagram in which both activities and object flow states have been assigned to swimlanes.

Activities and Other Views

Activity graphs do not show the full detail of a computation. They show the flow of activities but not the objects that perform the activities. Activity graphs are a starting point for design. To complete a design, each activity must be expanded as one or more operations, each of which is assigned to a specific class to implement. Such an assignment results in the design of a collaboration that implements the activity graph.

8

Interaction View

Overview

Objects interact to implement behavior. This interaction can be described in two complementary ways, one of them centered on individual objects and the other on a collection of cooperating objects.

A state machine is a narrow, deep view of behavior, a reductionist view that looks at each object individually. A state machine specification is precise and leads immediately to code. It can be difficult to understand the overall functioning of a system, however, because a state machine focuses on a single object at a time, and the effects of many state machines must be combined to determine the behavior of an entire system. The interaction view provides a more holistic view of the behavior of a set of objects. This view is modeled by collaborations.

Collaboration

A collaboration is a description of a collection of objects that interact to implement some behavior within a context. It describes a society of cooperating objects assembled to carry out some purpose. A collaboration contains slots that are filled by objects and links at run time. A collaboration slot is called a role because it describes the purpose of an object or link within the collaboration. A classifier role represents a description of the objects that can participate in an execution of the collaboration; an association role represents a description of the links that can participate in an execution of the collaboration. A classifier role is a classifier that is constrained by its part in the collaboration; an association role is an association that is constrained by its part in the collaboration. Relationships among classifier roles and association roles inside a collaboration are only meaningful in that context. In general, the same relationships do not apply to the underlying classifiers and associations apart from the collaboration.

The static view describes the inherent properties of a class. For example, a **Vehicle** has an owner. A collaboration describes the properties that an instance of a class has because it plays a particular role in a collaboration. For example, a **rental-Vehicle** in a **RentalCar** collaboration has a **rentalDriver**, something that is not relevant to a **Vehicle** in general but is an essential part of the collaboration.

An object in a system may participate in more than one collaboration. Collaborations in which it appears need not be directly related, although their execution is connected through the shared object. For example, one person may be both a **rentalDriver** and a **hotelGuest** as part of a **Vacation** model. Somewhat less often, an object may play more than one role in the same collaboration.

A collaboration has both a structural aspect and a behavioral aspect. The structural aspect is similar to a static view—it contains a set of roles and their relationships that define the context for its behavioral aspect. The behavioral aspect is the set of messages exchanged by the objects bound to the roles. Such a set of messages on a collaboration is called an interaction. A collaboration can include one or more interactions, each of which describes a series of messages exchanged among the objects in the collaboration to perform a goal.

Whereas a state machine is narrow and deep, a collaboration is broad but more shallow. It captures a more holistic view of behavior in the exchange of messages within a network of objects. Collaborations show the unity of the three major structures underlying computation: data structure, control flow, and data flow.

Interaction

An interaction is a set of messages within a collaboration that are exchanged by classifier roles across association roles. When a collaboration exists at run time, objects bound to classifier roles exchange message instances across links bound to association roles. An interaction models the execution of an operation, use case, or other behavioral entity.

A message is a one-way communication between two objects, a flow of control with information from a sender to a receiver. A message may have parameters that convey values between the objects. A message can be a signal (an explicit, named, asynchronous interobject communication) or a call (the synchronous invocation of an operation with a mechanism for later returning control to the sender).

The creation of a new object is modeled as an event caused by the creator object and received by the class itself. The creation event is available to the new instance as the current event on the transition from the top-level initial state.

Messages can be arranged into sequential threads of control. Separate threads represent sets of messages that are concurrent. Synchronization among threads is modeled by constraints among messages in different threads. One synchronization construct can model forks of control, joins of control, and branches.

Sequencing of messages can be shown in two kinds of diagrams: a sequence diagram (focusing on the time sequences of the messages) and a collaboration diagram (focusing on the relationships among the objects that exchange the messages).

Sequence Diagram

A sequence diagram displays an interaction as a two-dimensional chart. The vertical dimension is the time axis; time proceeds down the page. The horizontal dimension shows the classifier roles that represent individual objects in the collaboration. Each classifier role is represented by a vertical column—the lifeline. During the time an object exists, the role is shown by a dashed line. During the time an activation of a procedure on the object is active, the lifeline is drawn as a double line.

A message is shown as an arrow from the lifeline of one object to that of another. The arrows are arranged in time sequence down the diagram.

Figure 8-1 shows a typical sequence diagram with asynchronous messages.

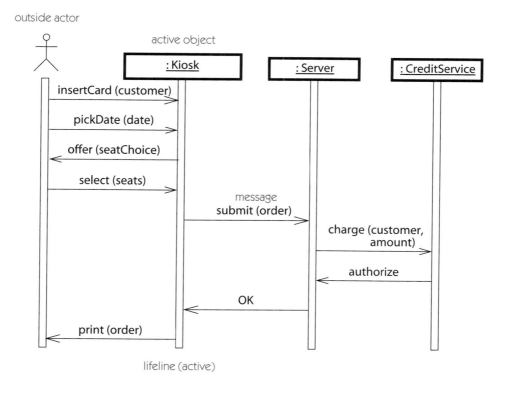

Figure 8-1. *Sequence diagram*

Activation

An activation is the execution of a procedure, including the time it waits for nested procedures to execute. It is shown by a double line replacing part of the lifeline in a sequence diagram. A call is shown by an arrow leading to the top of the activation the call initiates. A recursive call occurs when control reenters an operation on an object, but the second call is a separate activation from the first. Recursion or a nested call to another operation on the same object is shown in a sequence diagram by stacking the activation lines. Figure 8-2 shows a sequence diagram with procedural flow of control, including a recursive call and the creation of an object during the computation.

An active object is one that holds the root of a stack of activations. Each active object has its own event-driven thread of control that executes in parallel with other active objects. The objects that are called by an active object are passive objects; they receive control only when called, and they yield it up when they return.

If several concurrent threads of control have their own procedural flows of control using nested calls, the different threads must be distinguished using thread names, colors, or other means to avoid confusion when two threads come together

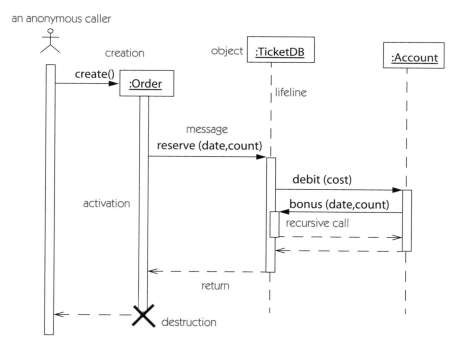

Figure 8-2. *Sequence diagram with activations*

on a single object (by a rendezvous, for example). Usually, it is best not to mix procedure calls with signals on a single diagram.

Collaboration Diagram

A collaboration diagram is a class diagram that contains classifier roles and association roles rather than just classifiers and associations. Classifier roles and association roles describe the configuration of objects and links that may occur when an instance of the collaboration is executed. When the collaboration is instantiated, objects are bound to the classifier roles and links are bound to the association roles. Association roles may also be played by various kinds of temporary links, such as procedure arguments or local procedure variables. Link symbols may carry stereotypes to indicate temporary links («**parameter**» or «**local**») or calls to the same object («**self**»). Only objects that are involved in the collaboration are represented, although there may be others in the entire system. In other words, a collaboration diagram models the objects and links involved in the implementation of an interaction and ignores the others. Figure 8-3 shows a collaboration diagram.

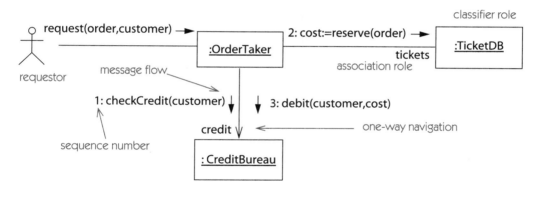

Figure 8-3. *Collaboration diagram*

It is useful to mark the objects in four groups: those that exist through the entire interaction; those created during the interaction (constraint {**new**}); those destroyed during the interaction (constraint {**destroyed**}); and those that are created and destroyed during the interaction (constraint {**transient**}). During design, you can start by showing the objects and links available at the start of an operation and then decide how control can flow to the correct objects within the graph to implement the operation.

Although collaborations directly show the implementation of an operation, they may also show the realization of an entire class. In this usage, they show the context needed to implement *all* of the operations of a class. This permits the modeler to see the multiple roles that objects may play in various operations. This view can be constructed by taking the union of all the collaborations needed to describe all the operations of the object.

Messages. Messages are shown as labeled arrows attached to links. Each message has a sequence number, an optional list of predecessor messages, an optional guard condition, a name and argument list, and an optional return value name. The sequence number includes the (optional) name of a thread. All messages in the same thread are sequentially ordered. Messages in different threads are concurrent unless there is an explicit sequencing dependency. Various implementation details may be added, such as a distinction between asynchronous and synchronous messages.

Flows. Usually, a collaboration diagram contains a symbol for an object during an entire operation. Sometimes, however, an object has different states that must be made explicit. For example, an object might change location, or its associations might differ significantly at different times. An object can be shown with both its class and its state—an object with a class-in-state. The same object can be shown multiple times, each with a different location or state.

The various object symbols that represent one object may be connected using become flows. A become flow is a transition from one object state to another. It is drawn as a dashed arrow with the stereotype «**become**» and may be labeled with a sequence number to show when it occurs (Figure 8-4). A become flow is also used to show migration of an object from one location to another.

Less commonly, the stereotype «**copy**» shows an object value produced by copying another object value.

Table 8-1 shows the kinds of object flow relationships.

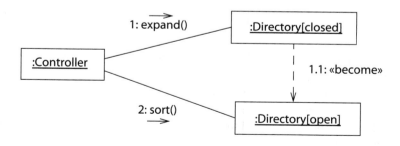

Figure 8-4. *Become flow*

Table 8-1: *Kinds of Flow Relationships*

Flow	Function	Notation
become	Transformation from one value of an object to another value	«become» - - - - - - ➤
copy	Copy of an object that is thereafter independent	«copy» - - - - - - ➤

Collaboration and sequence diagrams. Collaboration diagrams and sequence diagrams both show interactions, but they emphasize different aspects. Sequence diagrams show time sequences clearly but do not show object relationships explicitly. Collaboration diagrams show object relationships clearly, but time sequences must be obtained from sequence numbers. Sequence diagrams are often most useful for showing scenarios; collaboration diagrams are often more useful for showing detailed design of procedures.

Patterns

A pattern is a parameterized collaboration, together with guidelines about when to use it. A parameter can be replaced by different values to produce different collaborations. The parameters usually designate slots for classes. When a pattern is instantiated, its parameters are bound to actual classes within a class diagram or to roles within a larger collaboration.

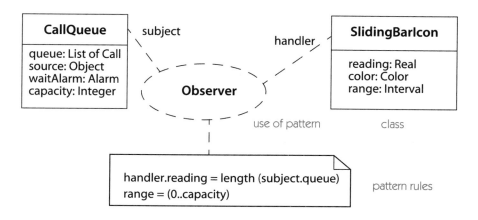

Figure 8-5. *Pattern usage*

The use of a pattern is shown as a dashed ellipse connected to each of its classes by a dashed line that is labeled with the name of the role. For example, Figure 8-5 shows the use of the **Observer** pattern from [Gamma-95]. In this use of the pattern, **CallQueue** replaces the **subject** role and **SlidingBarIcon** replaces the **handler** role.

Patterns may appear at the analysis, architecture, detailed design, and implementation levels. They are a way to capture frequently occurring structures for reuse. Figure 8-5 shows a use of the Observer pattern .

9

Physical Views

Overview

Much of a system model is intended to show the logical and design aspects of the system independent of its final packaging in an implementation medium. The implementation aspects are important, however, for both reusability and performance purposes. UML includes two kinds of views for representing implementation units: the implementation view and the deployment view.

The implementation view shows the physical packaging of the reusable pieces of the system into substitutable units, called components. An implementation view shows the implementation of design elements (such as classes) by components, as well as interfaces of and dependencies among components. Components are the high-level reusable pieces out of which systems can be constructed.

The deployment view shows the physical arrangement of run-time computational resources, such as computers and their interconnections. They are called nodes. At run time, nodes can contain components and objects. The assignment of components and objects to nodes can be static, or they can migrate among nodes. The deployment view may show performance bottlenecks if component instances with dependencies are placed on different nodes.

Component

A component is a physical unit of implementation with well-defined interfaces that is intended to be used as a replaceable part of a system. Each component embodies the implementation of certain classes from the system design. Well-designed components do not depend directly on other components but on interfaces that components support. In that case, a component in a system can be replaced by another component that supports the proper interfaces.

Components have interfaces they support and interfaces they require from other components. An interface is a list of operations supported by a piece of software or hardware. The use of named interfaces permits direct dependencies

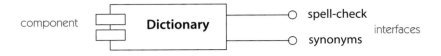

Figure 9-1. *Component with interfaces*

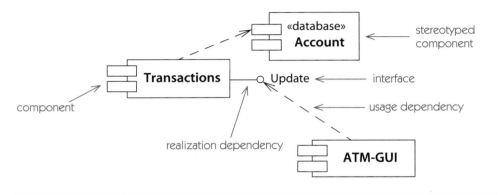

Figure 9-2. *Component diagram*

among components to be avoided, facilitating easier substitution of new components. The component view shows the network of dependencies among components. The component view can appear in two forms. It can show a set of available components (a component library) with their dependencies; this is the material out of which a system can be assembled. It can also show a configured system, with the selection of components (out of the entire library) used to build it. In this form, each component is wired to other components whose services it uses; these connections must be consistent with the interfaces of the components.

A component is drawn as a rectangle with two small rectangles on its side. It may be attached by solid lines to circles that represent its interfaces (Figure 9-1).

A component diagram shows dependencies among components (Figure 9-2). Each component realizes (supports) some interfaces and uses others. If dependencies among components are mediated through interfaces, components can be replaced by other components that realize the same interfaces.

Node

A node is a run-time physical object that represents a computational resource, generally having at least a memory and often processing capability as well. Nodes may have stereotypes to distinguish different kinds of resources, such as CPUs, devices, and memories. Nodes may hold objects and component instances.

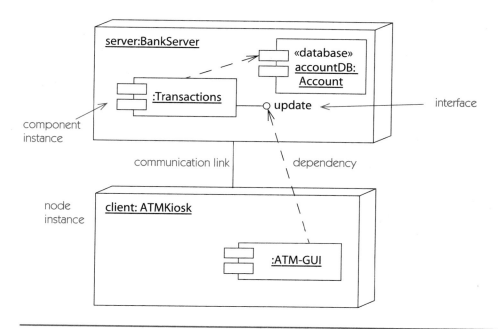

Figure 9-3. *Deployment diagram*

A node is shown as a stylized cube with the name of the node and, optionally, its classification (Figure 9-3).

Associations between nodes represent communication paths. The associations can have stereotypes to distinguish different kinds of paths.

Nodes may have generalization relationships to relate a general description of a node to a more specific variation.

The presence of an object on a node is shown by physically nesting the object symbol inside the node symbol. If that is not convenient, the object symbol may contain the tag **location** whose value is the name of the node on which the object resides (its location). Migration of objects or component instances among nodes may also be shown.

See become.

10
Model Management View

Overview

Any large system must be divided into smaller units so that humans can work with a limited amount of information at one time and so that work teams do not interfere with each other's work. Model management consists of packages (including special kinds of packages) and dependency relationships among packages.

Package

A package is a piece of a model. Every part of a model must belong to one package. The modeler may allocate the contents of a model to a set of packages. But to be workable, the allocation must follow some rational principle, such as common functionality, tightly coupled implementation, and a common viewpoint. UML does not impose a rule for composing packages, but a good decomposition into packages will greatly enhance model maintainability.

Packages contain top-level model elements, such as classes and their relationships, state machines, use case graphs, interactions, and collaborations—anything not contained in some other element. Elements such as attributes, operations, states, lifelines, and messages are contained in other elements and do not appear as direct contents of packages. Every top-level element has one package in which it is declared. This is its "home" package. It may be referenced in other packages, but the contents of the element are owned by the home package. In a configuration control system, a modeler must have access to the home package to modify the contents of an element. This provides an access control mechanism for working with large models. Packages are also the units for any versioning mechanisms.

Packages may contain other packages. There is a root package that indirectly contains the entire model of a system. There are several possible ways to organize the packages in a system. They may be arranged by view, by functionality, or by any other basis that the modeler chooses. Packages are general-purpose hierarchical organizational units of UML models. They can be used for storage, access control, configuration management, and constructing libraries containing reusable model fragments.

If the packages are well chosen, they reflect the high-level architecture of a system—its decomposition into subsystems and their dependencies. A dependency among packages summarizes the dependencies among the package contents.

Dependencies on Packages

Dependencies arise among individual elements, but in a system of any size, they must be viewed at a higher level. Dependencies among packages summarize dependencies among elements in them—that is, package dependencies are derivable from the dependencies among individual elements.

The presence of a dependency among packages implies that there exists in a bottom-up approach (an existence statement), or is permitted to exist later in a top-down approach (a constraint restricting any other relationship), at least one relationship element of the given kind of dependency among individual elements within the corresponding packages. It is an "existence statement" and does not imply that all elements of the package have the dependency. It is a flag to the modeler that there exists further information, but the package-level dependency does not contain the further information itself; it is only a summary.

The top-down approach reflects the overall system architecture. The bottom-up approach can be automatically generated from the individual elements. Both approaches have their place in modeling, even on a single system.

Multiple dependencies of the same kind among individual elements are aggregated to a single package-level dependency among the packages containing the elements. If the dependencies among individual elements contain stereotypes (such as different kinds of usage), the stereotype may be omitted in the package-level dependency in order to yield a single high-level dependency.

Packages are drawn as rectangles with tabs on them (desktop "folder" icons). Dependencies are shown as dashed arrows.

Figure 10-1 shows the package structure for a ticket-ordering subsystem. It has dependencies on outside packages and two variations of the **Seat selection** package. Any one implementation of the subsystem would only include one variation.

Access and Import Dependency

A package cannot, in general, access the contents of another package. Packages are opaque unless they are opened by an access or import dependency. The access dependency applies directly to packages and other containers. On the package level, the access dependency indicates that the contents of the supplier package may be referenced by the elements in the client package or by packages embedded within

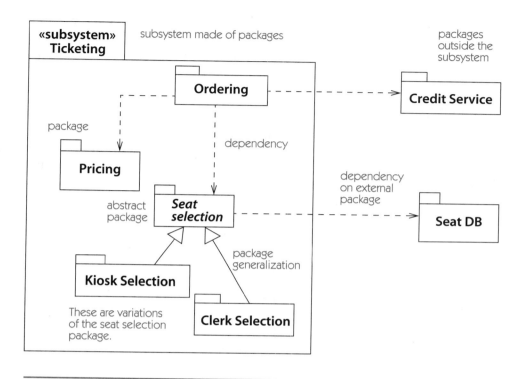

Figure 10-1. *Packages and their relationships*

the client. An element in the supplier must have sufficient visibility within its package to enable a client to see it. In general, a package can see only the elements of other packages that have been given public visibility by the package containing them. Elements with protected visibility are visible only to packages that are descendants of the package containing the elements. Elements with private visibility are visible only in the package containing them and any packages nested inside that package. Visibility also applies to the contents of classes (attributes and operations). A descendant of a class can see members of its ancestor with public or protected visibility; any other class may only see members with public visibility. Both access permission and the proper visibility are needed to reference an element. So for an element in one package to see an element in an unrelated package, the first package must access or import the second package, and the target element must have public visibility within the second package.

A package nested within another package is part of the container and has full access to its contents without the need of accesses. The container, however, may not see inside its nested packages without accessing them. Contents are encapsulated.

Note that an access dependency does not modify the namespace of the client or in any other way automatically create references. It merely grants permission to establish references. The import dependency is used to add names to the namespace of the client package as aliases for the full pathnames.

Model and Subsystem

A model is a package that encompasses a complete description of a particular view of a system. It provides a closed description of a system from one viewpoint. It does not have strong dependencies on other packages, such as implementation dependencies or inheritance dependencies. The trace relationship is a weak form of dependency among elements in different models that notes the presence of some connection without specific semantic implications.

Usually, a model is tree-structured. The root package contains in itself nested packages that constitute the full detail of the system from the given viewpoint.

A subsystem is a package that has separate specification and realization parts. It represents a coherent unit of the model with clean interfaces to the rest of the system. It usually represents the partition of the system on a functional or implementation boundary. Both models and subsystems are drawn as packages with stereotype keywords (Figure 10-1).

11

Extension Mechanisms

Overview

UML provides several extension mechanisms to allow modelers to make some common extensions without having to modify the underlying modeling language. These extension mechanisms have been designed so that tools can store and manipulate the extensions without understanding their full semantics. For this reason, the extensions can be stored and manipulated as strings. To a tool that does not understand the extension, it is just a string, but it can be entered, stored as part of a model, and passed to other tools. It is expected that back-end tools and add-ins will be written to process various kinds of extensions. These tools will define a particular syntax and semantics for their extensions that only they need understand.

This approach to extensions probably will not meet every need that arises, but we feel it would accommodate a large portion of the tailoring needed by most modelers in a simple manner that is easy to implement.

The extensibility mechanisms are constraints, tagged values, and stereotypes.

Keep in mind that an extension, by definition, deviates from the standard form of UML and may therefore lead to interoperability problems. The modeler should carefully weigh benefits and costs before using extensions, especially when existing mechanisms will work reasonably well. Typically, extensions are intended for particular application domains or programming environments, but they result in a UML dialect, with the advantages and disadvantages of all dialects.

Constraint

A constraint is a semantic restriction represented as a text expression. Each expression has an implicit interpretation language, which may be a formal mathematical notation, such as set-theoretic notation; a computer-based constraint language, such as OCL; a programming language, such as C++; or pseudocode or informal natural language. Of course, if the language is informal, then its interpretation is informal also and must be done by a human. Even if a constraint is expressed in a formal language, it does not mean that it will automatically be enforced. Full truth maintenance is beyond the state of the art of computing in most cases today, but at least the semantics will be precise.

Constraints can express restrictions and relationships that cannot be expressed using UML notation. They are particularly useful for stating global conditions or conditions that affect a number of elements.

Constraints are shown as expression strings enclosed in braces. They may be appended to a list element, attached to a dependency, or enclosed in a note. Figure 11-1 shows several kinds of constraints.

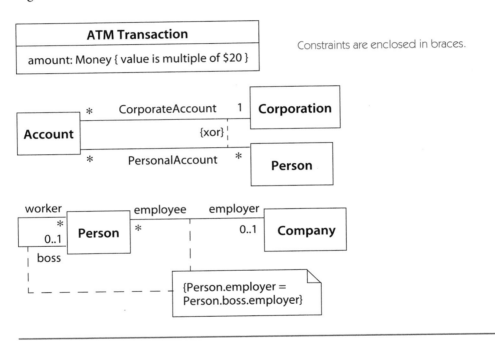

Figure 11-1. *Constraints*

Tagged Value

A tagged value is a pair of strings—a tag string and a value string—that stores a piece of information about an element. A tagged value may be attached to any individual element, including model elements and presentation elements. The tag is a name of some property the modeler wants to record, and the value is the value of that property for the given element. For example, the tag might be **author**, and the value might be the name of the person responsible for the element, such as **Charles Babbage**.

Tagged values can be used to store arbitrary information about elements. They are particularly useful for storing project management information, such as the creation date of an element, its development status, due dates, and test status. Any string may be used as a tag name, except that the names of built-in metamodel attributes should be avoided (because tags and attributes together can be considered properties of an element and accessed uniformly in a tool), and a number of tag names are predefined (see Chapter 14, Standard Elements).

Tagged values also provide a way to attach implementation-dependent add-in information to elements. For example, a code generator needs additional information about the kind of code to generate from a model. Often, there are several possible ways to correctly implement a model; the modeler must provide guidance about which choices to make. Certain tags can be used as flags to tell the code generator which implementation to use. Other tags can be used for other kinds of add-in tools, such as project planners and report writers.

Tagged values can also be used to store information about stereotyped model elements (discussed below).

Tagged values are shown as strings with the tag name, an equal sign, and the value. They are normally placed in lists inside braces (Figure 11-2). They will often be omitted on diagrams but shown on pop-up lists and forms.

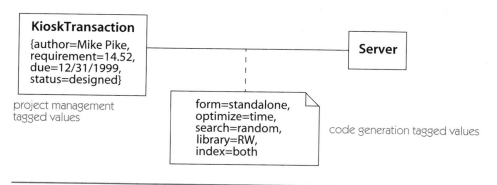

Figure 11-2. *Tagged values*

Stereotypes

Many modelers wish to tailor a modeling language for a particular application domain. This carries some risk, because the tailored language will not be universally understandable, but people nevertheless attempt to do it.

A stereotype is a kind of model element defined in the model itself. The information content and form of a stereotype are the same as those of an existing kind of base model element, but its meaning and usage is different. For example, modelers in the business modeling area often wish to distinguish business objects and business processes as special kinds of modeling elements whose usage is distinct within a given development process. These can be treated as special kinds of classes—they have attributes and operations, but they have special constraints on their relationships to other elements and on their usage.

A stereotype is based on an existing model element. The information content of the stereotyped element is the same as the existing model element. This permits a tool to store and manipulate the new element the same way it does the existing element. The stereotyped element may have its own distinct icon—this is easy for a tool to support. For example, a "business organization" might have an icon that looks like a group of persons. The stereotype may also have a list of constraints that apply to its usage. For example, perhaps a "business organization" can be associated only with another "business organization" and not with any class. Not all constraints can be automatically verified by a general-purpose tool, but they can be enforced manually or verified by an add-in tool that understands the stereotype.

Stereotypes may use tagged values to store additional properties that are not supported by the base element.

Stereotypes are shown as text strings surrounded by guillemets (« ») placed in or near the symbol for the base model element. The modeler may also create an icon for a particular stereotype, which replaces the base element symbol (Figure 11-3).

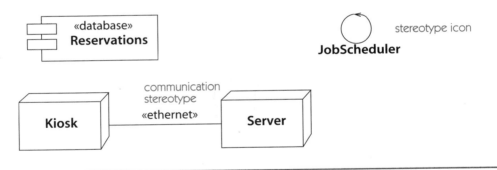

Figure 11-3. *Stereotypes*

Tailoring UML

The extension mechanisms of constraints, tagged values, and stereotypes make it possible to tailor UML profiles for special application domains. Several profiles have already been made and are described in Appendix C, Process Extensions. Others have been proposed by users. The ability to tailor the modeling language means that application domains can adapt the modeling language to their needs, yet still share the vast preponderance of concepts that are generic and common to all domains.

12

UML Environment

Overview

UML models are used within an environment. Most people use modeling as a means to an end—namely, the development of good systems—and not an end in itself. The purpose and interpretation of the model are affected by the rest of the environment. Other facilities in the wider environment include metamodels that cross many languages, model-editing tools, programming languages, operating systems and major system components, and the business and engineering world within which systems are used. The responsibility for giving meaning to a model and implementing its intent lies with all these facilities, including UML.

Models occur at various levels of concreteness. UML is a general-purpose modeling language that includes semantics and notation but is usable with different tools and implementation languages. Each level of usage introduces certain modeling considerations that appear in the UML to various degrees.

Semantics Responsibilities

A metamodel is the description of a model. A modeling language describes models; therefore, it can be described by a metamodel. A metamodel attempts to make a language precise by defining its semantics, but there is a tension to permit extensions for new situations. The actual form of the metamodel is important to tool implementation and model interchange but not very important to most users. We therefore have not covered it in this book. Those who are interested can consult the original standards documents [UML-98] available on the companion CD.

A metamodel and a language must cover a lot of ground and accommodate many interpretations. Existing systems have differing execution and memory models. It is impossible to choose one of them as the right interpretation. In fact, it is probably misleading to even consider such a choice. Instead, one can think of the different interpretations of execution models as semantic variation points. A semantic variation point is a point of difference about the detailed semantics of execution, but one that is orthogonal to other aspects of a system. For example, an environment may or may not choose to support dynamic classification, the ability of an object to change class at run time. Today, most programming languages do not permit it, mainly for programming-language implementation reasons, but some do. The difference is indistinguishable in the static semantics. The choice of static classification or dynamic classification can be identified as a semantic variation point with two options: static classification or dynamic classification. When such choices exist, people often argue about which is the right interpretation. Realize instead that this is a choice and give it a name so that either can be used.

A metamodel describes the contents of a well-formed model, just as a programming language describes a well-formed program. Only a well-formed model has a meaning and proper semantics; it does not make sense to ask the meaning of an ill-formed model. Much of the time, however, models under development are not well formed. They are incomplete and possibly inconsistent. But that is what model-editing tools must support—incomplete models, not just finished models. The UML metamodel describes correct, well-formed models. A separate metamodel can describe possible model fragments. We leave it to the tool makers to decide where to draw the line on supporting model fragments, and what kind of semantic support to give to ill-formed models.

UML includes some built-in extension mechanisms to tailor its use in specialized domains. The mechanisms include the ability to define stereotypes and tagged values. These mechanisms can be used to tailor a UML variant by defining a set of stereotypes and tags and adopting conventions for their use in order to build a model. For example, variants could be developed that are focused on the implementation semantics of various programming languages. Adding extensions can be powerful, but it carries some inherent dangers. Because their semantics are not defined within UML, UML cannot supply their meaning; the interpretation is up to the modeler. Furthermore, if you are not careful, some meanings may be ambiguous or even inconsistent. Modeling tools can provide automated support for stereotypes and tags defined by the tools, but not for user-defined extensions. Regardless of the support for extensions, any extension pulls the user away from the common center that the language standard provides and undercuts the goals of interchangeability of models and of the understandability of models. Of course, whenever you use a particular class library, you diverge from the perfect interchangeability of nothingness. So don't worry about it in the abstract. Use the extensions when they help, but avoid them when they are not needed.

Notation Responsibilities

Notation does not add meaning to a model, but it does help the user to understand the meaning in it. Notation does not have semantics, but it often adds connotations for a user, such as the perceived affinity of two concepts based on their nearness in a diagram.

The UML documents [UML-98] and this book define a canonical UML notation, what might be called the publication format for models. This is similar to many programming languages in which programs within journal articles are printed in an attractive format with careful layout, reserved words in boldface, and separate figures for each procedure. Real compilers have to accept messier input. We expect that editing tools will extend the notation to a screen format, including such things as the use of fonts and color to highlight items; the ability to easily suppress and filter items that are not currently of interest, to zoom into a diagram to show nested elements, to traverse hot links to other models or views; and animation. It would be hopeless to try to standardize all these possibilities and foolish to try, because there is no need and it would limit useful innovation. This kind of notational extension is the responsibility of a tool builder. In an interactive tool, there is less danger from ambiguity, because the user can always ask for a clarification. This is probably more useful than insisting on a notation that is totally unambiguous at first glance. The point is that a tool must be able to produce the canonical notation when requested, especially in printed form, but reasonable extensions should be expected in an interactive tool.

We expect that tools will also permit users to extend notation in limited but useful ways. We have specified that stereotypes can have their own icons. Other kinds of notational extensions might be permitted, but users need to use some discretion.

Note that notation is more than pictures; it includes information in text-based forms and the invisible hyperlinks among presentation elements.

Programming Language Responsibilities

UML must work with various implementation languages without incorporating them explicitly. We felt that UML should permit the use of any (or at least many) programming languages, for both specification and target-code generation. The problem is that each programming language has many semantic issues that we did not want to absorb into UML, because they are better handled as programming-language issues, and there is considerable variation in execution semantics. For example, the semantics of concurrency are handled in diverse ways among the languages (if they are handled at all).

Primitive data types are not described in detail in UML. This is deliberate as we did not wish to incorporate the semantics of one programming language in preference to all others. For most modeling purposes, this is not a problem. Use the semantic model applicable to your target language. This is an example of a semantic variation point.

The representation of detailed language properties for implementation raises the problem of capturing information about implementation properties without building their semantics into UML. Our approach was to capture language properties that go beyond UML's built-in capabilities by means of stereotypes and tagged values. These can be assigned to language properties and code-generation options by a tool or code generator. A generic editor need not understand them. Indeed a user could create a model using a tool that did not support the target language and transfer the final model to another tool for final processing. Of course, if the tool does not understand the stereotypes and tags, it cannot check them for consistency. But this is no worse than normal practice with text editors and compilers. If necessary, a tool can be created to use a particular set of extensions.

Code generation and reverse engineering for the foreseeable future will require input from the designer in addition to a UML model. Directives and hints to the code generator can be supplied as tagged values and stereotypes. For example, the modeler could indicate which kind of container class should be used to implement an association. Of course, this means that code-generation settings in tools might be incompatible, but we do not believe there currently is sufficient agreement on the right approach to standardize the actual settings. In any case, different tools will use their code generators as their competitive advantage. Eventually, default settings may emerge and become ripe for standardization.

Modeling with Tools

Models require tool support for realistic-sized systems. Tools provide interactive ways to view and edit models. They provide a level of organization that is outside the scope of the UML itself but that conveys understanding to the user and helps in accessing information. Tools help to find information in large models by searching and filtering what is presented.

Tool issues

Tools deal with the physical organization and storage of models. These must support multiple work teams on a single project, as well as reuse across projects. The following issues are outside the scope of canonical UML, but must be considered for actual tool usage.

Ambiguities and unspecified information. At early stages, many things are still unsaid. Tools must be able to adjust the precision of a model and not force every value to be specific. See the following sections "Inconsistent models for work in progress" and "Null and unspecified values."

Presentation options. Users do not want to see all the information all the time. Tools must support filtering and hiding of information that is unwanted at a given time. Tools will also add support for alternate visualizations by using the capabilities of the display hardware. This has been covered above in the section "Notation Responsibilities."

Model management. Configuration control, access control, and versioning of model units are outside the scope of UML, but they are crucial to the software engineering process and go on top of the metamodel.

Interfaces to other tools. Models need to be handled by code generators, metrics calculators, report writers, execution engines, and other back-end tools. Information for other tools needs to be included in the models, but it is not UML information. Tagged values are suitable for holding this information.

Inconsistent models for work in progress

The ultimate goal of modeling is to produce a description of a system at some level of detail. The final model must satisfy various validity constraints to be meaningful. As in any creative process, however, the result is not necessarily produced in a linear fashion. Intermediate products will not satisfy all the validity constraints at every step. In practice, a tool must handle not only semantically valid models, which satisfy the validity constraints, but also syntactically valid models, which satisfy certain construction rules but may violate some validity constraints. Semantically invalid models are not directly usable. Instead they may be thought of as "works in progress" that represent paths to the final result.

Null and unspecified values

A complete model must have values for all the attributes of its elements. In many cases, null (no value) is one of the possible values, but whether a value may be null is a part of the type description of the attribute; many types do not have a natural null value within their range of values. For example, null makes no sense as the upper bound on the size of a set. Either the set has a fixed upper size or there is no bound, in which case its maximum size is unlimited, so nullability is really just an augmentation to the range of possible values of a data type.

On the other hand, during early stages of design, a developer may not care about the value of a particular property. It might be a value that is not meaningful at a particular stage, for example, visibility when making a domain model. Or the value may be meaningful but the modeler may not have specified it yet, and the developer needs to remember that it still needs to be chosen. In this case, the value is unspecified. This indicates that a value will eventually be needed but that it has not yet been specified. It is not the same as a null value, which may be a legitimate value in the final model. In many cases, particularly with strings, a null value is a good way to indicate an unspecified value, but they are not the same. An unspecified value is not meaningful in a well-formed model. The UML definition does not handle unspecified values. They are the responsibility of tools that support UML and are considered part of a "work in progress" model that, by necessity, has no semantic meaning.

Part 3: Reference

13

Encyclopedia of Terms

abstract

A class, use case, signal, other classifier, or other generalizable element that cannot be directly instantiated. Also used to describe an operation that has no implementation. Antonym: concrete.

See abstract operation, generalizable element.

Semantics

An abstract class is a class that is not instantiable—that is, it may not have direct instances, either because its description is incomplete (such as lacking methods for one or more operations) or because it is not intended to be instantiated even though its description is complete. An abstract class is intended for specialization. To be useful, an abstract class must have descendants that may have instances; an abstract leaf class is useless. (It can appear as a leaf in a framework, but eventually, it must be specialized.)

A concrete class may not have any abstract operations (otherwise, it is necessarily abstract), but an abstract class may have concrete operations. Concrete operations are those that can be implemented once and used the same across all subclasses. In their implementation, concrete operations may use only features (attributes and operations) known to the class in which they are declared. One of the purposes of inheritance is to factor such operations into abstract superclasses so that they can be shared by all subclasses. A concrete operation may be polymorphic—that is, it can be overridden by a method in a descendant class—but it need not be polymorphic (it may be a leaf operation). A class, all of whose operations are implemented, may be abstract, but it must be explicitly declared as such. A class with one or more unimplemented operations is automatically abstract.

The same semantics apply to use cases. An abstract use case defines a fragment of behavior that cannot appear by itself, but it can appear in the definition of concrete use cases by the generalization, include, or extend relationships. By factoring the common behavior into an abstract use case, the model is made smaller and easier to understand.

A similar relationship exists with other classifiers and other generalizable elements.

Notation

The name of an abstract class or an abstract operation is shown in italics. Alternately, the keyword **abstract** may be placed in a property list below or after the name, for example, Account {abstract}.

See also class name.

Example

Figure 13-1 shows an abstract class Account with one abstract operation, computeInterest, and one concrete operation, deposit. Two concrete subclasses have been declared. Because the subclasses are concrete, each of them must implement the operation computeInterest. Attributes are always concrete.

Discussion

The distinction between modeling a class as abstract or concrete is not as fundamental or clear-cut as it might first appear. It is more a design decision about a model than an inherent property. During the evolution of a design, the status of a class may change. A concrete class may be modeled as abstract if subclasses that

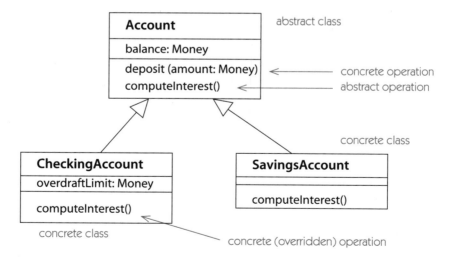

Figure 13-1. *Abstract and concrete classes*

enumerate all its possibilities are added. An abstract class may be modeled as concrete if distinctions among subclasses are found to be unnecessary and removed or are represented by attribute values instead of distinct subclasses.

One way to simplify the decision is to adopt the design principle that all nonleaf classes must be abstract (and all leaf classes must of necessity be concrete, except for an abstract leaf class intended for future specialization). This is not a UML rule; it is a style that may or may not be adopted. The reason for this "abstract superclasses" rule is that an inheritable method on a superclass and a method on a concrete class often have different needs that are not well served by a single method. The method on the superclass is forced to do two things: define the general case to be observed by all descendants and implement the general case for the specific class. These goals frequently conflict. Instead, any nonabstract superclass can be separated mechanically into an abstract superclass and a concrete leaf subclass. The abstract superclass contains all methods intended to be inherited by all subclasses; the concrete subclass contains methods that are needed for the specific instantiable class. Following the abstract superclass rule also allows a clean distinction between a variable or parameter that must hold the specific concrete type and one that can hold any descendant of the superclass.

In Figure 13-2, consider the declaration of class **Letter** that does not follow the abstract superclass rule. This class has an operation, **getNextSentence**, that returns the text for the next unread sentence, as well as an operation, **resetCursor**, that sets the cursor to the beginning. However, the subclass **EncryptedLetter** represents a letter that has been encrypted. The operation **getNextSentence** has been

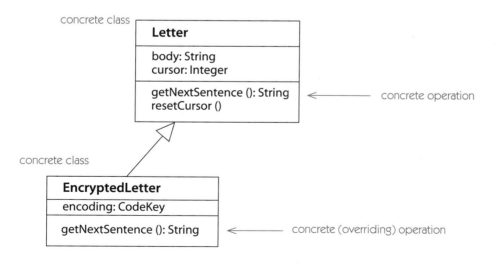

Figure 13-2. *Concrete superclass leads to ambiguity*

overridden because the text must be decrypted before it is returned. The implementation of the operation is completely different. Because **Letter** is a concrete superclass, it is impossible to distinguish a parameter that must be an ordinary **Letter** (nonoverridable) from one that could be either an ordinary **Letter** or an **EncryptedLetter**.

The abstract superclass approach is to distinguish abstract class **Letter** (which might be an encrypted letter or a nonencrypted letter) and to add class **NonEncryptedLetter** to represent the concrete case, as shown in Figure 13-3. In this case, **getNextSentence** is an abstract operation that is implemented by each subclass and **resetCursor** is a concrete operation that is the same for all subclasses. The model is symmetrical.

If the abstract superclass rule is followed, the declaration of abstract classes can be determined automatically from the class hierarchy and showing it on diagrams is redundant.

There is an exception to the statement that an abstract leaf class is useless: An abstract class may be declared in order to be a common namespace for a set of global class-scope attributes and operations. This is a relatively minor usage, mainly for programming convenience when dealing with non-object-oriented languages, and users are advised to avoid it in most cases. Global values violate the spirit of object-oriented design by introducing global dependencies. A singleton class can often provide the same functionality in a more extensible way.

See [Gamma-95], Singleton pattern.

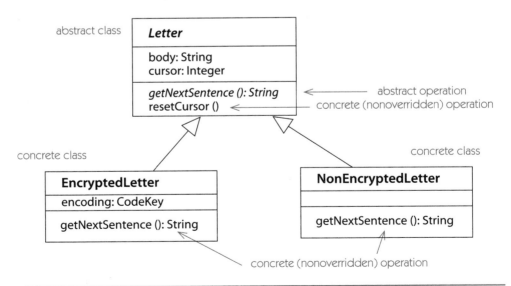

Figure 13-3. *Abstract superclass avoids ambiguity*

abstract class

A class that may not be instantiated.
See abstract.

Semantics

An abstract class may not have direct instances. It may have indirect instances through its concrete descendants.
See abstract for a discussion.

abstract operation

An operation that lacks an implementation—that is, one that has a specification but no method. An implementation must be supplied by any concrete descendant class.
See abstract, generalizable element, inheritance, polymorphic.

Semantics

If an operation is declared as abstract in a class, it lacks an implementation in the class, and the class itself is necessarily abstract. An implementation must be supplied for the operation by a concrete descendant. If the class inherits an implementation of the operation but declares the operation as abstract, the abstract declaration invalidates the inherited method in the class. If an operation is declared as concrete in a class, then the class must supply or inherit an implementation (a method or a call event) from an ancestor. If an operation is not declared at all in a class, then it inherits the operation declaration and implementation (or lack thereof) from its ancestors.

An operation may be implemented as a method or as a state machine transition triggered by a call event. Each class may declare its own method or call event for an operation or inherit a definition from an ancestor.

Notation

The name of an abstract operation is shown in italics (Figure 13-4). Alternately the keyword **abstract** may be placed in a property list after the operation signature.

Discussion

The most important use for the concept of inheritance is to support abstract operations that can be implemented differently by each concrete descendant class. An abstract operation permits a caller to invoke an operation without knowing precisely which class of object is the target, provided the target object is known to

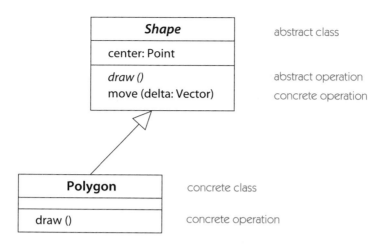

Figure 13-4. *Abstract operation and class*

support the operation by being an indirect instance of an abstract class that has a declaration of the abstract operation. The significance of such polymorphic operations is that the responsibility for determining the kind of object is shifted from the caller to the inheritance mechanism. Not only is the caller freed of the bother and cost of writing case statements, but the caller need not even be aware of which possible subclasses of an abstract class exist. This means that additional subclasses may be added later with new operation implementations. Abstract operations, polymorphism, and inheritance thereby facilitate updating of systems to add new kinds of objects and behaviors without having to modify the code that invokes the generic behavior. This greatly reduces the time needed to update a system and, even more important, it reduces the possibility of accidental inconsistencies.

abstraction

1. The act of identifying the essential characteristics of a thing that distinguish it from all other kinds of things. Abstraction involves looking for similarities across sets of things by focusing on their essential common characteristics. An abstraction always involves the perspective and purpose of the viewer; different purposes result in different abstractions for the same things. All modeling involves abstraction, often at many levels for various purposes.

2. A kind of dependency that relates two elements that represent the same concept at different abstraction levels.

See derivation, realization, refinement, trace.

Semantics

An abstraction dependency is a relationship between two elements at different abstraction levels, such as representations in different models, at different levels of precision, at different levels of concreteness, or at different levels of optimization. Generally the two representations would not be used simultaneously. Normally one element is more detailed than the other; the more detailed element is the client and the less detailed element is the supplier. If there is no clear understanding that either element is more detailed, then either element can be modeled as the client.

The stereotypes of abstraction dependency are trace, refinement (keyword **refine**), realization (keyword **realize**), and derivation (keyword **derive**).

Notation

An abstraction dependency is shown as a dashed arrow from the client element to the supplier element with the keyword «**trace**», «**refine**», or «**derive**». The realization dependency has its own special notation as a dashed arrow with a closed triangular arrowhead on the supplier element.

The mapping between elements can be attached to the relationship as a constraint.

Standard elements

derive, refine, trace

access

A permission dependency that permits one package to reference the elements of another package.

See friend, import, visibility.

Semantics

A package (the client) that references an element in another package (the supplier) must import the package containing the element using an «**access**» or an «**import**» dependency from the client package to the supplier package. A package implicitly gains access to all packages imported by any package within which it is nested (that is, nested packages can see everything that their containing packages see).

An element in a package has access to all elements that are *visible within the package*. The visibility rules may be summarized as follows.

- An element defined in a package is visible within the same package.

- If an element is visible within a package, then it is visible within all packages nested inside the package.

- If a package accesses or imports another package, then all elements defined with public visibility in the accessed or imported package are visible within the importing package.

- If a package is a child of another package, then all elements defined with public or protected visibility in the parent package are visible within the child package.

- Access and import dependencies are not transitive. If A can see B and B can see C, it does not necessarily follow that A can see C.

One consequence is that a package cannot see inside its own nested packages unless it accesses them and unless their contents are public within the nested packages.

The following are some further rules on visibility.

- The contents of a classifier, such as its attributes and operations as well as nested classes, are visible within the package if they have public visibility in the classifier. Note that the unstructured contents of a subsystem are governed by the package rules stated above, but any attributes or operations of the subsystem itself are governed by this rule.

- The contents of a classifier are visible within a descendant classifier if they have public or protected visibility in the classifier.

- All contents of a classifier are visible to elements within the classifier, including within methods or state machines of the classifier.

The normal simple case concerns elements in packages that are peers. In that case, an element can see all the elements in its own package and all the elements with public visibility in those packages imported by its package. A class can see the public features in other classes that it can see. A class can also see protected features in its ancestors.

Notation

An access dependency is shown by a dashed arrow, drawn with its tail on the client package and its head on the supplier package. The arrow uses the keyword «access» as a label.

Discussion

Figure 13-5 shows an example of peer-level access among two packages. Package P can access package Q, but package Q cannot access package P. Classes K and L in package P can see public class M in package Q, but they cannot see private class N. Classes M and N cannot see any class in package P, regardless of the public visibil-

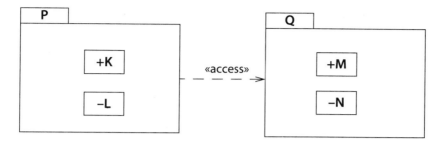

Figure 13-5. *Peer access*

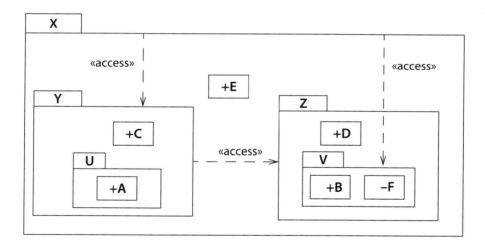

Figure 13-6. *Access rules*

ity of class K, because package Q has no access to package P. For a class to be visible in a peer package, the class must have public visibility and its package must be accessed or imported by the peer package.

Figure 13-6 shows a more complicated case of visibility and access declarations. The symbol in front of an element name represents the visibility of the element outside its own container: + for public, # for protected (visible only to descendants), – for private (not visible outside).

Class A can see C and E because they are in enclosing packages Y and X.

Classes C and A can see D because package Y imports package Z. Class A is nested inside package Y and can therefore see everything Y can see.

Classes A, C, and E can see B because they are nested in package X, which imports package V containing B. They cannot see F, however, because it has private visibility within its package V. Class F, therefore, cannot be seen outside package V.

Class E cannot see D because D is in package Z, which has not been imported by package X.

Class C cannot see A, and E cannot see A. Class A is in package U, which has not been imported by another package.

Classes B and F can see classes D and E, which are found in enclosing packages. They can also see C, which is in package Y, which is imported by enclosing package X. The fact that F is private does not prevent it from seeing other classes, but other classes cannot see F.

Classes B and F can see each other because they are in the same package. Class F is private to classes in outer packages, not to classes in its own package.

action

An executable atomic computation that results in a change in the state of the model or the return of a value. Contrast: activity.

See also entry action, exit action, transition.

Semantics

An action is an atomic computation—that it, it cannot be terminated externally. It can be attached to a transition in a state machine (between two states or within a single state) or to a step in an interaction. Usually, it is a primitive or near-primitive operation on the state of a system, often on the state of a single object. Typical actions include assignments to attribute values, accessing values of attributes or links, creation of new objects or links, simple arithmetic, and sending signals to other objects. Actions are the discrete steps out of which behavior is built. Actions are meant to be "fast" computations so that system response time is not impaired. The system can execute several actions simultaneously and time share among them, but their execution should be independent.

Actions may be attached to a transition. They are executed when the transition fires. They can also appear as entry actions and exit actions of states. These are actions triggered by transitions that enter or leave a state. All actions are atomic, that is, they are executed completely without interference from other operations.

An activity is also a computation, but it may have internal structure and may be terminated by a transition on an external event, therefore it can be attached to a state but not to a transition. Unlike actions, activities can persist indefinitely until externally terminated, although they may also terminate on their own. An action may not be externally terminated and can be attached to a transition or to the entry or exit of a state but not to a state itself.

Structure

An action has a target object set, a reference to the signal to be sent or the operation to be performed (collectively, these are called a *request*), a list of argument values, and an optional recurrence expression specifying possible iteration.

Object set. An object set expression that yields a set of objects. In many cases, the set contains a single fixed object. A copy of the message with the given list of arguments is sent concurrently to each object in the set (that is, it is "broadcast" to them). Each target independently receives and handles a separate instance of the message. If the set is empty, then nothing happens.

Request. Designates a signal or operation declaration. The signal is sent to the objects, or the operation is called (for an operation with a return value the set must contain a single object).

Argument list. A list of arguments. When evaluated, the values in the argument list must match the parameters of the signal or operation. The arguments are supplied as part of the send or call.

Recurrence. An iteration expression specifying how many times to perform the action, optionally specifying iteration variables. This expression can also describe a conditional action (an iteration with either zero or one repetition).

Kinds of actions

Assignment action. An assignment is an action that sets the value of an attribute in an object to a given value. The action has an expression for a target object, the name of an attribute within the object, and an expression for a value to be assigned to the attribute slot in the object.

Call action. A call action results in the invocation of an operation on an object; it is a call to an operation on an object. The action has a message name, a list of argument expressions, and a target object set expression. The target may be a set of objects. In that case the calls occur concurrently and the operation must not have a return value. If the operation has a return value, then it must have a single object as target.

A call action is synchronous. The caller waits for the completion of the invoked operation before receiving control again. If the operation is implemented as a call event, then the caller waits until the receiver executes the transition triggered by the call before receiving control again. If the operation execution returns values, the caller receives them when it receives control again.

Create action. A create action results in the instantiation and initialization of an object (see creation). The action has a reference to a class and an optional class-scope operation with an argument list. Execution of the action creates a new instance of the class; its attributes have the values obtained by evaluating their initial value expressions. If an explicit create operation is given, then it is executed. The operation may override the initialization of the attribute values, usually by using argument values of the create action.

Destroy action. A destroy action results in the destruction of a target object. The action has an expression that evaluates to an object. There are no other arguments. The result of executing the action is the destruction of the object, together with all links involving it and all composite parts of it (see composition).

Return action. A return action causes a transfer of control to the caller of an operation. This action is allowed only inside an operation that is invoked by a call. The action has an optional list of return values that are made available to the caller when it receives control. If the enclosing operation was invoked asynchronously, then the caller must explicitly choose to receive the return message (as a signal), or it is lost.

Send action. A send action creates an instance of a signal and initializes it with the arguments obtained by evaluating the argument expressions in the action. The signal is sent to the objects in the object set obtained by evaluating the target expression in the action. Each object in the set receives its own copy of the signal. The sender keeps its own thread of control and proceeds; sending a signal is asynchronous. The action has the name of a signal, a list of expressions for arguments of the signal, and an object set expression for the target objects.

If the object set is omitted, then the signal is sent to one or more objects determined by the signal and the system configuration. For example, an exception is sent to an enclosing scope determined by system policies.

Terminate action. A terminate action causes the destruction of the object owning the state machine that contains the action (that is, it commits suicide). The destruction of an object is an event to which other objects may respond.

Uninterpreted action. An uninterpreted action is a control construct or other construct not defined in UML.

Notation

UML does not have a fixed action language. It is expected that many modelers will choose to use an actual programming language to write actions. The following adaptation of OCL is used in this book to write action pseudocode, but it is not part of the standard.

Assignment action

    target := expression

Call action

    object-set . operation-name (argument$_{list}$)

Create action

   new class-name (argument$_{list,}$)

Destroy action

   object . destroy ()

Return action

   return expression$_{list,}$

Send action

   object-set . signal-name (argument$_{list,}$)

Terminate action

   terminate

Uninterpreted action

   if (expression) **then** (action) **else** (action)

If it is necessary to distinguish call and send explicitly, the keyword **call** or **send** may be prefixed to the expression. They are optional.

Discussion

The UML specification defines a set of actions with the expectation that others will be added in the actual implementation of support tools. This decision was a result of a trade-off between the desire for precision and the need for developers to work with various target languages, which have a wide range of semantic concepts. There is much more variation in execution semantics among programming languages than there is in data structure or in the set of available control constructs. Subtle differences are difficult to map in a practical way among languages, regardless of whether it is possible in theory. The selection of one programming language as the basis for an action language would, therefore, have the effect of discouraging the others, which we did not want to do. The semantics of actions have therefore been left somewhat incomplete and ambiguous within UML itself. To make the semantics precise, UML must be joined with the semantics of the action language (often a standard programming language) that is being used. Some critics have complained that UML is imprecise because of this freedom, but it is imprecise only to the degree that the chosen action language is imprecise. The real defect is that UML does not impose a lingua franca of actions and other expressions, but this is hardly possible in today's polyglot world of computation, regardless of its emotional appeal.

action expression

An expression that resolves to an action or an action sequence.

Discussion

The syntax of an action expression is not specified by UML. It is the responsibility of support tools. It is expected that different users may use programming languages, pseudocode, or even natural language to express actions. A more precise syntax is, of course, needed for detailed design, but this is where actual programming languages will be used by most users.

action sequence

A sequence of actions to be executed one after another. It is a kind of action.

Semantics

An action sequence is a list of actions. The actions are executed sequentially. The entire sequence is considered an atomic unit (that is, it is noninterruptible). An action sequence is an action and can therefore be attached to transitions and to interaction steps.

Notation

An action sequence is displayed as a string, which consists of a sequence of action strings separated by semicolons.

If actions are expressed in a particular programming language, then its syntax for statement sequences can be used instead.

Example

count := 0; reservations.clear(); **send** kiosk.firstScreen()

action state

A state whose purpose is to execute an action and then transition to another state. *See also* activity state, completion transition.

Semantics

An action state is a state whose purpose is to execute an entry action, after which it takes a completion transition to another state. An action state is atomic—that is, it may not be terminated by a transition on an external event. Conceptually, it represents a computation that completes in negligible time without interacting with other simultaneous actions. In practice, it may require time to complete, but the

time should be shorter than the response times required for events that might occur. It cannot have transitions triggered by events. An action state has no substructure, internal activities, or internal transitions. It is a kind of dummy state that is
useful for organizing state machines into logical structures. It usually has an outgoing completion transition. There may be multiple outgoing completion transitions if they have guard conditions (and therefore represent a branch).

Notation

There is no special notation for an action state. It can be shown as an ordinary
state with an entry action. It can also be shown as an activity state.

activation

The execution of an operation. An activation (also known as focus of control) represents the period during which an object performs an operation either directly or
through a subordinate operation. It models both the duration of the execution in
time and the control relationship between the execution and its callers. In a conventional computer and language, an activation corresponds to a value of the stack
frame.
See call, sequence diagram.

Semantics

An activation is an instance of executing an operation, including the period during
which the operation calls other subordinate operations (see call). Its context comprises a set of local variables that are accessible only to the activation, a current location within the method (or other behavioral description), and a reference (the
return reference) to the activation that represents the calling context, which regains
control when the current activation terminates. An activation with no return reference must be the result of a transition on the state machine of an active class object; when it completes, the state machine simply waits for the next event.

Note that this definition describes an ordinary procedure as implemented in a
typical von Neumann machine. But it is expressed in a general way meant to apply
also to a distributed environment in which there is no shared memory and in
which the stack frame comprises a linked list of activations in different memory
spaces.

Notation

An activation is shown on a sequence diagram as a tall, thin rectangle (a vertical
hollow bar), the top of which is aligned with its initiation time and whose bottom
is aligned with its completion time. The operation being performed is shown by a
text label next to the activation symbol or in the left margin, depending on style.

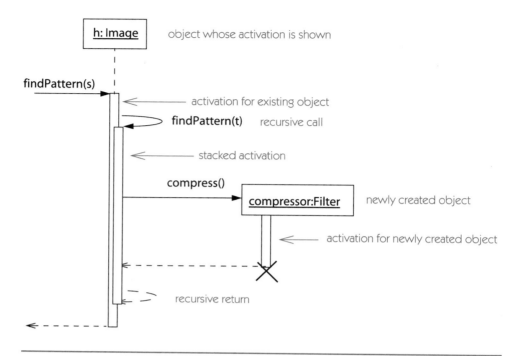

Figure 13-7. *Activations*

Alternately, the incoming message symbol may indicate the operation. In that case, the label may be omitted on the activation itself. If the flow of control is procedural, then the top of the activation symbol is at the tip of the incoming message arrow that initiates the action and the bottom of the symbol is at the tail of a return message arrow.

If there is concurrent activity by multiple objects, then each activation shows the execution of one concurrent object. Unless the objects communicate, the concurrent activations are independent and their relative execution times are irrelevant.

In the case of procedural code, an activation shows the duration during which a procedure is active in the object or a subordinate procedure called by the original procedure is active, possibly in some other object. In other words, all the active nested procedure activations are shown simultaneously. This set of simultaneous nested activations is the stack frame of the computation in a conventional computer. In the case of a second call to an object with an existing activation, the second activation symbol is drawn slightly to the right of the first one, so that they appear to "stack up" visually. Stacked calls may be nested to an arbitrary depth. The calls may be to the same operation (a recursive call) or to different operations on the same object.

Example

Figure 13-7 shows activations resulting from calls, including a recursive call.

active

A state that has been entered and has not yet been exited; one that is held by an object.

See also active class, active object.

Semantics

A state becomes active when a transition entering it fires. An active state ceases to be active when a transition leaving it fires. If an object has a thread of control, then at least one state is active. (In the degenerate case, a class may have only a single state. In that case, the response to an event is always the same.) If a state is active within the state machine for an object's class, the object is said to *hold* the state.

An object may hold multiple states at one time. The set of active states is called the active state configuration. If a nested state is active, then all states that contain it are active. If the object permits concurrency, then more than one concurrent substate may be active. Each transition affects, at most, a few states in the active state configuration. On a transition, unaffected active states remain active.

A composite state may be sequential or concurrent. If it is sequential and active, then exactly one of its immediate substates is active. If it is concurrent and active, then each of its immediate substates is active. In other words, a composite state expands into an AND-OR tree of active substates; at each level, certain states are active.

A transition across a composite state boundary must be structured to maintain these concurrency constraints. A transition into a sequential composite state usually has one source state and one destination state. Firing such a transition does not change the number of active states. A transition into a concurrent composite state usually has one source state and one destination state for each subregion of the concurrent composite state. Such a transition is called a fork. If one or more regions are omitted as destinations, the initial state from each omitted region is implicitly present as a destination; if one of the regions lacks an initial state, then the model is ill formed. Firing such a transition increases the number of active states. The situation is reversed on exit from a concurrent composite state.

See state machine, which contains a full discussion of the semantics of concurrent states and complex transitions.

Example

The top of Figure 13-8 shows a sample state machine with both sequential and concurrent composite states. The transitions have been omitted to focus on the states. The bottom of the figure shows the various configurations of states that can

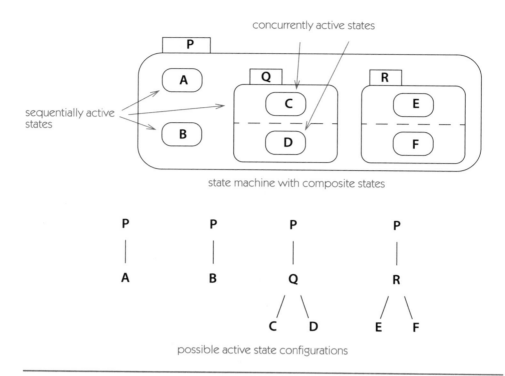

Figure 13-8. *Concurrently active states*

be active concurrently. In this example, there are four possible configurations of active states. Only the leaf states are concrete; the higher states are abstract—that is, an object may not be in one of them without also being in a nested leaf state. For instance, the object may not be in state Q without being in the substates of Q. Because Q is concurrent, both C and D must be active if Q is active. Each leaf state corresponds to a thread of control. In a larger example, the number of possible configurations may grow exponentially and it may be impossible to show them all, hence the advantage of the notation.

active class

A class whose instances are active objects.
See active object for details.

Semantics

An active class is a class whose instances are active objects. Stereotypes for an active class are process and thread.

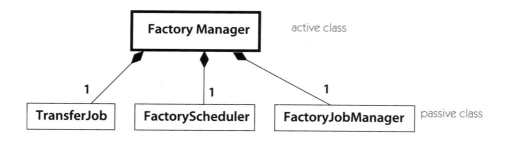

Figure 13-9. *Active class and passive parts*

Notation

An active class is shown with a heavy border.

Example

Figure 13-9 shows a class diagram with an active class and its passive parts. Figure 13-10 shows a collaboration that contains active objects corresponding to this model.

active object

An object that owns a thread of control and can initiate control activity; an instance of an active class.

See also passive object, process, thread.

Semantics

An active object does not run within another thread, stack frame, or state machine. It has an independent locus of control within the overall execution of a system. In a sense, it *is* the thread. Each active object is a distinct locus of execution; active objects are not reentrant, and recursive execution is not possible without the creation of additional objects.

An active object is the root of an execution stack frame in conventional computational terms. The creation of an active object initiates a new instance of a state machine. When the state machine performs a transition, an execution stack frame is created and continues until the action of the transition runs to its completion and the object waits for external input. An active object therefore does not run in the scope of another object. It can be created by an action of another object, but once created, it has an independent existence. The creator may be an active or a passive object. An active object is driven by events. Operations on it by other objects should be implemented by the active object as call events.

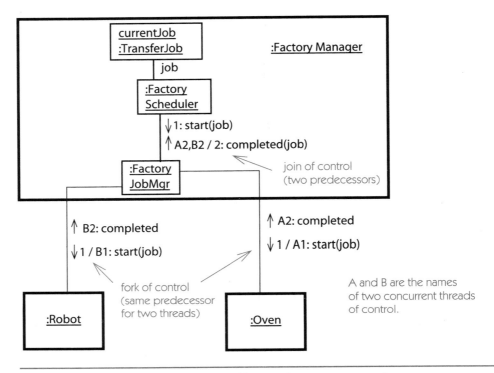

Figure 13-10. *Collaboration with active objects and concurrent control*

A passive object may be created as part of an action by another object. It has its own address space. A passive object has no thread of control. Its operations are called within the stack frame of an active object. It may be modeled by a state machine, however, to show the changes in its state caused by operations on it.

A conventional operating system process is best equated with an active object. An operating system thread may or may not be implemented by an active object.

The active-passive distinction is primarily a design decision and does not constrain the semantics of the objects. Both active and passive objects may have state machines and may exchange events.

Notation

A collaboration role for an active object is shown on a collaboration diagram as a rectangle with a heavy border. Frequently, active object roles are shown as composites with embedded parts.

An active object is also shown as an object symbol with a heavy border, with the name underlined, but active objects appear only within examples of execution and therefore are not so common.

The property keyword {active} may also be used to indicate an active object.

Example

Figure 13-10 shows three active objects in a factory automation system: a robot; an oven; and a factory manager, which is a control object. All three objects exist and execute concurrently. The factory manager initiates a thread of control at step 1, which then forks into two concurrent threads of control (A1 and B1) that are executed by the oven and the robot, respectively. When each has finished its execution, the threads join at step 2, in the factory manager. Each object remains alive and preserves its state until the next event arrives for it.

active state configuration

The set of states that are active at one time within a state machine. The firing of a transition changes a few states in the set; the others remain unchanged.

See active, complex transition, state machine.

activity

Ongoing nonatomic execution within a state machine. Contrast: action.

See also completion transition, state.

Semantics

An activity is the execution of substructure within a state machine, that is, substructure that has duration with possible interruption points. A transition that forces an exit from the controlling region aborts the activity. An activity is not terminated by the firing of an internal transition, because there is no change of state. The action of the internal transition may explicitly terminate it.

Activity can be modeled by nested states, by a submachine reference, or by an activity expression.

Example

Figure 13-11 shows an alarm system that illustrates the difference between an action and an activity. When the event **detect intrusion** occurs, the system fires a transition. As part of the transition, the action **call police** occurs. This is an action, therefore it is something that is atomic (and usually fast). No events may be accepted while the action is being executed. After the action is performed, the system enters the **Sounding** state. While the system is in this state, it performs the **sound alarm** activity. An activity takes time to complete, during which events might occur that interrupt the activity. In this case, the **sound alarm** activity does not terminate on its own; it continues as long as the system is in the **Sounding** state. When the **reset** event occurs, the transition fires and takes the system back to the

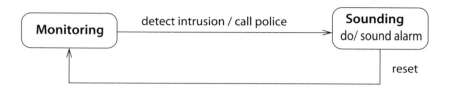

Figure 13-11. *Action and activity*

Monitoring state. When the Sounding state ceases to be active, its activity sound alarm is terminated.

activity diagram

A diagram that shows an activity graph.
See activity graph.

activity expression

A textual expression for a nonatomic computation, an activity. Such an expression is conceptually decomposable into atomic fragments, but it is convenient to permit a textual representation of the entire thing. The execution of an activity expression can be terminated by a transition that deactivates the controlling state.

Semantics

An activity expression is an effective procedure (algorithm) expressed in some language, such as a programming language or other formal language. It can also be expressed in human language. In that case, it will not be executable by tools and cannot be checked for errors or other properties. But it may be sufficient in the early stages of work. It may also represent a continuous real-world operation.

Notation

An activity expression is represented as text interpreted in some language.

Example

do / invertMatrix	Finite but takes time
do / computeBestMove (time-limit)	Compute until time runs out
do / sound siren	Continuous until stopped

activity graph

A special case of a state machine in which all or most of the states are activity states or action states and in which all or most of the transitions are triggered by completion of activity in the source states. An activity graph shows a procedure or a workflow. An activity graph is a complete unit in the model. An activity diagram is a diagram showing an activity graph.

See also state machine.

Semantics

An activity graph is a state machine that emphasizes the sequential and concurrent steps of a computational procedure. Workflows are examples of procedures that are often modeled by activity graphs. Activity graphs generally appear in the earlier stages of design before all implementation decisions have been made—in particular, before objects have been assigned to perform all activities. This type of graph is a variation of a state machine in which a state represents the performance of an activity, such as a computation or a real-world continuous operation, and the transitions are triggered by the completion of operations. An activity graph may be attached to the implementation of an operation as well as to the implementation of a use case.

In an activity graph the states are primarily activity states or action states. An activity state is a shorthand for a state with an internal computation and at least one outgoing completion transition that fires on the completion of activity in the state. There may be several outgoing transitions if they have guard conditions. Activity states should not have internal transitions or outgoing transitions based on explicit events. Use normal states for this situation. An action state is an atomic state—that is, one that may not be interrupted by transitions, even those on surrounding states.

The usual use of an activity state is to model a step in the execution of a procedure. If all the states in a model are activity states, then the result of the computation will not depend on outside events. The computation is deterministic if concurrent activities do not access the same objects and the relative completion times of concurrent activities do not affect the results.

Activity graphs may include ordinary wait states, whose exits are triggered by events, but such usage defeats the purpose of focusing on activities. Use an ordinary state model if there are more than a very few ordinary states.

Dynamic concurrency. An activity state with dynamic concurrency represents concurrent execution of multiple independent computations. The activity is invoked with a set of argument lists. Each member of the set is the argument list for a concurrent invocation of the activity. The invocations are independent of each other.

When all invocations have completed, the activity is complete and triggers its completion transition.

Object flow. Sometimes, it is useful to see the relationships between an operation and the objects that are its argument values or results. The input to and the outputs from an operation may be shown as an object flow state. This is a stereotype of a state that represents the existence of an object of a given class at a particular point in the computation. For added precision, the input or output object may be declared to be in a given state within its class. For example, the output of a "sign contract" operation will be an object flow state of the Contract class in the "signed" state. This object flow state may be an input of many other operations.

Swimlanes. The activities of an activity graph can be partitioned into groups, based on various criteria. Each group represents some meaningful partition of the responsibilities for the activities—for example, the business organization responsible for a given workflow step. Because of their graphical notation, the groups are called swimlanes.

Notation

An activity graph is notated as an activity diagram. Activity graphs are a variety of state machine, but several shorthand notations are particularly suitable for activity diagrams: activity states, branches, merges, swimlanes, object flow states, class-in-state, signal receipt and signal sending notation, and deferred events. See these entries for further details.

See control icons for some optional symbols that can be useful in activity diagrams.

Example

Figure 13-12 shows a workflow of the activities involved in processing an order at a theater box office. It includes a branch and subsequent merge based on whether the order is for a subscription or for individual tickets. The fork initiates concurrent activities that logically occur at the same time. Their actual execution may or may not overlap. The concurrency is terminated by a subsequent matching join. If there is only one person involved, then concurrent activities can be performed in any order (presuming they cannot be performed simultaneously, which is permitted by the model, but might be difficult in practice). For example, the box office personnel could assign the seats, then award the bonus, then debit the account; or they could award the bonus, assign the seats, then debit the account—but they cannot debit the account until after the seats have been assigned.

One output segment from the fork has a guard condition testing whether the subscriber is a member. This is a conditional thread. It is started only if the guard condition is satisfied. If the thread is not started, the input segment to the subse-

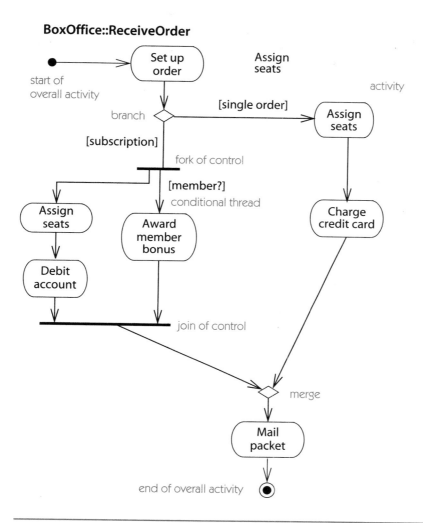

BoxOffice::ReceiveOrder

Figure 13-12. *Activity diagram*

quent matching join is considered completed. If the subscriber is not a member, only one thread is started. It assigns seats and debits the account, but does not wait for synchronization at the join.

Swimlanes. The activities in an activity graph can be partitioned into regions, which are called swimlanes from their visual appearance as regions on a diagram separated by dashed lines. A swimlane is an organizational unit for the contents of an activity graph. It has no inherent semantics, but can be used as the modeler desires. Often, each swimlane represents an organizational unit within a real-world organization.

Example

In Figure 13-13, the activities are divided into three partitions by swimlanes, each one corresponding to a different stakeholder. There is no UML requirement that the partitions correspond to objects, although in this example, there are obvious classes that would fall under each partition, and those classes would be the ones that perform the operations to implement each activity in the finished model.

The figure also shows the use of object flow symbols. The object flows correspond to different states of an order object as it works its way through a network of

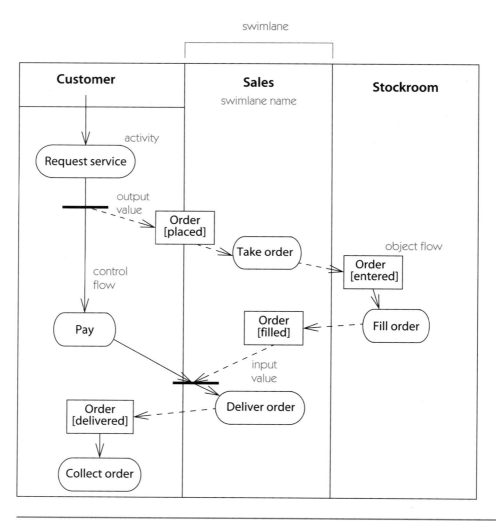

Figure 13-13. *Activity diagram with swimlanes*

activities. The symbol Order[placed], for example, means that at that place in the computation, an order has been advanced to the placed state in the Request Service activity but has not yet been consumed by the Take Order activity. After the Take Order activity completes, the order is then in the entered state, as shown by the object flow symbol on the output of the Take Order activity. All the object flows in this example represent the same object at different times in its life. Because they represent the same object, they cannot exist at the same time. A sequential control path can be drawn through all of them, as is apparent in the diagram.

Object flow. Objects that are input to or output by an action may be shown as object symbols. The symbol represents the object at the point in the computation at which it is suitable as an input or just produced as an output (usually an object does both). A dashed arrow is drawn from an outgoing transition of an activity state to an object flow that is one of its outputs, and a dashed arrow is drawn from an object flow to an incoming transition into an activity state that uses the object as one of its inputs. The same object may be (and usually is) the output of one activity and the input of one or more subsequent activities.

The control flow (solid) arrows may be omitted when the object flow (dashed) arrows supply a redundant constraint. In other words, when an action produces an output that is input by a subsequent action, that object flow relationship implies a control constraint.

Class in state. Frequently, the same object is manipulated by a number of successive activities that change its state. For greater precision, the object may be displayed multiple times on a diagram, each appearance denoting a different state during its life. To distinguish the various appearances of the same object, the state of the object at each point may be placed in brackets and appended to the name of the class—for example, PurchaseOrder[approved]. This notation may also be used in collaboration diagrams.

See also control icons for other symbols that can be used in activity diagrams.

Deferred events. Sometimes, there is an event whose occurrence must be "deferred" for later use while some other activity is underway. (Usually an event that is not handled immediately is lost.) A deferred event is an event that is placed on an internal queue until it is used or until it is discarded. Each state or activity may specify a set of events that are deferred if they occur during the state or activity. Other events must be handled immediately or they are lost. When the state machine enters a new state, all deferred events occur unless the new state also defers them. If a transition in the new state is triggered by an event that was deferred in the previous state, then the transition fires immediately. If several transitions are potentially enabled, it is undefined which of them will fire; imposing a rule to select one is a semantic variation point.

If an event occurs during a state in which it is deferred, it may trigger a transition, in which case it is not placed on the queue. If it does not trigger a transition, it is placed on the queue. If the active state changes, events on the queue may trigger transitions in the new state, but they remain on the queue if they are still deferred in the new state. The ability to undefer an event to trigger a transition is useful where an event must be deferred in a composite state but may enable transitions in one or more substates. Otherwise, it would have to be deferred in each substate in which it does not trigger a transition. Note that if a deferred event matches a trigger event on a transition but the guard condition is not satisfied, the event has not triggered the transition, and it is not removed from the queue.

A deferrable event is shown by listing it within the state, followed by a slash and the special operation **defer**. If the event occurs and does not trigger a transition, it is saved and recurs when the object transitions to another state, when it may be deferred again. When the object reaches a state in which the event is not deferred, it must be accepted or it will be ignored. The absence of a **defer** statement has the effect of cancelling a previous deferral. The **defer** indication may be placed on a composite state, in which case, the event is deferred throughout the composite state.

Action states are atomic and, therefore, implicitly defer any events that occur while they are active. It is unnecessary to mark them for deferral. An event that occurs is deferred until the action is completed, at which time the event may trigger a transition.

Example

Figure 13-14 shows steps in making a pot of coffee. In this example, the external object (**coffeePot**) is not shown, just the activities performed directly by the person. The act of turning on the pot is modeled as an event sent to the pot. The activity **Get Cups** occurs after turning on the coffee pot. After getting the cups, it is necessary to wait until the light goes out. There is a problem, however. If the **light goes out** event occurs before the **Get Cups** activity is complete, then the event is lost because the state machine is not ready to handle it. To avoid the danger of losing an event, the activity state **Get Cups** has been marked to defer the **light goes out** event. If the event occurs when the activity is still executing, the event will not be lost. Instead, it is saved on a queue until the state machine leaves the **Get Cups** state, at which point it is processed and triggers the transition.

Note that the **light goes out** event is not a trigger for the **Get Cups** state and, therefore, does not terminate the activity if it occurs. The event is a trigger for the signal receipt state that follows the completion of the **Get Cups** activity.

Dynamic concurrency. Dynamic concurrency with a value other than exactly one is shown by a multiplicity string in the upper-right part of the activity symbol (Figure 13-15). This indicates that multiple copies of the activity occur concurrently. The dynamic activity receives a set of argument lists. The details must be

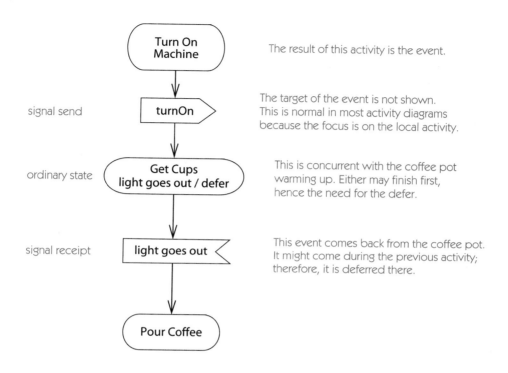

Figure 13-14. *Defer event and control icons*

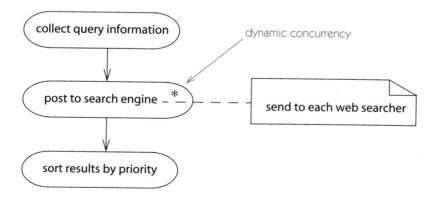

Figure 13-15. *Dynamic concurrency*

described textually. If the concurrency applies over several activities, they must be enclosed in a composite activity, which gets the multiplicity indicator.

Graph structure. A state machine must be well nested—that is, it is recursively partitioned into concurrent or sequential substates. For an activity graph, branches and forks must be well nested. Each branch must have a corresponding merge, and each fork must have a corresponding join. This is not always convenient for an activity graph. A common situation is a partial-order graph, in which there are no directed cycles, but forks and merges do not necessarily match. Such a graph is not well nested, but it can be transformed into a well-nested graph by assigning activities to threads and introducing synch state when transitions cross thread boundaries. The decomposition is not unique, but for a partial-order graph all decompositions yield identical executable semantics. Therefore, it is unnecessary to show an explicit decomposition or synch states for a simple partial-order graph. For more complicated graphs that involve conditionals and concurrency, it may be necessary to be more explicit about the decomposition.

activity state

A state that represents the execution of a pure computation with substructure, typically the invocation of an operation or a statement within it or the performance of a real-world procedure. An activity state can be externally terminated by an event that forces a transition out of the state. An activity state need not terminate on its own. There is no limit on how long it may be active.

See also activity, completion transition.

Semantics

An activity state is a state with an internal computation and, usually, at least one outgoing completion transition that fires on the completion of activity in the state (there may be several such transitions if they have guard conditions). Activity states should not have internal transitions or outgoing transitions based on explicit events. Use normal states for this situation. The normal use of an activity state is to model a step in the execution of an algorithm (a procedure). If all the states in a model are activity states and concurrent activities do not access the same values, then the computation is deterministic, even if it involves concurrent execution.

An activity state may reference a submachine, typically another activity graph. This is equivalent to expanding the activity state into a copy of the submachine network. It is a state machine subroutine.

An activity state is a state of the process of execution of a procedure rather than the state of a normal object.

An action state is an activity state that is atomic—that is, it may not be interrupted by a transition while it is active. It may be modeled as an activity state with only an entry action.

Activity states may be used in ordinary state machines, but they are more commonly used in activity graphs.

Transitions leaving an activity state usually should not include an event trigger. Outgoing transitions are implicitly triggered by the completion of the activity in the state. The transitions may include guard conditions and actions. Take care that all possible conditions are covered on the transitions departing an activity, or else the control may hang. If more than one guard condition evaluates to true, the choice is undefined. It may be nondeterministic, or a rule may be imposed as a semantic variation point.

For other situations use a normal state.

Notation

An activity state is shown as a shape with straight top and bottom and with convex arcs on the two sides (Figure 13-16). The activity expression is placed in the symbol. The activity expression need not be unique within the diagram.

Discussion

Action states are intended for short bookkeeping operations and activity states for computations of any duration or complexity. The implication is that an action might lock up the system so it must be brief, but an activity can be terminated so the system is not required to complete it if something urgent happens. UML semantics do not prevent long actions, but a code generator might legitimately assume that an action is intended to be completed at once, while an activity must be interruptible for other actions.

matrix.invert (tolerance)   drive to work

Figure 13-16. *Activities*

activity view

That aspect of the system dealing with the specification of behavior as activities connected by control flows. This view contains activity graphs and is shown on activity diagrams. It is loosely grouped with other behavioral views as the dynamic view.

See activity graph.

actor

An abstraction for entities outside a system, subsystem, or class that interact directly with the system. An actor participates in a use case or coherent set of use cases to accomplish an overall purpose.

See also use case.

Semantics

An actor characterizes and abstracts an outside user or related set of users that interact with a system or classifier. An actor is an idealization with a focused purpose and meaning and might not correspond exactly to physical objects. One physical object may combine disparate purposes and therefore be modeled by several actors. Different physical objects may include the same purpose, and that aspect of them would be modeled by the same actor. The user object may be a human, a computer system, another subsystem, or another kind of object. For example, actors in a computer network system might include **Operator, System Administrator, Database Administrator,** and plain **User.** There can also be nonhuman actors, such as **RemoteClient, MasterSequencer,** and **NetworkPrinter.**

Each actor defines a set of roles that users of a system may assume when interacting with the system. The complete set of actors describes all the ways in which outside users communicate with the system. When a system is implemented, the actors are implemented by physical objects. One physical object can implement more than one actor if it can fulfill all their roles. For example, one person can be both a salesclerk and a customer of a store. These actors are not inherently related, but they can both be implemented by a person. When the design of a system is performed, the various actors inside the system are realized by design classes (see realization).

The various interactions of actors with a system are quantized into use cases. A use case is a coherent piece of functionality involving a system and its actors to accomplish something meaningful to the actors. A use case may involve one or more actors. One actor may participate in one or more use cases. Ultimately, the actors are determined by the use cases and the roles that actors play in various use cases. An actor that participates in no use cases would be pointless.

A use case model characterizes the kinds of behavior provided by an entity, such as a system, subsystem, or class, in its interactions with outside entities. Outside entities are actors of the entity. In the case of a system, the actors may be realized both by human users and by other systems. In the case of a subsystem or class, the outside elements may be actors of the overall system, or they may be other elements within the system, such as other subsystems or classes.

Actor instances communicate with the system by sending and receiving message instances (signals and calls) to and from use case instances and, at realization level, to and from the objects that implement the use case. This is expressed by associations between the actor and the use case.

An actor may list the set of signals that it sends and receives. An actor may also have a list of interfaces that it supports and requires. The interfaces of an actor must be compatible with the interfaces of each use case that it communicates with. In other words, an actor must receive all the signals that a use case can send, and it must not send signals to a use case that the use case cannot receive. The interfaces of an actor constrain how the actor can be mapped onto classes. An actor may also have a list of attributes that characterize its state.

Generalization

Two or more actors may have similarities; that is, they may communicate with the same set of use cases in the same way. This similarity is expressed with generalization to another (possibly abstract) actor, which models the common aspects of the actors. The descendant actors inherit the roles and the relationships to use cases held by the ancestor actor. An instance of a descendant actor can always be used in cases in which an instance of the ancestor is expected (substitutability principle). A descendant includes the attributes and operations of its ancestors.

Notation

An actor may be shown as a class symbol (rectangle) with the stereotype «actor». The standard stereotype icon for an actor is the "stick man" figure, with the name of the actor below the figure. The actor may have compartments that show attributes and events that it receives, and it may have dependencies to show events that it sends. These are capabilities of a normal classifier (Figure 13-17).

Figure 13-17. *Actor symbol*

actual parameter

See argument.

aggregate

A class that represents the whole in an aggregation (whole-part) association.

aggregation

A form of association that specifies a whole-part relationship between an aggregate (a whole) and a constituent part.
See also composition.

Semantics

A *binary association* may be declared an aggregation—that is, a whole-part relationship. One end of the association is designated the aggregate while the other end is unmarked. Both ends may not be aggregates (or composites), but both ends can be unmarked (in which case, it is not an aggregation).

The links instantiated from aggregation associations obey certain rules. The aggregation relationship is transitive and antisymmetric across all aggregation links, even across those from different aggregation associations. Transitivity means that it makes sense to say that "B is part of A" if there is a path of aggregation links from B to A in the direction of traversal (in this example, from part to whole). Antisymmetry means that there are no cycles in the directed paths of aggregation links. That is, an object may not be directly or indirectly part of itself. Putting the two rules together, the graph of aggregation links from all aggregation associations forms a partial order graph, a graph without cycles (a tree is a special and common case of a partial order). Figure 13-18 shows an example.

A directed path of links from object B to object A implies that there is a directed path of aggregation associations from the class of B to the class of A, but the path of associations may involve cycles in which the same class appears more than once. A directed path of aggregation associations from a class to itself is a *recursion*.

There is a stronger form of aggregation, called composition. A composite is an aggregate with the additional constraints that an object may be part of only one composite and that the composite object has responsibility for the disposition of all its parts—that is, for their creation and destruction.

See composition for details.

In plain aggregation, a part may belong to more than one aggregate, and it may exist independently of the aggregate. Often the aggregate "needs" the parts, in the sense that it may be regarded as a collection of parts. But the parts can exist by themselves, without being regarded only as parts. For example, a path is little more

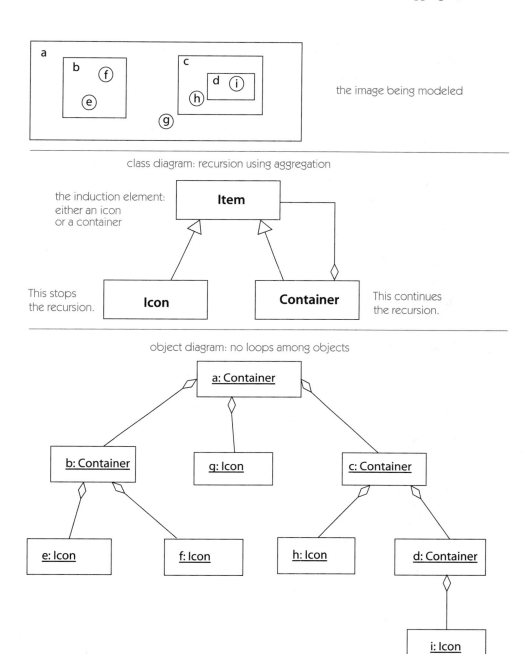

the image being modeled

class diagram: recursion using aggregation

the induction element:
either an icon
or a container

Item

This stops
the recursion.

Icon

Container

This continues
the recursion.

object diagram: no loops among objects

a: Container

b: Container

g: Icon

c: Container

e: Icon

f: Icon

h: Icon

d: Container

i: Icon

Figure 13-18. *Aggregations of objects are acyclic*

than a collection of segments. But a segment can exist by itself whether or not it is part of a path, and the same segment may appear in different paths.

See association and association end for most of the properties of aggregation.

Notation

An aggregation is shown as a hollow diamond adornment on the end of an association line at which it connects to the aggregate class (Figure 13-19). If the aggregation is a composition, then the diamond is filled (Figure 13-68). The ends in an association may not both have aggregation indicators.

An aggregate class can have multiple parts. The relation between the aggregate class and each part class is a separate association (Figure 13-20).

If there are two or more aggregation associations to the same aggregate class, they may be drawn as a tree by combining the aggregation ends into a single segment (Figure 13-21). This requires that all the adornments on the aggregation ends be consistent; for example, they must all have the same multiplicity. Drawing aggregations as a tree is purely a presentation option; there are no additional semantics to it.

Discussion

The distinction between aggregation and association is often a matter of taste rather than a difference in semantics. Keep in mind that aggregation is association. Aggregation conveys the thought that the aggregate is inherently the sum of its parts. In fact, the only real semantics that it adds to association is the constraint that chains of aggregate links may not form cycles, which is often important to know, however. Other constraints, such as existence dependency, are specified by the multiplicity, not the aggregation marker. In spite of the few semantics attached to aggregation, everybody thinks it is necessary (for different reasons). Think of it as a modeling placebo.

Several secondary properties are connected with aggregation, but not reliably enough to make them part of its required definition. These include propagation of operations from aggregate to parts (such as a move operation), and compact memory assignment (so that the aggregate and its recursive parts can be efficiently loaded with one memory transfer). Some authors have distinguished several kinds of aggregation, but the distinctions are fairly subtle and probably unnecessary for general modeling.

Aggregation is a property that transcends a particular association. One can compose aggregations over different pairs of classes, and the result is an aggregation. Aggregation imposes a constraint on the instances of all aggregation associations (including composition associations) that there may be no cycles of aggregation links, including links from different associations. In a sense, aggrega-

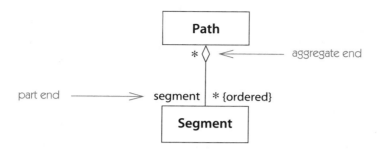

Figure 13-19. *Aggregation notation*

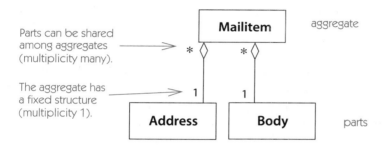

Figure 13-20. *One aggregate with several parts*

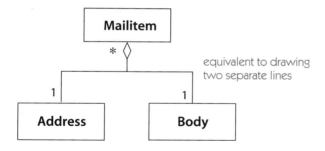

Figure 13-21. *Tree form of notation for multiple aggregations to the same class*

tion is a kind of generalization of association in which constraints and some operations apply to associations of many specific kinds.

Composition has more specific semantics that correspond to physical containment and various notions of ownership. Composition is appropriate when each part is owned by one object and when the part does not have an independent life separate from its owner. It is most useful when parts must be allocated and initialized at the time the owner is created, and the parts do not survive the destruction of their owner. The attributes of a class have these properties and can be considered a kind of composition, although they are not explicitly modeled as such. By using composition, the burden of memory management and the danger of dangling pointers or orphaned objects can be avoided. It is also appropriate for situations in which a bundle of attributes has been isolated into a distinct class for encapsulation and manipulation reasons, but the attributes really apply to the main class. Container classes used to implement associations are also obvious candidates for composite parts, although normally, they should be generated by a code generator and not modeled explicitly. Note that a composite part, such as a container class, may contain references (pointers) to noncomposite parts, but the referenced objects are not destroyed when the referencing object is destroyed.

analysis

That stage of a system that captures requirements and the problem domain. Analysis focuses on what to do; design focuses on how to do it. In an iterative process, the stages need not be performed sequentially. This results of this stage are represented by analysis-level models, especially the use case view and the static view. Contrast analysis, design, implementation, and deployment.

See stages of modeling, development process.

analysis time

A time during which an analysis activity of the software development process is performed. Do not assume that all the analysis for a system occurs at the same time or precedes other activities, such as design and implementation. The various activities are sequential for any single element, but different activities may be intermixed for the entire system.

See design time, modeling time.

ancestor

An element found by following a path of one or more parent relationships.

See generalization, parent.

architecture

The organizational structure of a system, including its decomposition into parts, their connectivity, interaction mechanisms, and the guiding principles that inform the design of a system.

See also package.

Semantics

Architecture is the set of significant decisions about the organization of a software system. It includes the selection of structural elements and the interfaces through which they are connected, the large-scale organization of structural elements and the topology of their connection, their behavior as specified in the collaborations among those elements, the important mechanisms that are available across the system, and the architectural style that guides their organization. For example, the decision to construct a system from two layers in which each layer contains a small number of subsystems that communicate in a particular way is an architectural decision. Software architecture is not only concerned with structure and behavior, but also with usage, functionality, performance, resilience, reuse, comprehensibility, economic and technology constraints and trade-offs, and aesthetic concerns.

Discussion

Architectural decisions about the decomposition of a system into parts can be captured using models, subsystems, packages, and components. The dependencies among these elements are key indicators of the flexibility of the architecture and the difficulty of modifying the system in the future.

Another major part of an architecture is the mechanisms that it provides to build upon. These may be captured with collaborations and patterns.

Nonstructural decisions can be captured using tagged values.

argument

A specific value corresponding to a parameter.

See also binding, parameter, substitutability principle.

Semantics

A run-time instance of a message has a list of argument values, each of which is a value whose type must be consistent with the declared type of the matching parameter in the signal or operation declaration. A value is consistent if its class or data type is the same or a descendant of the declared type of the parameter. By the substitutability principle, a value of a descendant may be used anywhere an ancestor type is declared. The implementation of a value depends on the simulator or execution environment in which it appears.

Within a collaboration or state machine, expressions may appear for actions. Within these expressions, calls and message sends require argument specifications. These argument specifications are also expressions. When these expressions are evaluated at run time, they must evaluate to values that are consistent with the declared parameters they match.

In a template binding, however, arguments appear within a UML model at modeling time. In these cases, arguments are represented as expressions in some language, usually a constraint language or programming language. Template arguments can include not only ordinary data values and objects, but also classifiers themselves. In the latter case, the corresponding parameter type must be **Classifier** or some other metatype. The value of a template argument must be fixed at modeling time; it may not be used to represent a run-time argument. Do not use templates if the parameters are not bound at modeling time.

artifact

A piece of information that is used or produced by a software development process, such as an external document or a work product. An artifact can be a model, description, or software.

association

The semantic relationship between two or more classifiers that involves connections among their instances.

See also association class, association end, association generalization, binary association, *n*-ary association.

Semantics

An association is a relationship among two or more specified classifiers that describes connections among their instances. The participating classifiers have ordered positions within the association. The same class may appear in more than one position in an association. Each instance of an association (a link) is a tuple (an ordered list) of references to objects. The extent of the association is a set of such links. A given object may appear more than once within the set of links, or even more than once within the same link (in different positions) if the definition of the association permits. Associations are the "glue" that holds together a system. Without associations, there is only a set of unconnected classes.

Structure

An association has a optional name, but most of its description is found in a list of association ends, each of which describes the participation of objects of a class in the association. Note that an association end is simply part of the description of an association and not a separable semantic or notational concept.

Name. An association has an optional name, a string that must be unique among associations and classes within the containing package. (An association class is both an association and a class; therefore, associations and classes share a single namespace). An association is not required to have a name; rolenames on its ends provide an alternate way of distinguishing multiple associations among the same classes. By convention, the name is read in the order that participating classes appear in the list: A Person works for a Company; a Salesman sells a Car to a Customer.

Association ends. An association contains an ordered list of two or more association ends. (By ordered, we mean that the ends are distinguishable and are not interchangeable.) Each association end defines the participation of one class at a given position (role) in the association. The same class may appear in more than one position; the positions are, in general, not interchangeable. Each association end specifies properties that apply to the participation of the corresponding objects, such as how many times a single object may appear in links in the association (multiplicity). Certain properties, such as navigability, apply only to binary associations, but most apply to both binary and *n*-ary associations.

See association end for full details.

Instantiation

A link is an instance of an association. It contains one slot for each association end. Each slot contains a reference to an object that is an instance (direct or indirect) of the class specified as the class of the corresponding association end. A link has no identity apart from the list of objects in it. The links in the extent of an association form a set; no duplicates may exist. The number of appearances of an object in the set of links must be compatible with the multiplicity on each end of the association. For example, if association **SoldTickets** connects many tickets to one performance, then each ticket may appear only once in a link, but each performance can appear many times, each time with a different ticket.

Links may be created and destroyed as the execution of a system proceeds, subject to restrictions on changeability of each end of the association. In some cases, a link can be created or changed from an object on one end of an association but not the other end. A link is created from a list of object references. A link has no identity of its own. It therefore makes no sense to talk about changing its value. It may be destroyed, and a new link may be created to take its place, however. A link of an association class does have one or more attribute values in addition to the list of objects that define its identity, and the attribute values can be modified by operations while preserving the references to the participating objects.

Notation

A binary association is shown as a solid path connecting the borders of two classes (Figure 13-22). An *n*-ary association is shown as a diamond connected by paths to each of its participant classes (Figure 13-129). (In the binary association, the

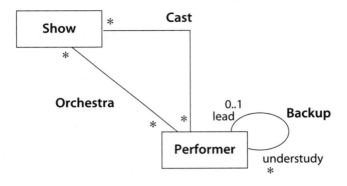

Figure 13-22. *Associations*

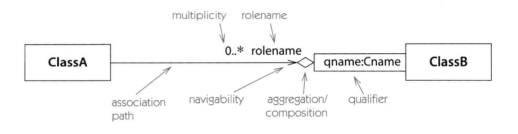

Figure 13-23. *Adornment order on association end*

diamond is suppressed as extraneous.) More than one end of the path may connect to a single class.

A path consists of one or more connected solid segments—usually straight line segments, but arcs and other curves are allowed, especially to show a self-association (an association in which one class appears more than once). The individual segments have no semantic significance. The choice of a particular set of line styles is a user choice.

See path.

The ends of the paths have adornments that describe the participation of a class in the association. Some adornments are displayed on the end of the path, between the line segment and the class box. If there are multiple adornments, they are placed in sequence from the end of the line to the class symbol—navigation arrow, aggregation/composition diamond, qualifier (Figure 13-23).

Other adornments, such as name labels, are placed near the thing they identify. Rolenames are placed near an end of the path.

See association end for full details on the notation of adornments.

Association name

A name for the association is placed near the path but far enough from an end so that there is no danger of confusion. (The danger of confusion is purely visual for a human. Within a graphic tool, the related symbols can be connected with unambiguous internal hyperlinks. It is a tool responsibility to determine how far is far enough.) The association name can be dragged from segment to segment of a multisegment association with no semantic impact. The association name may have a small filled triangle near it to show the ordering of the classes in the list. Intuitively, the name arrow shows which way to "read" the name. In Figure 13-24, the association **WorksFor** between class **Person** and class **Company** would have the name triangle pointing from **Person** to **Company** and would be read "Person works for Company." Note that the ordering triangle on the name is purely a notational device to indicate the ordering of the association ends. In the model itself, the ends are inherently ordered; therefore, the name in the model does not require or have an ordering property.

A stereotype on the association is indicated by showing the stereotype name in guillemets (« ») in front of or instead of the association name. A property list may be placed after or below the association name.

Example

Figure 13-24. *Association name*

Association class

An association class is shown by attaching a class symbol to the association path with a dashed line. For an *n*-ary association, the dashed line is connected to the association diamond. The class-like properties of the association are shown in the class symbol, and the association-like properties are shown on the path. Note, however, that the underlying modeling construct is a single element, even though the image is drawn using two graphic constructs.

See association class for more details.

Xor constraint

The constraint {xor} connects two or more associations that are connected to a single class (the base class) at one end. An instance of the base class may participate in exactly one of association connected by the constraint. The multiplicity of the chosen association must be observed. If any association multiplicity includes the cardinality 0, then an instance of the base class might have no link from the association; otherwise, it must have one.

An xor-constraint is shown as a dashed line connecting two or more associations, all of which must have a class in common, with the constraint string {or} labeling the dashed line (Figure 13-25). The rolenames on the ends away from the common class must be different. (This is simply a predefined use of the constraint notation using the standard constraint overlapping.)

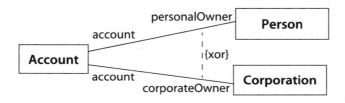

Figure 13-25. *Or association*

Discussion

An association need not have a name. Usually, rolenames are more convenient because they provide names for navigation and code generation and avoid the problem of which way to read the name. If it has a name, the name must be unique within its package. If it does not have a name and there is more than one association between a pair (or set) of classes, then rolenames must be present to distinguish the associations. If there is only one association between a pair of classes, then the class names are sufficient to identify the association.

An argument can be made that association names are most useful when the real-world concept has a name, such as **Marriage** or **Job.** When an association name is "directed" by reading in a given direction, it is usually better simply to use rolenames, which are unambiguous in the way they are read.

See transient link for a discussion of modeling instance relationships that exist only during procedure execution.

See composition for an example of generalization involving two associations.

Standard elements

implicit, persistence, xor

association (binary)

See binary association.

association (*n*-ary)

See *n*-ary association.

association class

An association class is an association that is also a class. An association class has both association and class properties. Its instances are links that have attribute values as well as references to other objects. Even though its notation consists of the symbols for both an association and a class, it is really a single model element.

See also association, class.

Semantics

An association class has the properties of both associations and classes—it connects two or more classes and it also has attributes and operations. An association class is useful when each link must have its own attribute values, operations, or references to objects. It may be regarded as a class with an extra class reference for each association end, which is the obvious and normal way to implement it. Each instance of the association class has object references as well as the attribute values specified by the class part.

An association class C connecting classes A and B is not the same as a class D with binary associations to A and B (see the discussion section). Like all links, a link of an association class such as C takes its identity from the object references in it. The attribute values are not involved in providing identity. Therefore, two links of C must not have the same pair of (a, b) objects, even if their attribute values differ, because they would have the same identity. That is, given attribute E, it is not permitted that (a, b, e1) and (a, b, e2) both be instances of C, because they share the same identity (a, b). Objects have inherent identity, however, so two objects can have the same attribute values or links to the same objects. In other words, an association, including an association class such as C, is a set of tuples and has no duplicates among its object references; whereas, an implicit relationship such as D is more like a bag, which can have duplicates. See the discussion for more details.

Association classes may have operations that modify the attributes of the link or add or remove links to the link itself. Because an association class is a class, it may participate in associations itself.

An association class may not have itself as one of its participating classes (although someone could undoubtedly find a meaning for this kind of recursive structure).

Notation

An association class is shown as a class symbol (rectangle) attached by a dashed line to an association path (Figure 13-26). The name in the class symbol and the name string attached to the association path are redundant. The association path may have the usual association end adornments. The class symbol may have attributes and operations, as well as participate in associations of its own as a class. There are no adornments on the dashed line; it is not a relationship but simply part of the overall association class symbol.

Style guidelines

The attachment point should not be near enough to either end of the path that it appears to be attached to the end of the path or to any of the role adornments.

Note that the association path and the association class are a single model element and therefore have a single name. The name can be shown on the path or the class symbol or both. If an association class has only attributes but no operations or other associations, then the name may be displayed on the association path and omitted from the association class symbol to emphasize its "association nature." If it has operations and other associations, then the name may be omitted from the path and placed in the class rectangle to emphasize its "class nature." In neither case is the actual semantics different.

Discussion

Figure 13-26 shows an association class representing employment. The employment relationship between a company and a person is many-to-many. A person may have more than one job, but only one job for a given company. The salary is not an attribute of either the company or the person because the association is many-to-many. It must be an attribute of the relationship itself.

The boss-worker relationship is not just a relationship between two people. It is a relationship between a person in one job and a person in another job—it is an association (**Manages**) between the association class and itself.

The following example shows the difference between an association class and a reified relationship modeled as a class. In Figure 13-27, the ownership of stock is modeled as an association between Person and Company. The association class attribute **quantity** represents the number of shares held. This relationship is modeled as an association class because there should be only one entry for any pairing of **Person** and **Company**.

To model purchases of stock, as shown in Figure 13-28, we do not use an association class, because there can be multiple purchases with the same Person and Company. Yet they must be distinguished because each purchase is distinct and

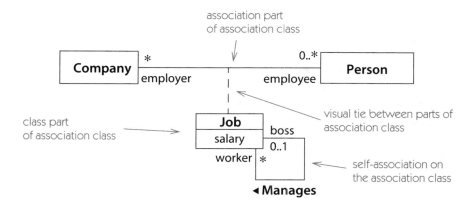

Figure 13-26. *Association class*

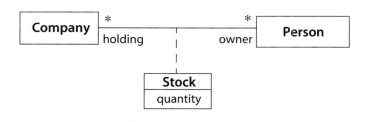

Figure 13-27. *Association class with attribute*

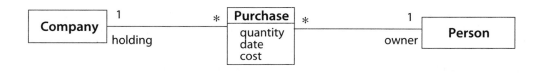

Figure 13-28. *Reified association*

has its own date and price in addition to quantity. The relationship must be *reified*—that is, made into distinct objects with their own identity. An ordinary class is the right way to model this case, because each purchase has its own identity, independent of the **Person** and **Company** classes that it relates. This is the way to model a relationship that is a bag rather than a set.

association end

A structural part of an association that defines the participation of a class in the association. One class may be connected to more than one end in the same association. The association ends within an association have distinct positions, have names, and, in general, are not interchangeable. An association end has no independent existence or meaning apart from its association.

See also association.

Semantics

Structure

An association end holds a reference to a target classifier. It defines the participation of the classifier in the association. An instance of the association (a link) must contain an instance of the given class or one of its descendants in the given position. Participation in an association is inherited by children of a class.

An association end has the following properties (see the individual entries for more information).

aggregation	Whether the attached object is an aggregate or composite, an enumeration with the values {none, aggregate, composite}. If the value is not none, then the association is called an aggregation or a composition. The default is none. Only a binary association can be an aggregation or composition, and only one end can be an aggregate or composite.
changeability	Whether the set of links related to an object may change, an enumeration with the values {changeable, frozen, addOnly}. The default is changeable.
interface specifier	An optional constraint on the specification type of the related object, a classifier (some people call this a *role*, although the term is used in other ways).
multiplicity	The possible number of objects that may be related to an object; normally specified as an integer range.
navigability	A Boolean value, indicating whether it is possible to traverse a binary association to obtain the object or set of objects associated with an instance of the class. The default is true (navigable).
ordering	Whether (and potentially how) the set of related objects is ordered, an enumeration with the values {unordered, ordered}. For design purposes, the value sorted may be used also.

qualifier	A list of attributes used as selectors for finding objects related by an association.
rolename	The name of the association end, an identifier string. This name identifies the particular role of the corresponding class within the association. The rolename must be unique within the association and also among direct and inherited pseudoattributes (attributes and other rolenames visible to the class) of the source class.
target scope	Whether the links relate objects or entire classes, an enumeration with the values {instance, classifier}. The default is instance (relates objects).
visibility	Whether the link is accessible to classes other than the one on the opposite end of the association. The visibility is placed on the end connected to the target class. Each direction of traversal has its own visibility value.

Notation

The end of the association path is connected to the edge of the rectangle of the corresponding class symbol. Association end properties are shown as adornments on or near the end of the path at which it attaches to a classifier symbol (Figure 13-29). The following list is a brief summary of adornments for each property. See the individual articles for more details.

aggregation	A small hollow diamond on the aggregate end, a filled diamond for a composition
changeability	The text property {frozen} or {addOnly} near the target end, usually omitted for {changeable} but permitted for emphasis
interface specifier	Text suffix on rolename, in the form :typename
multiplicity	Text label near the end of the path, in the form min..max
navigability	An arrowhead on the end of the path showing navigability in that direction. If neither end has an arrowhead, the assumption is that the association is navigable in both directions (because there is little need for associations that are not navigable in either direction).
ordering	The text property {ordered} near the target end; there is an ordered list of instances of the target class.
qualifier	A small rectangle between the end of the path and the source class in a traversal. The rectangle contains one or more attributes of the association—the qualifiers.

rolename	A text label near the target end
target scope	Class scope rolename is underlined, otherwise it is instance scope.
visibility	Visibility symbol (+ # −) prefixed to rolename

If there are multiple adornments on a single role, they are presented in the following order, reading from the end of the path attached to the class toward the bulk of the path (Figure 13-23):

qualifier

aggregation or composition symbol

navigation arrow

Rolenames and multiplicity should be placed near the end of the path so that they are not confused with a different association. They may be placed on either side of the line. It is tempting to require that they always be placed on one side of the line (clockwise or counterclockwise), but this is sometimes overridden by the need for clarity in a crowded layout. A rolename and a multiplicity may be placed on opposite sides of the same role, or they may be placed together (for example, * employee).

Standard elements

association, global, local, parameter, self

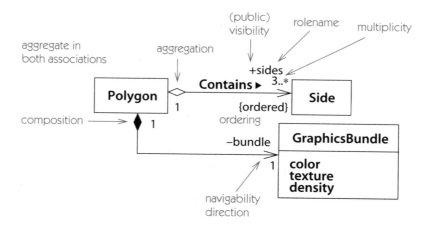

Figure 13-29. *Various adornments on association ends*

association generalization

A generalization relationship between two associations.
See also association, generalization.

Semantics

Generalization among associations is permitted, although it is somewhat uncommon. As with any generalization relationship, the child element must add to the intent (defining rules) of the parent and must subset the extent (set of instances) of the parent. Adding to the intent means adding additional constraints. A child association is more constrained than its parent. For example, in Figure 13-30, if the parent association connects classes **Subject** and **Symbol**, then the child association may connect classes **Order** and **OrderSymbol**, where **Order** is a child of **Subject** and **OrderSymbol** is a child of **Symbol**. Subsetting the extent means that every link of the child association is a link of the parent association, but not the reverse. The example obeys this rule. Any link connecting **Order** and **OrderSymbol** will also connect **Subject** and **Symbol**, but not all links connecting **Subject** and **Symbol** will connect **Order** and **OrderSymbol**.

Notation

A generalization arrow symbol (solid body, triangular hollow arrowhead) connects the child association to the parent association. The arrowhead is on the parent. Because of the lines connecting other lines, association generalization notation can be confusing and should be used with care.

Example

Figure 13-30 shows two specializations of the general **model-view** association between **Subject** and **Symbol**: The association between **Order** and **OrderSymbol** is a specialization, as is the association between **Customer** and **CustomerSymbol**. Each of these connects a **Subject** class to a **Symbol** class. The general **Subject-Symbol** association may be regarded as an abstract association whereas the two child associations are concrete.

This pattern of paired class hierarchies connected by associations is fairly common.

Standard elements

destroyed

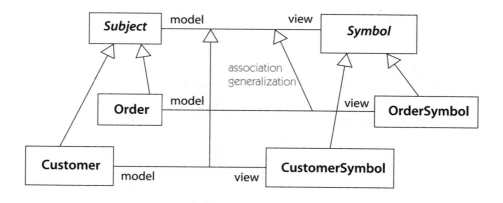

Figure 13-30. *Association generalization*

association role

The connection of two classifier roles within a collaboration; an association between two classifiers that applies only in a certain context as specified by a
collaboration.

See also association, collaboration.

Semantics

An association role is an association that is meaningful and defined only in the
context described by a collaboration. It is a relationship that is part of the collaboration but not an inherent relationship in other situations. Association roles are
the key structural part of collaborations. They permit the descriptions of contextual relationships.

Within a collaboration, a classifier role denotes an individual appearance of a
classifier, distinct from other appearances of the classifier and from the classifier
declaration itself. It is a classifier in its own right, one that represents a restriction
on the use of the base classifier, based on the context of a collaboration. Similarly,
an association role represents an association that is used in a particular context, often a restricted use of a normal association. An association role connects two classifier roles. When a collaboration is instantiated, objects are bound to classifier
roles and links are bound to the association roles. One object can play (be bound
to) more than one role.

An association role connects two or more classifier roles or classifiers within a
collaboration. It has a reference to an association—the base association—and it

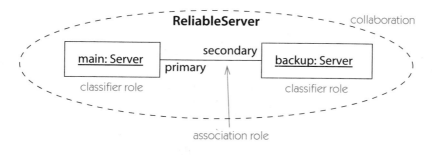

Figure 13-31. *Association role*

may have a multiplicity indicating how many links may play the role in an instance of the collaboration. In some cases, the connections within the collaboration can be regarded as uses of a general association between the participating classes. The collaboration shows one way of using the general association for a purpose within the collaboration.

In other cases, classifier roles are connected by associations that have no validity outside the collaboration. If an association role has no explicit base association, then it defines an implicit association valid only within the collaboration.

Notation

An association role is displayed in the same way as an association—namely, as a solid line between two classifier role symbols (Figure 13-31). The fact that it is an association role is clear because it involves classifier roles.

Standard elements

new, transient

asynchronous action

A request in which the sending object does not pause to wait for results; a send.
See send, synchronous action.

atomic

An action or operation whose execution must be completed as a unit; one that may not be partially executed or terminated by an external event. Usually, atomic operations are small and simple, such as assignments and simple arithmetic or string calculations. An atomic computation occurs at a definite point in the execution sequence.
See also action, activity, run to completion.

Semantics

The overall system can perform multiple actions simultaneously. When we call actions atomic, we do not imply that the entire system is atomic. The system can process hardware interrupts and time share between several actions. An action is atomic within its own thread of control. Once started, it must complete execution and it must not interact with other simultaneously active actions. The system can process interrupts and events, but they must not affect the atomic action. But actions should not be used as a long transaction mechanism. Their duration should be brief compared to the response time needed for external events. Otherwise, the system might be unable to respond in a timely manner.

attribute

An attribute is the description of a named slot of a specified type in a class; each object of the class separately holds a value of the type.

Semantics

An attribute is a named slot within a classifier that describes the values that instances of the classifier may hold. Every instance of the classifier or one of its descendants has a slot holding a value of the given type. All the slots are distinct and independent of each other (except for class-scope attributes, which are described later). As execution proceeds, the value held by a slot within an instance may be replaced by a different value of the type, provided the attribute is changeable.

A classifier forms a namespace for its attributes. Also included in the namespace are pseudoattributes, such as the rolenames of associations leaving the classifier and discriminators of generalizations involving the classifier.

Structure

An attribute has the following main constituents, which are described in detail under their proper entries.

changeability | Whether the value of the slot may change after initialization, an enumeration. The default is **changeable**. Possible values are

changeable | No restrictions on modification (the default)

addOnly | Additional values may be added to the set of values for the attribute. But once created, a value may not be removed or altered. (Meaningful only if the maximum multiplicity is greater than one.)

frozen	The value may not be altered after the object is initialized. No additional values may be added to a set of values.
initial value	An expression specifying the value that an attribute in an object holds just after it has been initialized. An expression is a text string, together with the name of a language used to evaluate the expression. The expression is evaluated in the context of the language when the object is instantiated. *See* expression for additional details. The initial value is optional. If it is absent, then the static model does not specify the value held by a new object (but some other part of the overall model may supply that information).
	Note that an explicit initialization procedure, such as a constructor, may supersede an initial value expression.
	The initial value of a class-scope attribute is used to initialize it once at the beginning of execution. UML does not specify the relative order of initialization of different class-scope attributes.
multiplicity	The possible number of values of the attribute that can exist simultaneously. The most common value "exactly one" denotes a scalar attribute. The value "zero or one" denotes an attribute with an optional value. A missing value is distinguishable from any value in the domain of the attribute type. (In other words, the absence of a value is different from the value zero. It is the empty set.) Other multiplicities denote potentially multivalued attributes. If the multiplicity is not a single integer, then the number of values held by the attribute can vary. The multiplicity "many" denotes an unlimited set of values.
name	The name of the attribute, a string, which must be unique within the class and its ancestors. It must also be unique among association rolenames reachable from the class.
owner scope	The value slot described by an attribute may be distinct in each object or it may be shared by all the objects of a class. The former is an instance-scope attribute; the latter is a class-scope attribute. Most attributes are instance-scope; they carry state information about a particular object. Class-scope attributes carry information about an entire class; there is a single value slot for the entire class.

	Whereas an instance-scope attribute is a description of a value that has no existence until an object is instantiated, a class-scope attribute represents the declaration of an individual discrete value that exists for the entire lifetime of a system.
target scope	The value held by an attribute may be an instance or a class itself. The former is instance scope; it is the default. The latter is class scope; it is rare and usually involves some kind of metamodeling.
type	Designates a class or data type that the values in the slot are instances of. A value can be an instance of a descendant of the given class or data type.
visibility	Whether the attribute can be seen by other classes, an enumeration with the choices **public**, **private**, and **protected**. Additional values might be added to model certain programming languages.

Notation

An attribute is shown as a text string that can be parsed into various properties. The default syntax is:

$$\text{«stereotype»}_{opt} \; \text{visibility}_{opt} \; \text{name multiplicity}_{opt} : \text{type}_{opt}$$
$$= \text{initial-value}_{opt} \{ \text{property-string} \}_{opt}$$

Visibility. The visibility is shown as a punctuation mark. Alternately the visibility can be shown as a keyword within the property string. The latter form must be used for user-defined or language-dependent choices. The predefined choices are

+ (public)	Any class that can see the class can also see the attribute.
# (protected)	The class or any of its descendents can see the attribute.
− (private)	Only the class itself can see the attribute.

Name. The name is shown as an identifier string.

Type. The type is shown as an expression string denoting a classifier. The name of a class or a data type is a legitimate expression string indicating that the values of the attribute must be of the given type. Additional type syntax depends on the language of the expression. Each language has syntax for constructing new data types out of simple ones. For example, C++ has syntax for pointers, arrays, and functions. Ada also has syntax for subranges. The language of the expression is part of the internal model, but it is not usually shown on a diagram. It is assumed that it is known for the entire diagram or obvious from its syntax.

The type string may be suppressed (but it still exists in the model).

Multiplicity. The multiplicity is shown as a multiplicity expression (see below) enclosed in square brackets ([ ]) placed after the attribute name. If the multiplicity is "exactly one," then the expression, including the brackets, may be omitted. This indicates that each object has exactly one slot holding a value of the given type (the most common case). Otherwise, the multiplicity must be shown. *See* multiplicity for a full discussion of its syntax. For example:

> colors [3]: Saturation   An array of 3 saturations
> points [2..*]: Point   An array of 2 or more points

Note that a multiplicity of 0..1 provides for the possibility of null values—the absence of a value, as opposed to a particular value from the range. A null value is not a value within the domain of most data types; it extends that domain with an extra value outside the domain. For pointers, however, the null value is often part of the implementation (although, even then, it is usually by convention—for example, the value 0 in C or C++, an artifact of memory addressing conventions). The following declaration permits a distinction between the *null* value and the empty string, a distinction supported by C++ and other languages.

> name [0..1]: String   If the name is missing, it is a null value.

Initial value. The initial value is shown as a string. The language of evaluation is usually not shown explicitly (but it is present in the model). If there is no initial value, then both the string and the equal sign are omitted. If the attribute multiplicity includes the value 0 (that is, optional) and no explicit initial value is given, then the attribute starts with a null value (zero repetitions).

Changeability. The changeability value is shown by a keyword—the name of the choice. If no choice is given, then the value is **changeable**.

Tagged value. Zero or more tagged values may be attached to an attribute (as to any model element). Each tagged value is shown in the form tag = value, where tag is the name of a tag and value is a literal value. Tagged values are included with property keywords as a comma-separated property list enclosed in braces.

Scope. A class-scope attribute is shown by underlining the name and type expression string; otherwise, the attribute is instance-scope. The notation justification is that a class-scope attribute is a value in the executing system, just as an object is an instance value, so both may be designated by underlining.

> class-scope-attribute

Figure 13-32 shows the declaration of some attributes.

Presentation options

Programming-language syntax. The syntax of the attribute string can be that of a programming language, such as C++ or Smalltalk. Specific tagged properties may be included in the string.

+size: Area = (100,100)	public, initial value
#visibility: Boolean = invisible	protected, initial value
+default-size: Rectangle	public
maximum-size: Rectangle	class scope
–xptr: XWindowPtr {requirement=4.3}	private, tagged value

Figure 13-32. *Attributes*

Style guidelines

Attribute names are shown in normal typeface.

Discussion

A similar syntax is used to specify qualifiers, template parameters, operation parameters, and so on (some of these omit certain terms).

Note that an attribute is semantically equivalent to a composition association. However, the intent and usage are usually different. Use attributes for data types—that is, for values with no identity. Use associations for classes—that is, for values with identity. The reason is that for objects with identity, it is important to see the relationship in both directions; for data types, the data type is usually subordinate to the object and has no knowledge of it.

Standard elements

persistence

background information

Each appearance of a symbol for a class on a diagram or on different diagrams may have its own presentation choices. For example, one symbol for a class may show the attributes and operations and another symbol for the same class may suppress them. Tools may provide style sheets attached to either individual symbols or entire diagrams. Style sheets would specify the presentation choices, and they would be applicable to most kinds of symbols, not just classes.

Not all modeling information is most usefully presented in a graphical notation. Some information is best presented in a textual or tabular format. For example, detailed programming information is often best presented as text lists. UML does not assume that all the information in a model will be expressed as diagrams; some of it may be available only as tables. This document does not attempt to prescribe the format of such tables or the forms that are used to access them. That is because the underlying information is adequately described in the UML metamodel, and the responsibility for presenting tabular information is a tool responsibility. It is assumed, however, that hidden links may exist from graphical items to tabular items.

become

A kind of flow dependency, used in an interaction, in which the target object represents a new version of the source object and thereafter replaces it.

See also class-in-state, copy, location.

Semantics

A become dependency is a kind of flow dependency that shows the derivation of one object from another object within an interaction. It represents an action that transforms an object. After a become flow executes, the new object replaces the original object within the computation. It is usually unnecessary to use this relationship just to show a change of value of an object. On the other hand, this relationship is useful for showing a qualitative change in an object, such as a change in state, a change in class, or a change in location. In this situation, the model contains two versions of the object, but the become relationship shows that they are really two versions of the same object over time; that is, they have the same identity.

A become transition within an interaction may have a sequence number to indicate when it occurs relative to other actions.

Notation

A become flow is shown by a dashed arrow whose tail is on the earlier version of the object and whose head is on the later version; the arrow carries the stereotype keyword «become». The arrow may have a sequence number within an interaction to show when the change occurs relative to other actions. Become transitions may appear in collaboration diagrams, sequence diagrams, and activity diagrams.

In an activity diagram, the become transition may be displayed as a dashed arrow to or from an object flow symbol. The **become** keyword may be omitted.

Example

Figure 13-33 shows a command to open a closed directory icon on a desktop, followed by a command to sort the items within the now-open directory. The directory is shown twice as a class-in-state object, with a become transition between the two versions.

Figure 13-132 in node shows a deployment diagram in which an object migrates between nodes.

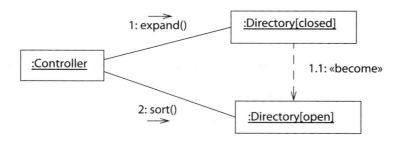

Figure 13-33. *Become flow*

behavior

The observable effects of an operation or event, including its results.

behavioral feature

A model element expressing dynamic behavior, such as an operation or method, that can be part of a classifier. The declaration that a classifier handles a signal is also a behavioral feature.

Standard elements

create, destroy, leaf

behavioral view

A view of a model that emphasizes the behavior of the instances in a system, including their methods, collaborations, and state histories.

binary association

An association between exactly two classes.
  See also association, *n*-ary association.

Semantics

A binary association is an association with exactly two association ends, by far the most common kind of association. Because an end in a binary association has a single other end, binary associations are particularly useful for specifying navigation paths from object to object. An association is navigable in a given direction if it can be traversed in that direction. Some other properties, such as multiplicity, are defined for *n*-ary associations, but they are more intuitive and useful for binary associations.

Notation

A binary association is shown as a solid path connecting two class symbols. Adornments can be attached to each end, and an association name may be placed near the line, far enough from either end so that it is not mistaken for a rolename. The notation for a binary association is the same as the notation for an *n*-ary association except for the suppression of the central diamond symbol. Binary associations, however, can have adornments that are not applicable to *n*-ary associations, such as navigability.

See association for details.

bind

Keyword for a binding dependency in the notation.
See binding.

binding

The assignment of values to parameters to produce an individual element from a parameterized element. The binding relationship is a kind of dependency. It is used to bind templates to produce new model elements.

See also bound element, template.

Semantics

A parameterized definition, such as an operation, signal, or template, defines the form of an element. A parameterized element cannot be used directly, however, because its parameters do not have specific values. Binding is a dependency that represents the assignment of values to parameters to produce a new, usable element. Binding acts on operations to produce calls, on signals to produce sent signals, and on templates to produce new model elements. The first two are bound during execution to produce run-time entities. These do not usually figure in models except as examples or simulation results. The argument values are defined within the execution system.

A template is bound at modeling time, however, to produce new model elements for use within the model. The argument values can be other model elements, such as classes, in addition to data values, such as strings and integers. The binding relationship binds values to a template, producing an actual model element that can be used directly within the model.

A binding relationship has a supplier element (the template), a client element (the newly generated bound element), and a list of values to bind to template parameters. The bound element is defined by substituting each argument value for its corresponding parameter within a copy of the template body. The classification of each argument must be the same as or a descendant of the declared classification of its parameter.

A binding does not affect the template itself. Each template can be bound many times, each time producing a new bound element.

Notation

Binding is indicated with the keyword «bind» attached to a dashed arrow that connects the generated element (on the tail of the arrow) to the template (on the arrowhead). The actual argument values are shown as a comma-separated list of text expressions enclosed in parentheses following the «bind» keyword on the arrow.

An alternative and more compact notation for binding uses name matching to avoid the need for arrows. To indicate a bound (generated) element, the name of a template is followed by a comma-separated list of text expressions enclosed in angle brackets (<argument$_{list,}$>).

In either case, each argument is stated as a text string that is evaluated statically at model-building time. It is not evaluated dynamically as an operation or signal argument is.

In Figure 13-34, the explicit form using the arrow declares a new class **Address-List**, whose name can be used in models and expressions. The implicit inline form **Varray<Point,3>** declares an "anonymous class" without a name of its own. It may be used in expressions using the inline syntax. In neither case can additional attributes or operations be declared. A subclass must be declared if extensions are needed.

Standard elements

bind

Boolean

An enumeration whose values are **true** and **false**.

Boolean expression

An expression that evaluates to a Boolean value. Useful in guard conditions.

bound element

A model element produced by binding argument values to the parameters of a template.

See also binding, template.

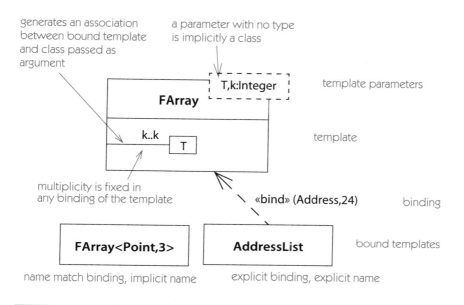

Figure 13-34. *Template declaration and binding*

Semantics

A template is a parameterized description of a group of potential elements. To obtain an actual element, the template's parameters must be *bound* to actual values. The actual value for each parameter is an expression supplied by the scope within which the binding occurs. Most arguments are classes or integers.

If the scope is itself a template, then the parameters of the outer template can be used as arguments in binding the original template, in effect reparameterizing it. But parameter names from one template have no meaning outside its body. Parameters in two templates cannot be assumed to correspond just because they have the same names, any more than subroutine parameters could be assumed to match based only on their names.

A bound element is fully specified by its template. Its content, therefore, may not be extended. Declaration of new attributes or operations for classes is not permitted, for example, but a bound class could be subclassed and the subclass extended in the usual way.

Example

Figure 13-35 shows the rebinding of a template. **PointArray** is a template with one parameter—the size **n**. We want to make it from the existing template **FArray**, which has two parameters—the type of element **T** and the size **k**. To make it, the parameter **k** from the **FArray** template is bound to the parameter **n** from the

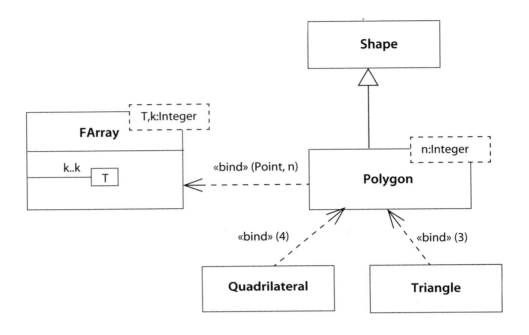

Figure 13-35. *Rebinding a template*

PointArray template. The parameter **T** from the **FArray** template is bound to the class **Point**. This has the effect of removing one parameter from the original template. To use the **PointArray** template to make a **Triangle** class, the size parameter **n** is bound to the value 3. To make a **Quadrilateral** class, it is bound to the value 4.

Figure 13-35 also shows the template **Polygon** as a child of class **Shape**. This means that each class bound from **Template** is a subclass of **Shape**—Triangle and Quadrilateral are both subclasses of Shape.

Notation

A bound element can be shown using a dashed arrow from the template to the bound element; the arrow has the keyword «**bind**». Alternately it can be shown using the text syntax TemplateName<argument$_{list,}$>, using name matching to identify the template. The text form avoids the need to show the template or to draw an arrow to it; this form is particularly useful when the bound element is used as a classifier for an attribute or operation parameter.

See binding for details. Figure 13-34 shows an example.

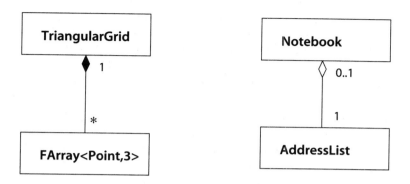

Figure 13-36. *Use of bound templates in associations*

The attribute and operation compartments are usually suppressed within a bound class because they must not be modified in a bound element.

A bound element name (either the inline "anonymous" form using angle brackets or the explicit "binding arrow" form) may be used anywhere an element name of the parameterized kind could be used. For example, a bound class name could be used as an attribute type or as part of an operation signature within a class symbol on a class diagram. Figure 13-36 shows an example.

Discussion

Classifiers are obvious candidates for parameterization. The types of their attributes, operations, or associated classifiers are common parameters in templates. Parameterized collaborations are patterns. Operations, in a sense, are inherently parameterized. The usefulness of parameterization of other elements is not so clear, but uses will likely be found.

branch

An element in a state machine in which a single trigger leads to more than one possible outcome, each with its own guard condition.

See also fork, join, junction state, merge.

Semantics

If the same event can have different effects that depend on different guard conditions, then they can be modeled as separate transitions with the same event trigger. In practice, however, it is convenient to permit a single trigger to drive multiple transitions. This is especially true in the common case in which the guard conditions cover every possibility, so that an occurrence of the event is guaranteed to trigger one of the transitions. A *branch* is a part of a transition that splits the transition path into two or more segments, each with a separate guard condition. The event trigger is placed on the first, common segment of the transition. The output of one branch segment can be connected to the input of another branch to form a tree. Each path through the tree represents a distinct transition. The conjunction of all the conditions on a path in a transition is equivalent to a single condition that is conceptually evaluated before the transition fires. A transition fires in a single step, despite its appearance as a tree of branches. The tree is merely a modeling convenience.

Within an activity graph, branches leaving an activity state are, usually, completion transitions—that is, they lack explicit event triggers, and they are triggered implicitly on the completion of activity within the state. If there are guard conditions or branches, it is important that they cover all possibilities so that some transition will fire. Otherwise, the execution of the activity graph would freeze, because the output transitions would never be reenabled.

Notation

A branch may be shown by repeating an event trigger on multiple transition arcs with different guard conditions. This may also be done with completion transitions, as in an activity diagram.

For greater convenience, however, the head of a transition arrow may be connected to a diamond symbol, which indicates a branch. The transition arrow is labeled with the trigger event, if any, but it should not have an action on it. Any actions go on the final segment of the transition.

A diamond symbol may have two or more arrows leaving it. Each arrow is labeled with a guard condition. The reserved word **else** can be used as a guard condition. Its value is true if all the other (explicit) guard conditions are false. The head of each arrow may be connected to another branch or to a state. An arrow connected to a state may have an action label attached.

The effect of a tree of branches is the same as expanding the tree into a separate transition arc for each path through the tree, all sharing the same trigger event but each with its own conjunction of guard conditions, action, and target state. Figure 13-37 shows two ways to draw the same situation.

Note that the diamond symbol can also be used for a merge (the inverse of a branch), in which two alternate paths come together, as shown in Figure 13-38. In the case of a merge, there are two or more input arrows and a single output arrow. No guard conditions are necessary.

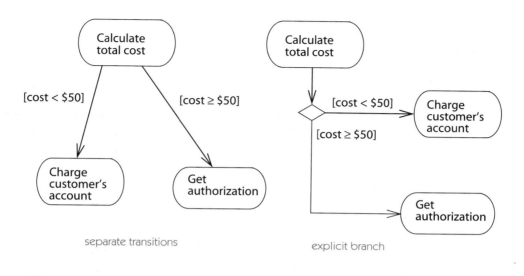

separate transitions   explicit branch

Figure 13-37. *Two ways to show a branch*

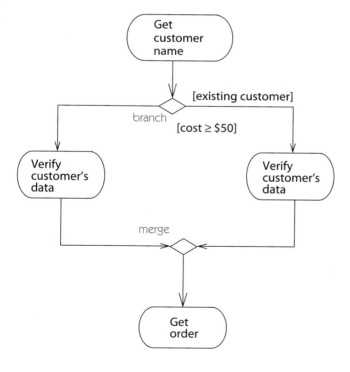

Figure 13-38. *Branch and merge*

call

To invoke an operation.

See also activation, call event, send.

Semantics

A call is the invocation of an operation at a point during the execution of a procedure. It moves a thread of control temporarily from the calling procedure to the called procedure. The execution of the calling procedure is blocked during the call. The caller yields control during the execution of the operation and regains it when the operation returns. The called procedure receives a list of arguments from the caller and also an implicit return pointer to the calling procedure, just past the point of the call. When the called procedure returns, it may supply a list of return values.

Often, a call is executed within the address space of the caller, but this is not necessary to the semantics of a call. Indeed, it is impossible in a distributed system, in which the receiver of the call may be physically separated from the caller. More important is the establishment of an implicit return link to the calling procedure location and environment, which enables control to be restored to the caller on a return. The calling procedure location may be modeled as a text line within a textual procedure or a state within a state machine. The calling environment may be modeled as an activation.

A call usage dependency models a situation in which an operation of the client class (or the operation itself) calls an operation of the supplier class (or the operation itself). It is represented with the «call» stereotype.

Notation

On a sequence diagram or a collaboration diagram, a call is shown as a text message directed to a target object or class.

A call dependency is shown as a dashed arrow from the caller to the called class or operation with the stereotype «call».

Most calls will be represented as part of text procedures in a programming language.

call event

The event of receiving a call for an operation that is implemented by actions on state machine transitions.

See also call, signal.

Semantics

A call event is a way of implementing an operation that is an alternative to the execution of a procedure. If a class specifies implementation of an operation as a call event, then a call of the operation is treated as an event that triggers a transition in the class's state machine. This permits a more dispersed implementation of an operation than a monolithic method procedure, which always does the same thing. (A procedure can have a case statement on the state of the object, so there is no real difference in power between the two approaches.)

If a class uses call events to implement an operation, then its state machine must have transitions triggered by the call event. The signature of a call event is the same as the operation: The name of the call event is the name of the operation; the parameters of the call event are the parameters of the operation.

When a call of the operation occurs, the state machine of the target object is consulted and the call event triggers a transition if it matches a trigger event on an active transition (one that departs from a currently active state). If a transition fires, its effect is executed. The effect may include any sequence of actions, including a **return**(value) action, whose purpose is to return a value to the caller.

When execution of the transition is complete, the caller regains control and may continue execution. If the operation requires a return value and the caller does not receive one, or if it receives a return value inconsistent with the declared type in the operation, then the model is in error. If the operation does not require a return value, then there is no problem. Note that if no transition is triggered by a call event, then control returns immediately to the caller. If the operation requires a return value, then the model is in error. Otherwise, the caller simply resumes immediately.

If the receiver is an active object, then a call event is handled when the state machine of the receiver is quiescent—that is, when any run-to-completion steps have been completed.

Notation

A call event is shown by an event trigger in a state diagram that matches an operation on the corresponding class. The action sequence on the transition may have a **return** statement in it; if so, the statement indicates the return value.

Example

Figure 13-39 shows an account that can be Locked and Unlocked. The **deposit** operation always adds money to the account, regardless of its state. The **withdraw** operation takes all of the money if the account is unlocked or none of the money if

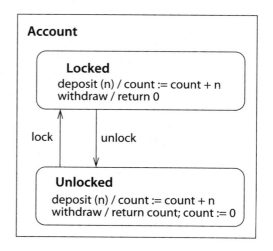

calling procedure text

    deposit (10);
    . . .
    amount := withdraw ( )

        Get all or nothing
        depending on whether
        the account is locked.

Figure 13-39. *Call events*

it is locked. The **withdraw** operation is implemented as a call event that triggers internal transitions in each state. When the call occurs, one or the other action sequence is executed, depending on the active state. If the system is locked, zero is returned; if the system is unlocked, all of the money in the account is returned and the count is reset to zero.

canonical notation

UML defines a canonical notation that uses monochromatic line drawings and text for displaying any model. This is the standard "publication format" of UML models and is suitable for printed diagrams.

Graphical editing tools can extend the canonical notation for convenience and to provide interactive capabilities. For example, a tool might provide the capability to highlight selected elements on the screen. Other interactive capabilities include navigation within the model and filtering of the displayed model according to selected properties. This kind of formatting is ephemeral and is not mandated by UML. With an interactive display, there is little danger of ambiguity as the user can simply ask for a clarification. Therefore, the focus of the UML standard is the printed canonical form, which every tool must support, with the understanding that an interactive tool may and should provide interactive extensions.

cardinality

The number of elements in a set. It is a specific number. Contrast with multiplicity, which is the range of possible cardinalities a set may hold.

Discussion

Note that the term *cardinality* is misused by many authors to mean what we call multiplicity, but the term cardinality has a long-standing mathematical definition as a number, not a range of numbers. This is the definition we use.

change event

The event of a Boolean expression becoming satisfied because of a change to one or more of the values it references.

See also guard condition.

Semantics

A change event contains a condition specified by a Boolean expression. There are no parameters to the event. The event occurs when the condition becomes true (after having been false) because of a change to one or more variables on which the condition depends.

This kind of event implies a continuous test for the condition. In practice, however, by analyzing the times at which the inputs to the condition can change, the developer can often perform the test at well-defined, discrete times so that continuous polling is usually not required.

The event occurs when the value of the expression changes from false to true (a positive-going state change). The event occurs once when this happens and does not recur unless the value first becomes false again.

Note the difference from a guard condition. A guard condition is evaluated *once* whenever the event on its transition occurs. If the condition is false, then the transition does not fire and the event is lost (unless it triggers some other transition). A change event is implicitly evaluated continuously and occurs once at the time when the value becomes true. At that time, it may trigger a transition or it may be ignored. If it is ignored, the change event does not trigger a transition in a subsequent state simply because the condition is still true. The change event has already occurred and been discarded. The condition must become false and then true again to cause another change event.

The values in the Boolean expression must be attributes of the object that owns the state machine containing the transition or values reachable from it.

Notation

Unlike signals, change events do not have names and are not declared. They are simply used as the triggers of transitions. A change event is shown by the keyword **when** followed by a Boolean expression in parentheses. For example:

    when (self.waitingCustomers > 6)

Discussion

A change event is a test for the satisfaction of a condition. It may be expensive to implement, although there are often techniques to compile it so that it need not be tested continuously. Nevertheless, it is potentially expensive and also hides the direct cause-and-effect relationship between the change of a value and the effects that are triggered by it. Sometimes, this is desirable because it encapsulates the effects, but change events should be used with caution.

A change event is meant to represent the test for values visible to an object. If a change to an attribute within an object is meant to trigger a change in another object that is unaware of the attribute itself, then the situation should be modeled as a change event on the attribute's owner that triggers an internal transition to send a signal to the second object.

Note that a change event is not explicitly sent anywhere. If an explicit communication with another object is intended, a signal should be used instead.

The implementation of a change event can be done in various ways, some of them by making tests within the application itself at appropriate times and some of them by means of underlying operating system facilities.

changeability

A property that indicates whether the value of an attribute or link can change.

Semantics

The property may be placed on an association end or an attribute. The property may also be applied to a class with the meaning that all its attributes and associations satisfy the property (for example, a value of frozen means that the value of an object of the class is unchangeable after initialization). Changeability is notated using a keyword in a property list with the following possible enumerated values.

changeable | Attribute values can change freely, including the addition and deletion of values if the multiplicity permits. Links can change freely and can be added and removed freely consistent with the multiplicity and other constraints. This is the default if another choice is not specified.

frozen | Attribute values may not change after initialization; no values can be added or deleted. No links may be added, deleted, or modified after the initialization of the object on the opposite end of the association (that is, the end opposite the end having the frozen value). However, when an object on the opposite end is created, new links to the frozen end may be added as part of its initialization.

addOnly   Additional attribute values may be added if the multiplicity is not a fixed number or already at maximum. After creation, values may not be modified or deleted while the containing object lives. New links may be added, but no links may be deleted or modified after their creation. If a participating object is destroyed, then the links containing it are deleted, despite its add-only status.

child

The more specific element in a generalization relationship. Called subclass for a class. A chain of one or more child relationships is a descendant. Antonym: parent.

Semantics

A child element inherits the features of its parent (and indirectly those of its ancestors) and may declare additional features of its own. It also inherits any associations and constraints that its ancestors participate in. A child element obeys the substitutability principle—that is, an instance of a descriptor satisfies any variable declaration classified as one of the ancestors of the descriptor. An instance of a child is an indirect instance of the parent.

class

The descriptor for a set of objects that share the same attributes, operations, methods, relationships, and behavior. A class represents a concept within the system being modeled. Depending on the kind of model, the concept may be real-world (for an analysis model), or it may also contain algorithmic and computer implementation concepts (for a design model). A classifier is a generalization of class that includes other class-like elements, such as data type, actor, and component.

Semantics

A class is the named description of both the data structure and the behavior of a set of objects. A class is used to declare variables. An object that is the value of a variable must have a class that is compatible with the declared class of the variable—that is, it must be the same class as the declared class or a descendant of it. A class is also used to instantiate objects. A creation operation produces a new instance of the given class.

An object instantiated from a class is a direct instance of the class and an indirect instance of the ancestors of the class. The object contains a slot to hold a value for each attribute; it accepts all the operations and signals of its class, and it may appear in links of associations involving the class or an ancestor of the class.

Some classes may not be directly instantiated, but instead are used only to describe structure shared among their descendants; such a class is an abstract class. A class that may be instantiated is a concrete class.

A class may also be regarded as a global object. Any class-scope attributes of the class are attributes of this implicit object. Such attributes have global scope, and each has a single value across the system. A class-scope operation is one that applies to the class itself, not to an object. The most common class-scope operations are creation operations.

In UML, a class is a kind of classifier. *Classifier* includes a number of class-like elements, but it finds its fullest expression in *class*.

Structure

A class has a class name and lists of operations, methods, and attributes. A class may participate in association, generalization, dependency, and constraint relationships. A class is declared within a namespace, such as a package or another class, and has various properties within its namespace, such as multiplicity and visibility. A class has various other properties, such as whether it is abstract or an active class. It may have a state machine that specifies its reactive behavior—that is, its response to the reception of events. A class may declare the set of events (including exceptions) that it is prepared to handle. It may provide the realization of the behavior specified by zero or more interfaces or types by providing an implementation for the behavior. An interface lists a set of operations that a class realizing the interface promises to support.

A class contains a list of attributes and a list of operations that each form a namespace within the class. Inherited attributes and inherited operations also appear within the respective namespaces. The namespace for attributes also includes pseudoattributes, such as rolenames of associations leaving the class and discriminators for generalizations involving the class or one of its ancestors. Each name must be declared only once within the class and its ancestors. Otherwise there is a conflict, and the model is ill formed. Operation names may be repeated provided they represent the same operation, otherwise there is a conflict.

A class is also a namespace and establishes the scope for nested classifier declarations. Nested classifiers are not structural parts of instances of the class. There is no data relationship between objects of a class and objects of nested classes. A nested class is a declaration of a class that may be used by the methods of the outer class. Classes declared within a class are private to it and are not accessible outside the class unless explicitly made visible. There is no visual notation to show nested class declarations. The expectation is that they will be made accessible within a tool by hyperlinks. Nested names must be referenced using pathnames.

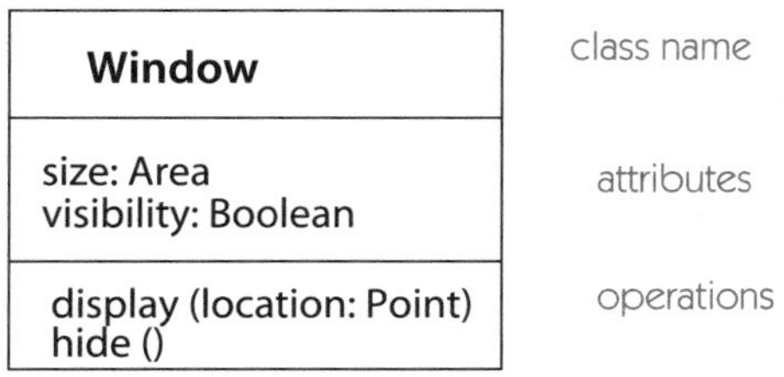

Window
size: Area visibility: Boolean
display (location: Point) hide ()

class name

attributes

operations

Figure 13-40. *Basic class declaration*

Notation

A class is shown as a solid-outline rectangle with three compartments separated by horizontal lines. The top compartment holds the class name and other properties that apply to the entire class. The middle compartment holds a list of attributes. The bottom compartment contains a list of operations. The middle and bottom compartments can be suppressed in a class symbol.

Usage. Classes are declared in class diagrams and used in many other diagrams. UML provides a graphical notation for declaring and using classes, as well as a textual notation for referencing classes within the descriptions of other model elements. The declaration of a class in a class diagram defines the contents of the class: its attributes, operations, and other properties. Other diagrams define additional relationships and attachments to a class.

Figure 13-40 shows a basic class declaration with attributes and operations.

Figure 13-41 shows the same class declaration with additional detail, much of it information of an implementation nature, such as visibility, class-level source scope creation operations, and implementation-dependent operations.

All internal information about the class is suppressed in Figure 13-42. The information is still present in the internal model and would usually be shown on at least one diagram.

Presentation options

Suppressing compartments. Either or both of the attribute and operation compartments may be suppressed (Figure 13-43). A separator line is not drawn for a missing compartment. If a compartment is suppressed, no inference can be drawn about the presence or absence of elements in it. Note that an empty compartment (that is, one with separator lines but no content) implies that there are no elements in the corresponding list. If some kind of filtering is in effect, then there are no elements that satisfy the filter. For example, if only public operations are visible, then the presence of an empty operation compartment indicates that there are no public operations. No conclusion can be drawn about private operations.

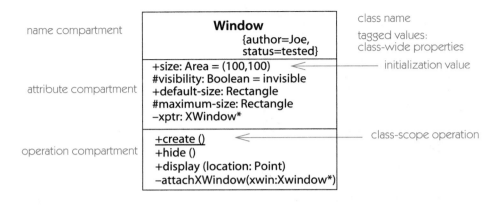

Figure 13-41. *Detailed class declaration with visibilities of features*

Figure 13-42. *Class symbol with all details suppressed*

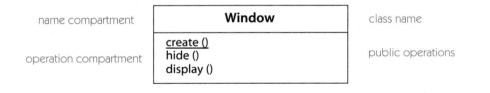

Figure 13-43. *Class declaration with attributes and non-public operations suppressed*

Additional compartments. Additional compartments may be supplied to show other predefined or user-defined model properties—for example, to show business rules, responsibilities, variations, signals handled, exceptions raised, and so on. An additional compartment is drawn with a compartment name at the top, shown in a distinctive font to identify its contents (Figure 13-44). The standard compartments (attribute, operation) do not require compartment names, although they may have names for emphasis or clarity if only one compartment is visible. Most compartments are simply lists of strings, in which each string encodes a property. Note that "string" includes the possibility of icons or embedded

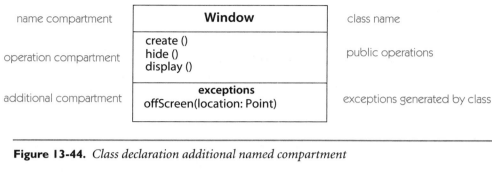

Figure 13-44. *Class declaration additional named compartment*

Figure 13-45. *Class with stereotype*

documents, such as spreadsheets and graphs. More complicated formats are possible, but UML does not specify such formats. They are a user and tool responsibility. If the nature of the compartment can be determined from the form of its contents, then the compartment name may be omitted.

See font usage, string.

Stereotype. A stereotype is shown as a text string in guillemets (« ») above the class name (Figure 13-45). Instead of the text string, an icon can be place in the upper right corner of the name compartment. A class symbol with a stereotype icon may be "collapsed" to show just the stereotype icon, with the name of the class either inside or below the icon (Figure 13-170). Other contents of the class are suppressed.

See stereotype.

Style guidelines

- Center a stereotype name in normal typeface within guillemets above the class name.

- Center or left-justify a class name in boldface.

- Left justify attributes and operations in normal typeface.

- Show the names of abstract classes or the signatures of abstract operations in italics.
- Show the attribute and operation compartments when needed (at least once in the diagram set) and suppress them in other contexts or in references. It is useful to define a "home" location for a class once in a set of diagrams and to give its full description there. In other locations, the minimal form is used.

Discussion

The concept of class applies to a range of usages in logical modeling, as well as implementation. It includes both the concept of type and the concept of implementation class. In UML, under certain semantic variation points, an object may have multiple classes, as well as be able to change its class at run time. Various more restrictive notions of class found in most programming languages can be thought of as special kinds of classes.

Standard elements

implementationClass, type

class diagram

A class diagram is a graphic presentation of the static view that shows a collection of declarative (static) model elements, such as classes, types, and their contents and relationships. A class diagram may show a view of a package and may contain symbols for nested packages. A class diagram contains certain reified behavioral elements, such as operations, but their dynamics are expressed in other diagrams, such as statechart diagrams and collaboration diagrams.

See also classifier, object diagram.

Notation

A class diagram shows a graphic presentation of the static view. Usually several class diagrams are required to show an entire static view. Individual class diagrams do not necessarily indicate divisions in the underlying model, although logical divisions, such as packages, are natural boundaries for forming diagrams.

class-in-state

A class, together with a state that objects of the class can hold.
See also activity graph.

Semantics

A class with a state machine has many states, each of which characterizes the behavior, values, and constraints of instances that are in the state. In some cases certain attributes, associations, or operations are valid only when an object is in a certain state or set of states. In other cases, an argument to an operation must be an object in a particular state. Often, these distinctions are simply part of the behavioral models. But sometimes, it is useful to model them directly on static views or interaction views.

A class-in-state is a class, together with a valid state that objects of the class can hold. If the class has concurrent substates, the state specification may be a set of substates that an object of the class can hold simultaneously. A class-in-state may be used as a classifier. It behaves like a subclass of the class itself. It may be used as the class of a variable or of a parameter. It may participate in associations that are valid only for objects in the given state. In Figure 13-46, consider the association **Assignment** between **SubmittedPaper** and **ConferenceSession**. This association is valid for a **SubmittedPaper** in the **accepted** state (target multiplicity one) but not in the **rejected** state. For any **SubmittedPaper**, the target multiplicity is zero-or-one, because the class includes both **accepted** and **rejected** papers. However, if the association is modeled between **SubmittedPaper** in state **accepted** and **ConferenceSession**, it has target multiplicity exactly one.

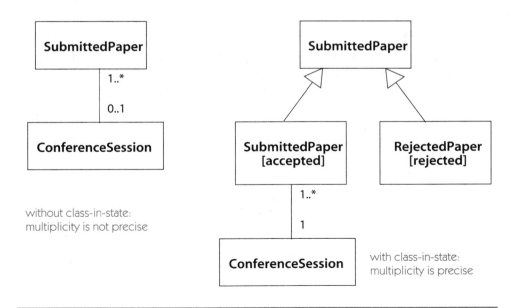

Figure 13-46. *Class-in-state*

Class-in-state elements are also useful for showing the input and output values of operations in activity graphs.

Notation

A class-in-state is shown as a class symbol in which the name of the class is followed by its state name within brackets (Classname[statename]). The brackets may also contain a comma-separated list of names of concurrent states to indicate that an object holds several of them.

Discussion

Class-in-state and dynamic classification are two ways to accomplish the same goal of allowing changes to the structure of an object during its life. Depending on the implementation environment, one or the other may be the more convenient mechanism.

class name

Each class must have a non-null name that is unique among classifiers within its container (such as a package or containing class). The scope of a name is its containing package and other packages that can see the containing package.

See name for a full discussion of naming and uniqueness rules.

Notation

The class name is shown in the top compartment of a class rectangle. The name compartment may also contain a keyword or stereotype name and/or a stereotype icon and a list of tagged values within braces (Figure 13-47).

An optional stereotype keyword may be placed above the class name within guillemets, and/or a stereotype icon may be placed in the upper-right corner of the compartment. The stereotype name must not match a predefined keyword, such as **enumeration**.

Figure 13-47. *Name compartment*

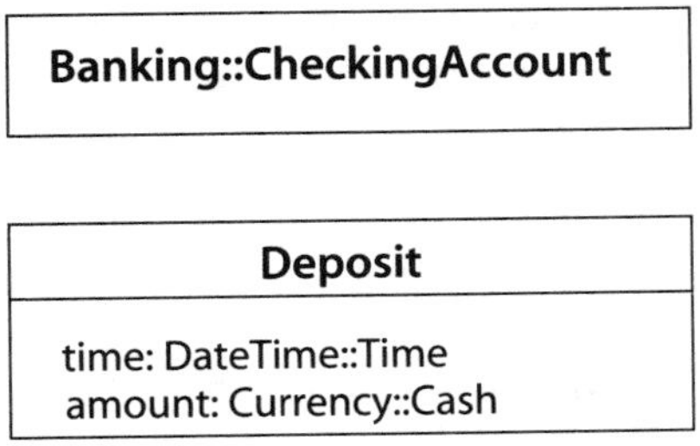

```
┌─────────────────────────────────────────┐
│  Banking::CheckingAccount               │
└─────────────────────────────────────────┘
```

```
┌─────────────────────────────────────────┐
│            Deposit                      │
├─────────────────────────────────────────┤
│  time: DateTime::Time                   │
│  amount: Currency::Cash                 │
└─────────────────────────────────────────┘
```

Figure 13-48. *Pathnames for classes in other packages*

The name of the class appears next. The class name is centered horizontally in boldface. If the class is abstract, its name appears in italics. But note that any explicit specification of generalization status (such as *abstract* or *concrete*) takes precedence over the name font.

An optional list of strings denoting properties (metamodel attributes or tagged values) may be placed in braces below the class name. The list may show class-level attributes for which there is no UML notation, and it may also show tagged values. Some keywords may be used without a value to denote a particular combination of property and value. For example, a leaf class shows the property {leaf}, which is equivalent to {isLeaf=true}.

By default a class shown within a package is assumed to be defined within that package. To show a reference to a class defined in another package, use the syntax

```
Package-name::Class-name
```

as the name string in the name compartment (Figure 13-48). A full pathname can be specified by chaining together package names separated by double colons (::). The same class name can be used for different classes in different packages, provided pathnames are used to distinguish them, but this duplication of names can lead to error and should be avoided if possible.

References to classes also appear in text expressions, most notably in type specifications for attributes and variables. In text expressions, a reference to a class is indicated simply by using the name of the class itself, including a possible package name, subject to the syntax rules of the expression.

classifier

A model element that describes behavioral and structural features. Kinds of classifiers include class, actor, component, data type, interface, node, signal, subsystem, and use case. Classes are the most general kind of classifier. Others can be intuitively understood as similar to classes, with certain restrictions on content or usage, although each kind of classifier is represented by its own metamodel class. Most properties of classes apply to classifiers, in general, with certain restrictions for each kind of classifier.

See also generalizable element, static view.

Standard elements

enumeration, location, metaclass, persistence, powertype, process, semantics, stereotype, thread, utility

classifier role

A slot in a collaboration that describes the role played by a participant in a collaboration.

See also collaboration.

Semantics

A collaboration describes a pattern of interaction among a set of participants, which are instances of classes or data types. A classifier role is the description of a participant. Each role is a distinct usage of the classifier in its own unique context. There may be multiple roles for the same classifier, each having a different set of relationships to other roles within a collaboration. A role is not an individual object, however, but a description of all the objects that may play a part in a collaboration instance. Each time the collaboration is instantiated, a different set of objects and links may play the roles.

A classifier role has a reference to a classifier (the base) and a multiplicity. The base classifier constrains the kind of object that can play the classifier role. The object's class can be the same as or a descendant of the base classifier. The multiplicity indicates how many objects can play the role at one time in one instance of the collaboration.

A classifier role may have a name, or it may be anonymous. It may have multiple base classifiers if multiple classification is intended.

A classifier role can be connected to other classifier roles by association roles.

Objects. A collaboration represents a group of objects that work together to accomplish a goal. A role represents the part of one of the objects (or a set of the objects) in carrying out that goal. An object is a direct or indirect instance of the base class of its role. All objects of the base class do not necessarily appear in collaborations, and objects of the same base class may play multiple roles in the same collaboration.

The same object may play different roles in different collaborations. A collaboration represents a facet of an object. A single physical object may combine different facets, thereby implicitly connecting the collaborations in which it plays roles.

Figure 13-49. *Classifier role*

Notation

A classifier role is shown by using the symbol for a classifier (a rectangle) with a role name and classifier name separated by a colon, that is, `rolename:BaseClass`. A role is not an object, however. It is a classifier that describes many objects that appear in different instances of the collaboration.

Either the role name or the classifier name may be omitted, but the colon must be included to distinguish it from an ordinary class. Within a collaboration there is little danger of confusion, as all the participants are roles.

A classifier role may display a subset of the features of the classifier, that is, the attributes and operations used in the given context. The rest of the features can be suppressed if they are not used.

Figure 13-49 shows various forms that a classifier role may take.

Standard elements

destroyed, new, transient

client

An element that requests a service from another element. The term is used to describe a role within a dependency. In the notation, the client appears at the tail of a dependency arrow. Antonym: supplier.

See dependency.

collaboration

A description of a general arrangement of objects and links that interact within a context to implement a behavior, such as a use case or operation. A collaboration has a static and a dynamic part. The static part describes the roles that objects and links may play in an instantiation of the collaboration. The dynamic part consists of one or more dynamic interactions that show message flows over time in the collaboration to perform computations.

See also association role, classifier role, interaction, message.

Semantics

Behavior is implemented by groups of objects that exchange messages within a context to accomplish a purpose. To understand the mechanisms used in a design, it is important to focus on the objects and messages involved in accomplishing a purpose or a related set of purposes, projected from the larger system within which they fulfill other purposes as well. An arrangement of objects and links that work together to accomplish a purpose is called a collaboration; a sequence of messages within a collaboration that implements behavior is called an interaction. A collaboration is a description of a "society of objects." It is a fragment of a larger, complete model, within which the collaboration is intended for a purpose.

For example, a commercial sale represents an arrangement of objects that have certain relationships to each other within the transaction. The relationships are not meaningful outside the transaction. Sale participants include a buyer, a seller, and a broker. To perform a specific interaction, such as selling a house, the participants exchange a certain sequence of messages, such as making an offer or signing a contract.

The message flows within the collaboration may optionally be specified by a state machine, which specifies legal behavior sequences. The events on the state machine represent messages exchanged among roles within the collaboration.

A collaboration consists of roles. A role is a part that a classifier or an association plays within the collaboration. A role is a slot that may hold an instance of a classifier or an association when instantiated. There may be different roles played by the same classifier or association; each would be filled by a different object or link. For example, within a commercial transaction, one party may be the seller and the other may be the buyer, even though they are both companies. The **seller** and **buyer** are roles of class **Company** within the collaboration **Sale**. Roles are meaningful only within a collaboration; outside they have no meaning. Indeed, in another collaboration, the roles may be reversed. An object may be a **buyer** in one instance of collaboration and a **seller** in another. The same object may play multiple roles in different collaborations. Contrast the restricted scope of a role with an association. An association describes a relationship that is globally meaningful for a class in all contexts, whether or not an object actually participates in the association. A collaboration defines relationships that are restricted to a context and which are meaningless outside of that context.

Realization. A collaboration realizes an operation or a use case. It describes the context in which the implementation of an operation or use case executes—that is, the arrangement of objects and links that exist when the execution begins, and the instances that are created or destroyed during execution. The behavior sequences may be specified in interactions, shown as sequence diagrams or collaboration diagrams.

A collaboration may also realize the implementation of a class. A collaboration for a class is the union of the collaborations for its operations. Different collaborations may be devised for the same class, system, or subsystem; each collaboration shows the subset of attributes, operators, and related objects that are relevant to one view of the entity, such as the implementation of a particular operation.

Patterns. A parameterized collaboration represents a design construct that can be reused in various designs. Usually the base classifiers are parameters. Such a parameterized collaboration captures the structure of a *pattern*.

See template.

A design pattern is instantiated by supplying actual classifiers for the base classifier parameters. Each instantiation yields a collaboration among a specific set of classifiers in the model. A pattern can be bound more than once to different sets of classifiers within a model, avoiding the need to define a collaboration for each occurrence. For example, a model-view pattern defines a general relationship among model elements; it can be bound to many pairs of classes that represent model-view pairs. Each pair of actual model-view classes represents one binding of the pattern. One such pair would be a house and a picture of the house, another pair would be a stock and a graphic showing the current price of the stock.

Note that a pattern also involves guidelines for use and explicit advantages and disadvantages. These can be put in notes or in separate text documents.

Layers of collaborations. A collaboration may be expressed at various levels of granularity. A coarse-grained collaboration may be refined to produce another collaboration that has a finer granularity. This is accomplished by expanding one or more operations from a high-level collaboration into distinct lower-level collaborations, one for each operation.

A collaboration may be implemented in terms of subordinate collaborations. Each subordinate collaboration implements a part of the overall functionality and has its own set of roles. Each role of the overall collaboration may be bound to one or more roles of the nested compositions. If an outer-level role is bound to more than one inner-level role, then it implicitly connects the behavior of the lower-level collaborations. This is the only way that use cases interact. One design approach is to work from the inside out. First construct the inner, narrow roles, and then combine them to produce outer, broader roles that have multiple responsibilities.

Run-time binding. At run time, objects and links are bound to the roles of the collaboration. An object can be bound to one or more roles, usually in different collaborations. If an object is bound to multiple roles, then it represents an "accidental" interaction between the roles—that is, an interaction that is not inherent in the roles themselves, but only a side effect of their use in a wider context. Often, one object plays roles in more than one collaboration as part of a larger collaboration. Such overlap between collaborations provides an implicit flow of control and information between them.

Structure

Roles. A collaboration contains a set of roles, each of which is a reference to one or more base classifiers (classifier role) or base associations (association role). A role is a slot in the collaboration that describes a use of a classifier or an association within the collaboration. A role is also a classifier itself; an object bound to the role in an instance of the collaboration is a transient instance of the role. Within an instance of the collaboration, an object is bound to each classifier role and a link is bound to each association role. One object may be bound to more than one classifier role in the same collaboration instance, although this is uncommon and can be prevented by a suitable constraint. Objects of the same class may appear in multiple roles in the same collaboration instance. Each object has the relationships appropriate to its role. Each classifier role may list a subset of the classifier's features that are used in the collaboration. The other features are irrelevant in the collaboration, although they may be used in other collaborations. If there are multiple roles involving the same base classifier, the roles should have names to distinguish them. If there is a single use of a base classifier in a collaboration, the role can be anonymous, as the classifier is sufficient to identify it. The roles define the structure of the collaboration.

If multiple classification is supported, then the role may have multiple base classifiers. An object bound to the classifier role is an instance of each of them.

Generalizations. A collaboration can also include generalizations and constraints. These are in addition to any relationships the participating classifiers may have on their own outside the collaboration. A generalization in a collaboration is necessary only when the classifiers in the collaboration are parameters. Otherwise, their generalization structure is specified as part of their definition as classifiers and may not be altered by a collaboration. In a parameterized collaboration (a pattern) some of the classifier roles may be parameters. A generalization between two parameterized classifier roles indicates that any classifiers that are bound to the roles must satisfy the generalization relationship. (The classifier bound to the parent role must be an ancestor of the classifier bound to the child role. They need not be parent and child.)

For example, the pattern **Composite** from [Gamma-95] represents a recursive tree of objects in which class **Component** is a generic element of the tree, **Composite** is a recursive element, and **Leaf** is a leaf element (Figure 13-50). **Component** is the parent of **Leaf** and **Composite**, the latter of which is an aggregate of **Component** elements (the recursion). **Component**, **Composite**, and **Leaf** are parameters within the pattern. They are replaced by actual classes when the pattern is used. Any set of actual classes bound to the pattern must observe the ancestor-descendant relationship between **Component** and its children **Composite** and **Leaf**. Sample substitutions would include **Graphic**, **Picture**, and **Rectangle**; **DirectoryEntry**,

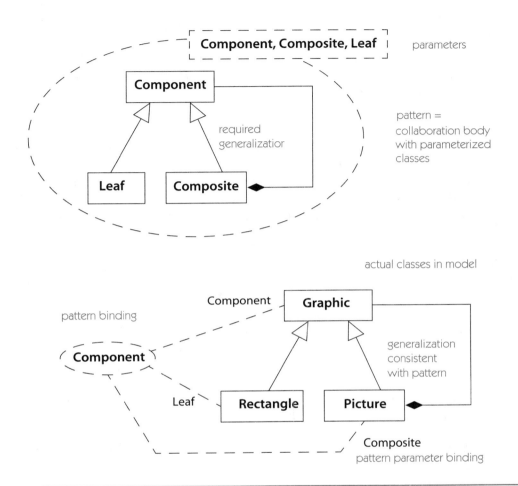

Figure 13-50. *Pattern: a parameterized collaboration*

Directory, and **File**; and any other recursive classes. If a binding does not fulfill the generalization constraint, it is ill formed.

Constraints. Constraints may be specified on parameterized and nonparameterized roles. These constraints are in addition to any that may exist on classifiers bound to the roles. The constraints apply to each instance of the collaboration.

Messages. A collaboration may have a set of messages to describe its dynamic behavior. A collaboration with messages is an interaction. There may be multiple interactions, each describing part of the same collaboration. One interaction can describe the implementation of one operation and another interaction can describe another operation, for example. Messages have sequencing information among them; the sequencing information is equivalent to specifying a state machine triggered by messages.

Source. A collaboration may represent a class, use case, or method (a collaboration is the implementation of an operation, not the specification of an operation). The collaboration describes the behavior of the source element.

Notation

A collaboration diagram is a graph of class symbols (rectangles) representing classifier roles and association paths (solid lines) representing association roles, with message symbols attached to its association role paths. A collaboration diagram without messages shows the *context* in which interactions can occur, without showing any interactions. It may be used to show the context for a single operation or even for all the operations of a class or group of classes. If messages are attached to the association lines, the diagram shows an interaction. Typically, an interaction represents the implementation of an operation or use case.

A collaboration diagram shows the slots for objects involved as classifier roles in an interaction. A classifier role is distinguished from a classifier because it has both a name and a class, with the syntax rolename :classname. Either the rolename or the class name may be omitted, but the colon is required. A diagram also shows the links among the objects as association roles, including transient links representing procedure arguments, local variables, and *self*-links. Multiple association roles can have the same association name, provided they connect different classifier roles. Arrows on link lines indicate navigability in the direction of the arrow. (An arrowhead *on* a line between object boxes indicates a link with one-way navigability. An arrow *next to* a line indicates a message flowing in the given direction over the link. A message cannot flow backward over a one-way link, so message flows must be compatible with navigability arrows.)

Individual attribute values in classifier roles are usually not shown explicitly. If messages must be sent to attribute values, the attributes should be modeled as objects using associations.

Tools may use other graphic markers in addition to or in place of the keywords. For example, each kind of lifetime might be shown in a different color. A tool may also use animation to show the creation and destruction of elements and the state of the system at various times.

Implementation of an operation

A collaboration that shows the implementation of an operation includes symbols for the target object role and the roles of other objects the target object uses, directly or indirectly, to perform the operation. Messages on association roles show the flow of control in an interaction. Each message shows a step within the method for the operation.

A collaboration describing an operation also includes role symbols representing arguments of the operation, and local variables created during its execution. Objects created during the execution may be designated as {new}; objects destroyed during the execution may be designated as {destroyed}; objects created during the execution and then destroyed may be designated as {transient}. Objects without a keyword exist when the operation begins and still exist when it is complete.

The internal messages that implement a method are numbered, starting with number 1. For a procedural flow of control, the subsequent message numbers use "dot" sequences nested in accordance with call nesting. For example, the second top-level step is message 2; the first subordinate step inside that step is message 2.1. For asynchronous messages exchanged among concurrent objects, all the sequence numbers are at the same level (that is, they are not nested).

See message for a full description of message syntax including sequencing.

A complete collaboration diagram shows the roles of all the objects and links used by the operation. If an object is not shown, the assumption is that it is not used. It is not safe to assume that all the objects on a collaboration diagram *are* used by the operation, however.

Example

In Figure 13-51, an operation **redisplay** is called on a **Controller** object. At the time when the operation is called, it already has a link to the **Window** object, where the picture will be displayed. It also has a link to a **Wire** object, the object whose image will be displayed in the window.

The top-level implementation of the **redisplay** operation has only one step—the calling of operation **displayPositions** on the **wire** object. This operation has sequence number 1, because it is the first step in the top-most method. This message flow passes along a reference to the **Window** object that will be needed later.

The **displayPositions** operation calls the **drawSegment** operation on the same **wire** object. The call, labeled with sequence number 1.1, is dispatched along the implicit **self** link. The star indicates an iterative call of the operation; the details are supplied in the brackets.

Each **drawSegment** operation accesses two **Bead** objects, one indexed by qualifier value **i-1** and one by value **i**. Although there is only one association from **Wire** to **Bead**, within the context of this operation, two links to two **Wire** objects are needed. The objects are labeled **left** and **right** (these are the classifier roles in the collaboration). One message is dispatched along each link. The messages are labeled 1.1.1a and 1.1.1b. This indicates that they are steps of operation 1.1; the letters at the end indicate that the two messages can be dispatched concurrently. In a

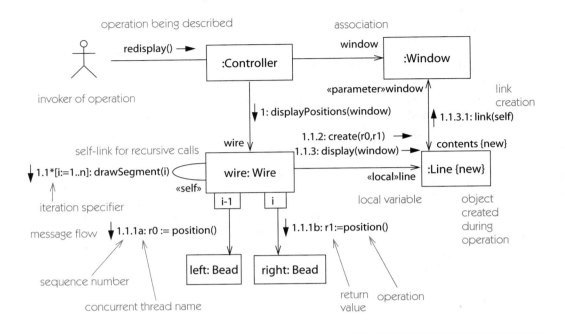

Figure 13-51. *Collaboration diagram with message flows*

normal implementation, they would probably not be executed in parallel, but because they are declared as concurrent, they can be executed in any convenient sequential order.

When both values (**r0** and **r1**) have been returned, the next step under operation 1.1 can proceed. Message 1.2 is a create message sent to a **Line** object. Actually it goes to the **Line** class itself (in principle, at least), which creates a new **Line** object linked to the sender. The new object has the label {**new**} to indicate that it is created during the operation but lives on afterward. The new link has the label «local», indicating that it is not an association but a local variable within the procedure. Local variables are inherently transient and disappear with the termination of the procedure. Therefore, it is unnecessary to label it with the keyword {**transient**}.

Step 1.3 uses the newly created link to send a **display** message to the newly created **Line** object. The pointer to the **window** object is passed along as an argument, making it accessible to the **Line** object as a «**parameter**» link. Note that the **Line** object has a link to the same **window** object that is associated with the original **Controller** object; this is important to the operation and it is shown by the diagram. In the final step 1.3.1, the **Window** object is requested to create a link to the **Line** object. This link *is* an association, so it has rolename **contents**, and is labeled {**new**}.

The final state of the system can be observed by mentally erasing all the temporary links. There is a link from **Controller** to **wire** and from **wire** to its **Bead** parts, from **Controller** to **window** and from **window** to its **contents**. Once the operation is complete, however, a **Line** has no access to the **Window** that contains it. The link in that direction is transient and disappears when the operation is complete. Similarly, a **Wire** object no longer has access to the **Line** objects used to display it.

Instance-level collaborations

Collaborations can be expressed as descriptors and as instances, similar to many model elements. A descriptor-level collaboration shows a potential relationship among objects; the collaboration can be instantiated many times to produce collaboration instances. Each collaboration instance shows a relationship among specific objects.

Which form should be used to model a situation? If the diagram shows contingency, then it must be a descriptor-level diagram. Object diagrams do not have contingency. They do not have conditionals or loops; such things are part of a generic description. An instance does not have a range of values or a set of possible control paths; it has a value and a history.

If the diagram shows specific values of attributes or arguments, if it shows a specific number of objects or links out of a variable-size multiplicity, or if it shows a particular choice of branches and loops during execution, then it must be an instance-level diagram.

In many cases either form can be used. This is true when the computation has no branches. Then any execution is prototypical, and there is not much difference between the descriptor form and the instance form.

collaboration diagram

A diagram that shows interactions organized around roles—that is, slots for instances and their links within a collaboration. Unlike a sequence diagram, a collaboration diagram explicitly shows the relationships among the roles. On the other hand, a collaboration diagram does not show time as a separate dimension, so the sequence of messages and the concurrent threads must be determined using sequence numbers. Sequence diagrams and collaboration diagrams express similar information, but show it in different ways.

See collaboration, pattern, sequence diagram.

collaboration role

A slot for an object or link within a collaboration. It specifies the kind of object or link that may appear in an instance of the collaboration.

See also association role, classifier role, collaboration.

Semantics

A collaboration role describes an object or a link. It does not, however, represent a single object or link, but rather a place where an object or link may be substituted when the collaboration is instantiated. A collaboration is either a classifier role or an association role. A classifier role has one or more base classifiers and may be instantiated as an object, which is an instance of the classifiers or one of their descendants. An association role may have a base association and may be instantiated as a link, which is an instance of the association or one of its descendants. In many cases, the association is defined only within the collaboration—that is, it occurs only for objects playing the roles and is not meaningful apart from the collaboration. In such a case, the base association can be omitted. The association is defined implicitly by its appearance in the collaboration, with the constraint that it is not usable elsewhere.

Notation

Collaboration roles may be classifier roles or association roles.

Classifier role. A classifier role is a classifier and is shown as a class rectangle symbol. Often, only the name compartment is shown. The name compartment contains the string

    classifierRoleName :BaseClassifierName$_{list,}$

The base classifier name can include a full pathname of enclosing packages, if necessary (a tool will normally permit shortened pathnames to be used when they are unambiguous). The package names precede the class name and are separated by double colons. For example:

    display_window:WindowingSystem::GraphicWindows::Window

A stereotype for a classifier role may be shown textually in guillemets above the name string or as an icon in the upper-right corner. The stereotype for a classifier role must match the stereotype for its base classifier.

A classifier role representing a set of objects includes a multiplicity indicator (such as '*') in the upper-right corner of the class box. This specifies the number of objects that may be bound to the role in one instance of the collaboration. If the indicator is omitted, the value is exactly one.

The name of the classifier role may be omitted. In this case, the colon should be kept with the class name. This represents an anonymous object of the class.

If multiple classification is supported, the role may have more than one classifier. The object is an instance of each of them.

The class of the classifier role may be suppressed (together with the colon).

An object or link that is created during an interaction has the keyword **new** as a constraint on its role. An object or link that is destroyed during an interaction has the keyword **destroyed** as a constraint on its role. The keywords may be used even if an element has no name. Both keywords may be used together, but the keyword **transient** may be used in place of **new destroyed**.

Association role. An association role is an association and is shown as a path between two classifier role symbols. The path may have an attached name of the form

```
associationRoleName : BaseAssociationName
```

If the name of the base association is omitted, then there is no base association. The rolenames and other adornments of the base association may be shown on the path.

If one end of the association role path is connected to a class role with a multiplicity other than one, then a multiplicity indicator may be placed on that end of the association to emphasize the multiplicity.

Figure 13-51 shows an example of collaboration roles.

combination

A kind of relationship that relates two parts of the description of a classifier that combine to make the full descriptor for the element.

See extend, include.

Semantics

One of the powerful capabilities of object orientation is the ability to combine description of model elements out of incremental pieces. Inheritance combines classifiers related by generalization to produce the effective full descriptor of a class.

Other ways of combining descriptors are the extend and include relationships. These are modeled as varieties of the combination relationship. (Generalization might well be considered in the same category, but because of its importance it is treated as a distinct fundamental relationship.)

Notation

A combination relationship is shown as a dashed arrow with a stereotype keyword attached. *See* extend and include for specific details of each one.

Discussion

Other kinds of combination relationship are possible. Some programming languages, such as CLOS, implement several powerful varieties of method combination.

comment

An annotation attached to an element or a collection of elements. A comment has no direct semantics, but it may display semantic information or other information meaningful to the modeler or to a tool, such as a constraint or method body.

See also note.

Semantics

A comment contains a text string but it may also include embedded documents if a modeling tool permits. A comment may be attached to a model element, a presentation element, or a set of elements. It provides a text description of arbitrary information, but it has no semantic impact. Comments provide information to modelers and may be used to search models.

Notation

Comments are displayed in note symbols, which are shown as rectangles with bent upper-right corners ("dog ears") attached by a dashed line or lines to the element or elements that the comment applies to (Figure 13-52). Modeling tools are free to provide additional formats for displaying comments and browsing them, such as pop-ups, special fonts, and so on.

Standard elements

requirement, responsibility

Figure 13-52. *Comment*

communication association

An association that describes a communication relationship between instances of the connected elements. In a deployment view, it is an association between nodes that implies a communication. In a use case model, it is an association between a use case and an actor that is a communication association.

See actor, use case.

compartment

A graphical division of a closed shape symbol, such as a class rectangle divided vertically into smaller rectangles. Each compartment shows properties of the element that it represents. Compartments come in three kinds: fixed, lists, and regions.

See also class, classifier.

Notation

A *fixed compartment* has a fixed format of graphical and text parts to represent a fixed set of properties. The format depends on the kind of element. An example is a class name compartment, which contains a stereotype symbol and/or name, a class name, and a property string that shows various class properties. Depending on the element, some of the information may be suppressible.

A *list compartment* contains a list of strings that encode constituents of the element. An example is an attribute list. The encoding depends on the constituent type. The list elements may be shown in their natural order within the model, or they may be sorted by one or more of their properties (in which case, the natural order will not be visible). For example, a list of attributes could be sorted first on visibility and then on name. List entries can be displayed or suppressed based on the properties of the model elements. An attribute compartment, for instance, might show only public attributes. Stereotypes and keywords may be applied to individual constituents by prepending them to the list entry. Stereotypes and keywords may be applied to all subsequent constituents by placing them on list entry by themselves. They affect all subsequent list entries until the end of the list or another such running declaration. The string «constructor» placed on a separate line in an operation list would stereotype the subsequent operations as constructors, but the string «query» further down the list would revoke the first declaration and replace it by the «query» stereotype.

A *region* is an area that contains a graphic subpicture showing substructure of the element, often potentially recursive. An example is a nested state region. The nature of the subpicture is peculiar to the model element. Including both regions and text compartments in a single symbol is legal, but can be messy. Regions are often used for recursive elements, and text is used for leaf elements with no recursive substructure.

A class has three predefined compartments: name, a fixed compartment; attributes, a list compartment; and operations, another list compartment. A modeler can add another compartment to the rectangle and place its name at the head of the compartment, in a distinctive font (for example, small boldface).

The graphical syntax depends on the element and the kind of compartment. Figure 13-53 shows a compartment for signals. Figure 13-157 shows a compartment for responsibilities.

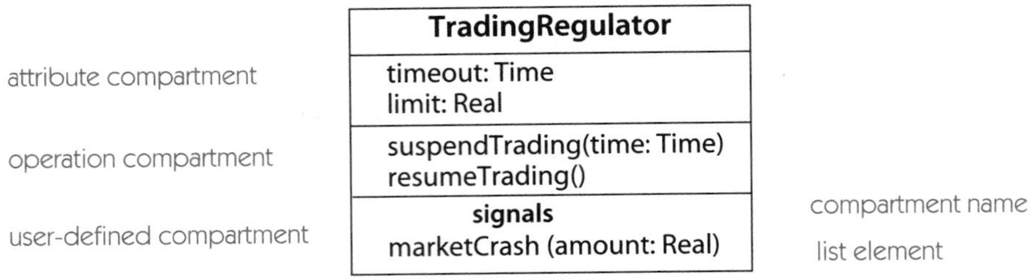

attribute compartment

operation compartment

user-defined compartment

TradingRegulator
timeout: Time
limit: Real
suspendTrading(time: Time)
resumeTrading()
signals
marketCrash (amount: Real)

compartment name

list element

Figure 13-53. *Named compartment in a class*

compile time

Refers to something that occurs during the compilation of a software module.
See modeling time, run time.

completion transition

A transition that lacks an explicit trigger event and is triggered by the completion of activity in the source state.
See also activity, transition, trigger.

Semantics

A completion transition is represented as a transition that has no explicit trigger event. The transition is triggered implicitly when its source state has completed any activity (including nested states). In a composite state, completion of activity is indicated by reaching the final state. If a state lacks internal activity or nested states, then the completion transition is triggered immediately after the entry action and exit action are executed, but no other events can intervene.

If a state has nested states or activity but lacks outgoing transitions with trigger events, the completion transition is not guaranteed to fire. An event might cause a triggered transition on one of the nested states to fire while the enclosing state is waiting to complete its activity, so the completion transition might be bypassed.

A completion transition may have a guard condition and an action. Usually, it is undesirable to have an isolated guarded completion transition, because if the guard condition is false, the transition will never fire (because the implicit trigger occurs only once). Occasionally, this may be useful to represent some kind of failure, provided a triggered transition eventually pulls the object out of the dead state. More commonly a set of guarded completion transitions have conditions that cover all possibilities so that one of them will fire immediately when the state terminates.

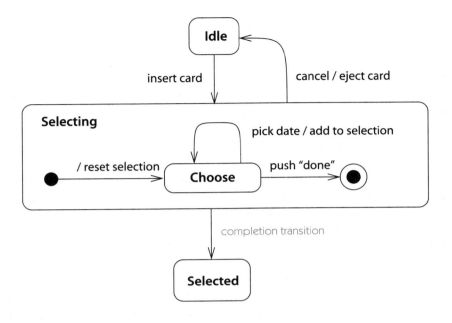

Figure 13-54. *Completion transition*

Completion transitions are also used to connect initial states and history states to their successor states, because these pseudostates may not remain active after the completion of activity.

Example

Figure 13-54 shows a state machine fragment of ticket-ordering application. The **Selecting** state remains active as long as the customer keeps picking dates. When the customer presses the "done" button, then the **Selecting** state reaches its final state. This triggers the completion transition, which goes to the **Selected** state.

complex transition

A transition with more than one source state and/or more than one target state. It represents a response to an event that causes a change in the amount of concurrency. It is a sychronization of control, a forking of control, or both, depending on the number of sources and targets.

See also branch, composite state, fork, join, merge.

Semantics

At a high level, a system passes through a series of states, but the monolithic view that a system has a single state is too restrictive for large systems with distribution and concurrency. A system may hold multiple states at one time. The set of active states is called the active state configuration. If a nested state is active, then all states that contain it are active. If the object permits concurrency, then more than one concurrent substate may be active.

In many cases, the activity of a system can be modeled as a set of threads of control that evolve independently of each other or that interact in limited ways. Each transition affects, at most, a few states in the active state configuration. When a transition fires, unaffected active states remain active. The progress of the threads at a moment can be captured as a subset of states within the active state configuration, one subset for each thread. Each set of states evolves independently in response to events. If the number of active states is constant, the state model is nothing but a fixed collection of state machines that interact. In general, however, the number of states (and therefore the number of threads of control) can vary over time. A state can transition to two or more concurrent states (a fork of control), and two or more concurrent states can transition to one state (a join of control). The number of concurrent states and their evolution is controlled by the state machine for the system.

A complex transition is a transition into or from a set of concurrent substates. A complex transition has more than one source state and/or target state. If it has multiple source states, it represents a join of control. If it has multiple target states, it represents a fork of control. If it has multiple source and target states, it represents a synchronization of parallel threads.

If a complex transition has multiple source states, all of them must be active before the transition is a candidate for triggering. The order in which they become active is irrelevant. If all the source states are active and the event occurs, the transition is triggered and may fire if its guard condition is true. Each transition is triggered by a single event, even if there are multiple source states. The concept of simultaneous occurrence of events is not supported by UML; each event must trigger a separate transition and then the resultant states can be followed by a join.

If a complex transition with multiple source states lacks a trigger event (that is, if it is a completion transition) then it is triggered when all its explicit source states become active. If its guard condition is satisfied at that time, it fires.

When a complex transition fires, all the source states and all their peers within the same composite state cease to be active, and all the target states and all their peers become active.

In more complicated situations, the guard condition may be expanded to permit firing when some subset of the states is active.

Example

Figure 13-55 shows a typical concurrent composite state with complex transitions entering and leaving it. Figure 13-56 shows a typical execution history of this machine (the active states are shown in blue). The history shows the variation in number of active states over time.

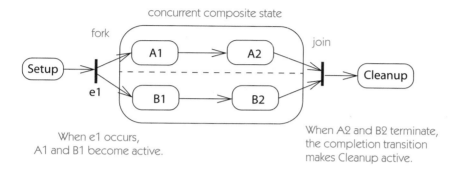

Figure 13-55. *Fork and join*

Concurrent states

Unless a state machine is carefully structured, a set of complex transitions can lead to inconsistencies, including deadlocks, multiple occupation of a state, and other problems. The problem has been extensively studied under Petri net theory, and the usual solution is to impose well-formedness rules on the state machine to avoid the danger of inconsistencies. These are "structured programming" rules for state machines. There are a number of approaches, each with advantages and disadvantages. The rules adopted by UML require that a state machine decompose into finer states using a kind of *and-or* tree. The advantage is that a well-nested structure is easy to establish, maintain, and understand. The disadvantage is that certain meaningful configurations are prohibited. On balance, this is similar to the trade-off in giving up goto's to get structured programming.

A complex state may be decomposed into a set of mutually exclusive substates (an "or" decomposition) or into a set of concurrently held substates (an "and" decomposition). The structure is recursive. Generally, "and" layers alternate with "or" layers. An "and" layer represents concurrent decomposition—all of the substates are active concurrently. An "or" state represents a sequential decomposition—one substate is active at a time. A legal set of concurrent states can be obtained by recursively expanding the nodes in the tree, starting with the root. Replace an "and" state by all of its children; replace an "or" state by one of its children. This corresponds to the nested structure of statecharts.

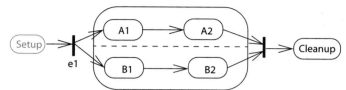

e1 occurs

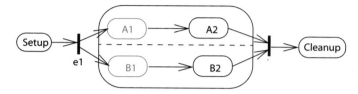

A1 completes

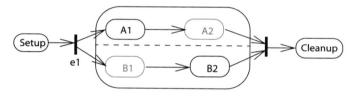

B1 completes

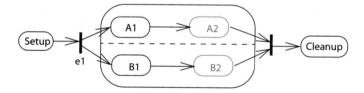

A2 and B2 complete

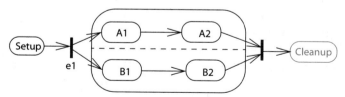

(Active states shown in blue)

Figure 13-56. *History of active states in a concurrent state machine*

Example

Figure 13-57 shows an and-or tree of states corresponding to the state machine in Figure 13-55. A typical set of concurrently active states is colored in blue. This corresponds to the third step in Figure 13-56.

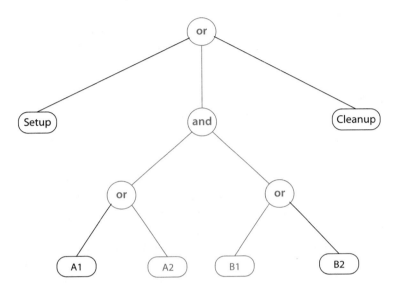

(Typical set of active states shown in blue)

Figure 13-57. *And-or tree of nested states*

If a transition enters a concurrent region, it enters all the substates. If a transition enters a sequential region, it enters exactly one substate. The active state within a sequential region can change. With a concurrent region all concurrent substates remain active as long as the region is active, but generally each concurrent substate is decomposed further as a sequential region.

Therefore, a simple transition (one that has one input and one output) must connect two states in the same sequential region or two states separated by or-levels only. A complex transition must connect all the substates within a concurrent region with a state outside the concurrent region (we omit more complicated cases, but they must follow the principles above). In other words, a transition entering a concurrent region must enter each substate; a transition leaving a concurrent region must leave each substate.

A shortcut representation is available: If a complex transition enters a concurrent region but omits one or more of the subregions, then there is implicitly a transition to the initial state of each omitted subregion. If some subregion has no initial state, the model is ill formed. If a complex transition leaves a concurrent region, there is an implicit transition from each omitted subregion. If the transition fires, any activity within the subregion is terminated—that is, it represents a forced exit. A transition can be connected to the enclosing concurrent region itself. It implies a transition to the initial state of each subregion—a common modeling situation. Similarly, a transition from an enclosing concurrent region implies the forced exit of each subregion (if it has an event trigger) or waiting for each subregion to complete (if it is triggerless).

The rules on complex transitions ensure that meaningless combinations of states cannot be active concurrently. A set of concurrent substates is a partition of the enclosing composite state. Either all of them are active or none of them is active.

Conditional thread

In an activity graph, a segment leaving a fork may have a guard condition. This is a conditional thread. When the transition fires, the thread headed by the guarded segment is initiated only if the guard condition is satisfied. Unguarded segments are always initiated when the transition fires. The concurrency in an activity graph must be well nested—each fork must correspond to a subsequent join. When a conditional thread fails to start because its guard condition is false, the activity at the corresponding input segment on the matching join is considered complete—that is, the transition does not wait for a flow of control on the conditional thread. If all the threads on a fork fail to start, then control resumes immediately at the matching join.

A conditional thread is equivalent to a graph with a branch and merge surrounding the conditional portion of the activity graph.

Example

Figure 13-58 shows an activity graph with two conditional threads. It represents the check-in procedure for an airline. Before anything can happen, the customer must present a ticket. Then there are three concurrent threads, two of which are conditional. Seat assignment is always performed, but baggage is checked only if the customer has baggage, and the passport is examined only if the flight is international. When all three threads are complete, control joins to a single thread in which the ticket and boarding pass are returned to the customer. If a conditional thread does not start, it is considered complete for the subsequent join.

Notation

A complex transition is shown as a short heavy bar (a synchronization bar, which can represent synchronization, forking, or both). The bar may have one or more

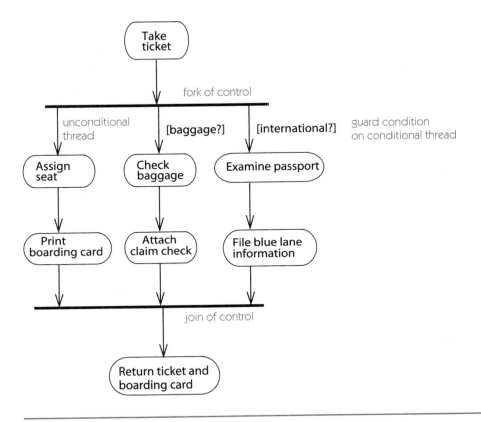

Figure 13-58. *Conditional threads*

solid transition arrows from states to the bar (the states are the source states); the bar may have one or more solid arrows from the bar to states (the states are the *target states*). A transition label may be shown near the bar, describing the trigger event, guard condition, and actions, as described under transition. Individual arrows do not have their own transition strings; they are merely part of the overall single transition.

Example

Figure 13-59 shows the state machine from Figure 13-55 with an additional exit transition. It also shows an implicit fork from state **Setup** to the initial states in each subregion and an implicit join from the final states in each subregion to state **Cleanup**.

If event **f1** occurs when state **B2** is active, then the transition to state **Cleanup** occurs. This transition is an implicit join; it terminates state **A2** as well as state **B2**.

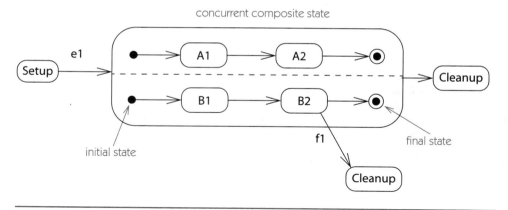

Figure 13-59. *Complex transitions (fork, join)*

component

A physical, replaceable part of a system that packages implementation and conforms to and provides the realization of a set of interfaces.

Semantics

A component represents a physical piece of implementation of a system, including software code (source, binary, or executable) or equivalents, such as scripts or command files. Some components have identity and may own physical entities, which include run-time objects, documents, databases, and so on. Components exist in the implementation domain—they are physical units on computers that can be connected to other components, replaced by equivalent components, moved around, archived, and so on. Models may show dependencies among components, such as compiler and run-time dependencies or information dependencies in a human organization. A component instance may be used to show implementation units that exist at run time, including their location on node instances.

Components have two aspects. They package the code that implements the functionality of a system, and some of them own instances of objects that constitute the system state. We call the latter identity components, because their instances have identity and state.

Code aspect. A component contains the code for implementation classes and other elements. (Code is taken broadly and includes scripts, hypertext structures, and other forms of executable descriptions.) A source-code component is a package for the source code of implementation classes. Some languages (such as C++) distinguish declaration files from method files, but they are all components. A binary-code component is a package for compiled code. A binary-code library is a component. An executable component contains executable code. Each kind of component contains the code for implementation classes that realize some logical classes and interfaces. The realization relationship relates a component to the logical classes and interfaces that its implementation classes implement.

The interfaces of a component describe the functionality that it supports. Each operation in the interface must eventually map to an implementation element supported by the component.

The static, executable structure of a system implementation can be represented as an interconnected set of components. Dependencies among components mean that implementation elements in one component require the services of implementation elements in other components. Such usage requires the supplier elements to be publicly visible in their components. A component may also have private elements, but these cannot be direct suppliers of services to other components.

Components may be contained by other components. A contained component is just another implementation element within its container.

A component instance is an instance of a component on a node instance. Source-code and binary-code component instances may reside on particular node instances, but executable component instances are most useful. If an executable component instance is located on a node instance, objects of implementation classes supported by the component can execute operations when they are located on the node instance. Otherwise, an object located on a node instance cannot execute operations and must be moved or copied to another node instance to execute operations.

If a component lacks identity, all instances of it are the same. It does not matter which of them supports the execution of a run-time object. All of them behave the same. Because they have no identity, the component instances themselves do not have values or state.

Identity aspect. An identity component has identity and state. It owns physical objects, which are located on it (and, therefore, on the node instance containing the component instance). It may have attributes, composition relationships to owned objects, and associations to other components. From this point of view, it *is* a class. However, all of its state must map onto its owned instances. That's what makes it a component, rather than an ordinary class. Often an implementation class is provided to represent the component as a whole. This is called a dominant class and is often equated with the component itself, although they are not the same thing.

An object requesting services of an identity component must select a specific instance of the component, usually by having an association to one of the objects owned by the component. Because each identity component instance has state, requests to different instances may produce different results.

Example

For example, a spelling checker may be a component. If it has a fixed dictionary, it can be modeled as a nonidentity component. All instances of it produce the same results and there is no memory of past requests. If the dictionary can be updated, however, then it must be modeled as an identity component. There can be different versions of the dictionary, corresponding to different instances of the spelling checker component. A requestor must address its request to a specific instance of the component. Often the target component is implicit within a particular context, but it is a choice that must be part of the design.

Structure

A component *supports* a set of implementation elements, such as implementation classes. This means that the component provides the code for the elements. An implementation element may be supported by multiple components.

A component may have operations and interfaces, which must be implemented by its implementation elements.

An identity component is a physical *container* for physical entities, such as run-time objects and databases. To provide handles to its contained elements, it may have attributes and outgoing associations, which must be implemented by its implementation elements. An identity component may designate a dominant class that supports all its public attributes and operations, but such a class is just one of its implementation elements.

Notation

A component is displayed as a rectangle with two smaller rectangles protruding from its side. The name of the component type is placed inside (Figure 13-60).

A component instance has an individual name separated from a component type name by a colon. The name string is underlined to distinguish it from a component type (Figure 13-61). A component instance symbol may be drawn inside a

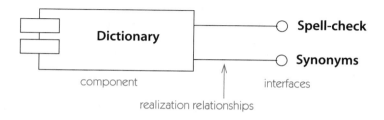

Figure 13-60. *Component*

node symbol to show that the component instance is located on the node instance (Figure 13-62). If the component does not have identity, the instance name is usually omitted. Objects owned by an identity component instance may be drawn inside it. A component with attributes or contained objects is automatically an identity component.

A dominant class subsumes the interface of the component. It may be drawn as a class with a component symbol in the upper right as a stereotype icon. In this

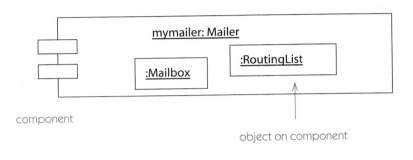

Figure 13-61. *Identity component instance with resident objects*

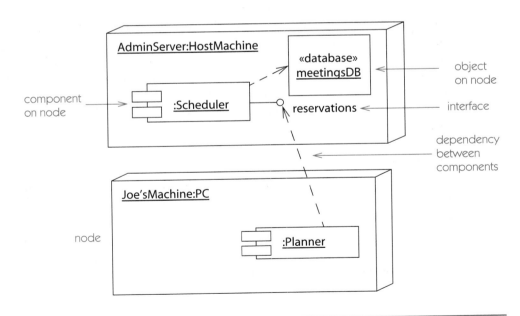

Figure 13-62. *Component instances on nodes*

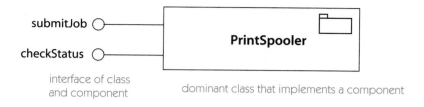

Figure 13-63. *Dominant class for a component*

case, the component and its dominant class share the same interface, and any objects contained in the component are reachable from the dominant class by composition links. Figure 13-63 shows an example.

Operations and interfaces available to outside objects may be shown directly in the class symbol. These are its class-like behavior. The contents of the subsystem are shown on a separate diagram. When the instantiable aspect of a subsystem need not be shown, the ordinary package notation can be used.

Dependencies from a component to other components or model elements are shown using dashed lines with arrowheads on the supplier elements (Figure 13-64). If a component is the realization of an interface, the shorthand notation of a circle attached to the component symbol by a line segment may be used. Realizing an interface means that the implementation elements in the component supply all the operations in the interface, at least. If a component uses an interface of another element, the dependency may be shown by a dashed line with an arrowhead on the interface symbol. Using an interface means that the implementation elements in the component require no more operations from a supplier component than the ones listed in the interface (but the client may depend on other interfaces, as well).

Discussion

The following expanded definition explains the intent behind a component and the considerations involved in deciding whether a piece of a system should be considered an interesting component.

- A component is nontrivial. It is functionally and conceptually larger than a single class or a single line of code. Typically, a component encompasses the structure and behavior of a collaboration of classes.

- A component is nearly independent of other components. It rarely stands alone, however. Rather, a given component collaborates with other components and in so doing, assumes an architectural context.

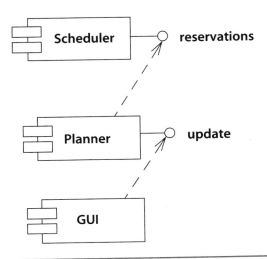

Figure 13-64. *Dependencies between components*

- A component is a replaceable part of a system. It is substitutable, making it possible to replace it with another one that conforms to the same interfaces. The mechanism of inserting or replacing a component to form a running system is typically transparent to the component user, enabled by object models that require little or no intervening transformation or by tools that automate the mechanism.

- A component fulfills a clear function and is logically and physically cohesive. It thus denotes a meaningful structural and/or behavioral chunk of a larger system.

- A component exists in the context of a well-defined architecture. It represents a fundamental building block on which systems can be designed and composed. This definition is recursive. A system at one level of abstraction may simply be a component at a higher level of abstraction.

- A component never stands alone. Every component presupposes an architectural and or technology context in which it is intended to be used.

- A component conforms to a set of interfaces. A component that conforms to an interface satisfies the contract specified by the interface and may be substituted in any context in which that interface applies.

Standard elements

document, executable, file, library, location, table

component diagram

A diagram that shows the organizations and dependencies among component types.

Semantics

A component diagram shows the dependencies among software components, including source code components, binary code components, and executable components (Figure 13-64). A software module may be represented as a component. Some components exist at compile time, some exist at link time, and some exist at run time; some exist at more than one time. A compile-only component is one that is meaningful only at compile time. The run-time component, in this case, would be an executable program.

A component diagram has only a descriptor form, not an instance form. To show component instances, use a deployment diagram.

Notation

A component diagram shows component classifiers, classes defined in them, and the relationships among them. Component classifiers may also be nested inside other component classifiers to show definition relationships.

A class defined within a component may be displayed inside it, although for systems of any size, it might be more convenient to provide a list of classes defined within a component, instead of showing symbols.

A diagram containing component classifiers and node classifiers may be used to show compiler dependencies, which are shown as dashed arrows (dependencies) from a client component to a supplier component that it depends on in some way. The kinds of dependencies are language-specific and may be shown as stereotypes of the dependencies.

The diagram may also be used to show interfaces and calling dependencies among components, using dashed arrows from components to interfaces on other components.

See component for examples of component diagrams.

composite aggregation

See composition.

composite class

A class that is related to one or more classes by a composition relationship.
See composition.

composite object

A composite object represents a high-level object made of tightly bound parts. It is an instance of a composite class, which implies the composition aggregation between the class and its parts. A composite object is similar to (but simpler and more restricted than) a collaboration. It is defined by composition in a static model, however, rather than by the context-dependent relationships of a collaboration.

See also composition.

Semantics

A composite object has a composition relationship to all of its composite parts. This means that it is responsible for their creation and destruction, and that no other object is similarly responsible. In other words, there are no garbage collection issues with the parts; the composite object can and must destroy them when it dies, or else it must hand over responsibility for them to another object.

The composition relationship is often implemented by physical containment within the same data structure as the composite object itself (usually a record). Physical containment ensures that the lifetime of the parts matches the lifetime of the composite object.

Notation

A network of objects and links may be nested within a graphic compartment inside an object symbol. The graphic compartment is shown as an addition compartment below the attribute compartment (the attribute compartment may be suppressed). The objects and links contained in the graphics region are composite parts of the composite object. A link whose path breaks the boundary of the object, however, is not a composite part of it; it is a link between separate objects.

Example

Figure 13-65 shows a composite object, namely a desktop window, composed of various parts. It contains multiple instances of the **ScrollBar** class. Each instance has its own name and role within the composite object. For example, the **horizontalBar** and the **verticalBar** are both scrollbars, but they behave differently within the composite. In this respect, they are like collaboration roles.

composite state

A state that consists of either concurrent (orthogonal) substates or sequential (disjoint) substates.

See also complex transition, simple state, state.

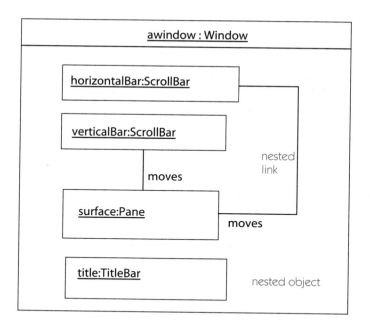

Figure 13-65. *Composite object*

Semantics

A composite state can be decomposed, using *and*-relationships, into concurrent substates, or, using *or*-relationships, into mutually exclusive disjoint substates. A state can be refined only in one of these two ways. Its substates can be refined in either way. If a sequential composite state is active, exactly one of its disjoint substates is active. If a concurrent composite state is active, all its orthogonal substates are active. The net effect is an *and-or tree*. Each state machine has a top-level state, which is a composite state.

A system may hold multiple states at one time. The set of active states is called the active state configuration. If a nested state is active, then all composite states that contain it are active. If the object permits concurrency, then more than one concurrent substate may be active.

See complex transition for a discussion of concurrent execution; Figure 13-57 shows an and-or tree.

A newly created object starts in its initial state, which the outermost composite state must have. The event that creates the object may be used to trigger a transition from the initial state. The arguments of the creation event are available to this initial transition.

An object that transitions to its outermost final state is destroyed and ceases to exist.

Structure

A composite state contains a set of substates. A composite state is either concurrent or sequential.

A sequential composite state may have, at most, one initial state and one final state. It may also have, at most, one shallow history state and one deep history state.

A concurrent composite state may not have an initial state, a final state, or history states, but any sequential composite states nested inside them may have such pseudostates.

Notation

A composite state is a state with subordinate detail. It has a name compartment, an internal transition compartment, and a graphic compartment that contains a nested diagram showing the subordinate detail. All of the compartments are optional. For convenience and appearance, the text compartments (name and internal transitions) may be shrunk as tabs within the graphic region, instead of spanning it horizontally.

An expansion of a concurrent composite state into concurrent substates is shown by tiling the graphic compartment of the state using dashed lines to divide it into subregions. Each subregion is a concurrent substate, which may have an optional name and must contain a nested state diagram with disjoint substates. The text compartments of the entire state are separated from the concurrent substates by a solid line.

An expansion of a state into disjoint substates is shown by a nested statechart diagram within the graphic region.

An initial state is shown as a small solid filled circle. In a top-level state machine, the transition from an initial state may be labeled with the event that creates the object. Otherwise, it must be unlabeled. If it is unlabeled, it represents any transition to the enclosing state. The initial transition may have an action. The initial state is a notational device. An object may not be *in* such a state but must transition to an actual state.

A final state is shown as a circle surrounding a small solid filled circle (a bull's eye). It represents the completion of activity in the enclosing state, and it triggers a transition on the enclosing state labeled by the implicit activity completion event (usually displayed as an unlabeled transition).

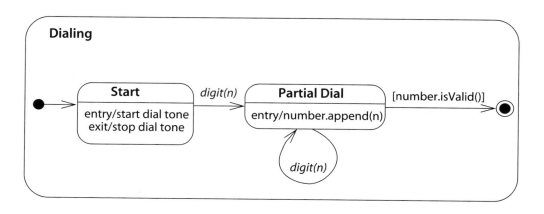

Figure 13-66. *Sequential composite state*

Example

Figure 13-66 shows a sequential composite state containing two disjoint substates, an initial state, and a final state. When the composite state becomes active, the substate **Start** (the target of the initial state) is activated first.

Figure 13-67 shows a concurrent composite state containing three orthogonal substates. Each concurrent substate is further decomposed into sequential substates. When the composite state **Incomplete** becomes active, the targets of the initial states become active. When all three subregions reach the final state, then the completion transition on the outer composite state **Incomplete** fires and the **Passed** state becomes active. If the **fail** event occurs while the **Incomplete** state is active, then all three concurrent subregions are terminated and the **Failed** state becomes active.

composition

A form of aggregation association with strong ownership and coincident lifetime of parts by the whole. A part may belong to only one composite. Parts with non-fixed multiplicity may be created after the composite itself. But once created, they live and die with it (that is, they share lifetimes). Such parts can also be explicitly removed before the death of the composite. Composition may be recursive.

See also aggregation, association, composite object.

Semantics

There is a strong form of aggregation association called composition. A composite is an aggregate association with the additional constraints that an object may be part of only one composite at a time and that the composite object has sole re-

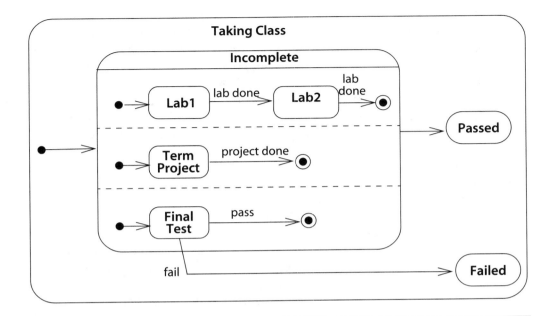

Figure 13-67. *Concurrent composite state*

sponsibility for the disposition of all its parts. As a consequence of the first constraint, the set of all composition relationships (over *all* associations with the composition property) forms a forest of trees made of objects and composition links. A composite part may not be shared by two composite objects. This accords with the normal intuition of physical composition of parts—one part cannot be a direct part of two objects (although it can indirectly be part of multiple objects at different levels of granularity in the tree).

By having responsibility for the disposition of its parts, we mean that the composite is responsible for their creation and destruction. In implementation terms, it is responsible for their memory allocation. During its instantiation, a composite must ensure that all its parts have been instantiated and correctly attached to it. It can create a part itself or it can assume responsibility for an existing part. But during the life of the composite, no other object may have responsibility for it. This means that the behavior for a composite class can be designed with the knowledge that no other class will destroy or deallocate the parts. A composite may add additional parts during its life (if the multiplicities permit), provided it assumes sole responsibility for them. It may remove parts, provided the multiplicities permit and responsibility for them is assumed by another object. If the composite is destroyed, it must either destroy all its parts or else give responsibility for them to other objects.

This definition encompasses most of the common logical and implementation intuitions of composition. For example, a record containing a list of values is a common implementation of an object and its attributes. When the record is allocated, memory for the attributes is automatically allocated also, but the values of the attributes may need to be initialized. While the record exists, no attribute can be removed from it. When the record is deallocated, the memory for the attributes is deallocated also. No other object can affect the allocation of a single attribute within the record. The physical properties of a record enforce the constraints of a composite.

This definition of composition works well with garbage collection. If the composite itself is destroyed, the only pointer to the part is destroyed and the part becomes inaccessible and subject to garbage collection. Recovery of inaccessible parts is simple even with garbage collection, however, which is one reason for distinguishing composition from other aggregation.

Note that a part need not be implemented as a physical part of a single memory block with the composite. If the part is separate from the composite, then the composite has responsibility for allocating and deallocating memory for the part, as needed. In C++, for example, constructors and destructors facilitate implementation of composites.

An object may be part of only one composite object at a time. This does not preclude a class from being a composite part of more than one class at different times or in different instances, but only one composition link may exist at one time for one object. In other words, there is an or-constraint among the possible composites that a part might belong to. Also, one object may be part of different composite objects during its life, but only one at a time.

Structure

The aggregation property on an association end may have the following values.

none	The attached classifier is not an aggregate or composite.
aggregate	The attached classifier is an aggregate. The other end is a part.
composite	The attached classifier is a composite. The other end is a part.

At least one end of an association must have the value **none**.

Notation

Composition is shown by a solid-filled diamond adornment on the end of an association path attached to the composite element (Figure 13-68). The multiplicity may be shown in the normal way. It must be 1 or 0..1.

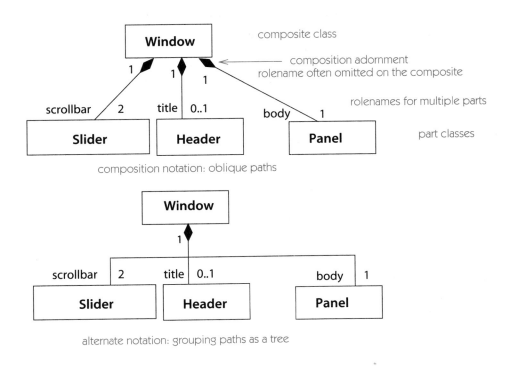

Figure 13-68. *Composition notation*

Alternately, composition may be shown by graphically nesting the symbols of the parts within the symbol of the composite (Figure 13-69). A nested classifier may have a multiplicity within its composite element. The multiplicity is shown by a multiplicity string in the upper-right corner of the symbol for the part. If the multiplicity mark is omitted, the default multiplicity is many. A nested element may have a rolename within the composition. The name is shown in front of its type in the syntax

rolename :classname

The rolename is the rolename on an implicit composition association from the composite to the part.

An association drawn entirely within a border of the composite is considered to be part of the composition. Any objects connected by a single link of the association must belong to the same composite. An association drawn so that its path breaks the border of the composite is not considered to be part of the composition. Any objects on a single link of the association may belong to the same or different composites (Figure 13-70).

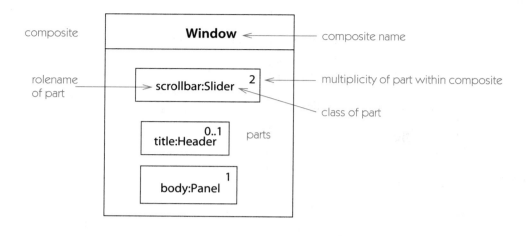

Figure 13-69. *Composition as graphical nesting*

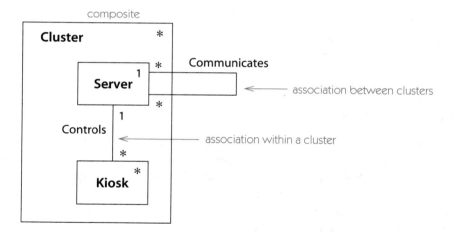

Figure 13-70. *Association within and among composites*

Note that attributes are, in effect, composition relationships between a class and the classes of its attributes (Figure 13-71). In general, however, attributes should be reserved for primitive data values (such as numbers, strings, and dates) and not references to classes, because any other relationships of the part classes cannot be seen in the attribute notation.

Note that the notation for composition resembles the notation for collaboration. A composition may be thought of as a collaboration in which all the participants are parts of a single composite object.

Figure 13-72 shows multilevel composition.

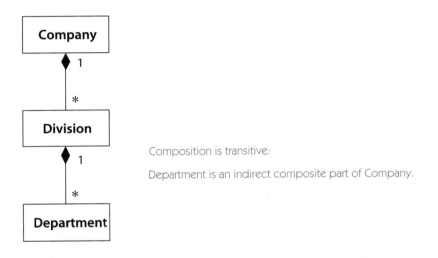

Window
scrollbar [2]: Slider title [0..1]: Header body: Panel

Avoid attributes for objects unless they are unshared and implementation-based.

Figure 13-71. *Attributes are a form of composition*

Composition is transitive:

Department is an indirect composite part of Company.

Figure 13-72. *Multilevel composition*

Discussion

(*See also* the discussion under aggregation for guidelines on when aggregation, composition, and plain association are appropriate.)

Composition and aggregation are metarelationships—they transcend individual associations to impose constraints in the entire set of associations. Composition is meaningful across composition relationships. An object may have at most one composition link (to a composite) although it might potentially come from more than one composition association. The entire graph of composition and aggregation links and objects must be acyclic, even if the links come from different associations. Note that these constraints apply to the instance domain—the aggregation associations themselves often form cycles, and recursive structures always require cycles of associations.

Consider the model in Figure 13-73. Every **Authentication** is a composite part of exactly one **Transaction**, which can be either a **Purchase** or a **Sale**. Every **Transaction** need not have an **Authentication**, however. From this fragment, we have

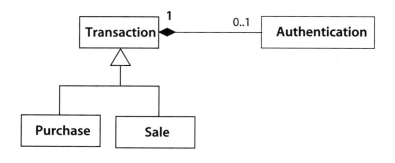

Figure 13-73. *Composition to an abstract composite class*

Figure 13-74. *Shared part class*

enough information to conclude that an **Authentication** has no other composition associations. Every authentication object must be part of a transaction object (the multiplicity is one); an object can be part of at most one composite (by definition); it is already part of one composite (as shown); so **Authentication** may not be part of any other composition association. There is no danger that an **Authentication** may have to manage its own storage. A **Transaction** is always available to take the responsibility, although not all **Transactions** have **Authentications** that they need to manage. (Of course, the **Authentication** can manage itself if the designer wants.)

Now consider Figure 13-74. An **Autograph** may optionally be part of either a **Transaction** or a **Letter**. It can't be part of both at one time (by the rules of composition). This model does not prevent an **Autograph** from starting as part of a **Letter** and then becoming part of a **Transaction** (at which time, it must cease being part of the **Letter**). In fact, an **Autograph** need not be part of anything. Also, from this model fragment, we cannot preclude the possibility that **Autograph** is optionally part of some other class that is not shown on the diagram or that might be added later.

What if it is necessary to state that every **Autograph** must be part of either a **Letter** or a **Transaction**? Then the model should be reformulated, as in Figure 13-73. A

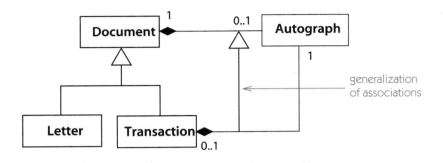

Figure 13-75. *Generalization of composition association*

new abstract superclass over **Letter** and **Transaction** can be added (call it **Document**), and the composition association with **Autograph** moved to it from the original classes. At the same time, the multiplicity from **Autograph** to **Document** is made one.

There is one minor problem with this approach: The multiplicity from **Document** to **Autograph** must be made optional, which weakens the original mandatory inclusion of **Autograph** within **Transaction**. The situation can be modeled using generalization of the composition association itself, as in Figure 13-75. The composition association between **Autograph** and **Transaction** is modeled as a child of the composition association between **Autograph** and **Document**. But its multiplicities are clarified for the child (note that they remain consistent with the inherited ones, so the child is substitutable for the parent). Alternately, the original model can be used by adding a constraint between the two compositions that one of them must always hold.

concrete

A generalizable element (such as a class) that can be directly instantiated. Of necessity, its implementation must be fully specified. For a class, all its operations must be implemented (by the class or an ancestor). Antonym: abstract.

See also direct class, instantiation.

Semantics

Only concrete classifiers can be instantiated. Therefore all the leaves of a generalization hierarchy must be concrete. In other words, all abstract operations and other abstract properties must eventually be implemented in some descendant. (Of course, an abstract class might have no concrete descendants if the program is incomplete, such as a framework intended for user extension, but such a class cannot be used in an implementation until concrete descendants are provided.)

Notation

The name of a concrete element appears in normal type. The name of an abstract element appears in italic type.

concurrency

The performance of two or more activities during the same time interval. There is no implication that the activities are synchronized. In general, they operate independently except for explicit synchronization points. Concurrency can be achieved by interleaving or simultaneously executing two or more threads.
See complex transition, composite state, thread.

concurrent substate

A substate that can be held simultaneously with other substates contained in the same composite state.
See composite state, disjoint substate.

conditional thread

A region of an activity graph that is started by a guarded output segment of a fork and concluded by an input segment of the corresponding join.
See composite state, complex transition.

conflict

The situation when the same-named attribute or operation is inherited from more than one class, or when the same event enables more than one transition, or any similar situation in which the normal rules yield potentially contradictory results. Depending on the semantics for each kind of model element, a conflict may be resolved by a conflict resolution rule, it may be legal but yield a nondeterministic result, or it may indicate that the model is ill formed.

Discussion

It is possible to avoid conflicts by defining them away with conflict resolution rules, such as: If the same feature is defined by more than one superclass, use the definition found in the earlier superclass (this requires that the superclasses be ordered). UML does not generally specify rules for resolving conflict on the principle that it is dangerous to count on such rules. They are easy to overlook and frequently are the symptom of deeper problems with a model. It is better to force the modeler to be explicit rather than depend on subtle and possibly confusing rules. In a tool or programming language, such rules have their place, if only to make the meaning deterministic. But it would be helpful for the tools to provide warnings when rules are used so that the modeler is aware of the conflict.

constraint

A semantic condition or restriction represented as an expression. Certain constraints are predefined in the UML, others may be defined by modelers. Constraints are one of three extensibility mechanisms in UML.

See also expression, stereotype, tagged value.

See Chapter 14, Standard Elements, for a list of predefined constraints.

Semantics

A constraint is a semantic condition or restriction expressed as a linguistic statement in some textual language.

In general, a constraint can be attached to any model element or list of model elements. It represents semantic information attached to a model element, not just to a view of it. Each constraint has a body and a language of interpretation. The body is a string encoding a Boolean expression for the condition in the constraint language. A constraint applies to an ordered list of one or more model elements. Note that the specification language may be a formal language or it may be a natural language. In the latter case, the constraint will be informal and not subject to automatic enforcement (which is not to say that automatic enforcement is always practical for all formal languages). UML provides the constraint language OCL [Warmer-99], but other languages can also be used.

Some common constraints have names to avoid writing a full statement each time they are needed. For example, the constraint **xor** between two associations that share a common class means that a single object of the shared class may belong to only one of the associations at one time.

See Chapter 14, Standard Elements, for a list of predefined UML constraints.

A constraint is an assertion, not an executable mechanism. It indicates a restriction that must be enforced by correct design of the system. How to guarantee a constraint is a design decision. Run-time constraints are meant to be evaluated at moments when an instantiated system is "stable"—that is, between the execution of operations and not in the middle of any atomic transactions. During the execution of an operation, there may be moments when the constraints are temporarily violated.

A constraint cannot be applied to itself.

An inherited constraint—a constraint on an ancestor model element or stereotype—must be observed even though additional constraints are defined on descendants. An inherited constraint may not be set aside or superseded. If you need to do this, the model is poorly constructed and must be reformulated. An inherited constraint can be tightened, however, by adding additional restrictions. If constraints inherited by an element conflict, then the model is ill formed.

Notation

A constraint is shown as a text string enclosed in braces ({ }). The text string is the encoded body written in a constraint language.

Tools are expected to provide one or more languages in which formal constraints may be written. One predefined language for writing constraints is OCL. Depending on the model, a computer language such as C++ may be useful for some constraints. Otherwise, the constraint may be written in natural language, with interpretation and enforcement remaining human responsibilities. The language of each constraint is part of the constraint itself, although the language is not generally displayed on the diagram (the tool keeps track of it).

For a list of elements represented by text strings in a compartment (such as the attributes within a class): A constraint string may appear as an entry in the list (Figure 13-76). The entry does not represent a model element. It is a *running constraint* that applies to all succeeding elements of the list until another constraint list element or the end of the list. The running constraint may be replaced by another running constraint later in the list. To clear the running constraint, replace it by an empty constraint. A constraint attached to an individual list element does not replace the running constraint but may augment it with additional restrictions.

For a single graphical symbol (such as a class or an association path): The constraint string may be placed near the symbol, preferably near the name of the symbol, if any.

ATM Transaction	
{ value ≥ 0 }	running constraint
amount: Money { value is multiple of $20 }	individual constraint and running constraint
balance: Money	only running constraint applies

Figure 13-76. *Constraints within lists*

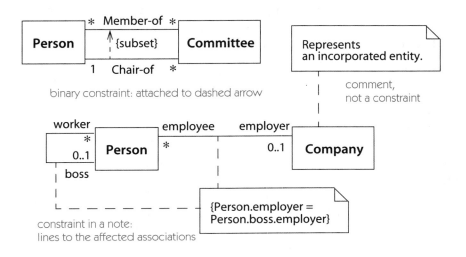

Figure 13-77. *Constraint notation*

For two graphical symbols (such as two classes or two associations): The constraint is shown as a dashed arrow from one element to the other element labeled by the constraint string (in braces). The direction of the arrow is relevant information within the constraint (Figure 13-77).

For three or more graphical symbols: The constraint string is placed in a note symbol and attached to each symbol by a dashed line (Figure 13-77). This notation may also be used for the other cases. For three or more paths of the same kind (such as generalization paths or association paths), the constraint may be attached to a dashed line crossing all the paths. In case of ambiguity, the various lines may be numbered or labeled to establish their correspondence to the constraint.

Discussion

A constraint makes a semantic statement about the model itself, whereas a comment is a text statement without semantic force and may be attached to either a model element or a presentation element. Both constraints and comments may be displayed using notes. In principle, constraints are enforceable by tools. In practice, some may be difficult to state formally and may require human enforcement. In the broad sense of the word, many elements in a model are constraints, but the word is used to indicate semantic statements that are difficult to express using the built-in model elements and that must be stated linguistically.

Constraints may be expressed in any suitable language or even in human language, although a human-language constraint cannot be verified by a tool. The

OCL language [Warmer-99] is designed for specifying UML constraints, but under some circumstances a programming language may be more appropriate.

Because constraints are expressed as text strings, a generic modeling tool can enter and maintain them without understanding their meaning. Of course, a tool or an add-in that verifies or enforces the constraint must understand the syntax and semantics of the target language.

A list of constraints can be attached to the definition of a stereotype. This indicates that all elements bearing the stereotype are subject to the constraint.

Enforcement. When the model contains constraints, it does not necessarily tell what to do if they are violated. A model is a declaration of what is supposed to happen. It is the job of the implementation to make it happen. A program might well contain assertions and other validation mechanisms, but a failure of a constraint must be considered a programming failure. Of course, if a model can help to produce a program that is correct by construction or can be verified as correct, then it has served its purpose.

Standard elements

invariant, postcondition, precondition

construction

The third phase of a software development process, during which the detailed design is made and the system is implemented and tested in software, firmware, and hardware. During this phase, the analysis view and the design view are substantially completed, together with most of the implementation view and some of the deployment view.

See development process.

constructor

A class-scope operation that creates and initializes an instance of a class. May be used as an operation stereotype.

See creation, instantiation.

container

An object that exists to contain other objects, and which provides operations to access or iterate over its contents, or a class describing such objects. For example, arrays, lists, and sets.

See also aggregation, composition.

Discussion

It is usually unnecessary to model containers explicitly. They are most often the implementation for the "many" end of an association. In most models, a multiplicity greater than one is enough to indicate the correct semantics. When a design model is used to generate code, the container class used to implement the association can be specified for a code generator using tagged values.

context

A view of a set of modeling elements that are related for a purpose, such as to execute an operation or form a pattern. A context is a piece of a model that constrains or provides the environment for its elements. A collaboration provides a context for its contents.

See collaboration.

control flow

A relationship among successive loci of control within an interaction, such as an activity graph or a collaboration.

See also action, activity graph, collaboration, completion transition, message, object flow state, transition.

Semantics

An interaction view graph represents the flow of control during a computation. The primitive elements of an interaction are simple actions and objects. A *control flow* represents the relationship between an action and its predecessor and successor actions, as well as between the action and its input and output objects. In an elided form, a control flow represents the computational derivation of one object from another or two versions of one object over time. (A control flow that involves an object as input or output is called an object flow.)

Notation

In a collaboration diagram, control flow is shown by messages attached to association roles (representing links) that connect classifier roles (representing objects and other instances). In an activity diagram, control flow is shown by the solid arrows between activity symbols. Object flow is shown by dashed arrows between an activity symbol or control flow arrow and an object flow state symbol. See those articles for more details.

control icons

Optional symbols that provide convenient shortcut notation for various control patterns.

See also activity graph, collaboration, state machine.

Notation

The following symbols are intended for use in activity diagrams, but they can also be used in statechart diagrams, if desired. These symbols do not permit anything that could not be shown using the basic symbols, but they may be convenient for certain common control patterns.

Branch. A branch is a set of transitions leaving a single state such that exactly one guard condition on one of the transitions must always be satisfied. In other words, if the trigger event occurs, exactly one transition is enabled to fire. The guard conditions essentially represent a branch of control. If the transition is a completion transition, then a branch is a pure decision. For convenience, one output of the branch may be labeled with the keyword **else**. This path is taken if no other path is taken.

A branch is notated as a diamond with one input arrow and two or more output arrows. The input transition arrow is labeled with the event trigger (if any). Each output is labeled with a guard condition (Figure 13-78).

Merge. A merge is a place at which two or more alternate paths of control come together. It is the inverse of a branch. A diamond is the symbol for either a branch or merge. It is a merge if there are multiple input arrows; it is a branch if there are multiple output arrows (Figure 13-78). Merges are not strictly necessary (multiple transitions that enter a single state are a merge), but they can be visually useful to show the match to previous branches.

Signal receipt. The receipt of a signal may be shown as a concave pentagon that looks like a rectangle with a triangular notch in its side (either side). The signature of the signal is shown inside the symbol. An unlabeled transition arrow is drawn from the previous action state to the pentagon, and another unlabeled transition arrow is drawn from the pentagon to the next action state. This symbol replaces the event label on the transition, which fires when the previous activity is complete and the event then occurs (Figure 13-79). Optionally, a dashed arrow may be drawn from an object symbol to the notch on the pentagon to show the sender of the signal.

Signal sending. The sending of a signal may be shown as a convex pentagon that looks like a rectangle with a triangular point on one side (either side). The signature of the signal is shown inside the symbol. An unlabeled transition arrow is drawn from the previous action state to the pentagon, and another unlabeled

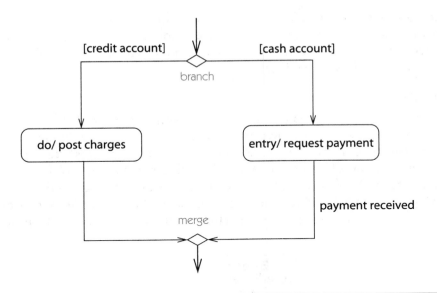

Figure 13-78. *Branch and merge*

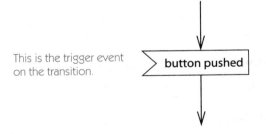

Figure 13-79. *Signal receipt*

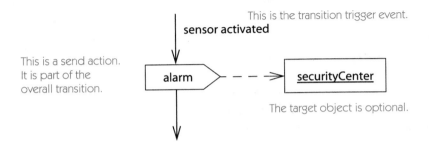

Figure 13-80. *Signal send*

transition arrow is drawn from the pentagon to the next action state. This symbol replaces the send-signal label on the transition (Figure 13-80). Optionally, a dashed arrow may be drawn from the point on the pentagon to an object symbol to show the receiver of the signal.

Example

In Figure 13-81, **EnterCreditCardData** and **ChargeCard** are activities. When they are completed, processing moves on to the next step. After **EnterCreditCardData** is completed, there is a branch on the amount of the request; if it is greater than $25, authorization must be obtained. A signal **request** is sent to the credit center. On a plain state machine, this would be shown as an action attached to the transition leaving **EnterCreditCardData**; they mean the same thing. **AwaitAuthorization** is a real wait state, however. It is not an activity that completes internally. Instead, it

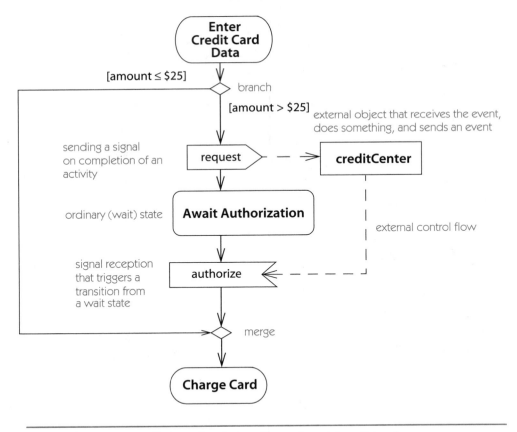

Figure 13-81. *Activity diagram showing sending and receiving of signals*

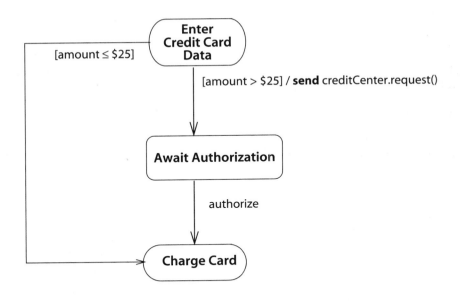

Figure 13-82. *Activity diagram without special symbols*

must wait for an external signal from the credit center (**authorize**). When the signal occurs, a normal transition fires and the system goes to the **ChargeCard** activity. The trigger event could have been shown as a label on the transition from **AwaitAuthorization** to **ChargeCard**. It is merely a variant notation that means the same thing.

Figure 13-82 shows the same example, without the special control symbols.

copy

A kind of flow relationship used in an interaction, in which the target object represents a copy of the source object, both of which are thereafter independent.

See also become.

Semantics

A copy relationship is a kind of flow relationship that shows the derivation of one object from another object within an interaction. It represents the action of making a copy. After a copy flow executes, there are two independent objects whose values can evolve independently.

A copy transition within an interaction may have a sequence number to indicate when it occurs relative to other actions.

Notation

A copy flow is shown by a dashed arrow from the original object to the newly produced copy (on the arrowhead). The arrow carries the stereotype keyword «copy» and may have a sequence number. Copy transitions may appear in collaboration diagrams, sequence diagrams, and activity diagrams.

Example

Figure 13-83 shows a file that has a backup on another node. First a copy is made («copy»), then the copy is moved to the secondary node («become» with a change of location).

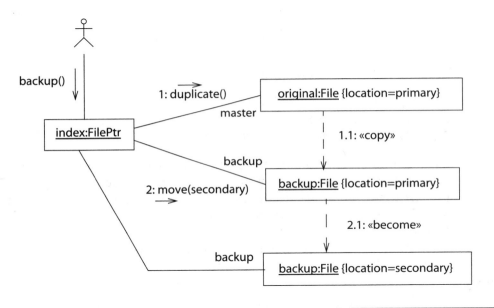

Figure 13-83. *Copy and become flow*

creation

The instantiation and initialization of an object or other instance (such as a use case instance). Antonym: destruction.
  See also instantiation.

Semantics

Creation of an object is the result of a message that instantiates the object. A creation operation may have parameters that are used for initialization of the new instance. At the conclusion of the creation operation, the new object obeys the constraints of its class and may receive messages.

A creation operation, or constructor, may be declared as a class-scope operation. The target of such an operation is (conceptually, at least) the class itself. In a programming language such as Smalltalk, a class is implemented as an actual run-time object and creation is therefore implemented as a normal message to such an object. In a language such as C++, there is no actual run-time object. The operation may be thought of as a conceptual message that has been optimized away at run time. The C++ approach precludes the opportunity to compute the class to be instantiated. Otherwise, each approach can be modeled as a message sent to a class.

The initial value expressions for the attributes of a class are (conceptually) evaluated at creation, and the results are used to initialize the attributes. The code for a creation operation can explicitly replace these values, so initial value expressions should be regarded as overridable defaults.

Within a state machine, the parameters of the constructor operation that created an object are available as an implicit current event on the transition leaving the top-level initial state.

Notation

In a class diagram, a creation operation (constructor) declaration is included as one of the operations in the operation list of the class. It may have a parameter list, but the return value is implicitly an instance of the class and may be omitted. As a class-scope operation, its name string must be underlined (Figure 13-84). It may show the «constructor» stereotype.

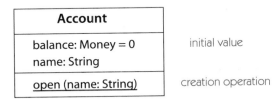

Figure 13-84. *Creation operation*

A creation operation execution within a sequence diagram is shown by drawing a message arrow, with its arrowhead on an object symbol (rectangle with underlined object name). Below the object symbol is the lifeline for the object (dashed line or double solid line, depending on whether it is active), which continues until the destruction of the object or the end of the diagram (Figure 13-85).

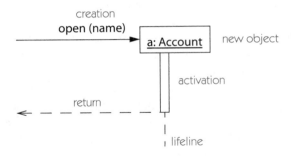

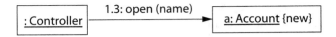

Figure 13-85. *Creation sequence diagram*

Figure 13-86. *Creation in a collaboration diagram*

The execution of a creation operation within a collaboration diagram is shown by including an object symbol with the property {new}. The first message to the object implicitly is the message that creates the object. Although the message is actually directed to the class itself, this flow is usually elided and the message is shown initializing the (newly instantiated, but uninitialized) instance, as shown in Figure 13-86.

See also collaboration and sequence diagram for notation to show creation within the implementation of a procedure.

current event

The event that triggered a run-to-completion step in the execution of a state machine.

See also run to completion, state machine, transition.

Semantics

For convenience, a state machine may traverse several connected transition segments in response to an event. All but the final transition segment go to pseudostates—that is, dummy states whose purpose is to help structure the state machine, but which do not wait for outside events. In principle, all the segments could be gathered into one transition, but the separation into multiple segments

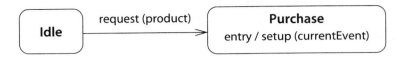

Figure 13-87. *Use of current event*

using pseudostates permits common subsequences to be shared among multiple transitions.

The execution of a chain of transition segments is atomic—that is, it is part of a single run-to-completion step that may not be interrupted by an outside event. During the execution of such a chain of transitions, actions and guard conditions attached to segments have implicit access to the event that triggered the first transition and to the parameters of that event. This event is known as the current event during a transition. The type of the current event may be discriminated by a polymorphic operation or a case statement. Once the exact type is known, then its parameters may be accessed.

The current event is particularly useful for the initial transition of a new object to obtain the creation parameters. When a new object is created, the event creating it becomes the current event and its parameters are available during the initial transition of the new object's state machine.

Example

Figure 13-87 shows a transition from the **Idle** state to the **Purchase** state triggered by the **request** event. The entry action of **Purchase** calls the **setup** operation, which uses the current event. The program can access the current event to obtain the **request** event and its parameter, **product**. If there are multiple possible bindings of the current event, the program may require a case statement to obtain the right trigger event. The syntax is programming-language specific.

Notation

The current event may be designated in an expression by the keyword **currentEvent**. A particular expression language may provide a more detailed syntax.

data type

A descriptor of a set of values that lack identity (independent existence and the possibility of side effects). Data types include primitive predefined types and user-definable types. Primitive types are numbers, strings, and time. User-definable types are enumerations. Anonymous data types intended for implementation in a programming language may be defined using language types.

See also classifier, identity.

Semantics

Data types are the predefined primitives needed as the foundation of user-definable types. Their semantics are mathematically defined outside the type-building mechanisms in a language. Numbers are predefined. They include integers and reals. Strings are also predefined. These data types are not user-definable.

Enumeration types are user-definable finite sets of named elements that have a defined ordering among themselves but no other computational properties. An enumeration type has a name and a list of enumeration constants. The enumeration type **Boolean** is predefined with the enumeration literals **false** and **true**.

Operations may be defined on data types, and operations may have data types as parameters. Because a data type has no identity and is just a pure value, operations on data types do not modify them; instead, they just return values. It makes no sense to talk of creating a new data type value, because they lack identity. All data type values are (conceptually) predefined. An operation on a data type is a query that may not change the state of the system but may return a value.

A data type may also be described by a language type—a data type expression in a programming language. Such an expression designates an anonymous data type in a target programming language. For example, the expression **Person* (*) (String)** denotes a type expression in C++ that does not correspond to a simple data type with a name.

data value

An instance of a data type, a value without identity.

See also data type, object.

Semantics

A data value is a member of a mathematical domain—a pure value. Two data values with the same representation are indistinguishable; data values have no identity. Data values are passed by value in a programming language. It makes no sense to pass them by reference. It is meaningless to talk about changing a data value; its value is fixed permanently. In fact, it *is* its value. Usually, when one talks of changing a data value, one means changing a variable that holds a data value so that it holds a new data value. But data values themselves are invariable.

default value

A value supplied automatically as part of some programming language or tool action. Default values for element properties are not part of the UML semantics and do not appear in models.

See also initial value, parameter, unspecified value.

deferred event

An event whose recognition is deferred while an object is in a certain state.

See also state machine, transition.

Semantics

A state may designate a set of events as *deferred*. If an event occurs while an object is in a state that defers the event and the event does not trigger a transition, the event has no immediate effect. It is saved until the object enters a state in which the given event is not deferred. If other events occur while the state is active, they are handled in the usual way. When the object enters a new state, saved events that are no longer deferred then occur one at a time and may trigger transitions in the new state (the order of occurrence of previously deferred events is indeterminate, and it is risky to depend on a particular order of occurrence). If no transition in the undeferred state is triggered by an event, it is ignored and lost.

Deferred events should be used with care in ordinary state machines. They can often be modeled more directly by a concurrent state that responds to them while the main computation is doing something else. They can be useful in activity states in which they allow computations to be sequentialized without losing asynchronous messages.

If a state has a transition triggered by a deferred event, then the transition overrides the deferral and the event triggers the transition.

Notation

A deferred event is indicated by an internal transition on the event with the special reserved action **defer**. The deferral applies to the state and its nested substates (Figure 13-88).

delegation

The ability of an object to issue a message to another object in response to a message. Delegation can be used as an alternative to inheritance. In some languages (such as *self*), it is supported by inheritance mechanisms in the language itself. In most other languages, such as C++ and Smalltalk, it can be implemented with an

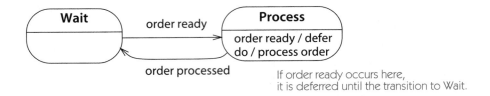

order processed   If order ready occurs here,
it is deferred until the transition to Wait.

Figure 13-88. *Deferred event*

association or aggregation to another object. An operation on the first object invokes an operation on the second object to accomplish its work. Contrast: inheritance.

See also association.

dependency

A relationship between two elements in which a change to one element (the supplier) may affect or supply information needed by the other element (the client). This is a term of convenience that groups together several different kinds of modeling relationships.

See relationship: Table 13-2 for a full chart of UML relationships.

Semantics

A dependency is a statement of relationship between two elements in a model or different models. The term, somewhat arbitrarily, groups together several different kinds of relationships, much as the biological term *invertebrate* groups together all phyla except *Vertebrata*.

In a case in which the relationship represents an asymmetry of knowledge, the independent elements are called supplier*s* and the dependent elements are called client*s*.

A dependency may have a name to indicate its role in the model. Usually, however, the presence of the dependency itself is sufficient to make the meaning clear, and a name is redundant. A dependency may have a stereotype to establish the precise nature of the dependency, and it may have a text description to describe itself in full detail, albeit informally.

A dependency between two packages indicates the presence of at least one dependency of the given kind between an element in each of the packages (except for access and import that relate packages directly). For example, a usage dependency between two classes may be shown as a usage dependency between the packages that contain them. A dependency among packages does not mean that all elements in the packages have the dependency—in fact, such a situation would be rare.

See package.

A dependency may contain a set of references to subordinate dependencies. For example, a dependency between two packages can reference the underlying dependencies among classes.

Dependencies are not necessarily transitive.

Note that association and generalization fit within the general definition of dependency, but they have their own model representation and notation and are not usually considered to be dependencies. A realization relationship has its own special notation, but it is considered a dependency.

Dependency comes in several varieties that represent different kinds of relationships: abstraction, binding, combination, permission, and usage.

Abstraction. An abstraction dependency represents a shift in the level of abstraction of a concept. Both elements represent the same concept in different ways. Usually one of the elements is more abstract, and the other is more concrete, although situations are possible when both elements are alternative representations at the same level of abstraction. From least specific to most specific relationships, abstraction includes the stereotypes trace, refinement (keyword **refine**), realization (which has its own special notation), and derivation (keyword **derive**).

Binding. A binding dependency relates an element bound from a template to the template itself. The arguments for the template parameters are attached to the binding dependency as a list.

Permission. A permission dependency (always shown as a specific stereotype) relates a package or class to a package or class to which it is granted some category of permission to use contents. The stereotypes of permission dependency are access, friend, and import.

Usage. A usage dependency (keyword «use») connects a client element to a supplier element, the change of which may require a change to the client element. Usage often represents an implementation dependency, in which one element makes use of the services of another element to implement its behavior. Stereotypes of usage include call, instantiation (keyword **instantiate**), parameter, and send. This is an open list. Other kinds of usage dependency may occur in various programming languages.

Notation

A dependency is shown as a dashed arrow between two model elements. The model element at the tail of the arrow (the client) depends on the model element at the arrowhead (the supplier). The arrow may be labeled with an optional keyword, to indicate the kind of dependency, and an optional name (Figure 13-89).

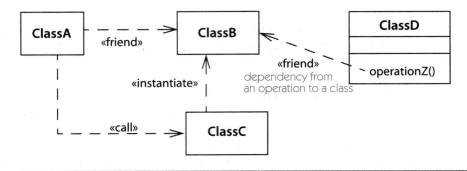

Figure 13-89. *Some dependencies among classes*

Several other kinds of relationships use a dashed arrow with a keyword, although they do not fit the definition of dependency. These include flow (become and copy), combination (extend and include), and the attachment of a note or constraint to the model element that it describes. If a note or constraint is one of the elements, the arrow may be suppressed because the note or constraint is always the source of the arrow.

Standard elements

become, bind, call, copy, create, derive, extend, friend, import, include, instanceOf, instantiate, powertype, send, trace, use

deployment

That stage of development that describes the configuration of the running system in a real-world environment. For deployment, decisions must be made about configuration parameters, performance, resource allocation, distribution, and concurrency. The results of this phase are captured in configuration files as well as the deployment view. Contrast analysis, design, implementation, and deployment.

See development process, stages of modeling.

deployment diagram

A diagram that shows the configuration of run-time processing nodes and the component instances and objects that live on them. Components represent run-time manifestations of code units. Components that do not exist as run-time entities (because they have been compiled away) do not appear on these diagrams; they should be shown on component diagrams. A deployment diagram shows instances whereas a component diagram shows the definition of component types themselves.

See also component, interface, node.

Semantics

The deployment view contains node instances connected by communication links. The node instances may contain run-time instances, such as component instances and objects. Component instances and objects can also contain other objects. The model may show dependencies among the instances and their interfaces, and may also model the migration of entities among nodes or other containers.

A deployment view has a descriptor form and an instance form. The instance form (described above) shows the location of specific component instances on specific node instances as part of a system configuration. This is the more common kind of deployment view. The descriptor form shows which kinds of components may live on which kinds of nodes and which kinds of nodes may be connected, similar to a class diagram.

Notation

A deployment diagram is a network of node symbols connected by paths showing communication associations (Figure 13-90). Node symbols may contain component instances, indicating that the component lives or runs on the node. Component symbols may contain objects, indicating that the object is part of the component. Components are connected to other components by dashed depen-

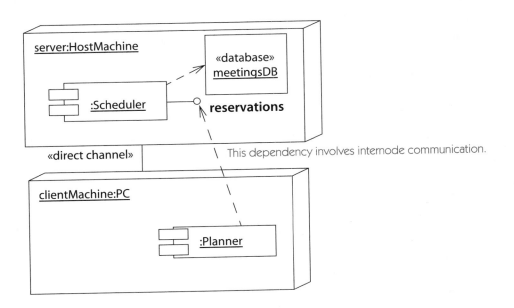

Figure 13-90. *Deployment diagram of client-server system*

dency arrows (possibly through interfaces). This indicates that one component uses the services of another component. A stereotype may be used to indicate the precise dependency, if needed.

Deployment diagrams are much like object diagrams. Usually, they show the individual node instances involved in a system. It is far less common to show a deployment diagram that defines the kinds of nodes that exist and their possible relationships to other kinds of nodes, like a class diagram.

Migration of components from node to node or objects from component to component may be shown using the «become» keyword on a dashed arrow. In this case, the component or object is resident on its node or component only part of the time. Figure 13-133 shows a deployment diagram in which an object moves between nodes.

See become.

deployment view

A view that shows the nodes in a distributed system, the components that are stored on each node, and the objects that are stored on components and nodes.

See deployment, deployment diagram.

derivation

A relationship between an element and another element that can be computed from it. Derivation is modeled as a stereotype of an abstraction dependency with the keyword **derive**.

See derived element.

derived element

A element that can be computed from other elements and is included for clarity or for design purposes even though it adds no semantic information.

See also constraint, dependency.

Semantics

A derived element is logically redundant within a model because it can be computed from one or more other elements. The formula for computing a derived element may be given as a constraint.

A derived element may be included in a model for several reasons. At the analysis level, a derived element is semantically unnecessary, but it may be used to provide a name or a definition for a meaningful concept, as a kind of macro. It is important to remember that a derived element adds nothing to the semantics of a model.

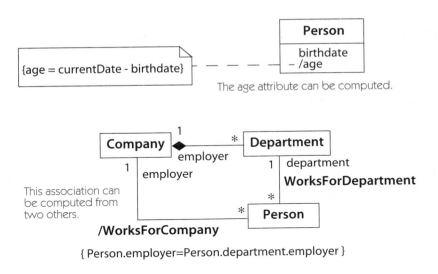

Figure 13-91. *Derived attribute and derived association*

In a design-level model, a derived element represents an optimization—an element that could be computed from other elements but is physically present in the model to avoid the cost or trouble of recomputing it. Examples are an intermediate value of a computation and an index to a set of values. The presence of a derived element implies the responsibility to update it if the values it depends on change.

Notation

A derived element is shown by placing a slash (/) in front of the name of the derived element, such as an attribute, a rolename, or an association name (Figure 13-91).

The details of computing a derived element can be specified by a dependency with the stereotype «derive». Usually, it is convenient in the notation to suppress the dependency arrow from the constraint to the element and simply place a constraint string near the derived element, although the arrow can be included when it is helpful.

Discussion

Derived associations are probably the most common kind of derived element. They represent virtual associations that can be computed from two or more fundamental associations. In Figure 13-91, for instance, derived association WorksForCompany can be computed by composing WorksForDepartment with the

employer composition. An implementation might explicitly include **Works-ForCompany** to avoid recomputing it, but it does not represent any additional information.

There is a difference with association generalization (Figure 13-30), which represents two levels of detail for an association. It would not usually be implemented at both levels. Usually only the child associations would be implemented. Sometimes only the parent association would be implemented, with the child associations constraining the kinds of objects that can be related.

descendant

A child or an element found by a chain of child relationships; the transitive closure of the specialization relationship. Antonym: ancestor.
See generalization.

descriptor

A model element that describes the common properties of a set of instances, including their structure, relationships, behavior, constraints, purpose, and so on. Contrast: instance.

Semantics

The word *descriptor* characterizes model elements that describe sets of instances. Most elements in a model are descriptors. The word includes all the elements of a model—classes, associations, states, use cases, collaborations, and so on. Sometimes, the word *type* is used in this meaning, but that word is often used in a more narrow sense to mean only class-like things. The word *descriptor* is meant to include every kind of descriptive element. A descriptor has an intent and an extent. The structure description and other general rules are the intent. Each descriptor characterizes a set of instances, which are its extent. There is no assumption that the extent is physically accessible at run time. The major dichotomy in a model is the descriptor-instance distinction.

Notation

The relationship between a descriptor and its instances is reflected by using the same geometric symbol for both, but underlining the name string of an instance. A descriptor has a name, whereas an instance has both an individual name and a descriptor name, separated by a colon, and the name string is underlined.

design

That stage of a system that describes how the system will be implemented, at a logical level above actual code. For design, strategic and tactical decisions are made to meet the required functional and quality requirements of a system. The results of this stage are represented by design-level models, especially the static view, state machine view, and interaction view. Contrast: analysis, design, implementation, and deployment.

See stages of modeling, development process.

design time

Refers to what occurs during a design activity of the software development process. Contrast: analysis time.

See modeling time, stages of modeling.

destroy

To eliminate an object and reclaim its resources. Usually this is an explicit action, although it may be the consequence of another action or constraint or of garbage collection.

See destruction.

destruction

The elimination of an object and the reclaiming of its resources. The destruction of a composite object leads to the destruction of its composite parts. Destruction of an object does not automatically destroy objects related by ordinary association or even by aggregation, but any links involving the object are destroyed with the object.

See also composition, final state, instantiation.

Notation

See collaboration and sequence diagram (Figure 13-162) for notation to show destruction within the implementation of a procedure. On a sequence diagram, the destruction of an object is shown by a large X on the lifeline of the object (Figure 13-92). It is placed at the message that causes the object to be destroyed or at the point where the object terminates itself. A message that destroys an object may be shown with the stereotype «destroy». On a collaboration diagram, the destruction of an object during an interaction is shown by the constraint {destroyed} on the object. If the object is created and destroyed in the interaction, the constraint {transient} is used instead.

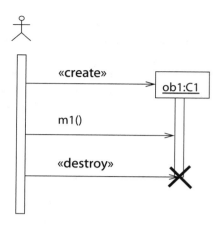

Figure 13-92. *Creation and destruction*

development process

A set of guidelines and a partially ordered set of work activities intended to produce software in a controlled, reproducible manner. The purpose of a software
development process is to ensure the success and quality of a finished system.

   See also stages of modeling.

Discussion

UML is a modeling language, not a process, and its purpose is to describe models
that may be produced by various development processes. For standardization, it is
more important to describe the resultant artifacts of a development than the process of producing them. That's because there are many good ways of building a
model, and a finished model can be used without knowing how it was produced.
Nevertheless, UML is intended to support a wide range of processes.

   For more details of the iterative, incremental, use-case-driven, architectural-
centric development process that the authors of this book endorse, see [Jacobson-
99].

Relationship of modeling stages and development phases

The stages of modeling fit within an iterative development process, which has the
phases inception, elaboration, construction, and transition (phase). The phases
are sequential within one release of an application, but each phase includes one or
more iterations. Within an iteration, individual model elements are moved along
the path from analysis toward deployment, each at its own appropriate pace. Although the development phases and the modeling stages are not synchronized,

there is a correlation. In the earlier development phases and the earlier iterations of a phase, there is more emphasis on the earlier model stages.

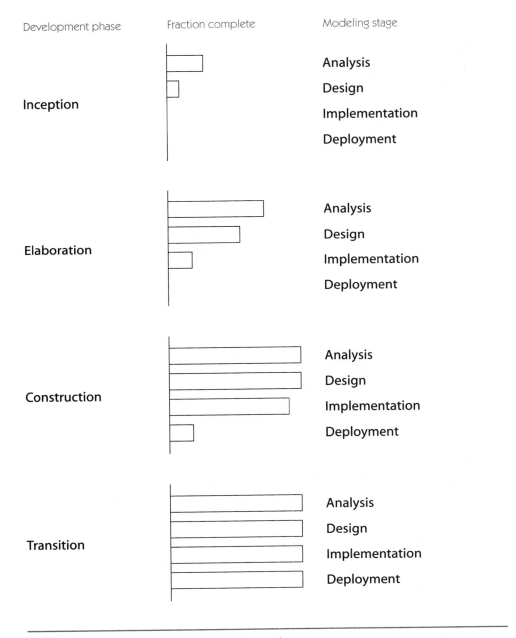

Figure 13-93. *Progress after each development phase*

Figure 13-93 shows the balance of effort during successive phases and iterations. During inception, the focus is mainly on analysis, with a skeleton of elements progressing toward design and implementation during elaboration. During construction and transition, all the elements must eventually be moved to completion.

diagram

A graphical presentation of a collection of model elements, most often rendered as a connected graph of arcs (relationships) and vertices (other model elements). UML supports class diagram, object diagram, use case diagram, sequence diagram, collaboration diagram, statechart diagram, activity diagram, component diagram, and deployment diagram.

See also background information, font usage, hyperlink, keyword, label, package, path, presentation element, property list.

Semantics

A diagram is not a semantic element. A diagram shows presentations of semantic model elements, but their meaning is unaffected by the way they are presented.

A diagram is contained within a package.

Notation

Most UML diagrams and some complex symbols are graphs that contain shapes connected by paths. The information is mostly in the topology, not in the size or placement of the symbols (there are some exceptions, such as a sequence diagram with a metric time axis). There are three important kinds of visual relationships: connection (usually of lines to 2-dimensional shapes), containment (of symbols by 2-dimensional closed shapes), and visual attachment (one symbol being "near" another one on a diagram). These geometric relationships map into connections of nodes in a graph in the parsed form of the notation.

UML notation is intended to be drawn on 2-D surfaces. Some shapes are 2-D projections of 3-D shapes, such as cubes, but they are still rendered as icons on a 2-D surface. In the near future, true 3-D layout and navigation may be possible on desktop machines but it is not currently common.

There are four kinds of graphical constructs used in UML notation: icons, 2-D symbols, paths, and strings.

An icon is a graphical figure of a fixed size and shape. It does not expand to hold contents. Icons may appear within area symbols, as terminators on paths, or as stand-alone symbols that may or may not be connected to paths. For example, the symbols for aggregation (a diamond), navigability (an arrowhead), final state (a bull's eye), and object destruction (a large *X*) are icons.

Two-dimensional symbols have variable height and width, and they can expand to hold other things, such as lists of strings or other symbols. Many of them are divided into compartments of similar or different kinds. Paths are connected to 2-D symbols by terminating the path on the boundary of the symbol. Dragging or deleting a 2-D symbol affects its contents and any paths connected to it. For example, the symbols for class (a rectangle), state (a rounded rectangle), and note (a dog-eared rectangle) are 2-D symbols.

A path is a sequence of line or curve segments whose endpoints are attached. Conceptually, a path is a single topological entity, although its segments may be manipulated graphically. A segment may not exist apart from its path. Paths are always attached to other graphic symbols at both ends (no dangling lines). Paths may have terminators—that is, icons that appear in a sequence on the end of the path and that qualify the meaning of the path symbol. For example, the symbols for association (solid lines), generalization (solid lines with a triangle icon), and dependency (dashed lines) are paths.

Strings present various kinds of information in an "unparsed" form. UML assumes that each usage of a string in the notation has a syntax by which it can be parsed into underlying model information. For example, syntaxes are given for attributes, operations, and transitions. These syntaxes are subject to extension by tools as a presentation option. Strings may exist as the content of a compartment, as elements in lists (in which case the position in the list conveys information), as labels attached to symbols or paths, or as stand-alone elements on a diagram. For example, class names, transition labels, multiplicity indications, and constraints are strings.

direct class

The class that most completely describes an object.

See also class, generalization, inheritance, multiple classification, multiple inheritance.

Semantics

An object may be an instance of many classes—if it is an instance of a class, then it is also an instance of the ancestors of the class. The direct class is the most specific description of an object, the one that most completely describes it. An object is a direct instance of its direct class and an indirect instance of the ancestors of the direct class. An object is not an instance of any descendants of the direct class (by definition).

If multiple classification is allowed in a system, no single direct class may completely describe an object. The object may be the combined direct instance of more than one class. An object is a direct instance of each class that contains part of its description, provided no descendant also describes the object. In other words, none of the direct classes of an object have an ancestor relationship to each other.

If a class is instantiated to produce an object, the object is a direct instance of the class.

direct instance

An instance, such as an object, whose most specific descriptor, such as a class, is a given class. Used in a phrase like, "Object O is a direct instance of class C." In this case, class C is the direct class of object O.

See direct class.

discriminator

A pseudoattribute that selects a child element from a set of children in a generalization relationship. All of the children represent a given quality by which to specialize the parent, in contrast to other potential qualities by which to specialize the same parent; it represents a dimension of specialization.

See also generalization, powertype, pseudoattribute.

Semantics

Sometimes, a model element can be specialized on the basis of different qualities. Each quality represents an independent orthogonal dimension of specialization. For example, a vehicle can be specialized on propulsion (gasoline motor, rocket engine, wind, animal, human), as well as on venue of travel (land, water, air, outer space). A discriminator is the name of a dimension of specialization. An element may be specialized on multiple dimensions, all of which must be present in a concrete instance.

A generalization relationship may have a discriminator, a string that represents a dimension of classifying the children of the parent. All the specialization relationships from a single parent with the same discriminator name form a group; each group is a separate dimension of specialization. The complete set of discriminator names represents the entire set of dimensions of specializing the parent. An instance must be simultaneously an instance of one child from each discriminator group. For example, a vehicle must have a propulsion and a venue.

Each discriminator represents an abstract quality of the parent, a quality that is specialized by the children bearing that discriminator relationship to the parent. But a parent with multiple discriminators has multiple dimensions, all of which must be specialized to produce a concrete element. Therefore, children within a discriminator group are inherently abstract. Each of them is only a partial description of the parent, a description that emphasizes one quality and ignores the rest.

For example, a subclass of vehicle that focuses on propulsion omits venue. A concrete element requires specializing all the dimensions simultaneously. This can occur by multiple inheritance of the concrete model element from a child in each of the dimensions, or by multiple classification of an instance from a child in each of the dimensions. Until all the discriminators are combined, the description remains abstract.

For example, an actual vehicle must have a means of propulsion and a venue. A wind-powered water vehicle is a sailboat. There is no particular name for an animal-powered air vehicle, but instances of the combination exist in fantasy and mythology.

The absence of a discriminator label indicates the "empty" discriminator, which is also considered a valid discriminator (the "default" discriminator). This convention permits the usual nondiscriminator case to be treated uniformly. In effect, if none of the generalization paths have discriminators, then all the children are in the same discriminator. In other words, there is one discriminator to which all the specializations belong, and it yields the same semantics as the discriminator-free case.

Structure

Each specialization (generalization) arc has a discriminator string, which may be the empty string.

The discriminator is a pseudoattribute of the parent. It must be unique among the attributes and association roles of the parent. The domain for the pseudoattribute is the set of child classes. Multiple occurrences of the same discriminator name are permitted among different children and the parent and indicate that the children belong to the same partition.

Notation

A discriminator is shown as a text label on a generalization arrow (Figure 13-94). If two generalization arcs with the same discriminator share an arrowhead, the discriminator may be placed on the arrowhead.

Example

Figure 13-94 shows a specialization of **Employee** on two dimensions: employee **status** and **locality**. Each dimension has a range of values represented by subclasses. But both dimensions are required to produce an instantiable subclass. **Liaison**, for example, is a class that is both a **Supervisor** and an **Expatriate**.

Any descendant of a single dimension is abstract, until the two dimensions are recombined in a multiply-inherited descendant.

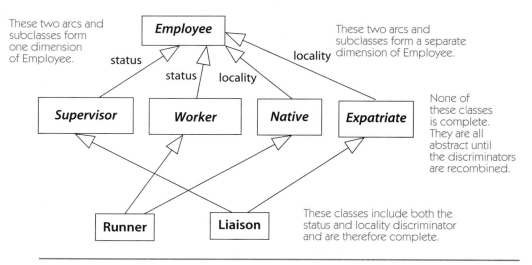

These two arcs and subclasses form one dimension of Employee.

These two arcs and subclasses form a separate dimension of Employee.

None of these classes is complete. They are all abstract until the discriminators are recombined.

These classes include both the status and locality discriminator and are therefore complete.

Figure 13-94. *Discriminators*

disjoint substate

A substate that cannot be held simultaneously with other substates contained in the same composite state. Contrast: concurrent substate.

See complex transition, composite state.

distribution unit

A set of objects or components that are allocated to an operating-system process or a processor as a group. A distribution unit can be represented by a run-time composite or by an aggregate. This is a design concept in the deployment view.

dynamic classification

A semantic variation of generalization in which an object may change type or role. Contrast: static classification.

See also multiple classification.

Semantics

In many programming languages, an object may not change the class from which it is instantiated. This static classification restriction simplifies implementation and optimization of compilers, but it is not a logical necessity. For example, under the static classification assumption, an object instantiated as a circle must remain a circle; it may not be scaled in the *x*-dimension, for example. Under the dynamic classification assumption, a circle that is scaled in one dimension becomes an ellipse. This is not regarded as a problem.

Either assumption may be used in a UML model. This is an example of a semantic variation point. The choice affects surprisingly little of a model, although the differences are important for execution. The same classes must be defined in either case, but the operations they support may differ in the two cases.

dynamic concurrency

An activity state that represents multiple concurrent executions when it is active.
See activity graph.

dynamic view

That aspect of a model dealing with the specification and implementation of behavior over time, as distinguished from static structure found in the static view. The dynamic view is a grouping term that includes the use case view, state machine view, activity view, and interaction view.

elaboration

The second phase of a software development process, during which the design for the system is begun and the architecture is developed and tested. During this phase, most of the analysis view is completed, together with the architectural parts of the design view. If an executable prototype is constructed, some of the implementation view is done.
See development process.

element

An atomic constituent of a model. This book describes elements that may be used in UML models—model elements, which express semantic information, and presentation elements, which provide graphic presentations of model-element information.
See also diagram, model element.

Semantics

The term *element* is so broad that it has little specific semantics.
All elements may have the following property.

tagged value	Zero or more tag-value pairs may be attached to any element. The tag is a name that identifies the meaning of the value. Tags are not fixed in UML but can be extended to denote various kinds of information meaningful to the modeler or to an editing tool.

Standard elements

documentation

entry action

An action performed when a state is entered.

See also exit action, run to completion, state machine, transition.

Semantics

A state may have an optional entry action attached to it. Whenever the state is entered in any way, the entry action is executed after any actions attached to outer states or transitions and before any actions attached to inner states. The entry action may not be evaded by any means. It is guaranteed to have been executed whenever the owning state or a state nested within it is active.

Execution order. On a transition between two states with exit and entry actions in which the transition also has an action, the execution order is: Any exit actions are executed on the source state and its enclosing states out to, but not including, the state that encloses both the source and target states. Then the action on the transition is executed, after which the entry actions are executed (outermost first) on the enclosing states inside the common state, down to and including the target state. Figure 13-117 shows some transitions with multiple actions.

Notation

An entry action is coded using the syntax for an internal transition with the dummy event name **entry** (which is therefore a reserved word and may not be used as an actual event name).

    entry / action-sequence

Only one entry action may be attached to a state, but the action may be a sequence so no generality is lost.

Discussion

Entry and exit actions are not semantically essential (the entry action could be attached to all incoming transitions) but they facilitate the encapsulation of a state so that the external use of it can be separated from its internal construction. They make it possible to define initialization and termination actions, without concern that they might be avoided. They are particularly useful with exceptions, because they define actions that must be performed even if an exception occurs.

An entry action is useful for performing an initialization that must be done when a state is first entered. One use is to initialize variables that capture information accumulated during a state. For example, a user interface to allow keypad input of a telephone number or an account number would clear the number on entry. Resetting an error counter, such as the number of password failures, is another example. Allocating temporary storage needed during the state is another use for an entry action.

Often, an entry action and an exit action are used together. The entry action allocates resources, and the exit action releases them. Even if an external transition occurs, the resources are released. This is a good way to handle user errors and exceptions. User-level errors trigger high-level transitions that abort nested states, but the nested states have an opportunity to clean up before they lose control.

enumeration

A data type whose instances form a list of named literal values. Usually, both the enumeration name and its literal values are declared.

See also classifier, data type.

Semantics

An enumeration is a user-definable data type. It has a name and an ordered list of enumeration literal names, each of which is a value in the range of the data type—that is, it is a predefined instance of the data type. For example, RGBColor = {red, green, blue}. The data type Boolean is a predefined enumeration with the literals false and true.

Notation

An enumeration is shown as a rectangle with the keyword «enum» above the enumeration name in the upper compartment (Figure 13-95). The second compartment contains a list of enumeration-literal names. The third compartment (if present) contains a set of operations on the type. They must all be queries (which, therefore, do not need to be explicitly declared as such).

event

The specification of a noteworthy occurrence that has a location in time and space.

See also state machine, transition, trigger.

Semantics

Within a state machine, an occurrence of an event can trigger a state transition. An event has a (possibly empty) list of parameters that convey information from the creator of the event to its receiver. The time at which the event occurred is

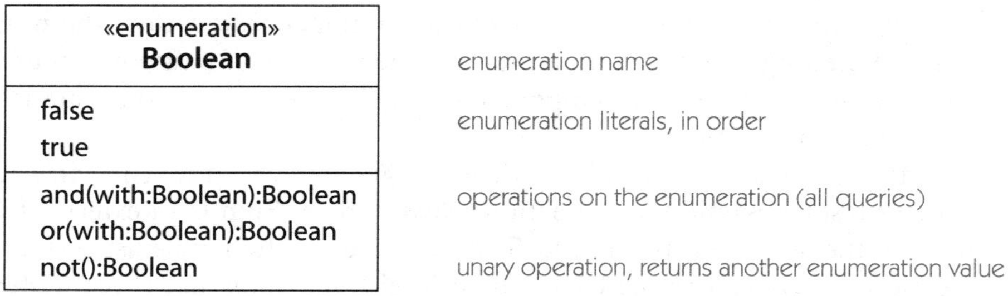

«enumeration» **Boolean**	enumeration name
false true	enumeration literals, in order
and(with:Boolean):Boolean or(with:Boolean):Boolean not():Boolean	operations on the enumeration (all queries) unary operation, returns another enumeration value

Figure 13-95. *Enumeration declaration*

implicitly a parameter of every event. Other parameters are part of the definition of an event.

An occurrence (instance) of an event has an argument (actual value) corresponding to each event parameter. The value of each argument is available to an action attached to a transition triggered by the event.

There are four kinds of events.

call event	The receipt of a request to invoke an operation. The expected result is the execution of the operation by triggering a transition in the receiver. The parameters of the event are a reference to the operation and the parameters of the operation and, implicitly, a return pointer. The caller regains control when the transition is complete (or immediately if no transition fires).
change event	The satisfaction of a Boolean condition specified by an expression in the event. There are no parameters. This kind of event implies a continuous test for the condition. The event occurs when the condition changes from false to true. In practice, however, the times at which the condition can be satisfied can often be restricted to the occurrence of other events, so that polling is usually not required.
signal event	The receipt of a signal, which is an explicit named entity intended for explicit communication between objects. A signal has an explicit list of parameters. It is explicitly sent by an object to another object or set of objects. A general broadcast of an event can be regarded as the sending of a signal to the set of all objects, although in practice, it

might be implemented differently for efficiency. The sender explicitly specifies the arguments of the signal at the time it is sent. A signal sent to a set of objects may trigger zero or one transition in each of them.

Signals are explicit means by which objects may communicate with each other asynchronously. To perform synchronous communication, two asynchronous signals must be used, one in each direction of communication.

Signals are generalizable. A child signal is derived from a parent signal; it inherits the parameters of the parent and may add additional parameters of its own. A child signal satisfies a trigger that requires one of its ancestors.

time event   The satisfaction of a time expression, such as the occurrence of an absolute time or the passage of a given amount of time after an object enters a state. Note that both absolute time and elapsed time may be defined with respect to a real-world clock or a virtual internal clock (in which case, it may differ for different objects).

Notation

See the specific kind of event for details on notation.

Standard elements

create, destroy

exception

A signal raised in response to behavioral faults by the underlying execution machinery.

See also composite state, signal.

Semantics

An exception is usually generated implicitly by underlying implementation mechanisms in response to a failure during execution. It may be regarded as a signal to the active object or procedure activation that caused the execution. The state machine of the object can take an appropriate action to deal with the exception, including aborting current processing and going to a known place in execution, executing an operation without a change of state, or ignoring the event. The ability to attach transitions to high-level states makes exception handling flexible and powerful.

An exception is a signal and therefore has a list of parameters that are bound to values when the exception occurs. The parameter values are set by the execution machinery that detects the fault, such as the operating system. The operation that handles the exception can read the parameters. In most languages, exceptions can be manipulated and retransmitted by operations that handle them.

Notation

The stereotype «exception» may be used to distinguish the declaration of an exception. No stereotype is necessary to use the event name in a state machine.

exit action

An action performed when a state is exited.

See also entry action, run to completion, state machine, transition.

Semantics

A state may have an optional exit action attached to it. Whenever the state is exited in any way, the exit action is executed after any actions attached to inner states or transitions and before any actions attached to outer states. The exit action may not be evaded by any means. It is guaranteed to be executed before control leaves the owning state.

Entry and exit actions are not semantically essential (the exit action could be attached to all outgoing transitions), but they facilitate the encapsulation of a state so that the external use of it can be separated from its internal construction. They make it possible to define initialization and termination actions, without concern that they might be avoided. They are particularly useful with exceptions, because they define actions that must be performed even if an exception occurs.

Notation

An exit action is coded using the syntax for an internal transition with the dummy event name **exit** (which is, therefore, a reserved word and may not be used as an actual event name).

exit / action-sequence

Only one exit action may be attached to a state. But the action may be an action sequence, so no generality is lost.

Discussion

An exit action is useful for performing a cleanup that must be done when a state is exited. The most significant use of exit actions is to release temporary storage and other resources allocated during execution of the state (usually, a state with nested detail).

Often, an entry action and an exit action are used together. The entry action allocates resources, and the exit action releases them. Even if an exception occurs, the resources are released.

export

In the context of packages, to make an element accessible outside its enclosing namespace by adjusting its visibility. Contrast with access and import, which make outside elements accessible within a package.

See also access, import, visibility.

Semantics

A package exports an element by setting its visibility to a level that permits it to be seen by other packages (public for packages importing it, protected for its own children).

Discussion

Two things are necessary for an element (such as a class) to be able to see an element in a peer package. The package containing the target element must export it by giving it public visibility. In addition, the package referencing the target element must access or import the package containing the target element. Both steps are necessary.

expression

A string that encodes a statement to be interpreted by a given language. Many kinds of expression yield values when interpreted; other kinds perform specific actions. For example, the expression "(7 + 5 * 3)" evaluates to a value of type number.

Semantics

An expression defines a statement that evaluates to a (possibly empty) set of instances or values or the performance of a specific action when executed in a context. An expression does not modify the environment in which it is evaluated. An expression consists of a string and the name of the language of evaluation.

An expression element contains the name of the language of interpretation and the string that encodes the expression in the syntax of the designated language. It is assumed that an interpreter is available for the language. Supplying an interpreter is the responsibility of the modeling tool. The language may be a constraint-specification language, such as OCL; it may be a programming language, such as C++ or Smalltalk; or it may be a human language. Of course, if an expression is written in a human language, then it cannot be evaluated automatically by a tool and it must be purely for human consumption.

Various subclasses of expressions yield different types of values. These include Boolean expressions, object set expressions, time expressions, and procedure expressions.

Expressions appear in UML models as actions, constraints, guard conditions, and others.

Notation

An expression is displayed as a string defined in a language. The syntax of the string is the responsibility of a tool and a linguistic analyzer for the language. The assumption is that the analyzer can evaluate strings at run time to yield values of the appropriate type, or can yield semantic structures to capture the meaning of the expression. For example, a type expression evaluates to a classifier reference, and a Boolean expression evaluates to a true or false value. The language itself is known to a modeling tool but is generally implicit on the diagram under the assumption that the form of the expression makes its purpose clear.

Example

self.cost < authorization.maxCost

forall (k in targets) { k.update ( ) }

extend

A relationship from an *extension* use case to a *base* use case, specifying how the behavior defined for the extension use case can be inserted into the behavior defined for the base use case. The extension use case incrementally modifies the base use case in a modular way.

See also extension point, include, use case, use case generalization.

Semantics

The extend relationship connects an extension use case to a base use case. The extension use case in this relationship is not necessarily a separate instantiable classifier. Instead, it consists of one or more segments that describe additional behavior sequences that incrementally modify the behavior of the base use case. Each segment in an extension use case may be inserted at a separate location in the base use case. The extend relationship has a list of extension point names, equal in number to the number of segments in the extension use case. Each extension point must be defined in the base use case. When the execution of a use case instance reaches a location in the base use case referenced by the extension point and any condition on the extension is satisfied, then execution of the instance may transfer to the behavior sequence of the corresponding segment of the extension use case; when the execution of the extension segment is complete, control returns to the original use case at the referenced point.

Multiple extend relationships may be applied to the same base use case. An instance of a use case may execute more than one extension during its lifetime. If several use cases extend one base use case at the same extension point, then their relative order of execution is nondeterministic. There may even be multiple extend relationships between the same extension and base use cases, provided the extension is inserted at a different location in the base. Extensions may even extend other extensions in a nested manner.

An extension use case in an extend relationship may access and modify attributes defined by the base use case. The base use case, however, cannot see the extensions and may not access their attributes or operations. The base use case defines a modular framework into which extensions can be added, but the base does not have visibility of the extensions. The extensions implicitly modify the behavior of the base use case. Note the difference with use case generalization. With extension, the effects of the extension use case are added to the effects of the base use case in an instantiation of the base use case. With generalization, the effects of the child use case are added to the effects of the parent use case in an instantiation of the child use case, whereas an instantiation of the parent use case does not get the effects of the child use case.

An extension use case may extend more than one base use case, and a base use case may be extended by more than one extension use case. This does not indicate any relationship among the base use cases.

An extension use case may itself be the base in an extend, include, or generalization relationship.

Structure (of extension use case)

An extension use case contains a list of one or more *insertion segments*, each of which is a behavior sequence.

Structure (of base use case)

A base use case defines a set of extension points, each of which references a location or set of locations in the base use case where additional behavior may be inserted.

Structure (of extend relationship)

The extend relationship has a list of extension point names, which must be present in the base use case. The number of names must equal the number of segments in the extension use case.

The extend relationship may have a condition, an expression in terms of attributes of the base use case, or the occurrence of events such as the receipt of a signal. The condition determines whether the extension use case is performed when the execution of a use case instance reaches a location referenced by the first extension point. If the condition is absent, then it is deemed to be always true. If the condition for an extension use case is satisfied, then execution of the extension use case proceeds. If the extension point references several locations in the base use case, the extension use case may be executed at any one of them.

The extension may be performed more than once, if the condition remains true. All segments of the extension use case are executed the same number of times. If the number of executions must be restricted, the condition can be defined accordingly.

Execution semantics

When a use case instance performing the base use case reaches a location in the base use case that is referenced by an extend relationship, then the condition on the extend relationship is evaluated. If it is true or if it is absent, then the extension use case is performed. In many cases, the condition includes the occurrence of an event or the availability of values needed by the extension use case segment itself—for example, a signal from an actor that begins the extension segment. The condition may depend on the state of the use case instance, including attribute values of the base use case. If the event does not occur or the condition is false, the execution of the extension use case does not start. When the performance of an extension segment is complete, the use case instance resumes performing the base use case at the location at which it left off.

Additional insertions of the extension use case may be performed immediately if the condition is satisfied. If the extension point references multiple locations in the base use case, the condition may be satisfied at any of them. The condition may become true at any location within the set.

If there is more than one insertion sequence in an extension use case, then all the insertion segments are executed if the condition is true at the first extension point. The condition is not reevaluated for subsequent segments., which are inserted when the use case instance reaches the corresponding locations within the base use case. The use case instance resumes execution of the base between insertions at different extension points. Once started, all the segments must be performed.

Note that, in general, a use case is a nondeterministic state machine (as in a grammar), rather than an executable procedure. That is because the conditions may include the occurrence of external events. To realize a use case as a collaboration of classes may require a transformation into explicit control mechanisms, just as the implementation of a grammar requires a transformation to an executable form that is efficient but harder to understand.

Note that *base* and *extension* are relative terms. An extension can itself serve as a base for a further extension. This does not present any difficulty, and the previous rules still apply—the insertions are nested. For example, suppose use case B extends use case A at extension point x, and suppose use case C extends use case B at extension point y (Figure 13-96). When an instance of A comes to extension point x, it begins performing use case B. When the instance then comes to extension point y within B, it begins performing use case C. When the execution of C is complete, it resumes performing use case B. When the execution of B is complete, it resumes performing A. It is similar to nested procedure calls or any other nested construct

Notation

A dashed arrow is drawn from the extension use case symbol to the base use case symbol with a stick arrowhead on the base.. The keyword «**extend**» is placed on

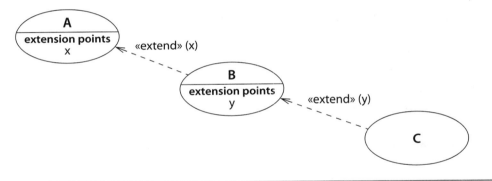

Figure 13-96. *Nested extends*

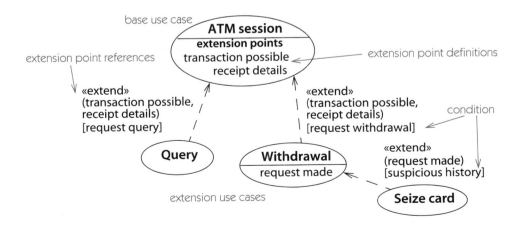

Figure 13-97. *Extend relationship*

the arrow. A list of extension point names may appear in parentheses after the keyword.

Figure 13-97 shows use cases with extend relationships, and Figure 13-98 shows the behavior sequences of the use cases.

Discussion

The extend, include, and generalization relationships all add behavior to an initial use case. They have many similarities, but it is convenient to separate them in practice. Table 13-1 compares the three viewpoints.

Base use case for ATM session:

    show advertisement of the day
    include (identify customer)   inclusion
    include (validate account)   inclusion
     (extension point references here)<--------- <transaction possible>
    print receipt header
     (another extension point target) <--------- <receipt details>
    log out

Extension use case for query:

    segment   first segment
      receive request query
      display query information

    segment   second segment
      print withdrawal information

Extension use case for withdrawal:

    segment   first segment
      receive request withdrawal
      specify amount
     (another extension point target) <--------- <request made>
    segment   second segment
      disburse cash

Extension use case for seize card:

    segment   only segment
      swallow the card
      end the session

Figure 13-98. *Behavior sequences for use cases*

Table 13-1: *Comparison of Use Case Relationships*

Property	Extend	Include	Generalization
Base behavior	Base use case	Base use case	Parent use case
Added behavior	Extension use case	Inclusion use case	Child use case
Direction of reference	Extension use case references the base use case.	Base use case references the inclusion use case.	Child use case references the parent use case.
Base modified by the addition?	The extension implicitly modifies the behavior of the base. The base must be well formed without the extension, but if the extension is present, an instantiation of the base may execute the extension.	The inclusion explicitly modifies the effect of the base. The base may or may not be well formed without the inclusion, but an instantiation of the base executes the inclusion.	The effect of executing the parent is unaffected by the child. To obtain the effects of the addition, the child, not the parent, must be instantiated.
Is the addition instantiable?	Extension is not necessarily instantiable. It may be a fragment.	Inclusion is not necessarily instantiable. It may be a fragment.	Child is not necessarily instantiable. It may be abstract.
Can the addition access attributes of the base?	The extension may access and modify the state of the base.	The inclusion may access the state of the base. The base must provide appropriate attributes expected by the inclusion.	The child may access and modify the state of the base (by the usual mechanisms of inheritance).
Can the base see the addition?	The base cannot see the extension and must be well formed in its absence.	The base sees the inclusion and may depend on its effects but may not access its attributes.	The parent cannot see the child and must be well formed in its absence.
Repetition	Depends on condition	Exactly one repetition	Child controls its own execution

extension point

A named marker that references a location or set of locations within the behavioral sequence for a use case, at which additional behavior can be inserted. An extension point declaration opens up the use case to the possibility of extension. An insertion segment is a behavior sequence in an extension use case (a use case related to a base use case by an extend relationship). The extend relationship contains a list of extension point names that indicate where the insertion segments from the extension use case insert their behavior.

See also extend, use case.

Semantics

An extension point has a name and references a set of one or more locations within a use case behavior sequence. An extension point may reference a single location between two behavior steps within a use case. In addition, it may reference a set of discrete locations. It may also reference a region within a behavior sequence (this is nothing more than the set of all locations between steps in the sequence).

A location is a state within a state machine description of a use case, or the equivalent in a different description—between two statements in a list of statements or between two messages in an interaction.

An extend relationship contains an optional condition and a list of extension point references equal in number to the number of insertion segments in the extension use case. An insertion segment may be performed if the condition is satisfied while a use case instance is executing the base use case at any location in the extension point corresponding to the insertion segment.

The location of an extension point can be changed without affecting its identity. The use of named extension points separates the specification of extension behavior sequences from the internal details of the base use case. The base use case can be modified or rearranged without affecting the extensions. Moreover, an extension point can be moved within the base without affecting the relationship or the extension use case. As with all kinds of modularity, this independence requires a good choice of extension points and is not guaranteed under all circumstances.

Notation

The extension points for a use case may be listed in a compartment named **extension points**.

The extension points must also reference locations within the behavior sequence of the use case. The net result is that extension point names serve as labels for states, statements, and regions within the behavior sequence. This does not

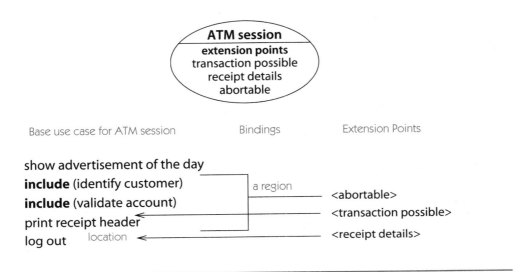

Figure 13-99. *Extension point declarations*

mean that they should be present in the original behavior sequence text. Extension points are names that permit separating the location from the choice to perform an insertion. An editing tool can place an extension point on an overlay of the behavior sequence text without modifying the original text, or it can have a separate table of extension point names mapped into statements (by statement number, internal labels, or direct graphics). In any case, the net effect corresponds to locating each extension point name between one or more steps in the behavior sequences. In the pseudocode example in Figure 13-99 an extension point name in single angle brackets references a location in the behavior sequence. There are many possible syntaxes for locating extension points within behavior sequences, depending on the language used to specify the sequence. This is an example, but not the only way.

extent

The set of instances described by a descriptor. Also sometimes called *extension*. Contrast: intent.

Semantics

A descriptor, such as a class or an association, has both a description (its intent) and a set of instances that it describes (its extent). The purpose of the intent is to specify the properties of the instances that compose the extent. There is no assumption that the extent is physically manifest or that it can be obtained at run time. For example, a modeler should not assume that the set of objects that are instances of a class can be obtained even in principle.

feature

A property, such as operation or attribute, which is encapsulated as part of a list within a classifier, such as an interface, a class, or a datatype.

final state

A special state within a composite state that, when active, indicates that the execution of the composite state has been completed. When a composite state reaches its final state, a completion transition leaving the composite state is triggered and may fire if its guard condition is satisfied.

See also activity, completion transition, destruction.

Semantics

To promote encapsulation, it is desirable to separate the outside view of a composite state from the inside details as much as possible. From the outside, the state is viewed as an opaque entity with an internal structure that is hidden. From the outside viewpoint, transitions go to and from the state itself. From the inside viewpoint, they connect to substates within the state. An initial state or a final state is a mechanism to support encapsulation of states.

A final state is a special state that indicates that the activity of the composite state is complete and that a completion transition leaving the composite state is enabled. A final state is not a pseudostate. A final state may be active for a period of time, unlike an initial state that immediately transitions to its successor. Control may remain within a final state while waiting for the completion of other concurrent substates of the composite state—that is, while waiting for sychronization of multiple threads of control to join together. Outgoing event-triggered transitions are not allowed from a final state, however (otherwise, it is just a normal state). A final state may have any number of incoming transitions from within the enclosing composite state, but no transitions from outside the enclosing state. The incoming transitions are normal transitions and may have the full complement of triggers, guard conditions, and actions.

If an object reaches its top-level final state, the state machine terminates and the object is destroyed.

Notation

A final state is displayed as a bull's-eye icon—that is, a small filled black disk surrounded by a small circle. The symbol is placed inside the enclosing composite

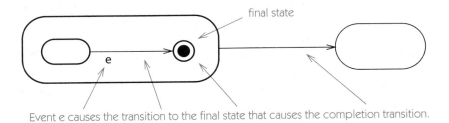

Event *e* causes the transition to the final state that causes the completion transition.

Figure 13-100. *Final state*

state whose completion it represents (Figure 13-100). Only one final state may oc-cur (directly) within a composite state. Additional final states may occur, however, within nested composite states. For convenience, the final state symbol may be re-peated within a state, but each copy represents the same final state.

fire

To execute a transition.
    See also run to completion, trigger.

Semantics

When an event required by a transition occurs, and the guard condition on the transition is satisfied, the transition performs its action and the active state changes.
    When an object receives an event, the event is saved if the state machine is exe-cuting a run-to-completion step. When the step is completed, the state machine handles an event that has occurred. A transition is *triggered* if its event is handled while the owning object is in the state containing the transition or is in a substate nested inside the state containing the transition. An event satisfies a trigger event that is an ancestor of the occurring event type. If a complex transition has multiple source states, all of them must be active for the transition to be enabled. A comple-tion transition is enabled when its source state completes activity. If it is a com-posite state, it is enabled when all its direct substates have completed or reached their final states.
    When the event is handled, the guard condition (if any) is evaluated. If the Boolean expression in the guard condition evaluates to true, then the transition is said to *fire*. The action on the transition is executed, and the state of the object

becomes the target state of the transition (no change of state occurs for an internal transition, however). During the state change, any exit actions and entry actions on the minimal path from the original state of the object to the target state of the transition are executed. Note that the original state may be a nested substate of the source state of the transition.

If the guard condition is not satisfied, nothing happens as a result of this transition, although some other transition might fire if its conditions are satisfied.

If more than one transition is eligible to fire, only one of them will fire. A transition in a nested state takes precedence over a transition in an enclosing state. Otherwise, the choice of transitions is undefined and may be nondeterministic. This is often a realistic real-world situation.

As a practical matter, an implementation may provide an ordering of transitions for firing. This does not change the semantics, as the same effect could be achieved by organizing the guard conditions so that they do not overlap. But it is often simpler to be able to say, "This transition fires only if no other transition fires."

Deferred events. If the event or one of its ancestors is marked for deferral in the state or in an enclosing state, and the event does not trigger a transition, the event is a deferred event until the object enters a state in which the event is not deferred. When the object enters a new state, any previously deferred events that are no longer deferred become *pending* and they occur in an indeterminate order. If the first pending event does not cause a transition to fire, it is ignored and another pending event occurs. If a previously deferred event is marked for deferral in the new state, it may trigger a transition, but it remains deferred if it fails to trigger a transition. If the occurrence of an event causes a transition to a new state, any remaining pending and deferred events are reevaluated according to the deferral status of the new state and a new set of pending events is established.

An implementation might impose stricter rules on the order in which deferred events are processed or supply operations to manipulate their order.

flow

A kind of relationship that relates two versions of the same object at successive points in time.

See also become, copy.

Semantics

A flow relationship relates two versions of the same object at successive points in time. It may relate two values of an object in an instance-level interaction, or it may relate two classifier roles describing the same object in a descriptor-level interaction. It represents the transformation of one state of an object into another. It may represent a change in value, of control state, or of location.

The stereotypes of flow dependency are become and copy. Other stereotypes may be added by users.

Notation

A flow relationship is shown as a dashed arrow with the appropriate stereotype keyword attached. A naked flow relationship without a stereotype may not be used.

Standard elements

become, copy

focus of control

A symbol on a sequence diagram that shows the period of time during which an object is performing an action, either directly or through a subordinate procedure.

See activation.

font usage

Text may be distinguished through the use of different fonts and other graphic markers.

See also graphic marker.

Discussion

Italics are used to indicate an abstract class, attribute, or operation. Other font distinctions are primarily for highlighting or to distinguish parts of the notation. It is recommended that names of classifiers and associations be shown in boldface and subsidiary elements, such as attributes, operations, rolename, and so on, be shown in normal type. Compartment names should be shown in a distinctive font, such as small boldface, but the choice is left to an editing tool. A tool is also free to use font distinctions for highlighting selected elements, to distinguish reserved words and keywords, and to encode selected properties of an element, or it may enable the use of such distinctions under user control. Similar considerations apply to color, although its use should be optional because many persons are color blind. All such uses are convenience extensions to the canonical notation described in this book, which is sufficient to display any model.

fork

A complex transition in which one source state is replaced by two or more target states, resulting in an increase in the number of active states. Antonym: join.

See also complex transition, composite state, join.

Semantics

A fork is a transition with one source state and two or more target states. If the source state is active and the trigger event occurs, the transition action is executed and all the target states become active. The target states must be in different regions of a concurrent composite state.

Notation

A fork is shown as a heavy bar with one incoming transition arrow and two or more outgoing transition arrows It may have a transition label (guard condition, trigger event, and action). Figure 13-101 shows an explicit fork into a concurrent composite state.

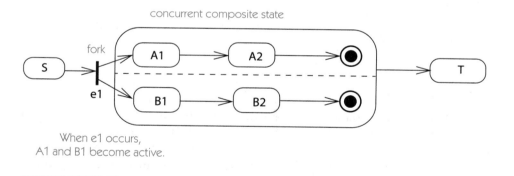

Figure 13-101. *Fork*

formal argument

See parameter.

framework

A generic architecture that provides an extensible template for applications within a domain.

See package.

friend

A usage dependency that grants the client permission to access the supplier, even though the client otherwise does not have sufficient visibility to access the supplier.

See also access, import, visibility.

Semantics

A friend dependency is used to grant an operation or a class permission to use the contents of a class, although there would otherwise be insufficient permission. It is an explicit exception to the usual permission rules between the affected elements. This capability should be used carefully and sparingly.

Notation

A friend dependency is shown as a dashed arrow from the operation or class gaining permission to the class whose contents are made available; the stereotype keyword «friend» is attached to the arrow.

full descriptor

The complete implicit description of a direct instance. The full descriptor is implicitly assembled by inheritance from all the ancestors.

See also direct class, inheritance, multiple classification.

Semantics

A declaration of a class or other model element is, in fact, only a partial description of its instances; call it the *class segment*. In general, an object contains more structure than described by the class segment of its direct class. The rest of the structure is obtained by inheritance from the ancestor classes. The complete description of all its attributes, operations, and associations is called the full descriptor. The full descriptor is usually not manifest in a model or program. The purpose of inheritance rules is to provide a way to automatically construct the full descriptor from the segments. In principle, there are various ways to do this, often called *metaobject protocols*. UML defines one set of rules for inheritance that cover most popular programming languages and are also useful for conceptual modeling. Be aware, however, that other possibilities exist—for example, the CLOS language.

functional view

A view dealing with the breakdown of a system into functions or operations that provide its functionality. A functional view is not usually considered object-oriented and can lead to an architecture that is hard to maintain. In traditional development methods, the data flow diagram is the heart of the functional view. UML does not directly support a functional view, although activity graphs have some functional characteristics.

generalizable element

A model element that may participate in a generalization relationship.
See also generalization, inheritance.

Semantics

A generalizable element may have parents and children. A variable that is classified with an element may hold an instance of a descendant of the element.

Generalizable elements include classes, use cases, other classifiers, associations, states, events, and collaborations. A generalizable element inherits the features of its ancestors. The definition of which parts of each kind of generalizable element are inherited depends on the kind of element. Classes, for instance, inherit attributes, operations, methods, participation in associations, and constraints. Associations inherit the participating classes (these may themselves be specialized) and the association-end properties. Use cases inherit attributes and operations, associations to actors, extend and include relationships to other use cases, and behavior sequences. States inherit transitions.

See generalization, association generalization, use case generalization.

Structure

A generalizable element has properties that declare where it may appear within a generalization hierarchy.

abstraction	Specifies whether the generalizable element describes direct instances or is an abstract element that must be specialized before it can be instantiated. **True** indicates that the element is abstract (may not have direct instances); **false** indicates that it is concrete (may have direct instances). To be usable, an abstract element must have concrete descendants. A class with an operation lacking a method is of necessity abstract.
leaf	Specifies whether the generalizable element may be specialized. **True** indicates that it may not have descendants (that is, it must be a leaf), **false** indicates that it may have descendants (whether or not it actually has any descendants at the moment). An abstract class that is a leaf is useless for anything but grouping global attributes and operations.

root   Specifies whether the element must be a root with no ancestors. True indicates that it must be a root and may not have ancestors; false indicates that it need not be a root and may have ancestors (whether or not it actually has any ancestors at the moment).

Note that declaring leaf and root classes does not affect the semantics, but such declarations may provide a statement of the designer's intent. They may also permit more efficient compilation of separate packages by avoiding the need for a global analysis or overly conservative assumptions about polymorphic operations.

Standard elements

leaf

generalization

A taxonomic relationship between a more general element and a more specific element. The more specific element is fully consistent with the more general element and contains additional information. An instance of the more specific element may be used where the more general element is allowed.

See also association generalization, inheritance, substitutability principle, use case generalization.

Semantics

A generalization relationship is a directed relationship between two generalizable elements of the same kind, such as classes, packages, or other kinds of elements. One element is called the parent, and the other is called the child. For classes, the parent is called the superclass and the child is called the subclass. The parent is the description of a set of (indirect) instances with common properties over all children; the child is a description of a subset of those instances that have the properties of the parent but that also have additional properties peculiar to the child.

Generalization is a transitive, antisymmetric relationship. One direction of traversal leads to the parent; the other direction leads to the child. An element related in the parent direction across one or more generalizations is called an ancestor; an element related in the child direction across one or more generalizations is called a descendant. No directed generalization cycles are allowed. A class may not have itself for an ancestor or descendant.

In the simplest case, a class (or other generalizable element) has a single parent. In a more complicated situation, a child may have more than one parent. The child inherits structure, behavior, and constraints from all its parents. This is called multiple inheritance (it might better be called multiple generalization). A child element references its parent and must have visibility to it.

Generalization may be applied to associations, as well as to classifiers, states, events, and collaborations.

For the application of generalization to associations, see association generalization.

For the application of generalization to use cases, see use case generalization.

Nodes and components are much like classes, and generalization applied to them behaves the same as it does for classes.

Constraints

A constraint may be applied to a set of generalization relationships and their children that share a common parent. The following properties can be specified.

disjoint	No element may have two children in the set as ancestors (in a multiple inheritance situation). No instance may be a direct or indirect instance of two of the children (in a multiple classification semantics).
overlapping	An element may have two or more children in the set as ancestors. An instance may be an instance of two or more children.
complete	All possible children have been enumerated in the set and no more may be added.
incomplete	All possible children have not been enumerated yet in the set. More are expected or known but not declared yet.

Notation

Generalization between classifiers is shown as a solid-line path from the child element (such as a subclass) to the parent element (such as a superclass), with a large hollow triangle at the end of the path where it meets the more general element (Figure 13-102). The lines to the parent may be combined to produce a tree (Figure 13-103).

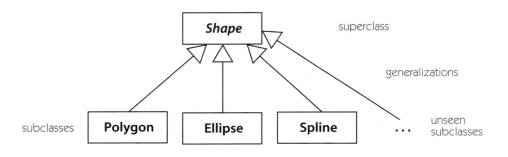

Figure 13-102. *Generalization*

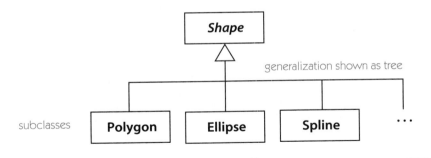

Figure 13-103. *Generalization using tree style*

Generalization may be applied to associations, as well as to classifiers, although the notation may be messy because of the multiple lines. An association can be shown as an association class for the purpose of attaching generalization arrows.

The existence of additional classes in the model that are not shown on a diagram may be shown using an ellipsis (…) in place of a class. (Note that this is not an indication that additional classes might be added in the future. It indicates that additional classes exist right now but are not being shown. This is a notational convention that means information has been suppressed. It is not a semantic element.) The presence of an ellipsis (…) as a subclass node of a class indicates that the semantic model contains at least one subclass of the class that is not visible on the current diagram. The ellipsis may have a discriminator. This indicator is intended to be automatically maintained by an editing tool, not entered manually.

Presentation options

A group of generalization paths for a given superclass may be shown as a tree with a shared segment (including triangle) to the superclass, branching into multiple paths to each subclass. This is merely a notational device. It does not indicate an *n*-ary relationship. In the underlying model, there is one generalization for each subclass-superclass pair. There is no semantic difference if the arcs are drawn separately.

If a text label is placed on a generalization triangle shared by several generalization paths to subclasses, the label applies to all the paths. In other words, all the subclasses share the given properties.

Example

Figure 13-104 shows the declaration of constraints on generalizations. It also illustrates the use of the "tree style" of generalization, in which the paths are drawn on an orthogonal grid and share a common parent arrow, as well as the "binary style," in which each parent-child relationship has its own oblique arrow.

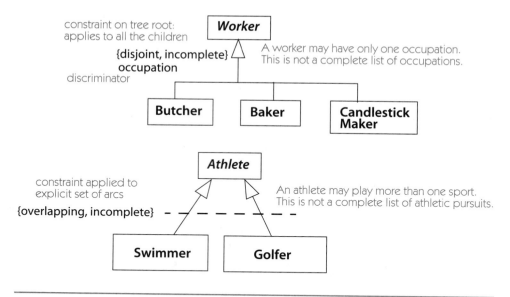

Figure 13-104. *Generalization constraints*

Discussion

The parent element in a generalization relationship can be defined without knowledge of the children, but the children must generally know the structure of their parents in order to work correctly. In many cases, however, the parent is designed to be extended by children and includes more or less knowledge of the expected children. One of the glories of generalization, however, is that new children are often discovered that had not been anticipated by the designer of the parent element, leading to an expansion in power that is compatible in spirit with the original intent.

The realization relationship is like a generalization in which only behavior specification is inherited rather than structure or implementation. If the specification element is an abstract class with no attributes, no associations, and only abstract operations, then generalization and realization are roughly equivalent as there is nothing to inherit but behavior specification. Note that realization does not actually populate the client, however; therefore, the operations must be in the client or inherited from some other element.

Standard elements

complete, disjoint, implementation, incomplete, overlapping

graphic marker

A notational element such as geometry, texture, fill pattern, font, color, and so on.
See also font usage.

Notation

Symbols for notation are constructed from various graphic markers. No one graphic marker has semantic significance by itself, but the goal of notation is to use graphic markers in a consistent and orthogonal way as much as possible.

Some graphic markers are used to construct predefined UML symbols, while other graphic markers are not used in the canonical notation. For example, no meaning has been assigned to color because many printers do not render it and some people cannot distinguish all colors. Unassigned graphic markers, such as colors, can be used within editing tools for whatever purpose the modeler or tool wishes.

UML permits limited graphical extension of its notation. A graphic icon or a graphic marker (such as texture or color) can be associated with a stereotype. The UML does not specify the form of the graphic specification. But many bitmap and stroked formats exist and might be used by a graphical editor (although their portability is a difficult problem).

More general forms of icon specification and substitution are conceivable, but we leave these to the ingenuity of tool builders—with the warning that excessive use of extensibility capabilities may lead to loss of portability among tools.

guard condition

A condition that must be satisfied in order to enable an associated transition to fire.
See also branch, conditional thread, junction state, transition.

Semantics

A guard condition is a Boolean expression that is part of the specification of a transition. When the trigger event for a transition is received, it is saved until the state machine has completed any current run-to-completion step. Then it is handled and the guard condition is evaluated. If the condition is true, the transition is enabled to fire (but if more than one transition is enabled, only one will fire). The test occurs at the moment the trigger event is handled. If the guard condition evaluates to false when the event is handled, it is not reevaluated unless the trigger event occurs again, even if the condition later becomes true.

A guard condition must be a query—that is, it may not modify the value of the system or its state; it may not have side effects.

A guard condition may appear on a completion transition. In that case, it selects one arm of a branch.

Notation

A guard condition is part of the string for a transition. It has the form of a Boolean expression enclosed in square brackets.

[boolean-expression]

Names used within the expression must be available to the transition. They are either parameters of the trigger event or attributes of the owning object.

guillemets

Small double angle marks (« ») used as quotation marks in French, Italian, Spanish, and other languages. In UML notation they are used to enclose keywords and stereotype names. For example: «bind», «instanceOf». Guillemets are available in most fonts, so there is really no excuse for not using them, but the typographically challenged could substitute two angle brackets (<< >>) if necessary.

See also font usage.

history state

A pseudostate that indicates that the enclosing composite state remembers its previously active substate after it exits.

See also composite state, pseudostate, state machine, transition.

Semantics

A history state allows a sequential composite state to remember the last substate that was active in it prior to a transition from the composite state. A transition to the history state causes the former active substate to be made active again. Any necessary entry actions are performed. A history state may have incoming transitions from outside the composite state or from the initial state. A history state may have one outgoing unlabeled transition. This transition indicates the initial stored history state. It is used if a transition goes to the history state when no stored state is present. The history state may not have incoming transitions from other states within the composite state because it is already active.

A history state may remember *shallow history* or *deep history*. A shallow history state remembers and reactivates a state at the same nesting depth as the history state itself. If a transition from a nested substate directly exited the composite state, the enclosing substate at the top level within the composite state is activated. A deep history state remembers a state that may have been nested at some depth within the composite state. To remember a deep state, a transition must have taken the deep state directly out of the composite state. If a transition from a deep state goes to a shallower state, which then transitions out of the composite state, then the shallower state is the one that is remembered. A transition to a deep history state restores the previously active state at any depth. In the process, entry actions are executed if they are present on inner states containing the remembered state. A composite state may have both a shallow history state and a deep history state. An incoming transition must be connected to one or the other.

If a composite state reaches its final state, then it loses its stored history and behaves as if it had not been entered for the first time.

Notation

A shallow history state is shown as a small circle containing the letter H, as in Figure 13-105. A deep history state is shown as a circle containing the letters H*.

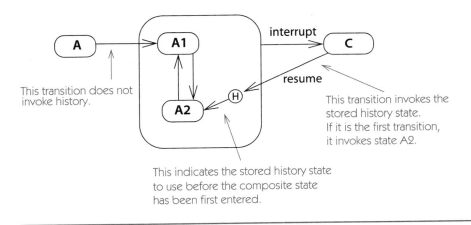

Figure 13-105. *History state*

hyperlink

An invisible connection between two notation elements that can be traversed by some command.

See also diagram.

Notation

A notation on a piece of paper contains no hidden information. A notation on a computer screen, however, may contain additional invisible hyperlinks that are not apparent in a static view but that can be invoked dynamically to access some other piece of information, either in a graphical view or in a textual table. Such dynamic links are as much a part of a *dynamic* notation as the visible information, but this document does not prescribe their form. We regard them as a tool responsibility. This document attempts to define a *static* notation for UML, with the understanding that some useful and interesting information may show up poorly or not at all in such a view. On the other hand, we do not know enough to specify the behavior of all dynamic tools, nor do we want to stifle innovation in dynamic presentation. Eventually, some dynamic notations may become well enough established to standardize, but we do not feel we should do so now.

identity

An object's inherent property of being distinguishable from all other objects.
See also data value, object.

Semantics

Objects are discrete and distinguishable from each other. The identity of an object is its conceptual handle, the inherent characteristic that allows it to be identified and referenced by other objects. Conceptually, an object does not need a key or other mechanism to identify itself, and such mechanisms should not be included in models. In an implementation, identity may be implemented by addresses or keys, but they are part of the underlying implementation infrastructure and need not be explicitly included as attributes in most models.

ill formed

Designation of a model that is incorrectly constructed, one that violates one or more predefined or model-specified rules or constraints. Antonym: well formed.
See also conflict, constraint.

Semantics

A model that violates well-formedness rules and constraints is not a valid model and therefore has inconsistent semantics. To attempt to use such a model may yield meaningless results. It is the responsibility of a modeling tool to detect ill-formed models and prevent their use in situations that might be troublesome. Because the use of some constructs extends the built-in UML semantics, automatic verification may not be possible in all cases. Also, automatic checking cannot be expected to verify consistency of operations, because that would involve solving the halting problem. Therefore, in practical situations, a combination of automatic verification and human verification is necessary.

Although a finished model must be well formed, intermediate versions of a model may be ill formed at times because they might be incomplete fragments of a final model. Editing a valid model to produce another valid model may require passing through intermediate models that are ill formed. This is no different from editing computer programs—the final program given to a compiler must be valid, but working copies in a text editor are often invalid. Therefore ill-formed models must be editable and storable by support tools.

implementation

1. A definition of how something is constructed or computed. For example, a class is an implementation of a type; a method is an implementation of an operation. Contrast: specification. The realization relationship relates an implementation to its specification.

See realization.

2. That stage of a system that describes the functioning of the system in an executable medium (such as a programming language, database, or digital hardware). For implementation, low-level tactical decisions must be made to fit the design to the particular implementation medium and to work around its limitations (all languages have some arbitrary limitations). If the design is done well, however, the implementation decisions will be local and none of them will affect a large portion of the system. This stage is captured by implementation-level models, especially the static view and code. Contrast analysis, design, implementation, and deployment.

See development process, stages of modeling.

implementation class

A stereotype for a class that provides a physical implementation, including attributes, associations to other classes, and methods for operations. An implementation class is intended for a traditional object-oriented language with static single classification. An object in such a system must have exactly one implementation class as its direct class. Contrast with type, a stereotype for a class that permits multiple classification. In a conventional language, such as Java, an object can have one implementation class and many types. The implementation class must be consistent with the types.

See type, which compares type and implementation class.

implementation inheritance

The inheritance of the implementation of a parent element—that is, its structure (such as attributes and operations) and its code (such as methods). By contrast, interface inheritance involves inheritance of interface specifications (that is, operations) but not methods or data structure (attributes and associations).

The normal meaning of generalization in UML includes the inheritance of *both* interface and implementation. To inherit *just* the implementation (private inheritance), use the «implementation» stereotype on a generalization. To support an interface without a commitment to implementation, use a realization relationship to an interface.

See also generalization, inheritance, interface inheritance, private inheritance.

implementation view

A view of a model that contains a static declaration of the components in a system, their dependencies, and possibly the classes that are implemented by the component.

See component diagram.

import

A stereotype of the permission dependency in which the names of the elements in the supplier package are added to the namespace of the client package.

See also access, package, visibility.

Semantics

The names found in the namespace of the supplier package are added to the namespace of the client package, under the same visibility rules as specified for access. If there are any conflicts between imported names and names already in the client namespace, the model is ill formed.

See access for the visibility rules for both access and import.

Notation

An import dependency is shown as a dashed arrow from the package gaining access to the package supplying elements; the stereotype keyword «import» is attached to the arrow.

inactive

A state that is not active; one that is not held by an object.

inception

The first phase of a software development process, during which the initial ideas for a system are conceived and evaluated. During this phase, some of the analysis view and small portions of other views are developed.

See development process.

include

A relationship from a *base* use case to an *inclusion* use case, specifying how the behavior defined for the inclusion use case can be inserted into the behavior defined for the base use case. The base use case can see the inclusion and can depend on the effects of performing the inclusion, but neither the base nor the inclusion may access each other's attributes.

See also extend, use case, use case generalization.

Semantics

The include relationship connects a base use case to an inclusion use case. The inclusion use case in this relationship is not a separate instantiable classifier. Instead, it explicitly describes an additional behavior sequence that is inserted into a use case instance that is executing the base use case. Multiple include relationships may be applied to the same base use case. The same inclusion use case may be included in multiple base use cases. This does not indicate any relationship among the base use cases. There may even be multiple include relationships between the same inclusion base case and base use cases, provided each insertion is at a different location in the base.

The inclusion use case may access attributes or operations of the base use case. The inclusion represents encapsulated behavior that potentially can be reused in multiple base use cases. The base use case sees the inclusion use case, which may set attribute values in the base use case. But the base use case must not access the attributes of the inclusion use case, because the inclusion use case will have terminated when the base use case regains control.

Note that additions (of all kinds) may be nested. An inclusion, therefore, may serve as the base for a further inclusion, extension, or generalization.

Structure

The include relationship has the following property.

location	A location within the body of the behavior sequence of the base use case, where the inclusion is to be inserted. When a use case instance reaches the location while performing the base use case, it performs the inclusion use case before resuming the base use case.
	The inclusion is an explicit statement within the behavior sequence of the base use case. The location is therefore implicit, unlike the situation with the extend relationship.

The inclusion is performed once. Other multiplicities can be achieved by loops in the behavior sequence for the base case that references the inclusion.

Notation

A dashed arrow is drawn from the base use case symbol to the inclusion use case symbol with a stick arrowhead on the inclusion. The keyword «include» is placed on the arrow (Figure 13-106). The location can be attached to the arrow as a property list in braces, but usually it is referenced as part of the text for the base use case and need not be shown on the diagram. Figure 13-107 shows the behavior sequences for these use cases.

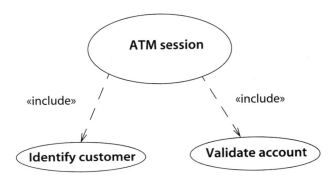

Figure 13-106. *Include relationship*

Base use case for ATM session:

show advertisement of the day	behavior step
include identify customer	inclusion
include validate account	another inclusion
print receipt header	behavior step
log out	behavior step

Inclusion use case for **Identify Customer:**

> get customer name
> **include** verify identity
> **if** verification failed **then** abort the session
> obtain account numbers for the customer

Inclusion use case for **Validate Account:**

> establish connection with account database
> obtain account status and limits

Figure 13-107. *Behavior sequences for use cases*

incremental development

The development of a model and other artifacts of a system as a series of versions, each complete to some degree of precision and functionality, but each adding incremental detail to the previous version. The advantage is that each version of the model can be evaluated and debugged based on the relatively small changes to the previous version, making it easier to make changes correctly. The term is closely allied with the concept of iterative development.

See development process.

indirect instance

An entity that is an instance of an element, such as a class, and is also an instance of a child of the element. That is, it is an instance but not a direct instance.

inheritance

The mechanism by which more specific elements incorporate structure and behavior defined by more general elements.

See also full descriptor, generalization.

Semantics

Inheritance allows a full description of a generalizable element to be automatically constructed by assembling declaration fragments from a generalization hierarchy. A generalization hierarchy is a tree (actually, a partial order) of declarations of model elements, such as classes. Each declaration is not the declaration of a complete, usable element, however. Instead, each declaration is an incremental declaration describing what the element declaration adds to the declarations of its ancestors in the generalization hierarchy. Inheritance is the (implicit) process of combining those incremental declarations into full descriptors that describe actual instances.

Think of each generalizable element as having two descriptions, a segment declaration and a full descriptor. The segment declaration is the incremental list of features that the element declares in the model—the attributes and operations declared by a class, for example. The segment declaration is the difference between the element and its parents. The full descriptor does not appear explicitly within the model. It is the full description of an instance of the element—for example, the complete list of attributes and operations held by an object of a class. The full descriptor is the union of the contents of the segment declarations in an element and all its ancestors.

That is inheritance. It is the incremental definition of an element. Other details, such as method lookup algorithms, vtables, and so on, are merely implementation mechanisms to make it work in a particular language, not part of the essential definition. Although this description may seem strange at first, it is free of the implementation entailments found in most other definitions, yet is compatible with them.

Conflicts

If the same feature appears more than once among the set of inherited segments, there may be a conflict. No attribute may be declared more than once in an inherited set. If this occurs, the declarations conflict and the model is ill formed. (This restriction is not essential for logical reasons. It is present to avoid the certain confusion that would occur if attributes had to be distinguished by pathnames.)

The same operation may be declared more than once, provided the declaration is exactly the same (the methods may differ, however) or a child declaration strengthens an inherited declaration (for example, by declaring a child to be a query or increasing its concurrency status). A method declaration on a child replaces (overrides) a method declaration on an ancestor. There is no conflict. If distinct methods are inherited from two different ancestors that are not themselves in an ancestor relationship, then the methods conflict and the model is ill formed.

Discussion

Generalization is a taxonomic relationship among elements. It describes what an element *is*. Inheritance is a mechanism for combining shared incremental descriptions to form a full description of an element. They are not the same thing, although they are closely related. The inheritance mechanism applied to the generalization relationship enables factoring and sharing of descriptions and polymorphic behavior. This is the approach taken by most object-oriented languages and by UML. But keep in mind that there are other approaches that could have been taken and that are used by some programming languages.

initial state

A pseudostate that indicates the default starting place for a transition whose target is the boundary of a composite state.

See also composite state, creation, entry action, initialization, junction state.

Semantics

To promote encapsulation, it is desirable to separate the outside view of a composite state from the inside details as much as possible. From the outside, the state is viewed as an opaque entity with hidden internal structure. From the outside viewpoint, transitions go to and from the state itself. From the inside viewpoint, they connect to substates within the state.

An initial state is a dummy state (pseudostate) that represents a connection point for an incoming transition to the boundary of the composite state. It is not a real state; control may not remain within it. Rather, it is a syntactic means of indicating where the control should go. An initial state must have an outgoing trigger-less transition (a transition with no event trigger, therefore automatically enabled as soon as the initial state is entered). The completion transition connects to a real state in the composite state. The completion transition may have an action on it. The action is executed when the state is entered after the entry action (if any) of the composite state. This allows an action to be associated with the default entry, in addition to the entry action (which is performed on all entries, default or otherwise). This action may access the implicit current event—that is, the event that triggered the first segment in the transition that ultimately caused the transition to the initial state.

An initial state may not have an outgoing transition with an event trigger. An incoming transition is equivalent to an incoming transition to the enclosing composite state and should be avoided. Connect such transitions to the composite state.

Most often the transition on the initial state is unguarded. In that case, it must be the only transition from the initial state. A set of outgoing transitions may be provided with guard conditions, but the guard conditions must completely cover all possible cases (or, more simply, one of them can have the guard condition **else**). The point is that control must leave the initial state immediately. It is not a real state, and some transition must fire.

The initial state in the top-level state of a class represents the creation of a new instance of the class. When its outgoing transition is taken, the implicit current event is the creation event of the object and has the argument values passed by the constructor operation. These values are available within actions on the outgoing transition.

Object creation

The initial state of the topmost composite state of a class is slightly different. It may have a trigger with the stereotype «create», together with a named event trigger with parameters. There may be multiple transitions of this kind with different triggers. The signature of each trigger must match a creation operation on the class. When a new object of the class is instantiated, the transition corresponding to its creation operation fires and receives the arguments from the call to the creation operation.

Notation

An initial state is displayed as a small filled black circle inside the symbol of its composite state. Outgoing transition arrows may be connected to it. Only one initial state may occur (directly) within a composite state. However, additional initial states may occur within nested composite states.

Example

In Figure 13-108, we start in state X. When event e occurs, the transition fires and action a is performed. The transition goes to state Y. Entry action b is performed, and the initial state becomes active. The outgoing transition immediately fires, performing action c and changing to state Z.

Instead, if event f occurs when the system is in state X, then the other transition fires and action d is performed. This transition goes directly to state Z. The initial state is not involved. Because control passes into state Y, action b is performed, but action c is not performed in this case.

In Figure 13-109, the initial state has a branch. Again, suppose the system starts in state X. When event e occurs, actions a is performed, the system changes to state Y, and the entry action b is performed. Control goes to the initial state. The size attribute of the owning object is tested. If it is 0, control goes to state Z; if it is not 0, control goes to state W.

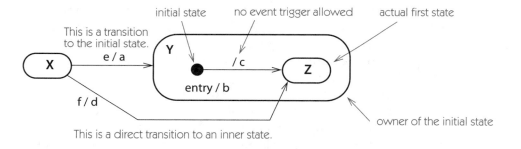

Figure 13-108. *Initial state*

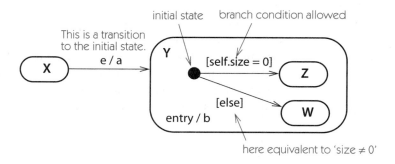

Figure 13-109. *Initial state with branch*

initial value

An expression specifying the value that an attribute in an object holds just after it has been initialized.

See also default value, initialization.

Semantics

An initial value is an expression attached to an attribute. The expression is a text string that also designates a language for interpreting the expression. When an object holding the attribute is instantiated, the expression is evaluated according to the given language and the current value of the system. The result of the evaluation is used to initialize the value of the attribute in the new object.

The initial value is optional. If it is absent, then the attribute declaration does not specify the value held by a new object (but some other part of the overall model may supply that information).

Note that an explicit initialization procedure for an object (such as a constructor) may supersede an initial value expression and overwrite the attribute value.

The initial value of a class-scope attribute is used to initialize it once at the beginning of execution. UML does not specify the relative order of initialization of different class-scope attributes.

initialization

Setting the value of a newly created object—namely, the values of its attributes, links of associations that it belongs to, and its control state.

See also instantiation.

Semantics

Conceptually, a new object is created complete in one step. It is easier, however, to think about the instantiation process in two steps: creation and initialization. First a new empty shell object is allocated with the proper structure of attribute slots, and the new raw object is given identity. Identity can be implemented in various ways, such as by the address of the memory block containing the object or by an integer counter. In any case, it is something that is unique across the system and can be used as a handle to find and access the object. At this point, the object is not yet legal—it may violate the constraints on its values and relationships. The next step is initialization. Any declared initial value expressions for attributes are evaluated, and the results are assigned to the attribute slots. The creation method may explicitly calculate the values for attributes, thereby overriding the default initial values. The resultant values must satisfy any constraints on the class. The creation method may also create links containing the new object. They must satisfy the declared multiplicity of any associations that the class participates in. When the initialization is complete, the object must be a legal object and must obey any constraints on its class. After initialization is complete, attributes or associations whose changeability property is **frozen** or **addOnly** may not be altered until the object is destroyed. The entire initialization process is atomic and may not be interrupted or interleaved.

instance

An individual entity with its own identity and value. A descriptor specifies the form and behavior of a set of instances with similar properties. An instance has identity and values that are consistent with the specification in the descriptor. Instances appear in models mainly as examples consistent with descriptor-level models.

See also descriptor, identity, link, object.

Semantics

An instance has identity. In other words, at different points in time during the execution of a system, the instance can be identified with the same instance at other points in time, even though the value of the instance changes. At any time, an instance has a value expressible in terms of data values and references to other instances. A data value is a degenerate case. Its identity is the same as its value, or considered from a different viewpoint, it has no identity.

In addition to identity and value, each instance has a descriptor that constrains the values that the instance can have. A descriptor is a model element that describes instances. This is the descriptor-instance dichotomy. Most modeling concepts in UML have this dual character. The main content of most models is descriptors of various kinds. The purpose of the model is to describe the possible values of a system in terms of its instances and their values.

Each kind of descriptor describes one kind of instance. An object is an instance of a class; a link is an instance of an association. A use case describes possible use case instances; a parameter describes a possible argument value; and so on. Some instances do not have familial names and are usually overlooked except in very formal settings, but they nevertheless exist. For example, a state describes possible occurrences of the state during an execution trace.

A model describes the possible values of a system and its behavior in progressing from value to value during execution. The value of a system is the set of all instances in it and their values. The system value is valid if every instance is the instance of some descriptor in the model, and if all the explicit and implicit constraints in the model are satisfied by the set of instances.

The behavior elements in a model describe how the system and the instances in it progress from value to value. The concept of identity of instances is essential to this description. Each behavioral step is the description of the change of the values of a small number of instances in terms of their previous values. The remainder of the instances in the system preserve their values unchanged. For example, a local operation on one object can be described by expressions for the new values of each attribute of the object without changes to the rest of the system. A nonlocal function can be decomposed into local functions on several objects.

Note that the instances in an executing system are not model elements. Usually, they are not part of the model at all. When instances appear in a model, they appear as illustrations or examples of typical structure and behavior, snapshots of system value or execution traces of its history. These are useful for human insight, but they are usually points in a large or infinite set of possible values and do not *define* anything.

Direct instance. Each object is the direct instance of some class and the indirect instance of the ancestors of the class. This is also the case for instances of other generalizable elements. An object is a direct instance of a class if the class describes the instance and no descendant class also describes the object. In the case of multiple classification, an instance may be a direct instance of more than one classifier, none of which is an ancestor of any of the others. Under some execution semantics, one of the classifiers is designated the implementation class and the others are designated types or roles. The full descriptor is the implicit full description of an instance—all its attributes, operations, associations, and other properties—whether obtained by an instance from its direct classifier or from an ancestor classifier by inheritance. In case of multiple classification, the full descriptor is the union of the properties defined by each direct classifier.

Creation. *See* instantiation for a description of how instances are created.

Notation

Although descriptors and instances are not the same, they share many properties, including the same form (because the descriptor must describe the form of the instances). Therefore, it is convenient to choose notation for each descriptor-instance pair so that the correspondence is immediately visually obvious. There are a limited number of ways to do this, each with its advantages and disadvantages. In UML the descriptor-instance distinction is shown by using the same geometrical symbol for each pair of elements and by underlining the name string of an instance element. This visual distinction is generally easily apparent without being overpowering even when an entire diagram contains instance elements.

Although Figure 13-110 shows objects, the underlining convention can be used for other kinds of instances, such as use case instances, component instances, and node instances.

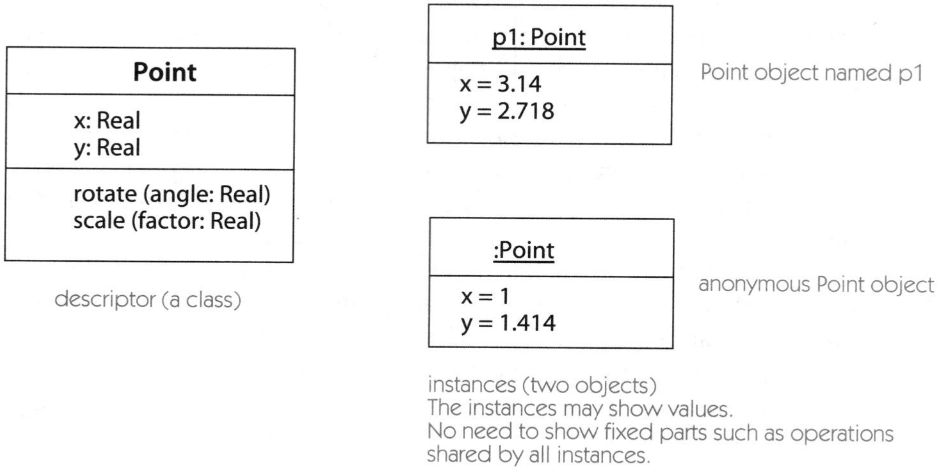

Figure 13-110. *Descriptor and instances*

Because instances appear in models as examples, usually only details relevant to a particular example are included. For example, the entire list of attribute values need not be included; or the entire list of values can be omitted if the focus is on something else, such as message flow between objects.

instance of

Relationship between an instance and its descriptor.
See instance.

instantiable

Able to have instances. Synonym: concrete.
See also abstract, direct instance, generalizable element.

Semantics

Generalizable elements may be declared as abstract or instantiable. If they are instantiable, then direct instances can be created.

instantiate

To create an instance of a descriptor.
See instantiation.

instantiation

The creation of new instances of model elements.

See also initialization.

Semantics

Instances are created at run time as a result of primitive create actions or creation operations. First an identity is created for the new instance; then its data structure is allocated as prescribed by its descriptor; and then its property values are initialized as prescribed by the descriptor and the creation operator.

The instantiation usage dependency shows the relationship between an operation that creates instances or a class containing such an operation and the class of objects being instantiated.

Objects. When a new object is instantiated (created), it is created with identity and memory and it is initialized. The initialization of an object defines the values of its attribute, its association, and its control state.

Usually, each concrete class has one or more class-scope constructor operations the purpose of which is to create new objects of the class. Underlying all the constructor operations is an implicit primitive operation that creates a new raw instance that is then initialized by the constructor operations. After a raw instance has been created, it has the form prescribed by its descriptor, but its values have not yet been initialized, so they may be semantically inconsistent. An instance is therefore not available to the rest of the system until it has been initialized, which occurs immediately after creation of the raw instance.

Links. Similarly, links are created by creation actions or operations, usually by instance-scope operations attached to one of the participating classes, rather than by constructor operations on the association element itself (although this is a possible implementation technique under some circumstances). Again, there is an underlying implicit primitive operation that creates a new link among a specific tuple of objects. This operation has no effect if a link of the same association already exists among the tuple of objects (because the extent of an association is a set and may not contain duplicate values). With an ordinary association, there is nothing more to do. A link of an association class, however, requires initialization of its attribute values.

Use case instances. The instantiation of a use case means that a use case instance is created, and the use case instance begins executing at the beginning of the use case controlling it. The use case instance may temporarily follow another use case related by extend or include relationships before it resumes executing the original use case. When the use case instance comes to the end of the use case it is following, the use case instance terminates.

Other instances. Instances of other descriptors may be created in a similar two-step process: First perform a raw creation to establish identity and to allocate data structure, then initialize the values of the new instance so that it obeys all relevant constraints. For example, an activation is created implicitly as the direct consequence of a call to an operation.

The exact mechanisms of creating instances are the responsibility of the run-time environment.

Notation

An instantiation dependency is shown as a dashed arrow from the operation or class performing the instantiation to the class being instantiated; the stereotype «instantiate» is attached to the arrow.

Discussion

Instantiation is sometimes used to mean binding a template to produce a bound element, but binding is more specific for this relationship.

intent

The formal specification of the structural and behavioral properties of a descriptor. Sometimes called *intension.* Contrast: extent.

See also descriptor.

Semantics

A descriptor, such as a class or an association, has both a description (its intent) and a set of instances that it describes (its extent). The purpose of the intent is to specify the structural and behavioral properties of the instances in an executable manner.

interaction

A specification of how messages are sent between objects or other instances to perform a task. The interaction is defined in the context of a collaboration.

See also interaction diagram.

Semantics

Objects or other instances in a collaboration communicate to accomplish a purpose (such as performing an operation) by exchanging messages. The messages may include signals and calls, as well as more implicit interactions through conditions and time events. A pattern of message exchanges to accomplish a specific purpose is called an interaction.

Structure

An interaction is a behavioral specification that comprises a sequence of message exchanges among a set of objects to accomplish a purpose, such as the implementation of an operation. An interaction is a collaboration plus a sequenced set of message flows imposed on the links in the collaboration. To specify an interaction, it is first necessary to specify a collaboration—that is, to define the objects that interact and their relationships to each other. Then the possible interaction sequences are specified, in a single description containing conditionals (branches or conditional signals), or as multiple descriptions, each describing one path among the possible execution paths. The complete description of the behavior of a collaboration can be given as a state machine, whose states are the states of the execution of an operation or other procedure.

Notation

Interactions are shown as sequence diagrams or as collaboration diagrams. Both diagram formats show the execution of collaborations. Sequence diagrams show the behavioral view of collaborations explicitly, including the time sequencing of messages and an explicit representation of method activations. However, sequence diagrams show only the participating objects and not their relationships to other objects or their attributes. Therefore, they do not fully show the contextual view of a collaboration. Collaboration diagrams show the full context of an interaction, including the objects and their relationships relevant to an interaction, so they are often better for design purposes than sequence diagrams.

interaction diagram

A generic term that applies to several types of diagrams that emphasize object interactions. These include collaboration diagrams and sequence diagrams. Closely related are activity diagrams.

See also collaboration, interaction.

Notation

A pattern of interaction among objects is shown on an interaction diagram. Interaction diagrams come in various forms all based on the same underlying information but each emphasizing one view of it: sequence diagrams, collaboration diagrams, and activity diagrams.

A sequence diagram shows an interaction arranged in time sequence. In particular, it shows the objects participating in the interaction by their lifelines and the messages they exchange, arranged in time sequence. A sequence diagram does not show the links among the objects. Sequence diagrams come in several formats intended for different purposes.

A sequence diagram can exist in a generic form (describing all possible sequences) and in an instance form (describing one execution sequence consistent with the generic form). In cases without loops or branches, the two forms are isomorphic; the descriptor is a prototype for its instances.

A collaboration diagram shows an interaction arranged around the objects that perform operations. It is similar to an object diagram that shows the objects and the links among them needed to implement a higher-level operation.

The time sequence of messages is indicated by sequence numbers on message flow arrows. Both sequential and concurrent sequences can be shown using appropriate syntax. Sequence diagrams show time sequences using the geometric order of the arrows in the diagram. Therefore, they do not require sequence numbers, although sequence numbers may be included for convenience or to permit switching to a collaboration diagram.

Sequence diagrams and collaboration diagrams express similar information but show it in different ways. Sequence diagrams show the explicit sequence of messages and are better for real-time specifications and for complex scenarios. Collaboration diagrams show the relationships among objects and are better for understanding all the effects on an object and for procedural design.

Discussion

An activity diagram shows the procedural steps involved in performing a high-level operation. It is not an interaction diagram, as it shows the flow of control between procedural steps rather than the flow of control between objects. An activity diagram is primarily focused on the steps in the procedure. It does not show assignment of operations to target classes. An activity graph is a form a state machine; it models the state of execution of a procedure. A number of special icons used in activity diagrams are equivalent to basic UML constructs subject to some additional constraints, but they are provided for convenience.

interaction view

A view of a model that shows the exchange of messages among objects to accomplish some purpose. It consists of collaborations and interactions and is shown using collaboration diagrams and sequence diagrams.

interface

A named set of operations that characterize the behavior of an element.
See also classifier, realization.

Semantics

An interface is a descriptor for the externally visible operations of a class, component, or other entity (including summarization units, such as packages) without specification of internal structure. Each interface often specifies only a limited part of the behavior of an actual class. A class may support many interfaces, either disjoint or overlapping in their effect. Interfaces do not have implementation; they lack attributes, states, and associations; they have only operations and signals received. Interfaces may have generalization relationships. A child interface includes all the operations and signals of its ancestors but may add additional operations. An interface is essentially equivalent to an abstract class with no attributes and no methods and only abstract operations. All the operations in an interface have public visibility (otherwise, there would be no point to including them, as an interface has no "inside" that could use them).

The following extended definition indicates the purpose of an interface.

- An interface is a collection of operations used to specify a service of a class or a component.

- An interface serves to name a collection of operations and to specify their signatures and their effects. An interface focuses upon the effects, not the structure, of a given service. An interface offers no implementation for any of its operations. The operation list may also include signals the class is prepared to handle.

- An interface is used for specifying a service the supplier provides and that other elements can request. An interface gives a name to a collection of operations that work together to carry out some logically interesting behavior of a system or a part of a system.

- An interface defines a service offered by a class or a component. It defines a service that is in turn implemented by a class or a component. As such, an interface spans the logical and physical boundaries of a system. One or more classes (which are likely a part of some component subsystem) may provide a logical implementation of an interface. One or more components may provide a physical packaging that conforms to that same interface.

- If a class realizes (implements) an interface, then it must declare or inherit all the operations in the interface. It may contain additional operations (see realization). If the class realizes more than one interface, it must contain each operation found in any of its interfaces. The same operation may appear in more than one interface. If their signatures match, they must represent the same operation or they are in conflict and the model is ill formed. (An implementation may adopt language-specific rules for matching signatures. For example, in C++, parameter names and return types are ignored.) An interface makes no statement about the attributes or associations of a class; they are part of its implementation.

• An interface is a generalizable element. A child interface inherits all the operations of its parent and may add some operations. Realization may be considered behavior inheritance; a class inherits the operations of another classifier, but not its structure. A class may realize another class. The class serving as the specification acts as an interface in that only its operations affect the relationship.

• Interfaces do participate in associations. An interface may not have an association that is navigable starting from the interface. An interface may be the target of an association, however, provided the association is navigable only toward the interface.

Notation

An interface is a classifier and may be shown using the rectangle symbol with the keyword «interface». A list of operations supported by the interface is placed in the operation compartment. Signals bearing the «signal» stereotype may also be included in the operation list, or they may be listed in their own compartment. The attribute compartment may be omitted because it is always empty.

An interface may also be displayed as a small circle with the name of the interface placed below the symbol. The circle may be attached by a solid line to classes (or to other elements) that support it. It may also be attached to higher-level containers, such as packages, that contain the classes. This indicates that the class provides all the operations in the interface type (and possibly more). The circle notation does not show the list of operations that the interface supports. Use the full rectangle symbol to show the list of operations. A class that uses or requires operations supplied by the interface may be attached to the circle by a dashed arrow pointing to the circle. The dashed arrow implies that the class requires the operations specified in the interface for some purpose, but the client class is not required to use *all* the interface operations. A service is usually specified by a sufficiency test. If a supplier provides the operations contained in a set of interfaces, then it satisfies the requirements of the clients.

The realization relationship is shown by a dashed line with a solid triangular arrowhead (a "dashed generalization symbol") from a class to an interface it supports. This is the same notation used to indicate realization of a type by an implementation class. In fact, this symbol can be used between any two classifier symbols, indicating that the client (at the tail of the arrow) supports all the operations defined in the supplier (at the head of the arrow), but with no necessity to support any data structure of the supplier (attributes and associations).

Example

Figure 13-111 shows a simplified view of financial components that deal with prices of securities. The FinancialPlanner is a personal finance application that keeps track of investments, as well as personal expenses. It needs the ability to update securities prices. The MutualFundAnalyzer examines mutual funds in detail. It needs the ability to update the prices of the underlying securities, as well as the prices of the funds. The ability to update securities prices is shown by the interface UpdatePrices. There are two components that implement this interface, shown by the solid lines connecting them to the interface symbol. Component ManualPriceEntry allows a user to manually enter prices of selected securities. Component QuoteQuery retrieves security prices from a quote server using a modem or the Internet.

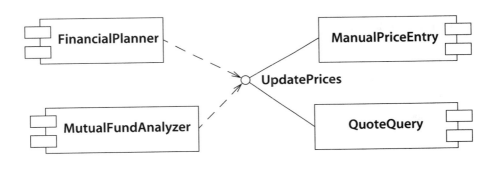

Figure 13-111. *Interface suppliers and clients*

Figure 13-112 shows the full notation for an interface as a keyword on a class symbol. We see that this interface involves two operations—asking the price of a security and getting a value; and submitting a list of securities and receiving a list of prices that have changed. In this diagram the QuoteQuery component is connected to the interface using a realization arrow, but it is the same relationship shown in the previous diagram, just a more explicit notation.

This diagram also shows a new interface, PeriodicUpdatePrices, which is a child of the original interface. It inherits the two operations and adds a third operation that submits a request for a periodic, automatic update of prices. This interface is realized by the component QuoteServer, a subscription service. It implements the same two operations as QuoteQuery but in a different way. It does not share the implementation of QuoteQuery (in this example) and therefore does not inherit implementation from it.

Figure 13-112 shows the difference between interface inheritance and full inheritance. The latter implies the former, but a child interface may be implemented in

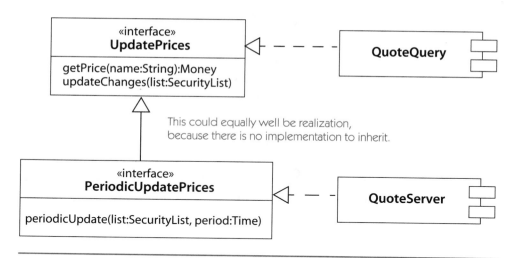

Figure 13-112. *Full interface notation*

```
┌─────────────────────────┐
│      «interface»        │
│      DoorOpener         │
├─────────────────────────┤
│         signals         │
│  close                  │
│  open                   │
│  stop                   │
└─────────────────────────┘
```

Figure 13-113. *Interface with signals*

a different way than the parent interface. **QuoteServer** supports the interface that **QuoteQuery** implements, namely **UpdatePrices**, but it does not inherit the implementation of **QuoteQuery**. (In general, it is convenient to inherit implementation, as well as interface, so the two hierarchies are often identical.)

An interface may also contain a list of the signals it handles (Figure 13-113).

Interfaces are used to define the behavior of classes, as well as components, without restricting the implementation. This permits distinguishing interface inheritance, as declared in Java, from implementation inheritance.

interface inheritance

The inheritance of the interface of a parent element but not its implementation or data structure. The intention to support an interface without a commitment to implementation is modeled using realization.

Note that in UML, generalization implies inheritance of *both* interface and implementation. To inherit just the implementation without the interface, use private inheritance.

See also implementation inheritance, inheritance, private inheritance, realization.

interface specifier

A specification of the behavior required of an associated class to satisfy the intent of the association. It consists of a reference to an interface, class, or other classifier that specifies the required behavior.

See also association role, rolename, type.

Semantics

In many cases, an associated class may have more functionality than needed to support a particular association. For example, the class may participate in other associations, and its overall behavior is the behavior needed to support all of them together. It may be desirable to specify more precisely the functionality needed from a class to support an association. An interface specifier is a classifier attached to an association end that indicates the functionality needed to support the association, without regard for uses of the target class by other associations.

An interface specifier is not required. In many or even most cases, a class participating in an association has just the functionality required and nothing more need be said. If an interface specifier is omitted, the association may be used to obtain full access to the functionality of the associated class.

The specifier can be a set of classifiers, each of which states behavior the target class must support. The target class must support all of them but may do more than is required by the specifiers.

Notation

An interface specifier is shown by the syntax

rolename : iname$_{list,}$

in place of a plain rolename, where **iname** is the name of an interface or other classifier. If there is more than one specifier, their names are given as a comma-separated list.

Example

In Figure 13-114, class **Server** stores requests in an **Array** class. For this purpose, however, it requires only the functionality of a **Queue** class. It doesn't make random access to the information, for example. The actual class **Array** satisfies the

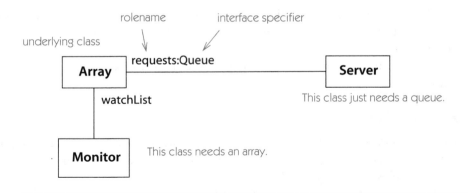

Figure 13-114. *Interface specifier*

needs of the interface specifier Queue—an array includes the functionality of a queue. The Monitor, however, has an Array that it uses to display the status of requests. The Monitor uses the full functionality of an Array.

Discussion

The use of a rolename and an interface specifier are equivalent to creating a small collaboration that includes just an association role and two classifier roles, the structure of which is defined by the rolename and role classifier on the original association. The original association and classes are therefore a use of the collaboration. The original class must be compatible with the interface specifier (which can be an interface or a type).

internal transition

A transition attached to a state that has an action but does not involve a change of state.
See also state machine.

Semantics

An internal transition allows an event to cause an action without a change of state. An internal transition has a source state but no target state. If it fires, its action is executed but the state does not change, even if the internal transition is attached to and inherited from an enclosing state of the current state. Therefore, no entry action or exit action are executed. In this respect, it differs from a self-transition, which causes the exit of nested states and the execution of exit and entry actions.

Notation

An internal transition is shown as a text entry within the internal transition compartment of a state. The entry has the same syntax as the text label for an external transition. Because there is no target state, there is no need to attach it to an arrow.

event-name / action-expression

The event names **entry**, **exit**, **do**, and **include** are reserved words and may not be used as event names. These reserved words are used to declare an entry action, an exit action, the execution of an activity, or the execution of a submachine, respectively. For uniformity, these special actions use internal transition syntax to specify the action. They are not internal transitions, however, and the reserved words are not event names.

Figure 13-115 shows the notation.

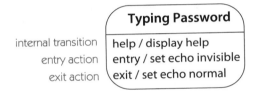

Figure 13-115. *Internal transition syntax*

Discussion

An internal transition may be thought of as an "interrupt" that causes an action but does not affect the current state, and therefore does not invoke exit or entry actions. Attaching an internal transition to a composite state is a good way to model an action that must occur over a number of states but must not change the active state—for example, displaying a help message or counting the number of occurrences of an event. It is not the right way to model an abort or an exception. These should be modeled by transitions to a new state, as their occurrence invalidates the current state.

invariant

A constraint that must be true at all times (or, at least, at all times when no operation is incomplete).

Semantics

An invariant is a Boolean expression that must be true at all times that no operation is active. It is an assertion, not an executable statement. Depending on the exact form of the expression, it might or might not be possible to verify it automatically in advance.

See also precondition, postcondition.

Structure

An invariant is modeled as a constraint with the stereotype «invariant» attached to an element.

Notation

A postcondition can be shown in a note with the keyword «invariant». The note is attached to a classifier, attribute, or other element.

iteration expression

An expression that yields a set of iteration cases. Each iteration case specifies an execution of an action within an iteration. An iteration case may include the assignment of values to an iteration variable. The action is performed once for each iteration case.

See also message.

Semantics

The iteration expression represents conditional or iterative execution. It represents the execution of zero or more messages depending on the conditions involved. The choices are

* [iteration-clause]	An iteration
[condition-clause]	A branch

An iteration represents a sequence of messages. The iteration-clause shows the details of the iteration variable and test, but it may be omitted (in which case the iteration conditions are unspecified). The iteration-clause is meant to be expressed in pseudocode or an actual programming language. UML does not prescribe its format. An example would be

*[i := 1..n]

A condition represents a message whose execution is contingent on the truth of the condition-clause. The condition-clause is meant to be expressed in pseudocode or an actual programming language. UML does not prescribe its format. An example would be

[x > y]

Note that a branch is notated the same as an iteration without a star. You can think of it as an iteration restricted to a single occurrence.

The iteration notation assumes that the messages in the iteration will be executed sequentially. There is also the possibility of executing them concurrently. That notation is a star followed by a double vertical line, for parallelism (*||). For example,

*[i:=1..n]|| q[i].calculateScore ()

Note that in a nested control structure, the iteration expression is not repeated at inner levels of the sequence number. Each level of structure specifies its own iteration within its enclosing context.

iterative development

The development of a system by a process broken into a series of steps, or iterations, each of which provides a better approximation to the desired system than the previous iteration. The result of each step must be an executable system that can be executed, tested, and debugged. Iterative development is closely allied with the concept of incremental development. In iterative incremental development, each iteration adds incremental functionality to the previous iteration. The order of adding functionality is chosen to balance the size of the iterations and to attack potential sources of risk early, before the cost of fixing problems is large.

See development process.

join

A place in a state machine, activity diagram, or sequence diagram at which two or more concurrent threads or states combine to yield one thread or state; an and-join or "unfork." Antonym: fork.

See complex transition, composite state.

Semantics

A join is a transition with two or more source states and one target state. If all the source states are active and the trigger event occurs, the transition action is executed and the target state becomes active. The source states must be in different regions of a concurrent composite state.

Notation

A join is shown as a heavy bar with two or more incoming transition arrows and one outgoing transition arrow. It may have a transition label (guard condition, trigger event, and action). Figure 13-116 shows an explicit join from states in a concurrent composite state.

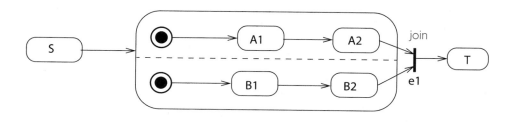

Figure 13-116. *Join*

Discussion

See merge.

junction state

A pseudostate that is part of a single overall transition in a state machine. It does not break a single run-to-completion step in the execution of a transition.
See also branch, merge.

Semantics

A transition in a state machine can cross several composite state boundaries from the source state to the target state. In executing such a transition, one or more entry actions or exit actions may be invoked. Sometimes, it is necessary to interleave one or more actions on the transition with the entry actions and exit actions attached to the nested states. This is not possible with a simple transition, which has a single action attached.

It is also convenient to allow several triggers to have a single outcome, or to allow a single trigger to have several possible outcomes with different guard conditions.

A junction state is a pseudostate that makes it possible to build a single overall transition from a series of transition fragments. A junction state may have one or more incoming transition segments and one or more outgoing transition segments. It may not have an internal activity, a submachine, or any outgoing transitions with event triggers. It is a dummy state to structure transitions and not a state that can be active for any finite time.

A junction state is used to structure a transition from several segments. Only the first segment in a chain of junction states may have an event trigger, but all of them may have guard conditions. Subsequent segments must be triggerless. The effective guard condition is the conjunction of all the individual guard conditions. The transition does not fire unless the entire set of conditions is met. In other words, the state machine may not remain at the junction state.

If multiple transitions enter a single junction state, they may each have a different trigger or may be triggerless. Each path through a set of junction states represents a distinct transition.

An outgoing transition may have a guard condition. If there are multiple outgoing transitions, each must have a distinct guard condition. This is a branch.

An outgoing transition may have an action attached. (The junction state may have an internal action, but this is equivalent to attaching an action to the outgoing transition, which is the preferred form.) The action is executed provided all guard conditions are satisfied, even those found in subsequent segments. A transition may not "partially fire" so that it stops at a junction state. It must reach a normal state.

When an incoming transition fires, the outgoing transition will fire immediately. Any attached action is then executed. The execution of the incoming transition and the outgoing transition are part of a single atomic step (a run-to-completion step)—that is, they are not interruptible by an event or other actions.

Notation

A junction state is shown in a state machine as a small circle. It has no name. It may have incoming and outgoing transition arrows.

Example

Figure 13-117 shows two complete transitions from state S to state T—a single-segment transition triggered by event f, and a multisegment transition triggered by event e, which is structured using two junction states. The annotations show the interleaving of the transition actions with the exit and entry actions.

Note that the placement of the action label on the transition line has no significance. If action d had been placed inside state X, it would nevertheless be executed after state X is exited and before state Y is entered. Therefore, it should be drawn at the outermost location along the transition.

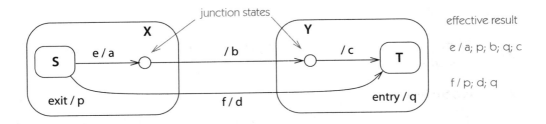

Figure 13-117. *Junction states*

For other examples, see Figure 13-179 and Figure 13-184.

See also control icons for other shortcut symbols that may be included in state-chart diagrams and activity diagrams.

keyword

A keyword is a textual adornment that categorizes a model element that lacks its own distinct syntax.

See also graphic marker, stereotype.

Notation

Keywords are used for built-in model elements that lack a unique notation, as well as for user-definable stereotypes. The general notation for the use of a keyword is to enclose it in guillemets (« »).

«keyword»

When the keyword is part of an area symbol, such as a class rectangle, the keyword is placed within the symbol boundary.

Some predefined keywords are described in the text of this document and are treated as reserved words in the notation. Other names are available for users to employ as stereotype names. The use of a stereotype name that matches a predefined keyword is not allowed.

Discussion

The number of easily distinguishable visual symbols is limited. The UML notation therefore makes use of text keywords to distinguish variations on a common theme, including metamodel subclasses of a base class, stereotypes of a metamodel base class, and groups of list elements. From the user's perspective, the metamodel distinction between metamodel subclasses and stereotypes is often unimportant, although it is, of course, important to tool builders and others who implement the metamodel.

label

A term for a use of a string on a diagram. It is purely a notational term.

See also diagram.

Notation

A label is a graphic string that is logically attached to another symbol on a diagram. Visually, the attachment is usually a matter of containing the string in a closed region or placing the string near the symbol. For some symbols the string is placed in a definite position (such as below a line), but for most symbols, the string must be "near" a line or icon. An editing tool can maintain an explicit internal graphic linkage between a label and a graphic symbol so that the label remains logically connected to the symbol even if they become separated visually. But the final appearance of the diagram is a matter of aesthetic judgment and should be made so that there is no confusion about which symbol a label is attached to. Although the attachment may not be obvious from a visual inspection of a diagram, the attachment is clear and unambiguous at the graphic structure level (and therefore poses no ambiguity in the semantic mapping). A tool may visually show the attachment of a label to another symbol using various aids (such as a colored line or flashing of matched elements) as a convenience.

language type

An anonymous data type defined in the syntax of a programming language.
See also data type.

Semantics

A language type is an expression to be interpreted as a programming-language data type. It may be used as the type of an attribute, variable, or parameter. It does not have a name and does not declare a new data type.

For example, the C++ data type "**Person* (*)(Contract*, int)**" could be defined as a C++ language type.

The intent of a language type is implementation in a programming language. Associations should be used for more logical relationships.

layer

An architectural pattern of grouping packages in a model at the same level of abstraction. Each layer represents a virtual world at some level of reality.

leaf

A generalizable element that has no children in the generalization hierarchy. It must be concrete (fully implemented) to be of any use.
See also abstract, concrete.

Semantics

The leaf property declares that an element *must* be a leaf. The model is ill formed if it declares a child of such an element. The purpose is to guarantee that a class cannot be modified, for example, because the behavior of the class must be well established for reliability. The leaf declaration also permits separate compilation of parts of a system by ensuring that methods cannot be overridden and facilitating inlining of method code. An element for which the property is false may indeed *be* a leaf but might have children in the future if the model is modified. Being a leaf or being constrained to be a leaf are not fundamental semantic properties.

lifeline

A dashed line in a sequence diagram that shows the existence of an object over a period of time. The line is parallel to the time axis.

See also sequence diagram.

Semantics

The lifeline indicates the period during which an object exists. An object is active if it owns a thread of control—that is, if it is the root of the thread. A passive object is temporarily active during the time when it has a thread of control passing through it—that is, during the period of time during which it has a procedure call outstanding. The latter is called an activation. It includes the time during which a procedure is calling a lower-level procedure.

Notation

An object or a classifier role is shown on a sequence diagram as a vertical dashed line, called the lifeline. The lifeline represents the existence of the object at a particular time.

Arrows between lifelines indicate messages between objects. An arrow with its head on a lifeline is a message received by the object, an operation that it has responsibility for; an arrow with its tail on a lifeline is a message sent by the object, an operation that it invokes. The geometric order of the message arrows along the lifeline indicates the relative time order of the messages.

If the object is created or destroyed during the period of time shown on the diagram, then its lifeline starts or stops at the appropriate point. Otherwise, it goes from the top to the bottom of the diagram. An object symbol is drawn at the head of the lifeline. If the object is created during the time shown on the diagram, then the object symbol is drawn at the head of the message that creates it. Otherwise, the object symbol is drawn above any message arrows. If the object is destroyed during the diagram, then its destruction is marked by a large X, either at the arrowhead of the message that causes the destruction or (in the case of self-destruction) at the final return message from the destroyed object. An object that exists when the transaction starts is shown at the top of the diagram (above the first arrow). An object that exists when the transaction finishes has its lifeline continue beyond the final arrow.

The lifeline may split into two or more concurrent lifelines to show conditionality. Each track corresponds to a conditional branch in the message flow. The lifelines may join at some subsequent point. See Figure 13-162 for an example. This notation can be confusing and should be used sparingly.

The period of time during which an object is permanently or temporarily active is shown by a solid double line that hides the lifeline. A second double line is overlaid to show recursion. *See* activation for more details. Because an active object is always active, the double line is sometimes omitted because it adds no information.

A lifeline may be interrupted by a state symbol to show a change of state. This corresponds to a become transition within a collaboration diagram. An arrow may be drawn to the state symbol to indicate the message that caused the change of state. See Figure 13-163 for an example.

link

A tuple of object references that is an instance of an association or an association role.

Semantics

A link is an individual connection among two or more objects. It is a tuple (ordered list) of object references. It is an instance of an association. The objects must be direct or indirect instances of the classes at corresponding positions in the association. An association may not contain duplicate links from the same association—that is, two identical tuples of object references.

A link that is an instance of an association class may have a list of attribute values in addition to the tuple of object references. Duplicate links with the same tuple object references are not permitted, even if their attribute values are distinct. The identity of a link comes from its tuple of object references, which must be unique.

A link may be used for navigation. In other words, an object appearing in one position in a link may obtain the set of objects appearing in another position. It may then send them messages (called "sending a message across an association"). This process is efficient if the association has the navigability property in the target direction. Access may or may not be possible if the association is nonnavigable, but it will probably be inefficient. Navigability in opposite directions is specified independently.

Within a collaboration, an association role is a contextual, often transient, relationship between classifiers. An instance of an association role is also a link, but typically one whose life is limited to the duration of the collaboration.

Notation

A binary link is shown as a path between two objects—that is, one or more connected line segments or arcs. In the case of a reflexive association, the path is a loop, with both ends on a single object.

See association for details of paths.

A rolename may be shown at each end of the link. An association name may be shown near the path. If present, the name is underlined to indicate an instance. Links do not have instance names. They take their identity from the objects they relate. Multiplicity is *not* shown for links because instances do not have multiplicity; multiplicity is a property of the descriptor that limits how many instances can exist. Other association adornments (aggregation, composition, and navigation) may be shown on the link roles.

A qualifier may be shown on a link. The value of the qualifier may be shown in its box. Figure 13-118 shows both ordinary and qualified links.

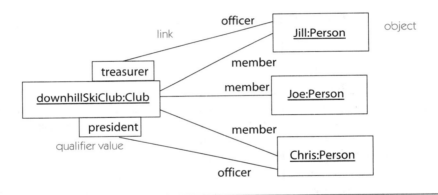

Figure 13-118. *Links*

Other adornments on links can show properties of their associations, including directionality of navigation, aggregation or composition, implementation stereotypes, and visibility.

N-*ary link*. An *n*-ary link is shown as a diamond with a path to each participating object. The other adornments on the association and the adornments on the roles have the same possibilities as the binary link.

Discussion

How should a dependency be shown on an object diagram? In general, a dependency represents a relationship among classes, not among objects and belongs on a class diagram, not an object diagram. What about procedure arguments, local variables of procedures, and the caller of an operation? These must exist as actual data structures, not simply dependencies. Therefore, they can be shown as links. The caller of a procedure requires a reference to the target object—this is a link. Some links may be instances of association roles in collaborations, such as most parameters and local variables. Remaining dependencies are relevant to the class itself and not its individual objects.

link end

An instance of an association end.

list

An ordered variable-length collection of model elements owned by and nested within another model element.

See also classifier, state.

Semantics

A classifier contains several lists of subordinate elements, including attributes, operations, and methods. A state contains a list of internal transitions. Other kinds of elements contain lists of other elements. Each kind of list is described individually. This article describes the properties of embedded lists, in general. In addition to lists of attributes and operations, optional lists can show other predefined or user-defined values, such as responsibilities, rules, or modification histories. UML does not define these optional lists. The manipulation of user-defined lists is tool-dependent.

An embedded list and the elements in the list belong exclusively to the containing class or other container element. Ownership is not shared among multiple containers. Other classes may be able to access the list elements—for example, by inheritance or association—but ownership of the contained lists for model editing belongs to the immediate container. Owned elements are stored, copied, and destroyed along with their containers.

The elements in a list have an order determined by the modeler. The order may be useful to the modeler—for example, it may be used by a code generator to generate a list of declarations in a programming language. If the modeler doesn't care about the order, maybe because the model is in the analysis stage or because the language ignores the ordering, then the order still exists in the model but can simply be ignored as irrelevant.

Notation

An embedded list appears within its own compartment as a list of strings, one string per line for each list element. Each string is the encoded representation of a feature, such as an attribute, operation, internal transition, and so on. The nature of the encoding is described in the article for each kind of element.

Ordering. The canonical order of the strings is the same as for the list elements within the model, but the internal ordering may be optionally overridden and the strings sorted according to some internal property, such as name, visibility, or stereotype. Note, however, that the items maintain their original order in the underlying model. The ordering information is merely suppressed in the view.

Ellipsis. An ellipsis (. . .) as the final element of a list or the final element of a delimited section of a list indicates that there are additional elements in the model that meet the selection criteria but are not shown in that list. In a different view of the list, such elements may appear.

Stereotype. A stereotype may be applied to a list element. A stereotype keyword enclosed in guillemets (« ») precedes the element string.

Property string. A property string may specify a list of properties of an element. A comma-separated list of properties or constraints, all enclosed in braces ({ }), follows the element.

Group properties. Stereotypes and other properties may also be applied to groups of list elements. If a stereotype, keyword, property string, or constraint appears on a line by itself, then the line does not represent a list element. Instead, the restrictions apply to each successive list element as if they had been placed directly on each line. This default applies until another group property line occurs in the list. All group properties can be cancelled by inserting a line with an empty keyword («»), but it is generally clearer to place all entries that are not subject to group properties at the head of the list. Figure 13-119 shows the application of stereotypes to multiple list elements

Note that group properties are merely a notational convenience and that each model element has its own distinct value for each property.

Compartment name. A compartment may display a name indicating which kind of compartment it is. The name is displayed in a distinctive font (such as boldface in a smaller size) centered at the top of the compartment. This capability is useful if some compartments are omitted or if additional user-defined compartments are added. For a class, the predefined compartments are named **attributes** and **operations**. An example of a user-defined compartment might be **requirements**. The name compartment in a class must always be present and therefore does not require or permit a compartment name. Figure 13-119 and Figure 13-120 show named compartments.

Presentation options

Ordering. A tool may present the list elements in a sorted order. In that case, the inherent ordering of the elements is not visible. A sort is based on some internal property and does not indicate additional model information. Typical sort rules include alphabetical order, ordering by stereotype (such as constructors, destruc-

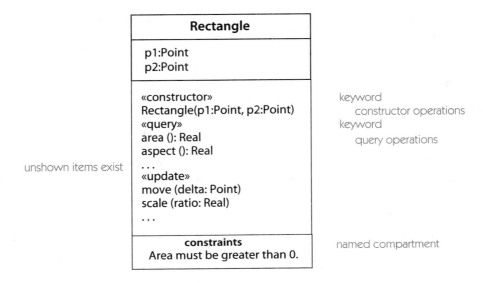

Figure to the right of the Rectangle box contains labels:
keyword
   constructor operations
keyword
   query operations

named compartment

unshown items exist

Rectangle box:

Rectangle

p1:Point
p2:Point

«constructor»
Rectangle(p1:Point, p2:Point)
«query»
area (): Real
aspect (): Real
. . .
«update»
move (delta: Point)
scale (ratio: Real)
. . .

constraints
Area must be greater than 0.

Figure 13-119. *Stereotype keyword applied to groups of list elements*

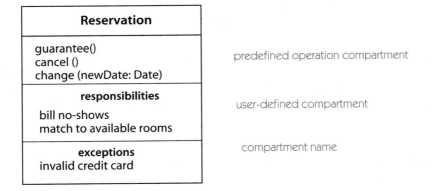

Reservation box:

Reservation

guarantee()
cancel ()
change (newDate: Date)

responsibilities
bill no-shows
match to available rooms

exceptions
invalid credit card

Labels to the right:
predefined operation compartment

user-defined compartment

compartment name

Figure 13-120. *Compartments with names*

tors, then ordinary methods), ordering by visibility (public, then protected, then private), and so on.

Filtering. The elements in the list may be filtered according to some selection rule. The specification of selection rules is a tool responsibility. If a filtered list shows no elements, there are no elements that meet the filter criterion, but the original list may or may not contain other elements that do not meet the criterion and are therefore invisible. It is a tool responsibility whether and how to indicate the presence of either local or global filtering, although a stand-alone diagram should have some indication of such filtering if it is to be understandable.

If a compartment is suppressed, no inference can be drawn about the presence or absence of its elements. An empty compartment indicates that no elements meet the selection filter (if any).

Note that attributes may also be shown by composition (see Figure 13-71).

location

The physical placement of a run-time entity, such as an object or a component, within a distributed environment. In UML, location is discrete and the units of location are nodes.

See also component, node.

Semantics

The concept of location requires the concept of a space within which things can exist. UML does not model the full complexity of the three-dimensional universe. Instead, it supports a topological model of spaces connected by communications paths. A node is a computing resource at which a run-time entity can live. Nodes are connected by communications paths modeled as associations. The location of an entity is specified by referencing a node. Within a node, some entities live inside other nested entities. For example, an object lives inside a component or inside another object. The location of these entities is the containing entity.

An object or component instance may move to a new location. This may be modeled using the become relationship, which indicates that at some point the first entity is replaced by the second entity, which has a different location.

Notation

The location of an instance (including objects, component instances, and node instances) within another instance may be shown by physical nesting, as shown in Figure 13-121. Containment may also be shown by composition arrows. Alternately, an instance may have a property tag **location** the value of which is the name of the containing instance.

If an object moves during an interaction, it may appear as two or more versions with a **become** transition between the versions, as in Figure 13-121. The become arrow may have a sequence number attached to it to show the time when the object moves. Each object symbol represents a version of the object during a portion of the overall time. Messages must be connected to the correct version of the object (Figure 13-117).

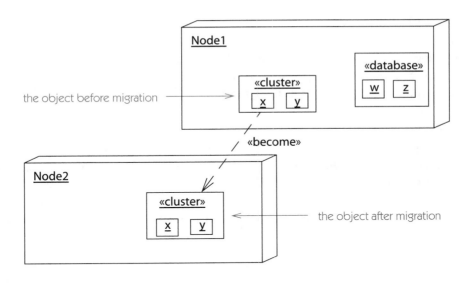

Figure 13-121. *Nodes and migration of objects*

many

An abbreviation for the multiplicity 0..*—that is, zero or more without limit. In other words, totally unrestricted in size.

See multiplicity.

member

Name for a named structural inheritable constituent of a classifier, either an attribute, operation, or method. Each classifier may have a list of zero or more of each kind of member. A list of members of a given kind is notated as a list of strings within a compartment of the classifier symbol.

See also list.

merge

A place in a state machine, activity diagram, or sequence diagram where two or more alternate control paths come together; an or-merge or "unbranch." Antonym: branch.

See also junction state.

Semantics

A merge is simply a situation in which two or more control paths come together. In a state machine, one state has more than one input transition. No special model construct is required or provided to indicate a merge. It may be indicated by a junction state if it is part of a single run to completion path.

Notation

A merge may be indicated in a statechart diagram, activity diagram, or sequence diagram by a diamond with two or more input transitions and a single output transition. No conditions are necessary. Figure 13-122 shows an example.

A diamond is also used for a branch (the inverse of a merge), but a branch is clearly distinguished because it has one input transition and multiple output transitions, each with its own guard condition.

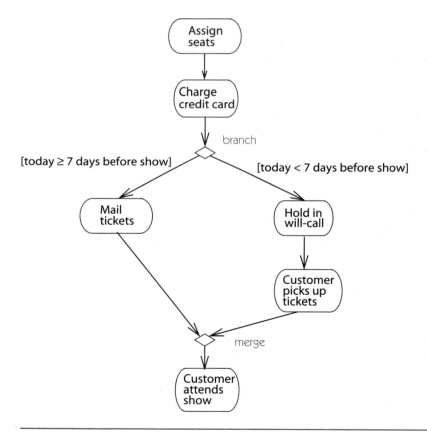

Figure 13-122. *Merge*

A combination branch and merge is legal but of limited usefulness. It would have multiple input transitions and multiple, labeled output transitions.

Note that a merge is merely a notational convenience and can be omitted without loss of information. A branch and merge are usually paired in a nested fashion.

Discussion

Be sure to distinguish merge and join. Merge combines two or more alternate paths of control. In any execution, only one path will be taken at a time. No synchronization is necessary.

Join combines two or more concurrent paths of control. In any execution, all the paths will be taken, and the join will fire only when all of them have reached the source states of the join.

message

The conveyance of information from one object (or other instance) to another, with the expectation that activity will ensue. A message may be a signal or the call of an operation. The receipt of a message instance is normally considered an instance of an event.

See also call, collaboration, interaction, operation, send, signal.

Semantics

A message is the sending of a signal from one object (the *sender*) to one or more other objects (the *receivers*), or it is the call of an operation on one object (the *receiver*) by another object (the *sender* or *caller*). The implementation of a message may take various forms, such as a procedure call, interprocess communication between active threads, explicit raising of events, and so on. At a logical level, sending a signal and calling an operation are similar. They both involve a communication from a sender to a receiver that passes information by value that the receiver uses to determine what to do. A call can be considered a pattern of signals that involves a send with an implicit return pointer argument that is later used to send a return signal to the caller. A call can be modeled as two messages, a call message and a later return message. At an implementation level, signals and calls have different properties and detailed behavior, so they are distinguished as UML elements.

The receipt of a signal may trigger a state machine transition for the receiver. A call may be handled in two possible ways at the choice of the receiver (the choice must be made in the model for the receiver). An operation may be implemented as a procedure body (method) that is invoked when a call arrives. When execution of the procedure is complete, then the caller resumes control, with an optional return value. Alternately, for an active object, a call of an operation may cause a call event, which triggers a state machine transition. In this case there is no method body, instead transition can have actions. The transition can also supply a return value for the caller. When the transition is complete, or immediately if the call event does not trigger a transition, the caller resumes control.

A message includes an expression for a set of target objects. The message is sent to each object in the set. Unless specified otherwise (by a constraint), the messages are sent concurrently to all the objects in the set. This means that the execution order is completely arbitrary and could be parallel. If messages must be sent in a particular order, they should be sent within a loop. In case of a call, the caller regains control when all the calls have completed.

The time a message is sent or received may be represented by an expression on the message name.

See timing mark.

Structure

A message has a sender, a receiver, and an action.

Within an interaction, the sender is the classifier role that sends the message. The receiver is the classifier role that receives the message. The action is a call; a signal; a local operation on the sender; or a primitive action, such as a create or destroy. The action includes a list of arguments, an expression for a set of receivers, and a reference to the operation or signal involved. It may also include a specification of conditionality and iteration of the message execution.

Within an interaction, messages are related by the predecessor-successor relationship and the caller-called relationship. The latter relationship is applicable to procedural methods. Each call adds a level of nesting to the sequence. Within a call, messages are ordered sequentially, with the possibility of concurrent subsequences.

The predecessor-successor (sequencing) relationship organizes the messages of a thread into a linear sequence. A message can have multiple predecessors or successors. If two messages have a common predecessor and are not otherwise sequenced, then they may be executed concurrently. If a message has multiple predecessors, it must wait until all of them complete. Such a message is a synchronization point.

The caller-called (activator) relationship defines nested procedure structure. The message that calls a procedure (using a call action) is the activator of all of the messages that make up the body of the called procedure. Among themselves the called messages have a predecessor-successor relationship to establish their relative order (which may permit concurrency).

If a message is a call, then the caller is blocked until the called procedure completes and returns. If the receiver handles the operation as a call event, however, the return occurs when the initial transition completes, after which the caller resumes control and the receiver can continue its own execution.

The sequencing and activator relationships relate messages within the same interaction only.

Notation

The notation for sequence diagrams and collaboration diagrams is different.

Sequence diagrams

On a sequence diagram, a message is shown as a solid arrow from the lifeline of one object (the sender) to the lifeline of another object (the target). If the arrow is perpendicular to the lifelines, the message transmission is regarded as instantaneous or at least fast, compared with external messages. If the arrow is slanted, then the message transmission is regarded as having duration, during which other messages might be sent. In case of a message from an object to itself, the arrow may start and finish on the same lifeline. The message arrows are arranged in sequential order from top to bottom, vertically. If two messages are concurrent, their relative order is not significant. Messages may have sequence numbers, but because the relative order of messages in shown visually, the sequence numbers are often omitted.

Transmission delay. Usually message arrows are drawn horizontally, indicating the duration required to send the message is atomic—that is, it is brief compared with the granularity of the interaction and that nothing else can "happen" during the message transmission. This is the correct assumption within many computers. If the message requires some time to deliver, during which something else can occur (such as a message in the opposite direction), then the message arrow may be slanted downward so that the arrowhead is below the arrow tail.

Branching. A branch is shown by multiple arrows leaving a single point, each labeled by a guard condition. Depending on whether the guard conditions are mutually exclusive, the construct may represent conditionality or concurrency.

Iteration. A connected set of messages may be enclosed and marked as an iteration. An iteration marker indicates that the set of messages can occur multiple times. For a procedure, the continuation condition for the iteration may be specified at the bottom of the iteration. If there is concurrency, then some messages in the diagram may be part of the iteration and others may be singly executed.

Collaboration diagrams

On a collaboration diagram, a message is shown as a small labeled arrow attached to a path between the sender and the receiver objects. The path is the one used to access the target object. The arrow points along the path in the direction of the target object. In the case of a message from an object to itself, the message appears on a path looping back to the same object and the target end has the keyword «self».

More than one message may be attached to one link, in the same or different directions. The relative order of messages is shown by the sequence number portion of the message label.

Both diagrams

The message arrow is labeled with the name of the message (operation or signal name) and its argument values. The arrow may also be labeled with a sequence number to show the sequence of the message in the overall interaction. Sequence numbers may be omitted in sequence diagrams, in which the physical location of the arrow shows the relative sequence, but they are necessary in collaboration diagrams. Sequence numbers are useful on both kinds of diagrams for identifying concurrent threads of control. A message may also be labeled with a guard condition.

Control flow type. The following arrowhead variations may be used to show various kinds of message control flow.

Filled solid arrowhead

> Procedure call or other nested flow of control. The entire nested sequence is completed before the outer-level sequence resumes. May be used with ordinary procedure calls. May also be used with concurrently active objects when one of them sends a signal and waits for a nested sequence of behavior to complete.

Stick arrowhead

> Flat flow of control. Each arrow shows the progression to the next step in sequence. In the case of nested procedures, this corresponds to a bottom-across scan of the leaves of the tree of actions.

Half stick arrowhead

> Asynchronous flow of control. Used instead of the stick arrowhead to show explicitly an asynchronous message between two objects in a procedural sequence.

Dashed arrow with stick arrowhead

> Return from a procedure call. The return arrow may be suppressed as it is implicit at the end of an activation.

Other variations

> Other kinds of control may be shown, such as "balking" or "time-out," but these are treated as extensions to the UML core.

Message label. The label has the following syntax:

predecessor$_{opt}$ guard-condition$_{opt}$ sequence-expression$_{opt}$

return-value-list :=$_{opt}$ message-name (argument$_{list,}$)

The label indicates the message sent, its arguments and return values, and the sequencing of the message within the larger interaction, including call nesting, iteration, branching, concurrency, and synchronization.

Predecessor. In a collaboration, the predecessor is a comma-separated list of sequence numbers followed by a slash (/).

sequence-number$_{list,}$ /

The clause is omitted if the list is empty.

Each sequence-number is a sequence-expression without any recurrence terms. It must match the sequence-number of another message.

The meaning is that the message flow is not enabled until all the message flows whose sequence numbers are listed have occurred (a thread can go beyond the required message flow and the guard remains satisfied). Therefore, the guard condition represents a synchronization of threads.

Note that the message corresponding to the numerically preceding sequence number is an implicit predecessor and need not be explicitly listed. All the sequence numbers with the same prefix form a sequence. The numerical predecessor is the one in which the final term is one less. That is, number 3.1.4.5 is the predecessor of 3.1.4.6.

In a sequence diagram the visual ordering determines the sequencing, and a synchronization is shown by the presence of multiple messages to the same object before the object sends any messages of its own.

Sequence expression. The sequence-expression is a dot-separated list of sequence-terms followed by a colon (':'). Each term represents a level of procedural nesting within the overall interaction. If all the control is concurrent, then nesting does not occur. Each sequence-term has the following syntax.

label recurrence$_{opt}$

where label is

integer

or

name

The integer represents the sequential order of the message within the next higher level of procedural calling. Messages that differ in one integer term are sequentially related at that level of nesting. An example is: Message 3.1.4 follows message 3.1.3 within activation 3.1.

The name represents a concurrent thread of control. Messages that differ in the final name are concurrent at that level of nesting. An example is: Message 3.1a and message 3.1b are concurrent within activation 3.1. All threads of control are equal within the nesting depth.

The recurrence represents conditional or iterative execution. This represents zero or more messages that are executed, depending on the conditions. The choices are

* [iteration-clause]	an iteration
[condition-clause]	a branch

An iteration represents a sequence of messages at the given nesting depth. The iteration-clause may be omitted (in which case, the iteration conditions are unspecified). The iteration-clause is meant to be expressed in pseudocode or an actual programming language; UML does not prescribe its format. An example would be: *[i := 1..n].

A condition represents a message whose execution is contingent on the truth of the condition clause. The condition-clause is meant to be expressed in pseudocode or an actual programming language; UML does not prescribe its format. An example would be: [x > y].

Note that a branch is notated the same as an iteration without a star. One might think of it as an iteration restricted to a single occurrence.

The iteration notation assumes that the messages in the iteration will be executed sequentially. There is also the possibility of executing them concurrently. The notation for this is to follow the star with a double vertical line, for parallelism (*||).

Note that in a nested control structure, the recurrence is not repeated at inner levels. Each level of structure specifies its own iteration within the enclosing context.

Signature. A signature is a string that indicates the name, arguments, and return value of an operation, message, or signal. These have the following properties.

return-value-list	A comma-separated list of names that designates the values returned by the message within the subsequent execution of the overall interaction. These identifiers can be used as arguments to subsequent messages. If the message does not return a value, then the return value and the assignment operator are omitted.
message-name	The name of the event raised in the target object (often the event of requesting an operation to be performed). It may be implemented in various ways, *one* of which is an operation call. If it is implemented as a procedure call,

then this is the name of the operation and the operation must be defined on the class of the receiver or inherited by it. In other cases, it may be the name of an event that is raised on the receiving object. In normal practice with procedural overloading, both the message name and the argument list types are required to identify an operation.

argument-list   A comma-separated list of arguments enclosed in parentheses. The parentheses can be used even if the list is empty. Each argument is an expression in pseudocode or an appropriate programming language (UML does not prescribe). The expressions may use return values of previous messages (in the same scope) and navigation expressions starting from the source object (that is, attributes of it and links from it and paths reachable from them).

Example

The following are samples of control message label syntax.

2: display (x, y)	Simple message
1.3.1: p:= find(specs)	Nested call with return value
[x < 0] 4: invert (x, color)	Conditional message
3.1*: update ( )	Iteration
A3,B4/ C2: copy(a,b)	Synchronization with other threads

Presentation options

Instead of text expressions for arguments and return values, data tokens may be shown near a message (Figure 13-123). A token is a small circle labeled with the argument expression or return value name. It has a small arrow on it that points along the message (for an argument) or opposite the message (for a return value). Tokens represent arguments and return values. The choice of text syntax or tokens is a presentation option, but text is more compact and is recommended for most purposes.

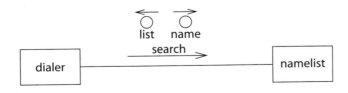

Figure 13-123. *Value flow tokens*

The syntax of messages may be expressed in the syntax of a programming language, such as C++ or Smalltalk. All the expressions on a single diagram should use the same syntax, however.

metaclass

A class whose instances are classes. Metaclasses are typically used to construct metamodels. A metaclass can be modeled as a stereotype of a class using the keyword «metaclass».
See also powertype.

meta-metamodel

A model that defines the language for expressing a metamodel. The relationship between a meta-metamodel and a metamodel is analogous to the relationship between a metamodel and a model. This level of indirection is usually relevant only to tool builders, database builders, and the like. UML is defined in terms of a meta-metamodel, called the Meta-Object Facility (MOF).

metamodel

A model that defines the language for expressing a model; an instance of a meta-metamodel. The UML metamodel defines the structure of UML models.

metaobject

A generic term for all entities in a metamodeling language. For example, metatypes, metaclasses, meta-attributes, and meta-associations.

metarelationship

A term grouping relationships that connect descriptors to their instances. These include the instance relationship and the powertype relationship.

method

The implementation of an operation. It specifies the algorithm or procedure that produces the results of an operation.
See also concrete, operation, realization.

Semantics

A method is an implementation of an operation. If an operation is not abstract, it must have a method or a call event, either defined on the class with the operation or inherited from an ancestor. A method is specified as a procedural expression, a linguistic string in a designated language (such as C++, Smalltalk, or a human language) that describes an algorithm. The language must be matched to the purpose, of course. A human language, for instance, may be adequate for early analysis but not suitable for code generation.

An operation declaration implies the presence of a method unless the operation is declared as abstract. In a generalization hierarchy, each repeated declaration of the operation implies a new method that overrides any inherited method of the same operation. Two declarations represent the same operation if their signatures match.

Note that a method is an executable procedure—an algorithm—not simply a specification of results. A before-and-after specification is not a method, for example. A method is a commitment to implementation and addresses issues of algorithm, computational complexity, and encapsulation.

In some respects, a method may have stricter properties than its operation. A method can be a query even though the operation is not declared as a query. But if the operation is a query, then the method must be a query. Similarly, a method may strengthen the concurrency property. A sequential operation may be implemented as a guarded or concurrent method. In these cases, the method is consistent with the declarations of its operation. It just strengthens the constraints.

Notation

The presence of a method is indicated by an operation declaration that lacks the abstract property (Figure 13-124). If the operation is inherited, the method can be shown by repeating the operation declaration in normal (nonitalic) text to show a concrete operation. The text of the method body may be shown as a note attached

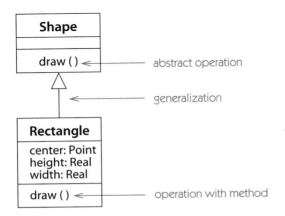

Figure 13-124. *Method on nonabstract operation*

to the operation list entry, but usually method bodies are not shown at all on diagrams. They remain hidden for a text editor to show on command.

model

A semantically complete abstraction of a system.

See also package, subsystem.

Semantics

A model is a more or less complete abstraction of a system from a particular viewpoint. It is complete in the sense that it fully describes the system or entity, at the chosen level of precision and viewpoint. Different models provide mostly independent viewpoints that can be manipulated separately.

A model may comprise a containment hierarchy of packages in which the top-level package corresponds to the entire system. The contents of a model are the transitive closure of its containment (ownership) relationships from top-level packages to model elements.

A model may also include relevant parts of the system's environment, represented, for example, by actors and their interfaces. In particular, the relationship of the environment to the system elements may be modeled. A system and its environment form a larger system at a higher level of scope. Therefore, it is possible to relate elements at various levels of detail in a smooth way.

Elements in different models do not directly affect each other, but they often represent the same concepts at different levels of detail or stages of development. Therefore, relationships among them, such as trace and refinement, are important to the development process itself and often capture important design decisions.

Notation

A model can be shown as a package with the stereotype «model». There is little notational detail to show about models, however. Tools can show lists of models, but models have few relationships among themselves. Most useful is the ability to traverse from a model name to its top package or to a map of its overall contents.

Discussion

No one view of a system, or indeed no system itself, is ever complete in and of itself. There are always connections to the wider world, and a model always falls short of reality. Therefore, the concept of a closed model is always an approximation in which arbitrary lines must be drawn for practical work.

A UML model is represented as a package hierarchy that emphasizes one view of a system. Each model may have its own leveling hierarchy that may be similar or different to the leveling hierarchy of other views of the system.

model element

An element that is an abstraction drawn from the system being modeled. Contrast with presentation element, which is a (generally visual) presentation of one or more modeling elements for human interaction.

Semantics

All elements that have semantics are model elements, including real-world concepts and computer-system implementation concepts. Graphic elements whose purpose is to visualize a model are presentation elements. They are not model elements, as they do not add semantics to the model.

Model elements may have names, but the use and constraints on names vary by kind of model element and are discussed with each kind. Each model element belongs to a namespace appropriate to the kind of element. All model elements may have the following attached properties.

tagged value	Zero or more tag-value pairs may be attached to any model element or presentation element. The tag is a name that identifies the meaning of the value. The tags are not fixed in UML but can be extended to denote various kinds of information meaningful to the modeler or to an editing tool.
constraint	Zero or more constraints may be attached to a model element. Constraints are restrictions that are expressed as linguistic strings in a constraint language.
stereotype	Zero or one stereotype name may be attached to a model element, provided the stereotype is applicable to the base model element. The stereotype does not alter the structure of the base class, but it may add constraints and tagged values that apply to the model elements bearing the stereotype.

In addition, model elements may participate in dependency relationships.

See Chapter 14, Standard Elements, for a list of predefined tags, constraints, and stereotypes.

model management view

That aspect of a model dealing with the organization of the model itself into structured parts—namely, packages, subsystems, and models. The model management view is sometimes considered to be a part of the static view and is often combined with the static view on class diagrams.

modeling time

Refers to something that occurs during a modeling activity of the software development process. It includes analysis and design. Usage note: When discussing object systems, it is often important to distinguish between modeling-time and run-time concerns.

See also development process, stages of modeling.

module

A software unit of storage and manipulation. Modules include source code modules, binary code modules, and executable code modules. The word does not correspond to a single UML construct, but rather includes several constructs.

See component, package, subsystem.

multiobject

A classifier role that denotes a set of objects rather than a single object.

See also classifier role, collaboration, message.

Semantics

A multiobject is a classifier role that denotes a set of objects, usually the set of objects on the *many* side of an association. A multiobject is used within a collaboration to show operations that address the entire set of objects as a unit rather than a single object in it. For example, an operation to find an object within a set operates on the entire set, not on an individual object. The underlying static model is unaffected by this grouping.

Notation

A multiobject is shown as two rectangles in which the top rectangle is shifted slightly vertically and horizontally to suggest a stack of rectangles (Figure 13-125). A message arrow to the multiobject symbol indicates a message to the set of objects—for example, a selection operation to find an individual object.

To perform an operation on each object in a set of associated objects requires two messages: an iteration to the multiobject to extract links to the individual objects, then a message sent to each object using the (temporary) link. This may be elided on a diagram by combining the messages into one that includes an iteration and an application to each object. The target rolename takes a *many* indicator (*) to show that many links are implied. Although this may be written as a single message, in the underlying model (and in any actual code), it requires the two layers of structure (iteration to find links, message using each link) mentioned previously.

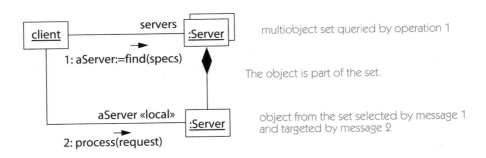

Figure 13-125. *Multiobject*

An object from the set is shown as a normal object symbol, but it may be attached to the multiobject symbol using a composition link to indicate that it is part of the set. A message arrow to the simple object symbol indicates a message to an individual object.

Typically, a selection message to a multiobject returns a reference to an individual object, to which the original sender then sends a message.

multiple classification

A semantic variation of generalization in which an object may belong directly to more than one class.

Semantics

This is a semantic variation point under which an object may be a direct instance of more than one class. When used with dynamic classification, objects may acquire and lose classes during run time. This allows classes to be used to represent temporary roles an object may play.

Although multiple classification matches logic and everyday discourse well, it complicates implementation of a programming language and is not supported by the popular programming languages.

multiple inheritance

A semantic variation point of generalization in which an element may have more than one parent. This is the default assumption within UML and is necessary for proper modeling of many situations, although modelers may choose to restrict its use for certain kinds of elements. Contrast: single inheritance.

multiplicity

A specification of the range of allowable cardinality values—the size—that a set may assume. Multiplicity specifications may be given for association ends, parts within composite classes, repetitions of messages, and other purposes. Essentially, a multiplicity is a (possibly infinite) subset of the nonnegative integers. Contrast: cardinality.

See also multiplicity (of association), multiplicity (of class).

Semantics

Multiplicity is a constraint on the cardinality (size) of a set. In principle, it is a subset of the nonnegative integers. In practice, it is usually a finite set of integer intervals, most often a single interval with a minimum and a maximum value. Any set must be finite, but the upper bound can be finite or unbounded (an unbounded multiplicity is called "many"). The upper bound must be greater than zero; or, at any rate, a multiplicity comprising only zero is not very useful, as it permits only the empty set. Multiplicity is coded as a string.

In most cases, a multiplicity may be specified as an integer range—a minimum and a maximum cardinality—but in general, it may be a discontinuous subset of the nonnegative integers. The set of integers may be infinite—that is, the upper bound may be unlimited (but note that any particular cardinality in the set is finite).

For most practical purposes, this set of integers can be specified as a finite list of disjoint, disconnected integer intervals. An interval is a set of contiguous integers characterized by its minimum and maximum values. Some infinite sets cannot be specified this way—for example, the set of even integers—but usually little is lost by simply including the gaps. For most design purposes, in fact, a single interval with a minimum and maximum value suffices for the entire multiplicity specification, because a major purpose of the multiplicity is to bound the amount of storage that might be needed.

See multiplicity (of association) and multiplicity (of class) for specific details of using multiplicity with these elements.

Notation

Multiplicity is specified by a text expression consisting of a comma-separated list of integer intervals, each in the form

minimum..maximum

where minimum and maximum are integers, or maximum can be a "*" which indicates an unbounded upper limit. An expression such as **2..*** is read "2 or more."

An interval can also have the form

number

where number is an integer representing an interval of a single size.

The multiplicity expression consisting of a single star

*

is equivalent to the expression 0..*—that is, it indicates that the cardinality is unrestricted ("zero or more, without limit"). This frequently encountered multiplicity is read "many."

Example

0..1

1

0..*

*

1..*

1..6

1..3,7..10,15,19..*

Style guidelines

- Preferably intervals should monotonically increase. For example, 1..3,7,10 is preferable to 7,10,1..3.
- Two contiguous intervals should be combined into a single interval. For example, 0..1 is preferable to 0,1.

Discussion

A multiplicity expression can include variables, but they must resolve to integer values when the model is complete—that is, they must be parameters or constants. Multiplicity is not meant to be dynamically evaluated within a run-time scope like a dynamic array bound. It is meant to specify the possible range of values (worst case) a set might assume and the application must therefore accommodate in its data structures and operations. It is a model-time constant. If the bound is variable at run time, then the proper choice of multiplicity is *many* (0..*).

The multiplicity may be suppressed on a diagram, but it exists in the underlying model. In a finished model, there is no meaning to an "unspecified" multiplicity. Not knowing the multiplicity is no different from saying that it is many, because in the absence of any knowledge, the cardinality might take any value, which is just the meaning of many.

See unspecified value.

multiplicity (of association)

The multiplicity specified on an association end.
See multiplicity.

Semantics

The multiplicity attached to an association end declares how many objects may fill the position defined by the association end.

For a binary association, the multiplicity on the target end constrains how many objects of the target class may be associated with a given single object from the other (source) end. Multiplicity is typically given as a range of integers. (*See* multiplicity for a more general definition.) Common multiplicities include exactly one; zero or one; zero or more, without limit; and one or more, without limit. The phrase "zero or more, without limit" is usually called many.

In an *n*-ary association, the multiplicity is defined with respect to the other *n-1* ends. For example, given a ternary association among classes (A, B, C), then the multiplicity of the C end states how many C objects may appear in association with a particular pair of A and B objects. If the multiplicity of this association is (many, many, one), then for each possible (A, B) pair, there is a unique value of C. For a given (B, C) pair, there may be many A values, however, and many values of A, B, and C may participate in the association.

See *n*-ary association for a discussion of *n*-ary multiplicity.

Notation

The multiplicity is shown by a multiplicity string near the end of the path to which it applies (Figure 13-126). A range of numbers has the form n1..n2.

See multiplicity for further details on syntax and more general forms for specifying it (although these are probably more general than needed for most practice).

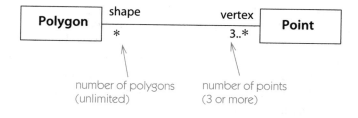

Figure 13-126. *Multiplicity of association*

multiplicity (of attribute)

The possible number of values of an attribute in each object.

Semantics

The multiplicity attached to an attribute declares how many values may be held by an object having the attribute.

The usual multiplicity is exactly one (1..1), meaning that every object has one value for the attribute. Other common multiplicities include zero or one (an optional, or "nullable," value); zero or more, without limit (a set of values); and one or more, without limit (a nonempty set of values). The phrase "zero or more, without limit" is usually called many.

Notation

The multiplicity is shown by a multiplicity string in brackets after the attribute name and preceding the colon (Figure 13-127). If there are no brackets, then the multiplicity is exactly one (a scalar value, the default).

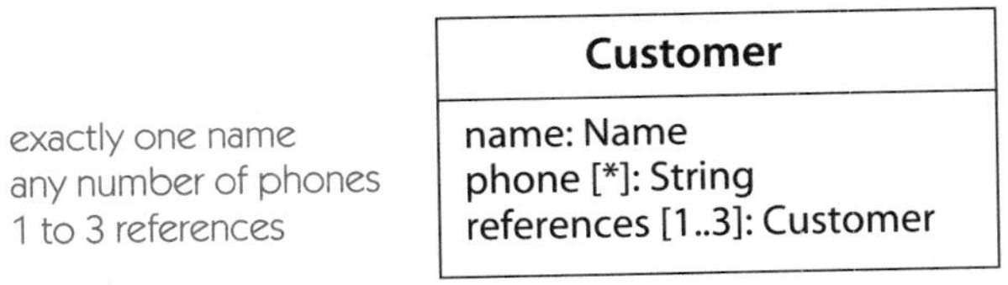

```
                              ┌──────────────────────────┐
                              │         Customer         │
                              ├──────────────────────────┤
exactly one name              │ name: Name               │
any number of phones          │ phone [*]: String        │
1 to 3 references             │ references [1..3]: Customer │
                              └──────────────────────────┘
```

Figure 13-127. *Multiplicity of attributes*

multiplicity (of class)

The range of possible cardinalities of the instances of a class—that is, how many instances may legitimately exist at one time.

Semantics

When applied to a class, multiplicity declares how many instances of the class may exist. The usual default is unlimited, but a finite multiplicity is useful in some cases, particularly to declare a singleton class—that is, a class that may have only one instance, usually needed to establish the context and parameters of the entire system.

The other use of multiplicity with classes is within a collaboration, in which it may be attached to a classifier role to specify how many instances may be bound to the role in an instance of the collaboration.

Figure 13-128. *Multiplicity of class*

Notation

Multiplicity of a class or classifier role is shown by placing a multiplicity string in the upper right corner of the rectangle symbol (Figure 13-128). The string may be omitted if the multiplicity is many (unlimited).

n-ary association

An association among three or more classes. Contrast: binary association.

Semantics

Each instance of the association is an *n*-tuple of values from the respective classes. A single class may appear in more than one position in the association. A binary association is a special case with its own simpler notation and certain additional properties (such as navigability) that are meaningless (or at least hopelessly complicated) for an *n*-ary association.

Multiplicity for *n*-ary associations may be specified but is less obvious than binary multiplicity. The multiplicity on an association end represents the potential number of values at the end, when the values at the other *n-1* ends are fixed. Note that this definition is compatible with binary multiplicity.

Aggregation (including composition) is meaningful only for binary associations. An *n*-ary association may not contain the aggregation or composition marker on any role.

There is no semantic difference between a binary association and an *n*-ary association with two ends, regardless of representation. An association with two ends is deemed to be a binary association, and one with more than two ends is deemed to be an *n*-ary association.

Notation

An *n*-ary association is shown as a large diamond (that is, large compared with a terminator on a path), with a path from the diamond to each participant class. The name of the association (if any) is shown near the diamond. Adornments may appear on the end of each path as with a binary association. Multiplicity may be indicated, but qualifiers and aggregation are not permitted.

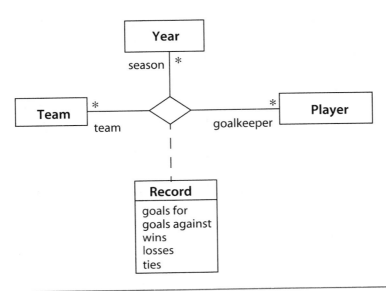

Figure 13-129. *Ternary association that is also an association class*

An association class symbol may be attached to the diamond by a dashed line. This indicates an *n*-ary association that has attributes, operations, and/or associations.

Example

Figure 13-129 shows the record of a team in each season with a particular goalkeeper. It is assumed that the goalkeeper might be traded during the season and might have a record with different teams. In a record book, each link would be a separate line.

Style guidelines

Usually, the lines are drawn from the points on the diamond or from the midpoint of a side.

Discussion

In an *n*-ary association, the multiplicity is defined with respect to the other *n-1* ends. For example, given a ternary association among classes (A, B, C), the multiplicity of the C end states how many C objects may appear in association with a particular pair of A and B objects. If the multiplicity of this association is (many, many, one), then for each possible (A, B) pair there is a unique C value. For a given (B, C) pair, there may be many A values, however, and individually many values of

A, B, and C may participate in the association. In a binary association this rule reduces to the multiplicity of each end defined with respect to the other end.

There is no point in defining multiplicity with respect to one end only (as some authors have proposed) because the multiplicity would be many for any meaningful *n*-ary association. If not, the association could be partitioned into a binary association between the single class and an association class that includes all the remaining classes, with a gain in both precision and efficiency of implementation. In general it is best to avoid *n*-ary associations, because binary associations are simpler to implement and they permit navigation. Generally, *n*-ary associations are useful only when all the values are needed to uniquely determine a link. An *n*-ary association will almost always be implemented as a class whose attributes include pointers to the participant objects. The advantage of modeling it as an association is the constraint that there can be no duplicate links within an association.

Consider the example of a student taking a course from a professor during a term (Figure 13-130). A student will not take the same course from more than one professor, but a student may take more than one course from a single professor, and a professor may teach more than one course. The multiplicities are shown in the diagram. The multiplicity on **Professor** is optional (0..1), the other multiplicities are many (0..*).

Each multiplicity value is relative to a pair of objects from other ends. For a (course, student) pair, there is zero or one professor. For a (student, professor) pair, there are many courses. For a (course, professor) pair, there are many students.

Note that if this association is reified into a class, then it would be possible to have more than one copy of the same (student, course, professor) combination, which is not desirable.

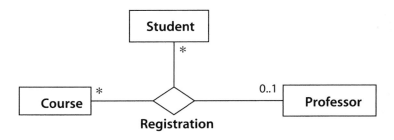

Figure 13-130. *Multiplicity on* n-*ary association*

name

A string used to identify a model element.

See also namespace.

Semantics

A name is an identifier—a sequence of characters from a finite, predefined alphabet in some defined language. An implementation may impose restrictions on the form of names, such as the exclusion of certain characters (for example, punctuation marks), restrictions on initial characters, and so on. In particular, it is assumed that names are usable as selectors and search keys within various data sets. For example, names from the Roman alphabet usually include upper and lower case letters; numerals; and one or more separators, such as underscore and hyphen, while other punctuation marks are implementation-dependent.

Tools and languages may impose reasonable limits on the length of strings and the character set they use for names, possibly more restrictive than those for arbitrary strings, such as comments.

Names are defined within a namespace, such as a package or class. Within a namespace, a name must be unique within its own semantic group, such as classifiers, states, attributes, and so on, but names of different groups may coincide (although this should be avoided to prevent confusion). Each namespace, except the entire system, is contained within another namespace. The names of all the nested namespaces and the final element name are composable into a single pathname string.

Notation

A name is displayed as a string. A name is usually displayed on a single line and contains only nonprintable characters. The canonical notation for names includes alphabetic characters, numerals, and underscores. If additional characters are allowed within a particular implementation, then it is possible that certain characters may have to be encoded for display to avoid confusion. This is an implementation responsibility of a tool.

Individual names from a namespace hierarchy separated by double colons may be composed into a pathname.

namespace

A part of the model in which the names may be defined and used. Within a namespace, each name has a unique meaning.

Semantics

All named elements are declared in a namespace, and their names have scope within it. The top-level namespaces are packages (including subsystems), containers whose purpose is to group elements primarily for human access and understandability, and also to organize models for computer storage and manipulation during development. Primary model elements, including classes, associations, state machines, and collaborations, act as namespaces for their contents, such as attributes, association ends, states, and collaboration roles. The scope of each model element is discussed as part of its description. Each of these model elements has its own distinct namespace.

Names defined within a namespace must be unique (after all, that is its purpose). Given a namespace and a name, a particular element in the namespace can be found (if it has a name—some elements are anonymous and must be found by relationship to named elements). Namespaces can be nested. It is possible to search inward over a list of nested namespaces by giving their names.

To gain access to other namespaces, a package can access or import another package.

The system itself defines the outermost namespace that provides the base for all absolute names. It is a package, usually with packages nested within it to several levels until primitive elements are finally obtained.

Notation

The notation for a pathname, a path over several nested namespaces, is obtained by concatenating the names of the namespaces (such as packages or classes) separated by pairs of double colons (::).

UserInterface::HelpFacility::HelpScreen

navigability

Navigability indicates whether it is possible to traverse a binary association within expressions of a class to obtain the object or set of objects associated with an instance of the class. The concept does not apply to *n*-ary associations (see text). The navigability property is an enumeration with the values **true** (navigable) and **false** (not navigable).

See also navigation efficiency.

Semantics

Navigability indicates whether a rolename may be used in expressions to traverse an association from an object to an object or set of objects of the class attached to the end of the association bearing the rolename. If navigability is true, then the association defines a pseudoattribute of the class that is on the end opposite the rolename—that is, the rolename may be used in expressions similar to an attribute of the class to obtain values. The rolename may also be used to express constraints.

A lack of navigability implies that the class opposite the rolename cannot "see" the association and therefore cannot use it to form an expression. An association without navigability does not create a dependency from the source to the target class, but a dependency may be created by some other cause.

Lack of navigability does not imply that there is no way to traverse the association. If it is possible to traverse the association in the other direction, it may be possible to search all the instances of the other class to find those that lead to an object, thereby inverting the association. This approach may even be practical in small cases.

Navigability is not defined on *n*-ary associations, because it would require specifying sets of classes from which or to which to navigate. This could be done, but it is too complicated to be useful as a basic property. This does not mean that *n*-ary associations cannot be traversed, but merely that the specification of their traversal is complicated and not suited to a simple Boolean definition.

Navigation usually carries the connotation of navigation efficiency, although this is not strictly required by the UML rules.

Notation

A navigable association is shown with an arrowhead on the end of the association path attached to the target class. The arrow indicates the direction of traversal (Figure 13-131). The navigability adornment may be suppressed (usually, on all associations in a diagram). Arrowheads may be attached to zero, one, or both ends of an association.

As a convenience, the arrowheads may be omitted on associations that are navigable in both directions. In theory, this can be confused with an association that is not navigable in either direction, but such an association is unlikely in practice and can be explicitly noted if it occurs.

There is no need for a notation for "undecided" navigability. If navigability has not been decided, then it is bidirectional in the general case. Any decision on navigability can only restrict it or leave it fully general.

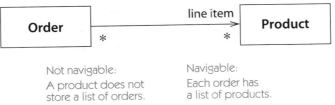

Figure 13-131. *Navigability*

navigable

An association or link that can be traversed in an expression. Its navigability property is **true**. Such a link is often implemented as a pointer or set of pointers.
See navigability, navigation efficiency.

navigation

To traverse connections in a graph, especially to traverse binary links and attributes in an object model to map an object into a value. In the latter case, the navigation path can be expressed as a sequence of attribute names or rolenames.
See navigability.

navigation efficiency

Indicates whether it is possible to efficiently traverse a binary association starting from one object to obtain the object or set of objects associated with it. The concept does not apply to *n*-ary associations. Navigation efficiency is related to navigability but not its defining property.
See also navigability.

Semantics

Navigation efficiency can be defined in a general manner so that it is applicable to abstract design, as well as to various programming languages. A binary association is efficiently navigable if the average cost of obtaining the set of associated objects is proportional to the number of objects in the set (*not* to the upper limit on multiplicity, which may be unlimited) plus a fixed constant. In computational complexity terms, the cost is $O(n)$. If the multiplicity is one or zero-one, then the access cost must be constant, which precludes searching a variable-length list. A slightly looser definition of navigation efficiency would permit a minimum cost of $log(n)$.

Although a navigable association of multiplicity-one is usually implemented using a pointer embedded in the block containing the attributes of the object, an external implementation is possible using hash tables, which have a constant average access cost. Thus, an association can be implemented as a look-up-table object external to the participating classes and can still be considered navigable. (In some real-time situations, the worst-case cost rather than the average cost must be limited. This doesn't require a change to the basic definition other than substituting the worst-case time, but probabilistic algorithms such as hash tables may be ruled out.)

If an association is not navigable in a given direction, it does not mean that it cannot be traversed at all but that the cost of traversal may be significant—for example, requiring a search through a large list. If access in one direction is infrequent, a search may be a reasonable choice. Navigation efficiency is a design concept that allows a designer to design object access paths with an understanding of the computational complexity costs. Usually, navigability implies navigational efficiency.

It is possible (if somewhat rare) to have an association that is not efficiently navigable in either direction. Such an association might be implemented as a list of links that must be searched to perform a traversal in either direction. It would be possible but inefficient to traverse it. Nevertheless, the use for such an association is small.

Discussion

Navigation efficiency indicates the efficiency of obtaining the set of related objects to a given object. When the multiplicity is 0..1 or 1, then the obvious implementation is a pointer in the source object. When the multiplicity is many, then the usual implementation is a container class containing a set of pointers. The container class itself may or may not reside within the data record for an object of the class, depending on whether it can be obtained at constant cost (the usual situation for pointer access). The container class must be efficient to navigate. For example, a simple list of all the links for an association would not be efficient, because the links for an object would be mixed with many other uninteresting links and would require a search. A list of links stored with each object would be efficient, because no unnecessary search is required.

In a qualified association, a navigable setting in the direction away from the qualifier usually indicates that it is efficient to obtain the object or set of objects selected by a source object and qualifier value. This is consistent with an implementation using hash tables or perhaps a binary tree search indexed by the qualifier value (which is exactly the point of including qualifiers as a modeling concept.

node

A node is a run-time physical object that represents a computational resource, which generally has at least a memory and often processing capability. Run-time objects and run-time component instances may reside on nodes.

See also location.

Semantics

Nodes include computing devices but also (in a business model, at least) human resources or mechanical processing resources. Nodes may be represented as descriptors and as instances. A node defines a location at which run-time computational instances, both objects and component instances, may reside.

Physical nodes have many additional properties, such as capacity, throughput, and reliability. UML does not predefine these properties, as there are a great number of possibilities, but they can be modeled in UML using stereotypes and tagged values.

Nodes may be connected by associations to show communication paths. The associations can be given stereotypes to distinguish various kinds of communication paths or various implementations of them.

A node is inherently part of the implementation view and not the analysis view. Node instances rather than node types generally appear in deployment models. Although node types are potentially meaningful, the types of the individual nodes often remain anonymous.

A node is a classifier and may have attributes. Most of the time, node instances are shown in deployment diagrams. Node descriptors have a more limited use.

Notation

A node is shown as a figure that looks like an off-center projection of a cube.

A node descriptor has the syntax

`node-type`

where `node-type` is a classifier name.

A node instance has a name and a type name. The node may have an underlined name string in it or below it. The name string has the syntax

`name :node-type`

The `name` is the name of the individual node (if any). The `node-type` says what kind of a node it is. Either or both elements are optional.

Dependency arrows (dashed arrows with the arrowhead on the component) may be used show the ability of a node type to support a component type. A stereotype may be used to state the precise kind of dependency.

Component instances and objects may be contained within node instance symbols. This indicates that the items reside on the node instances. Containment may also be shown by aggregation and composition association paths.

Nodes may be connected by association symbols to other nodes. An association between two nodes indicates a communication path between them. The association may have a stereotype to indicate the nature of the communication path (for example, the kind of channel or network).

Example

Figure 13-132 shows two nodes containing an object (cluster) that migrates from a component in one node to a component in the other.

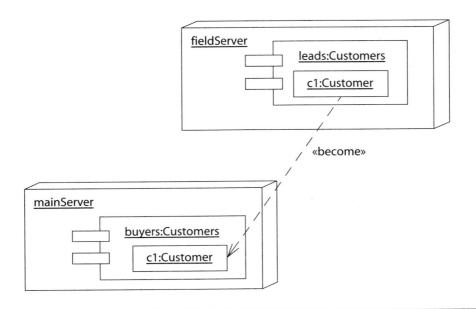

Figure 13-132. *Migration between nodes*

note

A symbol for displaying a comment or other textual information, such as a method body or a constraint.

Notation

A note is a dog-eared rectangle with its upper-right corner bent over. It contains text or extended text (such as an embedded document) that is not interpreted by UML. A note can present information from various kinds of model elements, such as a comment, a constraint, or a method. The note does not usually explicitly indicate the kind of element represented, but that is generally apparent from its form and usage. Within a modeling tool, the underlying element will be explicit in the model. A note can be attached with a dashed line to the element that it describes. If the note describes multiple elements, a dashed line is drawn to each of them.

A note may have a keyword in guillemets to clarify its meaning. The keyword «constraint» indicates a constraint.

Example

Figure 13-133 shows notes used for several purposes, including a constraint on an operation, a constraint on a class, and a comment.

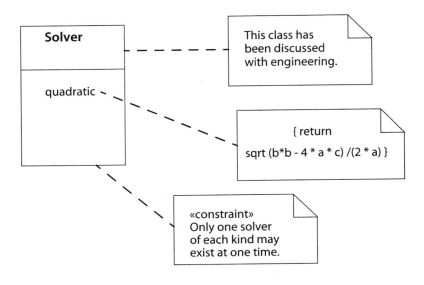

Figure 13-133. *Notes*

object

A discrete entity with a well-defined boundary and identity that encapsulates state and behavior; an instance of a class.

See also class, identity, instance.

Semantics

An object is an instance of a class, which describes the set of possible objects that can exist. An object can be viewed from two related perspectives: as an entity at a particular point in time with a specific value and as a holder of identity that has different values over time. The first view is appropriate to a snapshot, which represents a system at a point in time. An object in a snapshot has a location (in a distributed system) and has values for each of its attributes. An object is attached to a set of links that connect it to other objects.

Each object has its own unique identity and may be referenced by a unique handle that identifies it and provides access to it. The view of an object as an identity is appropriate to a collaboration instance, in which the object has run-time relationships to other objects that it uses to exchange message instances.

An object contains one attribute slot for each attribute in its full descriptor—that is, for each attribute declared in its direct class and in every ancestor class. When instantiation and initialization of an object are complete, each slot contains a value that is an instance of the classifier declared as the attribute type. As the system executes, the value in an attribute slot may change unless the attribute changeability property forbids it to change. At all times between the execution of operations, the values in an object must satisfy all implicit and explicit constraints imposed by the model. During execution of an operation, constraints may be temporarily violated.

If multiple classification is allowed in an execution environment, then an object may be the direct instance of more than one class. The object contains one attribute slot for each attribute declared in any of its direct classes or any of their ancestors. The same attribute may not appear more than once, but if two direct classes are descendants of a common ancestor, only one copy of each attribute from the ancestor is inherited, regardless of the multiple paths to it.

If dynamic classification is allowed, an object may change its direct class during execution. If attributes are gained in the process, then their values must be specified by the operation that changes the direct class.

If both multiple classification and dynamic classification are allowed, then an object may gain and lose direct classes during execution. However, the number of direct classes may never be less than one (it must have some structure, even if it is transient).

An object may be called to execute any operation that appears in the full descriptor of any direct class—that is, it has both direct and inherited operations.

An object may be used as the value of any variable or parameter whose declared type is the same class or an ancestor of the direct class of the object. In other words, an instance of any descendant of a class may appear as the value of a variable whose type is declared to be the class. This is the substitutability principle. This principle is not a logical necessity but exists to simplify the implementation of programming languages.

Notation

An object is an instance of a class. The general rule for the notation for instances is to use the same geometrical symbol as the descriptor but to underline the name of the instance to distinguish it as an individual. Any values are shown in the instance, but properties shared by all instances are notated only in the descriptor.

The canonical notation for an object is a rectangle with two compartments. The top compartment contains the object name and class, and the bottom compartment contains a list of attribute names and values (Figure 13-134). There is no need to show operations because they are the same for all objects of a class.

The top compartment shows the name of the object and its class, all underlined, using the syntax

objectname :classname

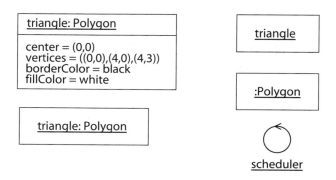

Figure 13-134. *Object notation*

The classname can include the full pathname of the enclosing package, if necessary. The package names precede the classname and are separated by double colons. For example

displayWindow: WindowingSystem::GraphicWindows::Window

A stereotype for the class may be shown textually (in guillemets above the name string) or as an icon in the upper-right corner. The stereotype for an object must match the stereotype for its class.

To show multiple classes of which the object is an instance, use a comma-separated list of classnames. Some of the classes can be transient roles that the object plays during a collaboration. For example

aPerson: Professor, Skier

To show the presence of an object in a particular state of a class, use the syntax

objectname : classname [statename-list]

The list must be a comma-separated list of names of states that can legally occur concurrently.

To show a change of class (dynamic classification), the object must be displayed twice, once with each class. The two symbols are connected by a become relationship to show that they represent the same object.

The second compartment shows the attributes for the object and their values as a list. Each value line has the syntax

attributename : type = value

The type is redundant with the attribute declaration in the class and may be omitted. The value is specified as a string that represents the value. The attribute names are not underlined.

The name of the object may be omitted. In this case, the colon should be kept with the class name. This represents an anonymous object of the class, given identity by its relationships. Each symbol that contains an anonymous object denotes a distinct object distinguished by its relationships to other objects.

The class of the object may be suppressed (together with the colon), but it should be shown when possible to avoid confusion.

The attribute value compartment as a whole may be suppressed.

Attributes whose values are not of interest may be suppressed.

To show the changes in value of attributes during a computation, show two versions of the same object with a become relationship between them.

object diagram

A diagram that shows objects and their relationships at a point in time. An object diagram may be considered a special case of a class diagram in which instances, as well as classes, may be shown. Also related is a collaboration diagram, which shows prototypical objects (classifier roles) within a context.

See also diagram.

Notation

Tools need not support a separate format for object diagrams. Class diagrams can contain objects, so a class diagram with objects and no classes is an "object diagram." The phrase is useful, however, to characterize a particular usage achievable in various ways.

Discussion

An object diagram shows a set of objects and links that represent the state of a system at a particular moment in time. It contains objects with values, not descriptors, although they can, of course, be prototypical in many cases. To show a general pattern of objects and relationships that can be instantiated many times, use a collaboration diagram, which contains descriptors (classifier roles and association roles) for objects and links. If a collaboration diagram is instantiated, it yields an object diagram.

An object diagram does not show the evolution of the system over time. For that purpose, use a collaboration diagram with messages, or a sequence diagram to represent an interaction.

object flow

A variety of control flow that represents the relationship between an object and the object, operation, or transition that creates it (as an output) or uses it (as an input).

See also control flow, object flow state.

Semantics

An object flow is a kind of control flow with an object flow state as an input or an output.

Notation

An object flow is shown as a dashed line from the source entity to the target entity. One or both entities may be object flow states, displayed as object symbols. The arrow may have a keyword to indicate what kind of object flow it is (become or copy). If there is no label on the arrow, it is a become relationship.

See object flow state, become, and copy for examples.

object flow state

A state that represents the existence of an object of a particular class at a point within a computation, such as an interaction view or an activity graph.

See also control flow, class-in-state.

Semantics

Both activity graphs and interaction views represent the flow of control among operations in target objects by messages, but messages do not show the flow of the objects that are arguments to operations. This kind of information flow can be represented in behavioral models using object flow states.

An object flow state represents an object of a class that exists at a point within a computation, such as an activity graph or an interaction view. The object may be the output of one activity and the input of many other activities. In an activity graph, it may be the target of a transition (often a fork, the other branch being the main control path), and it may be the source of a completion transition to an activity. When the preceding transition fires, the object flow state becomes active. This represents the creation of on object of the class. To show the passage of an object into a state, rather than the creation of a new object, an object flow state can be declared as a class in a state, a class-in-state.

An object flow state must match the type of the result or parameter that it represents. If it is the output of an operation, it must match the type of the result. If it is the input of an operation, it must match the type of a parameter.

If the object flow state is followed by a completion transition to an activity, then the activity can be performed as soon as the object value is available. No additional control input is necessary. In other words, the creation of data in the right form is the trigger for performing the activity.

To show that an activity requires both a control path and the presence of a value, the previous action of the control path and an object flow state for the value can lead into a complex transition. The activity is performed when all the input transitions are ready. Multiple paths to a transition indicate synchronization.

Object flow states are usually useful to document input-output relationships for human understanding rather than to specify a computation precisely. The information shown by object flow states is already available.

The production of an event by an activity in an activity graph can be modeled as an object flow state whose classifier is a signal. The stereotype «signal» may be used. The object flow state is an output of the activity. If the activity produces multiple events, the object flow states are targets of a fork.

Notation

An object of a class in a state is shown in an activity diagram by a rectangle containing the underlined class name followed by the state name in square brackets

Classname [Statename]

An example is

Order [Placed]

An object flow symbol represents the existence of the object in a state of the procedure itself and not simply the object itself, as data. The object flow symbol (which represents a state) may appear as the target of one transition arrow and as the source of multiple transition arrows. To distinguish these from ordinary transitions in an activity diagram, they are drawn as dashed arrows rather than solid arrows. They represent object flows.

Example

Figure 13-135 shows object flow states in an activity diagram. An object flow state is created by the completion of an operation. For example, Order[Placed] is created by the completion of **Request Service**. Because that activity is followed by another activity, the object flow state **Order[Placed]** is an output of a fork symbol. State **Order[Entered]**, on the other hand, is the result of completing activity **Take Order**, which has no other successor activities.

Figure 13-136 shows a portion of an activity diagram concerned with building a house. When the frame has been built, the carpenter is free to work on the roof and the house is ready for the plumbing to be installed. These events are modeled as object flow states of signals—Carpenter free and Frame ready. As a result of these events, the roof can be built and the plumbing can be installed. Therefore the object flow states are shown as inputs of the activities. In the model, the production of an event by the completion of one activity and its use to trigger the next activity are implicit in the connection of the activities. The need for a manifest event has been elided. Therefore, the appearance of the signals as object flow states is for information, rather than implementation structure.

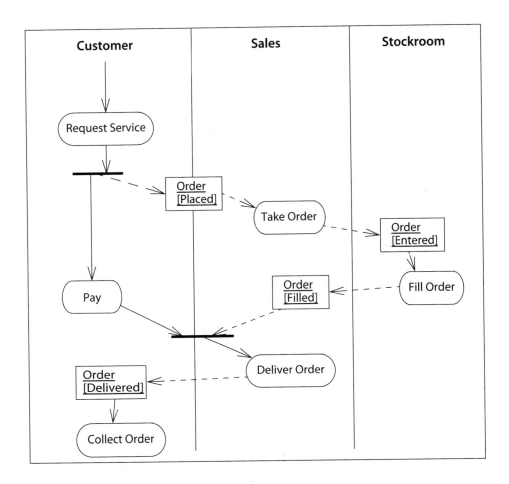

Figure 13-135. *Object flow states in an activity diagram*

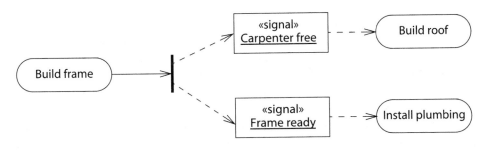

Figure 13-136. *Signal production in activity diagram*

Discussion

An object flow state represents the data flow view of a computation. Unlike traditional data flow, however, it exists at a definite point within a control flow model (a state machine or an activity graph), rather than within a data flow model. This places it squarely into an object-oriented framework. Object orientation unites the data structure, control flow, and data flow viewpoints into a single model.

object lifeline

A line in a sequence diagram that represents the existence of an object over a period of time.

object set expression

An expression that yields a set of objects when evaluated at run time.

Semantics

The target of a send action is an object set expression. When such an expression is evaluated at run time, it yields a set of objects to which a designated signal is sent in parallel. An object set expression may yield a single element, in which case the send action is an ordinary sequential action. It may even yield no element (that is, an empty set) in which case no send occurs.

OCL

Object Constraint Language, a text language for specifying constraints and queries. OCL is not intended for writing actions or executable code. For a full definition, see the book [Warmer-99].

Semantics

The Object Constrain Language (OCL) is a text language for writing navigation expressions, Boolean expressions, and other queries. It may be used to construct expressions for constraints, guard conditions, actions, preconditions and postconditions, assertions, and other kinds of UML expressions. A complete description of the OCL syntax and semantics can be found in [Warmer-99]. The following selected summary contains the most useful OCL syntax for creating navigation expressions and Boolean conditions. The full language contains a large number of predefined operators on collections and on primitive types.

Notation

Syntax for some common navigation expressions is shown below. These forms can be chained together. The left-most element must be an expression for an object or a set of objects. The expressions are meant to work on sets of values when applicable. For more details and syntax, see the OCL description.

item . selector

> selector is the name of an attribute in the item or the name of a role of the target end of a link attached to the item. The result is the value of the attribute or the related object(s). The result is a value or a set of values, depending on the multiplicities of the item and the association.

item . selector (argument$_{list,}$)

> selector is the name of an operation on the item. The result is the return value of the operation applied to the item.

item . selector [qualifier-value]

> selector designates a qualified association that qualifies the *item*. qualifier-value is a value for the qualifier attribute. The result is the related object selected by the qualifier. Note that this syntax is applicable to array indexing as a form of qualification.

set -> set-property

> set-property is the name of a built-in OCL function on sets. The result is the property of the set. Illegal if set-property is not a predefined OCL function. Several of the properties are listed below.

set -> select (boolean-expression)

> boolean-expression is written in terms of objects within the set. The result is the subset of objects in the set for which the Boolean expression is true.

set -> size

> The number of elements in the set.

self

> Denotes the current object (may be omitted if the context is clear).

operator

> The usual arithmetic and Boolean operators:
> = < > <= >= <> + – * / not

Example

flight.pilot.training_hours >= flight.plane.minimum_hours
The set of pilots who have enough training hours

company.employees–>select (title = "Boss" and self.reports–>size > 10)
The number of bosses who have more than 10 reports

operation

An operation is a specification of a transformation or query that an object may be called to execute. It has a name and a list of parameters. A method is a procedure that implements an operation. It has an algorithm or procedure description. An operation on an active class may also be implemented using a call event.

See also call, call event, method.

Semantics

An operation specifies a transformation on the state of the target object (and possibly the state of the rest of the system reachable from the target object) or a query that returns a value to the caller of the operation. An operation may be implemented as a a method or as a call event that causes a transition in the state machine of an active object. An operation is invoked by a call, which suspends the caller until the execution of the operation is complete, after which the caller resumes control beyond the point of the call, receiving a return value if one is supplied by the operation.

An operation is declared in a class. The declaration is inherited by the descendants of the class. If another declaration has the same "matching signature," it is the same operation. An implementation may specify a rule for matching signatures to test for conflict, but by default, it includes the name of the operation and the classes (but not the names or directions) of the parameters, not including return parameters. The same operation can appear in a descendant class. In that case, it is treated as a repetition of the inherited declaration and ignored. The purpose is to permit an operation to be declared multiple times in classes that are developed in different packages, using name matching. The operation declaration that is the common ancestor of all other declarations of it is called the *origin* (after Bertrand Meyer). It represents the governing declaration of the operation that is inherited by the others.

If two operation declarations have the same name and ordered list of parameter types (not including return parameters) but the other properties differ (for example, a parameter is an in-parameter in one operation and is an out-parameter in another), then the declarations conflict and the model is ill formed.

A method is the implementation of an operation (it may also be implemented by a call event). If an operation is declared in a class without the abstract property, then it has a method definition in the class. Otherwise, the operation may be abstract (and there is no method), or it may be concrete with an inherited method.

Structure

An operation has the following main constituents.

concurrency — The semantics of concurrent calls to the same passive instance, an enumeration. Possible values are

sequential — Callers must coordinate so that only one call to an object (on any sequential operation) may execute at once. If concurrent calls occur, then the semantics and integrity of the system cannot be guaranteed.

guarded — Multiple calls from concurrent threads may occur simultaneously to one object (on any guarded operation), but only one is allowed to commence at a time. The others are blocked until the execution of the first operation is complete. It is the responsibility of the modeler to ensure that deadlocks do not occur because of simultaneous blocks. Guarded operations must perform correctly (or block themselves) in the case of a simultaneous sequential operation, or guarded semantics cannot be claimed.

concurrent — Multiple calls from concurrent threads may occur simultaneously to one object (on concurrent operations). All of them may proceed concurrently with correct semantics. Concurrent operations must be designed so that they perform correctly in the case of a concurrent, sequential, or guarded operation on the same object. Otherwise, concurrent semantics cannot be claimed.

polymorphism — Whether the implementation of the operation (the method or call event) may be overridden by descendant classes. If true, the implementation can be overridden by a descendant class that provides a new definition of the method or a different state machine transition. The implementation takes on different forms—that is, it is polymorphic. If false, the current implementation is inherited unchanged by all descendants. It has a single form.

query	Whether the execution of the operation leaves the state of the system unchanged—that is, whether it is a query. If true, the operation returns a value, but it has no side effects. If false, it may alter the state of the system, but a change is not guaranteed.
name	The name of the operation, a string. The name together with the list of parameter types (not including parameter names or return types), is called the matching signature of the operation. The matching signature must be unique within the class and its ancestors. If there is a duplication, it is taken as a redeclaration of the operation, which must match completely. If they match, all but the operation declaration in the highest ancestor are ignored. If they do not match, the model is ill formed.
parameter list	The list of declarations of the parameters of the operation. *See* parameter list.
return type	A list of the types of the values returned by a call of the operation, if any. If the operation does not return values, then this property has the value null. Note that many languages do not support multiple return values, but it remains a valid modeling concept that can be implemented in various ways, such as by treating one or more of the parameters as output values.
scope	Whether the operation applies to individual objects or to the class itself (owner scope). Possible values are
instance	The operation may be applied to individual objects.
class	The operation applies to the class itself—for example, an operation that creates an instance of a class.
specification	An expression describing the effects produced by executing the operation—for example, a before-and-after condition. The format of the specification is not prescribed by UML and can take various forms.
visibility	The visibility of the operation by classes other than the one defining it. *See* visibility.

A method has the same constituents as an operation. In addition, it may have one or more of

behavior
: An optional state machine describing the implementation of the method.

body
: An expression describing the procedure for the method. This may be represented as a string or possibly a parsed format. Usually, this would be expressed in a programming language, although a natural language expression is possible for informal specifications. Generally, this value would not be supplied if the state machine is supplied.

collaboration
: A set of collaborations describing the implementation of the method as an ordered set of messages among roles (an interaction).

A call event has the same constituents as an operation. The implementation of the operation must be specified by one or more transitions that have the call event as a trigger.

Notation

An operation is shown as a text string that can be parsed into properties of the operation. The default syntax is

«stereotype»$_{opt}$ visibility$_{opt}$ name (parameter-list) :return-type$_{opt}$
{ property-string }$_{opt}$

The stereotype, visibility, return-type-expression, and property string are optional (together with their delimiters). The parameter list may be empty. Figure 13-137 shows some typical operations.

Name. A string that is the name of the operation (not including parameters).

Parameter list. A comma-separated list of parameter declarations, each comprising a direction, name, and type. The entire list is enclosed in parentheses (including an empty list). *See* parameter list and parameter for full details.

```
+display (): Location
+hide ()
«constructor» +create ()
-attachXWindow(xwin:Xwindow*)
```

Figure 13-137. *Operation list with a variety of operations*

Return type. A string containing a comma-separated list of names of classifiers (classes, data types, or interfaces). The type string follows a colon (:) that follows the parameter list of the operation. The colon and return-type string are omitted if the operation does not return any values (e.g., C++ **void**). Some, but not all, programming languages support multiple return values.

Visibility. The visibility is shown as one of the punctuation marks '+', '#', or '−', representing **public**, **protected**, or **private**. Alternately, visibility can be shown as a keyword within the property string (for example, {visibility=private}). This form must be used for user-defined or language-dependent choices.

Method. An operation and a method are declared using the same syntax. The topmost appearance of an operation signature within a generalization hierarchy is the declaration of an operation. Identical signatures in descendant classes are redundant declarations of the operation, but these may be useful for declaring methods or for declaring operations when the classes are developed separately. If an operation declaration has the abstract property (notated by operation name in italics or the keyword **abstract**), then there is no method corresponding to the declaration. Otherwise, the declaration represents both an operation declaration and a method implementing it.

In matching operations and methods, the name of the operation and the ordered list of parameter types are used, not including return parameters. If the remaining properties are inconsistent (for example, an in-parameter is matched to an out-parameter), then there is a conflict and the model is ill formed.

If two identical operation declarations have no common ancestor operation declaration, yet are inherited by a common class, then the model is ill formed. In this situation, the declarations would yield a conflict in a class that inherits both of them.

Method body. The body of a method may be shown as a string within a note attached to an operation declaration. The text of the specification should be enclosed in braces if it is a formal specification in some language (a semantic constraint). Otherwise, it should be normal text if it is just a natural-language description of the behavior (a comment). The connection of a method declaration and its state machine or collaboration has no visual representation, but it would generally be represented by a hyperlink within an editing tool.

Specification. An expression describing the effects of performing the operation. This may be stated in various ways, including text, before-after conditions, and invariants. In any case, the specification should be expressed in terms of the observable effects of the operation on the state of the system, not in terms of the execution algorithm. The algorithm is the business of the method.

The specification is shown by a string constraint within a note attached to the operation entry.

Query. The choice is shown by a property string of the form isQuery=true or isQuery=false. The choice true may also be shown by the keyword query. The absence of an explicit choice indicates the choice false—that is, the operation may alter the system state (but it does not guarantee to alter it).

Polymorphism. The choice is shown by a property string of the form isPolymorphic=true (overridable) or isPolymorphic=false (not overridable). The absence of an explicit choice indicates the choice true—that is, overridable.

Scope. An instance-scope operation is indicated by not underlining the operation string. A class-scope operation is indicated by underlining the name string.

Concurrency. The choice is shown by a property string of the form concurrency=value, where the value is one of sequential, guarded, or concurrent.

Signals. To indicate that a class accepts a signal, the keyword «signal» is placed in front of an operation declaration within the list of operations. The parameters are the parameters of the signal. The declaration may not have a return type. The response of the object to the reception of the signal is shown with a state machine. Among other uses, this notation can show the response of objects of a class to error conditions and exceptions, which should be modeled as signals.

Presentation options

The argument list and return type may be suppressed (together, not separately).

A tool may show the visibility indication in a different way, such as by using a special icon or by sorting the elements by group.

The syntax of the operation signature string can be that of a particular programming language, such as C++ or Smalltalk. Specific tagged properties may be included in the string.

Style guidelines

* Operation names typically begin with a lowercase letter.
* Operation names are shown in plain face.
* An abstract operation is shown in italics.

Standard elements

semantics

ordering

A property of a set of values, such as the set of objects related to an object across an association, stating whether the set is ordered or unordered.

See also association, association end, multiplicity.

Semantics

If the multiplicity upper bound on an association end is greater than one, then a set of objects is associated with each object on the other end of a binary association. The ordering property declares whether the set is ordered or unordered. If it is unordered, the objects in the set have no explicit order; they form an ordinary set. If it is ordered, the elements in the set have an explicitly imposed order. The element order is part of the information represented by the association—that is, it is additional information beyond the information in the elements themselves. The elements can be obtained in that order. When a new link is added to the association, its position in the sequence must be specified by the operation adding it. The position may be an argument of the operation or it may be implicit. For example, a given operation may place a new link at the end of the existing list of links, but the location of the new link must be specified somehow.

Note that an ordered set is not the same as a set whose elements are sorted by one or more attributes of the elements. A sorting is totally determined by the values of the objects in the set. Therefore, it adds no information, although it may certainly be useful for access purposes. The information in an ordered association, on the other hand, is additional to the information in the elements themselves.

The ordering property applies to any element that takes a multiplicity, such as an attribute with a multiplicity greater than one.

An ordered relationship may be implemented in various ways, but the implementation is usually stated as a language-specified code generation property. An implementation extension might substitute the data structure to hold the elements for the generic specification **ordered**.

A sorted set requires a separate specification of the sorting rule itself, which is best given as a constraint.

Notation

Ordering is specified by a keyword in braces near the end of the path to which it applies (Figure 13-138). The absence of a keyword indicates unordered. The keyword {ordered} indicates an ordered set. For design purposes, the keyword {sorted} may be used to indicate a set arranged by internal values.

For an attribute with multiplicity greater than one, one of the ordering keywords may be placed after the attribute string, in braces, as part of a property string.

If an ordering keyword is omitted, then the set is unordered.

Discussion

An ordered set has information in the ordering, information that is additional to the entities in the set itself. This is real information. Therefore, it is not derivable but must be specified when an entity is added. In other words, on any operation

The list of requests is ordered.   The set of reservations is unordered.

Figure 13-138. *Ordered and unordered sets*

that adds an entity, its position within the list of entities must be specified. Of course, an operation can be implemented so that the new entity is inserted in an implicit location, such as the beginning or the end of the list. And just because a set is ordered does not mean that any ordering of entities will be allowed. These are decisions that the modeler must make. In general, the position of the new entity within the list is a parameter of the creation operation.

Note that the ordering of a binary association must be specified independently for each direction. Ordering is meaningless unless the multiplicity in a direction is greater than one. An association can be completely unordered, it can be ordered in one direction and not the other, or it can be ordered in both directions.

Assume an association between classes A and B that is ordered in the B direction. Then, usually, a new link will be added as an operation on an A object, specifying a B object and a position in the list of existing B objects for the new link. Frequently, an operation on an A object creates a new B object and also creates a link between A and B. The list must be added to the list of links maintained by A. It is possible to create a new link from the B side, but generally the new link is inserted at a default position in the A-to-B list, because the position within that list has little meaning from the B end. Of course, a programmer can implement more complicated situations if needed.

An association that is ordered in both directions is somewhat unusual, because it can be awkward to specify the insertion point in both directions. But it is possible, especially if the new links are added at default locations in either direction.

Note that a sorted set does not contain any extra information beyond the information in the set of entities. Sorting saves time in an algorithm, but it does not add information. It may be regarded as a design optimization and need not be included in an analysis model. It may be specified as a value of the ordering property, but it does not require that an operation specify a location for a new entity added to the set. The location of the new entity must be determined automatically by the method by examining the attributes on which the list is sorted.

orthogonal substate

One of a set of states that partition a composite state into substates, all of which are concurrently active.

See composite state, concurrent substate.

owner scope

An indication of whether the feature applies to an individual object or is shared by an entire class.

See also scope, target scope.

Semantics

Owner scope indicates whether there is a distinct attribute slot for each instance of a class, or if there is one slot for the entire class itself. For an operator, owner scope indicates whether an operation applies to an instance or to the class itself (such as a creation operator). Sometimes called simply *scope*. Possible values are

instance	Each classifier instance has its own distinct copy of an attribute slot. Values in one slot are independent of values in other slots. This is the normal situation.
	For an operator, the operator applies to an individual object.
class	The classifier itself has one copy of the attribute slot. All the instances of the classifier share access to the one slot. If the language permits classes as real objects, then this is an attribute of the class itself as an object.
	For an operator, the operator applies to the entire class, such as a creation operator or an operator that returns statistics about the entire set of instances.

Notation

A class-scope attribute or operator is underlined (Figure 13-139). An instance-scope attribute or operator is not underlined.

Discussion

For an association, this would say whether the source position of a link holds instances or classifiers. But this information can be specified as the target scope in the other direction, so the owner scope is unnecessary and therefore not used for associations.

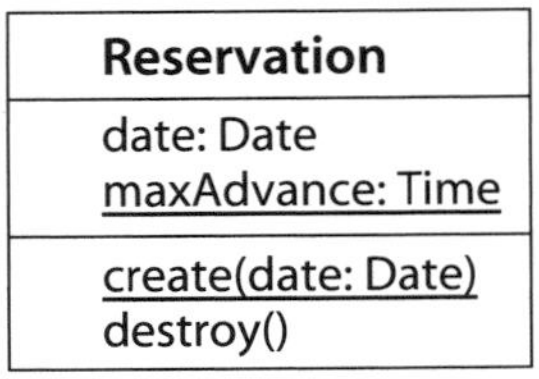

Reservation
date: Date maxAdvance: Time
create(date: Date) destroy()

Figure 13-139. *Class-scope attribute and operation*

package

A general-purpose mechanism for organizing elements into groups. Packages may be nested within other packages. A system may correspond to a single high-level package, with everything else in the model contained in it recursively. Both model elements and diagrams may appear in a package.

See also access, dependency, import, model, namespace, subsystem.

Semantics

A *package* is a grouping of model elements and diagrams. Every model element that is not part of another model element must be declared within exactly one namespace; the namespace containing the declaration of an element is said to *own* the element. A package is a general-purpose namespace that can own any kind of model element that is not restricted to one kind of owner. Each diagram must be owned by exactly one package, which may be nested within (and therefore owned by) another package. A package may contain subordinate packages and ordinary model elements. Some packages may be subsystems or models. The entire system description can be thought of as a single high-level subsystem package with everything else in it. All kinds of UML model elements and diagrams can be organized into packages.

Packages own model elements, subsets of the model, and diagrams. Packages are the basis for configuration control, storage, and access control. Each element can be directly owned by another model element or by a single package, so the ownership hierarchy is a strict tree. However, model elements (including packages) can reference other elements in other packages, so the usage network is a graph.

The special kinds of package are model, subsystem, and system. A system denotes a subsystem that is the root of the package hierarchy. It is the only model element not owned by some other model element. It indirectly includes everything in the model. There are several predefined stereotypes of model and subsystem.

See Chapter 14, Standard Elements, for details.

Packages may have dependency relationships to other packages. In most cases these summarize dependencies among the contents of the packages. A usage dependency between two packages means that there exists at least one usage dependency between elements of the two packages (not that every pair of elements has the dependency).

The access dependency is particular to packages themselves and is not a summarization of dependencies on their elements. It indicates that elements in the client package are granted permission to have relationships to elements in the supplier package. The relationships are also subject to visibility specifications. Access does not mean that the names of the elements in the target package occupy the namespace of the source package—the namespaces are distinct and elements can be uniquely identified by pathnames that include nested packages. The access dependency variation import is like an Ada **uses** statement. It adds the names from the supplier namespace to the client namespace (they must not conflict). But the access dependency does not alter the client namespace. It is mainly an access control mechanism in larger development projects, rather than a fundamental semantic relationship.

A nested package has access to any elements directly contained in outer packages (to any degree of nesting), without needing either import dependencies or visibility. A package must import its contained packages to see inside them, however. A contained package is, in general, an encapsulation boundary.

A package defines the visibility of its contained elements as **private, protected,** or **public.** Private elements are not available at all outside the containing package (regardless of imports). Protected elements are available only to packages with generalizations to the containing package, and public elements are available to importing packages and to descendants of the package.

See access for a full description of the visibility rules for elements in various packages.

Notation

A package is shown as a large rectangle with a small rectangle (a "tab") attached on one corner (usually, the left side of the upper side of the large rectangle). It is a folder icon.

If contents of the package are not shown, then the name of the package is placed within the large rectangle. If contents of the package are shown, then the name of the package may be placed within the tab.

A keyword string may be placed above the package name. Keywords may include subsystem, system, and model. User-defined stereotypes are also notated with keywords, but they must not conflict with the predefined keywords.

A list of properties may be placed in braces after or below the package name. Example: {abstract}.

The contents of the package may be shown within the large rectangle.

The visibility of a package element outside the package may be indicated by preceding the name of the element by a visibility symbol ('+' for public, '–' for private, '#' for protected).

Relationships may be drawn between package symbols to show relationships among at least some of the elements in the packages. In particular, dependency among packages (other than permission dependencies, such as access and import) implies that there exist one or more dependencies among the elements.

Presentation options

A tool may also show visibility by selectively displaying those elements that meet a chosen visibility level, for instance, all the public elements only.

A tool may show visibility by a graphic marker, such as color or font.

Style guidelines

It is expected that packages with large contents will be shown as simple icons with names, in which the contents may be dynamically accessed by "zooming" to a detailed view.

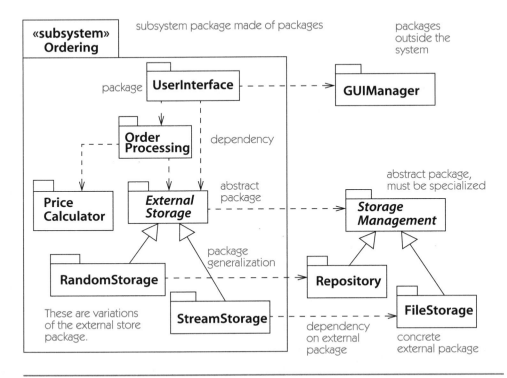

Figure 13-140. *Packages and their relationships*

Example

Figure 13-140 shows the package structure of an order-processing subsystem. The subsystem itself is shown as a package with a stereotype. It contains several ordinary packages. The dependencies among the packages are shown by dashed arrows. The figure also shows some external packages on which the subsystem depends. These may be off-the-shelf components or library elements.

Generalization among packages shows variations of a generic package. For instance, the **ExternalStore** package may be implemented as a **RandomStore** or a **StreamStore**.

Discussion

Packages are primarily intended as access and configuration control mechanisms to permit developers, particularly in large work groups, to organize large models and evolve them without getting in each other's way. Inherently, they mean what the developers want them to mean. More practically, packages should follow some kind of semantic boundary if they are to be useful. Because they are intended as configuration control units, they should contain elements that will likely evolve together. Packages also group elements that must be compiled together. If a change to one element forces the recompilation of other elements, then they might also be placed in one package.

Every model element must be owned by exactly one package or other model element. Otherwise, model maintenance, versioning, and configuration control become impossible. The package that owns a model element controls its definition. It can be referenced and used in other packages, but a change to it requires access permission and update right to the package that owns it.

Standard elements

access, extend, facade, framework, stub, system

parameter

The specification of a variable that can be changed, passed, or returned. A parameter may include a name, type, and direction. Parameters are used for operations, messages, events, and templates. Contrast: argument.

A parameter usage dependency relates an operation having a parameter or a class containing such an operation to the class of the parameter.

See also argument, binding.

Semantics

A parameter is a placeholder for an argument that is bound to it when the enclosing element is used. It constrains the values that the argument can take. It has the following parts.

default value   An expression for a value to be used if no argument is supplied for the parameter. The expression is evaluated when the parameter list is bound to arguments.

direction   The direction of information flow of the parameter, an enumeration with the following values.

in   An input parameter passed by value. Changes to the parameter are not available to the caller.

out   An output parameter. There is no input value. The final value is available to the caller.

inout   An input parameter that may be modified. The final value is available to the caller.

return   A return value of a call. The value is available to the caller. Semantically, no different from an out parameter, but the result is available for use in an inline expression.

The preceding choices may not all be directly available in every programming language, but the concept behind each of them makes sense in most languages and can be mapped into a sensible implementation.

name   The name of the parameter. It must be unique within its parameter list.

type   A reference to a classifier (a class, data type, or interface in most procedures). An argument bound to the parameter must be an instance of the classifier or one of its descendants.

Notation

Each parameter is shown as a text string that can be parsed into the various properties of a parameter. The default syntax is

direction name : type = default-value

Direction. The direction is shown as a keyword preceding the operation name. If the keyword is absent, then the direction is in. The choices are in, out, inout, and return. Return parameters are usually shown in a different position in an operation signature, where they need not be marked for direction.

Name. The name is shown as a string.

Type. The type is notated as a string that is the name of a class, an interface, or a data type.

Default value. The value is shown as an expression string. The language of the expression would be known by (and specifiable to) a tool but is not shown in the canonical format.

Scope. If the scope is class, then the operation string is underlined. If the scope is instance, the operation string is not underlined.

Parameter dependency. A parameter dependency is shown as a dashed arrow from the operation having the parameter or the class containing the operation to the class of the parameter; the arrow has the stereotype «parameter» attached.

Example

Matrix::transform (**in** distance: Vector, **in** angle: Real = 0): **return** Matrix

All of the direction labels here may be omitted.

parameter list

A specification of the values that an operation or template receives. A parameter list is an ordered list of parameter declarations. The list may be empty, in which case the operation is called with no parameters.

See parameter.

Notation

A parameter list is a comma-separated list of parameter declarations enclosed in parentheses.

(parameter$_{list,}$)

The parentheses are shown even if the list is empty.

( )

parameterized element

See template.

parent

The more general element in a generalization relationship. Called superclass for a class. A chain of one or more parent relationships (that is, the transitive closure) is an ancestor. The opposite is child.

See generalization.

participates

The connection of a model element to a relationship or to a reified relationship. For example, a class participates in an association, a classifier role participates in a collaboration.

passive object

An object that does not have its own thread of control. Its operations execute under a control thread anchored in an active object.

Semantics

An active object is one that owns a thread of control and may initiate control activity. A passive object is one that has a value but does not initiate control. However, an operation on a passive object may send messages while processing a request that it has received on an existing thread.

Notation

A passive object is shown as a class rectangle with the object name underlined. A passive class is shown as a class rectangle with the class name not underlined. The rectangle has a normal border (not bold). An active object or class is drawn with a bold border.

path

A connected series of graphic segments that connects one symbol to another, usually used to show a relationship.

Notation

A *path* is a graphical connection between symbols on a diagram. Paths are used in the notation for relationships of various kinds, such as associations, generalizations, and dependencies. The endpoints of two connected segments coincide. A segment may be a straight line segment, an arc, or some other shape, although many tools support only lines and arcs (Figure 13-141). Lines can be drawn at any angle, although some modelers prefer to restrict lines to orthogonal angles and possibly force them onto a regular grid for appearance and ease of layout. Generally, the routing of a path has no significance, although paths should avoid crossing closed regions, because crossing the boundary of a graphic region may have semantic significance. (For example, an association between two classes in a collaboration should be drawn within the collaboration region to indicate an association between objects from the same collaboration instance; whereas, a path that made an excursion from the region would indicate an association between objects from different collaboration instances.) More precisely, a path is topological. Its exact routing has no semantics, but its connection to and intersection with other symbols has significance. The exact layout of paths matter greatly to understandability and aesthetics, of course, and may subtly connote the importance of relationships and other things. But such considerations are for humans and not computers. Tools are expected to support the easy routing and rerouting of paths.

On most diagrams, the crossing of lines has no significance. To avoid ambiguity about the identity of crossing lines, a small semicircle or gap can be drawn in one of them at the crossing point (Figure 13-142). More commonly, modelers just treat a crossing as two independent lines and agree to avoid the confusion of having two right angles touch at their corners.

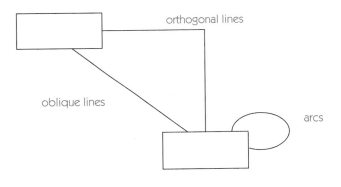

Figure 13-141. *Paths*

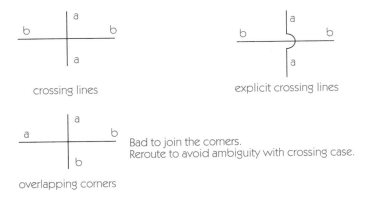

Figure 13-142. *Path crossings*

In some relationships (such as aggregation and generalization), several paths of the same kind may connect to a single symbol. If the properties of the various model elements match, then the line segments connected to the symbol can be combined into a single line segment so that the path from that symbol branches into several paths as a kind of tree (Figure 13-143). This is purely a graphical presentation option. Conceptually, the individual paths are distinct. This presentation option may not be used when the modeling information on the various segments is not identical.

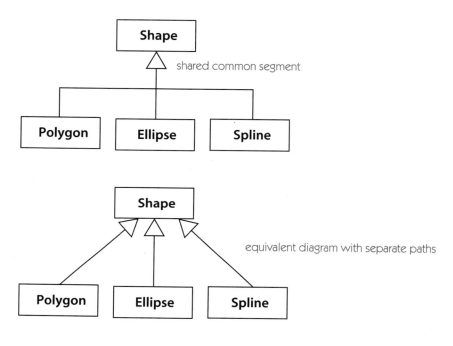

Figure 13-143. *Paths with shared segment*

pathname

A string composed by concatenating the names of the nested namespaces containing an element, starting from the implicit unnamed namespace that contains the entire system and ending with the name of the element itself.

Semantics

A pathname uniquely identifies a model element, such as an attribute or a state, within a system and may be used within an expression to reference an element. Not every kind of element has a name.

Notation

A pathname is displayed as a list of nested namespace and element names separated by double colons (::). A namespace is a package or an element with nested declarations.

Accounting::Personnel::Employee::address

An attribute **address** in class **Employee** in package **Personnel** in package **Accounting**

A pathname is a reference to an element in the package named by the path prefix.

pattern

A parameterized collaboration that represents a set of parameterized classifiers, relationships, and behavior that can be applied to multiple situations by binding elements from the model (usually classes) to the roles of the pattern. It is a collaboration template.

Semantics

A pattern represents a parameterized collaboration that can be used multiple times within one or more systems. To be a pattern, the collaboration must be usable in a wide range of situations to justify giving it a name. A pattern is a solution that has been shown to work in a number of situations. It is not necessarily the only solution to a problem, but it is a solution that has been effective in the past. Most patterns have advantages and disadvantages that depend on various aspects of the wider system. The modeler must consider these advantages and disadvantages before making a decision to use a pattern.

A UML parameterized collaboration represents the structural and behavioral views of certain kinds of patterns. Patterns involve other aspects that are not modeled directly by UML, such as the list of advantages and disadvantages and examples of previous use. Many of these other aspects can be expressed in words. See [Gamma-95] for a fuller treatment of patterns, as well as a catalog of some proven design patterns.

Generating collaborations from patterns. A collaboration can be used to specify the implementation of design constructs. The same kind of collaboration may be used many times by parameterizing its constituents. A pattern is a parameterized collaboration. Generally, the classes of the roles in the collaboration are parameters. A pattern is instantiated as a collaboration by binding values, usually classes, to its parameters. For the common case of parameterized roles, the template is bound by specifying a class for each role. Typically, the association roles in a pattern are not parameterized. When the template is bound, they represent implicit associations between the classes bound to the collaboration—that is, the binding of the template to make a collaboration generates additional associations.

Notation

The binding of a pattern to produce a collaboration is shown as a dashed ellipse containing the name of the pattern (Figure 13-144). A dashed line is drawn from the pattern binding symbol to each of the classes (or other model elements) that participate in the collaboration. Each line is labeled by the name of the parameter. In most cases, the name of a role in the collaboration can be used as a parameter name. Therefore, a pattern binding symbol can show the use of a design pattern, together with the actual classes that occur in that use of the pattern. The pattern binding usually does not show the internal structure of the collaboration that is generated by the binding. This is implied by the binding symbol.

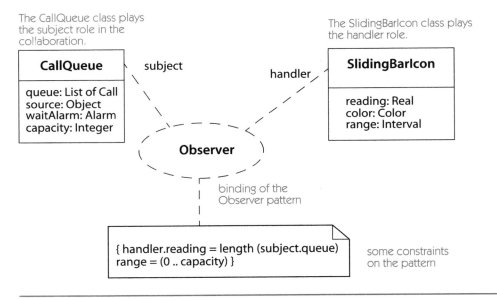

Figure 13-144. *Binding of a pattern to make a collaboration*

permission

A kind of dependency that grants the client element permission to use the contents of the supplier element (subject to visibility declarations of the content elements).

Semantics

The stereotypes of permission dependency are access, friend, and import. A naked permission dependency without a stereotype is never used. The access and import dependencies are used with packages. The friend dependency is used with classes or operations as clients and classes as suppliers.

Notation

A permission dependency is shown as a dashed arrow from the client (the element gaining permission) to the supplier (the element granting permission) with the appropriate stereotype keyword attached to the arrow.

Standard elements

friend, import

persistent object

An object that exists after the thread that created it has ceased to exist.

polymorphic

Indicates an operation whose implementation (a method or state machine triggered by a call event) may be supplied by a descendant class. An operation that is not polymorphic is a leaf operation.

See also abstract operation, generalization, inheritance, method.

Semantics

If an operation is polymorphic, then a method may be supplied for it in a descendant class (whether or not a method has already been supplied by the original class). Otherwise, a method must be available for the operation in the class declaring the operation, and the method cannot be overridden in a descendant class. A method is available if it is declared by a class or inherited from an ancestor. An abstract operation must be polymorphic (because it has no direct implementation). An operation is nonpolymorphic if it is declared to be a leaf operation.

If an operation is declared polymorphic in a class—that is, if it is not declared as a leaf—it may be declared to be a leaf in a descendant class. This prevents it from being overridden in a further descendant. A leaf operation may not be declared polymorphic in a descendant class. It may not be overridden at any depth.

UML does not mandate the rules for method combination if a method is declared in a class and overridden in a descendant class (see discussion following). Mechanisms, such as declaring before, after, and around methods, may be handled in a language-specific manner using tagged values. Actions such as explicitly calling the inherited method are, of course, dependent on the action language in any case.

Notation

A nonpolymorphic operation is declared using the keyword {leaf}. Otherwise, it is assumed to be polymorphic.

Discussion

An abstract operation is necessarily polymorphic. Otherwise, it could not be implemented at all. Bertrand Meyer calls this a deferred operation, because its specification is defined in a class but its implementation is deferred to subclasses. This is an essential, probably the most essential, use of inheritance in both modeling and programming. Using inheritance, operations can be applied to sets of objects of mixed classes. The caller need not know or determine the class of each object. It is only necessary that all of the objects conform to an ancestor class defining the desired operations. The ancestor class need not implement the operations. It must simply define their signatures. The caller need not know even the list of possible subclasses. This means that new subclasses can be added later, without disrupting polymorphic operations on them. Source code that invokes operations need not change when new subclasses are added. The ability to add new classes after the original code is written is one of the key pillars of object-oriented technology.

A more problematic use of polymorphism is the replacement (overriding) of a method defined in a class by a different method defined in a subclass. This is often cited as a form of sharing, but it is dangerous. Overriding is not incremental, so everything in the original method must be reproduced in the child method, even to make a small change. This kind of repetition is error-prone. In particular, if the original method is changed later, there is no guarantee that the child method will be changed also. There are times when a subclass can use a completely different implementation of an operation, but many experts would discourage such overriding because of the inherent danger. In general, methods should be either completely inherited without overriding or deferred; in the latter case there is no implementation in the superclass, so there is no danger of redundancy or inconsistency.

To permit a subclass to extend the implementation of an operation without losing the inherited method, most programming languages provide some form of method combination that uses the inherited method but allows additional code to be added to it. In C++, an inherited method must be explicitly invoked by class and operation name, which builds the class hierarchy into the code rigidly—not a very object-oriented approach. In Smalltalk, a method can invoke an operation on super, which causes the operation to be handled by the inherited method. If the class hierarchy changes, then the inheritance still works, possibly with a method from a different class. However, the overriding method must explicitly provide a call to super. Errors can and do happen, because programmers forget to insert the calls when a change occurs. Finally, CLOS provides very general and complicated automatic method combination rules that may invoke several methods during the execution of a single operation call. The overall operation is implemented from several fragments rather than being forced to be a single method. This is very general but harder to manage for the user.

UML does not force a single method combination approach. Method combination is a semantic variation point. Any of these approaches may be used. If the programming language is weak on method combination, then a modeling tool may be able to provide help in generating the appropriate programming-language code or in warning about possible oversights if method overriding is used.

postcondition

A constraint that must be true at the completion of an operation.

Semantics

A postcondition is a Boolean expression that must be true after the execution of an operation completes. It is an assertion, not an executable statement. Depending on the exact form of the expression, it might be possible to verify it automatically in advance. It can be useful to test the postcondition after the operation, but this is in the nature of debugging a program. The condition is supposed to be true, and anything else is a programming error. A postcondition is a constraint on the implementor of an operation. If it is not satisfied, then the operation has been implemented incorrectly.

See also invariant, precondition.

Structure

A postcondition is modeled as a constraint with the stereotype «postcondition», which is attached to an operation.

Notation

A postcondition can be shown in a note with the keyword «postcondition». The note is attached to the affected operation.

Example

Figure 13-145 shows a postcondition on an array sort operation. The new value of the array (a') is related to the original value (a). This example is expressed in structured natural language. Specification in a more formal language is also possible.

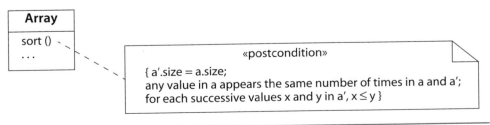

Figure 13-145. *Postcondition*

powertype

A metaclass whose instances are subclasses of a given class.
See also metaclass.

Semantics

The subclasses of a given class may themselves be considered instances of a meta-class. Such a metaclass is called a powertype. For example, class **Tree** may have sub-classes **Oak**, **Elm**, and **Willow**. Considered as objects, those subclasses are instances of metaclass **TreeSpecies**. **TreeSpecies** is a powertype that ranges over **Tree**.

Notation

A powertype is shown as a class with the stereotype «**powertype**». It is connected to a set of generalization paths by a dashed arrow with the stereotype «**powertype**» on the arrow (Figure 13-146).

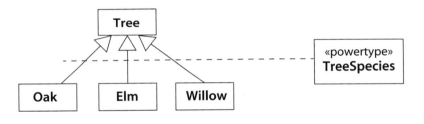

Figure 13-146. *Powertype*

precondition

A constraint that must be true when an operation is invoked.

Semantics

A precondition is a Boolean expression that must be true when an operation is called. It is the responsibility of the caller to satisfy the condition. It is not a condi-tion that the receiver should have to check. A precondition is not a guard condi-tion; it is a condition that *must* be true, not a way to optionally execute an operation. It can be useful to test the precondition at the beginning of the opera-tion for reliability, but this is in the nature of debugging a program. The condition is supposed to be true, and anything else is a programming error. If the condition is not satisfied, no statement can be made about the integrity of the operation or the system. It is liable to utter failure. In practice, explicitly checking preconditions by the receiver may detect many errors.

See also invariant, postcondition.

Structure

A precondition is modeled as a constraint with the stereotype «precondition», which is attached to an operation.

Notation

A precondition can be shown in a note with the keyword «precondition». The note is attached to the affected operation.

Example

Figure 13-147 shows a precondition on a matrix product operator.

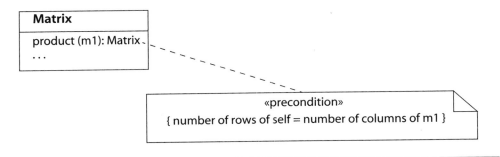

Figure 13-147. *Precondition*

presentation element

A textual or graphical projection of one or more model elements.
   See also diagram.

Semantics

Presentation elements (sometimes called view elements, although they include nongraphical forms of presentation) present the information in a model for human perception. They are the notation. They show part or all of the semantic information about a model element. They may also add aesthetic information useful to humans, for example, by grouping conceptually related elements together. But the added information has no semantic content. The expectation is that a presentation element is responsible for maintaining itself correctly despite changes to the underlying model elements; whereas, the model elements need not be aware of presentation elements to operate correctly.

The descriptions of UML notation in this book define the mapping from model elements to graphical presentations on a screen. The implementation of presentation elements as objects is the responsibility of a tool implementation.

primitive type

A predefined basic data type, such as an integer or a string.
See also enumeration.

Semantics

Instances of primitive types do not have identity. If two instances have the same representation, then they are indistinguishable and can be passed by value with no loss of information.

Primitive types include numbers and strings, and possibly other system-dependent data types, for example, dates, and money, whose semantics are predefined outside UML.

It is expected that primitive types will correspond closely to those found in the target programming language.

See also enumerations, which are user-definable data types that are not predefined primitive types.

private

A visibility value indicating that the given element is not visible outside its own namespace even to descendants of the namespace.

private inheritance

The inheritance of structure in a situation in which behavioral specification is not inherited.

See also implementation inheritance, interface inheritance, substitutability principle.

Semantics

A generalization may have the stereotype «implementation». This indicates that the client element (usually a class) inherits the structure (attributes, associations, and operations) of the supplier element but does not necessarily make this structure available to its own clients. Because the ancestry of such a class (or other element) is not visible to other classes, an instance of the class may not be used for a variable or parameter declared with the supplier class. In other words, the class is not substitutable for its privately inherited suppliers. Private inheritance does not follow the substitutability principle.

Notation

Private inheritance is indicated by the keyword «implementation» on a generalization arrow from the inheriting element (the client) to the element supplying the structure to be inherited (the supplier).

Discussion

Private inheritance is purely an implementation mechanism and should not be thought of as a use of generalization. Generalization requires substitutability. Private inheritance is not particularly meaningful in an analysis model, which does not involve implementation structure. Even for implementation, it should be used with care, as it involves a nonsemantic use of inheritance. A cleaner alternative is often an association to the supplier class. Many authors (including this one) would argue that it should never be used at all, because it uses inheritance in a nonsemantic way that is dangerous when changes are made to a model.

procedure expression

An expression whose evaluation represents the execution of a procedure that may affect the state of the running system.

Semantics

A procedure expression is an encoding of an executable algorithm. Its execution may (and usually does) affect the state of the system—that is, it has side effects. A procedure expression does not generally return a value. The purpose of its execution is to alter the system state.

process

1. A heavyweight unit of concurrency and execution in an operating system. *See* thread, which includes heavyweight and lightweight processes. If necessary, an implementation distinction can be made using stereotypes.
2. A software development process—the steps and guidelines by which to develop a system.
3. To execute an algorithm or otherwise handle something dynamically.

product

The artifacts of development, such as models, code, documentation, work plans; a work product.

projection

A mapping from a set to a subset of it. Most models and diagrams are projections from the full set of information that is potentially available.

property

A generic term denoting a named value conveying information about a model element. A property has semantic impact. Certain properties are predefined in the UML; others may be user defined.

See attribute, relationship, tagged value.

Semantics

Properties include built-in attributes (UML defined), as well as tagged values (user defined) and relationships (user defined) attached to an element. From a user's viewpoint, it often doesn't matter if a property is built in or it is implemented as a tagged value.

Discussion

Note that we use *property* in a general sense to mean any value attached to a model element, including attributes, associations, and tagged values. In this sense, it can include indirectly reachable values that can be found starting at a given element.

property list

A text syntax for showing a property or properties attached to an element, especially tagged values, but also including built-in attributes of model elements.

Notation

One or more comma-separated property specifications enclosed in braces ({ }). Each property declaration has the form

    property-name = value

or

    property-literal

where the property literal is a unique enumerated value whose appearance implies a unique property name.

Example

    { abstract, author=Joe, visibility=private }

Presentation options

A tool may present property specifications on separate lines with or without the enclosing braces, provided they are appropriately marked to distinguish them from other information. For example, properties for a class might be listed under the class name in a distinctive typeface, such as italics or a different font family. This is a tool issue.

Note that property strings may be used to display built-in attributes, as well as tagged values, but such usage should be avoided if the canonical form is simple.

protected

A visibility value indicating that the given element is visible outside its own namespace only to descendants of the namespace.

pseudoattribute

A value related to a class that behaves like an attribute—namely, it has a unique value for each instance.

See also discriminator, rolename.

Semantics

Pseudoattributes include association rolenames and generalization discriminators. An association rolename is a pseudoattribute in the class on the other end of the association. A generalization discriminator is a pseudoattribute in the parent element. In each child element, the value of the discriminator is the name of the child element.

A pseudoattribute can be used as a name in an expression to retrieve a value from an object. Because attribute names and pseudoattribute names may be used in expressions, they are in the same namespace and must be unique in that namespace. The names must also be unique with respect to inherited attribute and pseudoattribute names.

pseudostate

A vertex in a state machine that has the form of a state but does not behave as a full state. *See* history state, initial state, junction state, stub state.

Semantics

When a pseudostate is active, a state machine has not completed its run to completion step and will not process events. Pseudostates include initial state, junction state, stub state, and history state. Pseudostates are used to chain transition segments, and a transition to one implies a further automatic transition to another state without requiring an event.

A final state and a synch state are not pseudostates. They are special states that may remain active when a state machine has completed its run to completion step, but they have restrictions on the transitions that can depart from them.

public

A visibility value indicating that the given element is visible outside its own namespace.

qualifier

A slot for an attribute or list of attributes on a binary association, in which the values of the attributes select a unique related object or a set of related objects from the entire set of objects related to an object by the association. It is an index on the traversal of an association.

See association class, association end.

Semantics

A binary association maps an object to a set of related objects. Sometimes, it is desirable to select an object from the set by supplying a value that distinguishes the objects in the set. This value could be an attribute of the target class. In general, however, the selector value may be part of the association itself, an association attribute whose value is supplied by the creator when a new link is added to the association class. Such an attribute on a binary association is called a qualifier. An object, together with a qualifier value, determines a unique related object or (somewhat less often) a subset of related objects. The value qualifies the association. In an implementation context, such an attribute has been called an index value.

A qualifier is used to select an object or objects from the set of objects related to a object (called the *qualified object*) by an association (Figure 13-148). The object selected by the qualifier value is called the *target object*. A qualifier always acts on an association whose multiplicity is *many* in the target direction. In the simplest case, each qualifier value selects a single object from the target set of related objects. In other words, a qualified object and a qualifier value yield a unique related target object. Given a qualified object, each qualifier value maps into a unique target object.

Many kinds of names are qualifiers. Such a name within a context maps to a unique value. The qualified object supplies the context, the qualifier is the name, and the target object is the result. Any ID or other unique code is a qualifier; its purpose is to uniquely select a value. An array can be modeled as a qualified asso-

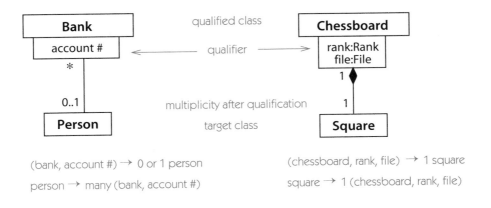

Figure 13-148. *Qualified associations*

ciation. The array is the qualified object, the array index is the qualifier, and the array element is the target object. For an array, the qualifier type is an integer range.

A qualifier may be used in a navigation expression to select a subset of objects related to an object across an association—namely, those bearing a particular value for the qualifier attribute value or list of values. The qualifier serves as a selector within the set of objects related by the association. It partitions the set into subsets by qualifier value. In most cases, the purpose of a qualifier is to select a unique object from the set of related objects so that a qualified association behaves like a lookup table.

Structure

Qualifier. A qualifier attribute is an optional part of a binary association end. The qualifier qualifies the class attached to the association end. An object of the class and a qualifier value select an object or set of objects from the class at the other end of the binary association. It is possible for both ends of a binary association to have qualifiers, but it is rare.

A qualifier is an association attribute or list of attributes. Each attribute has a name and a type but no initial value, as qualifiers are not free-standing objects, and each qualifier value must be explicit when a link is added to the association.

Qualifiers are not used with *n*-ary associations.

Multiplicity. The multiplicity of the qualified relationship is placed on the opposite end of the binary association from the qualifier. (The mnemonic is that the qualified class and qualifier together form a composite value that is related to the target class.) In other words, the qualifier is attached to the "near end" of the association, and the multiplicity and rolename are attached to the "far end."

The multiplicity attached to the target association end denotes how many target objects might be selected by a (source object, qualifier value) pair. Common multiplicity values include 0..1 (a unique value may be selected, but every possible qualifier value does not necessarily select a value), 1 (every possible qualifier value selects a unique target object, therefore the domain of qualifier values must be finite), and * (the qualifier value is an index that partitions the target objects into subsets).

In the majority of cases, the multiplicity is zero-or-one. This choice means that an object and qualifier value may yield, at most, one related object. A multiplicity of one means that every possible qualifier value yields exactly one object. This obviously requires the qualifier type to be a finite domain (in a computer implementation anyway). This multiplicity can be useful for mapping finite enumerated types—for example, a **Pixel** qualified by **PrimaryColor** (enumeration of red, green, and blue) would yield the red-green-blue value triplet for each pixel in an image.

The multiplicity of the unqualified association is not stated explicitly. But it is usually assumed to be many, or at least more than one. Otherwise, there would be no need for a qualifier.

A multiplicity of many on a qualified association has no significant semantic impact, because the qualifier does not reduce the multiplicity of the target set. Such a multiplicity represents a design statement that an index to traverse the association must be provided. In that case, the qualifier partitions the set of target objects into subsets. Semantically, this adds nothing beyond having an association attribute, which also (implicitly) partitions the links. The design connotation of a qualifier in a design model is that the traversal should be efficient—that is, it must not require a linear search among all the target values. Usually it is implemented by some kind of lookup table. An index in a database or data structure is properly modeled as a qualifier.

In the reverse direction across a qualified association (that is, going from the target class to the qualified object), the multiplicity indicates the number of (qualified object, qualifier) pairs that can relate to a target object, not the number of qualified objects. In other words, if several (qualified object, qualifier) pairs map into the same target object, then the reverse multiplicity is many. A reverse multiplicity of one from target to qualifier means that there is exactly one pairing of qualified object and qualifier value that relates to the target object.

Notation

A qualifier is shown as a small rectangle attached to the end of an association path between the final path segment and the symbol of the qualified class. The qualifier rectangle is part of the association path, not part of the class. The qualifier is attached to the class that it qualifies—that is, an object of the qualified class together with a value of the qualifier uniquely selects a set of target class objects on the other end of the association.

Qualifier attributes are listed within the qualifier box. There may be one or more attributes in the list. Qualifier attributes have the same notation as class attributes, except that initial value expressions are not meaningful.

Presentation options

A qualifier may not be suppressed (it provides essential detail, the omission of which would modify the inherent character of the relationship).

A tool may use a thinner line for qualifier rectangles than for class rectangles to distinguish them clearly.

The qualifier rectangle, preferably, should be smaller than the class rectangle to which it is attached, although this is not always practical.

Discussion

The multiplicities on a qualified association are treated as if the qualified object and the qualifier are a single entity, a composite key. In the forward direction, the multiplicity on the target end represents the number of objects related to the composite value (qualified object + qualifier value). In the reverse direction, the multiplicity describes the number of composite values (qualified object + qualifier) related to each target object, not the number of qualified objects related to each target object. This is why the qualifier is placed on the very end of the association path adjacent to the class symbol—you can think of the association path connecting the composite value to the target class.

There is no provision for specifying the multiplicity of the unqualified relationship. In practice, however, it is usually many in the forward direction. There is no point to have a qualified association unless many target objects are related to one qualified object. For logical modeling, the purpose of the qualifier is to reduce the multiplicity to one by adding the qualifier so that a query can be assured of returning a single value rather than a set of values. The uniqueness of the qualifier value is frequently a crucial semantic condition that is difficult to capture without qualifiers. Almost all applications have many qualified associations. Many names are really qualifiers. If a name is unique within some context, it is a qualifier and the context should be identified and modeled appropriately. Not all names are qualifiers. Names of persons, for example, are not unique. Because personal names are ambiguous, most data processing applications use some kind of identification number, such as a customer number, a Social Security number, or an employee number. If an application requires the lookup of information or the retrieval of data based on search keys, the model should generally use qualified associations. Any context in which names or identification codes are defined to select things out of sets should usually be modeled as a qualified association.

Note that the qualifier value is a property of the link, not of the target object. Consider a Unix file system, in which each directory is a list of entries whose names are unique within the directory, although the same names can be used in other directories. Each entry points to a file, which may be a data file or another directory. More than one entry can point to the same file. If this happens, the file has several aliases. The Unix directory system is modeled as a many-to-one association in which the directory qualified by the filename yields a file. Note that the filename is not part of the file; it is part of the relationship between a directory and a file. A file does not have a single name. It may have many names in many directories (or even several names in the same directory). The filename is not an attribute of the file.

A major motivation for qualified associations is the need to model an important semantic situation that has a natural and important implementation data structure. In the forward direction, a qualified association is a lookup table—for a qualified object, each qualifier value yields a single target object (or a null value if the qualifier value is absent in the set of values). Lookup tables are implementable by data structures, such as hash tables, b-trees, and sorted lists that provide much greater efficiency than unsorted lists, which must be searched linearly. In almost all cases, it is poor design to use a linked list or other unsorted data structure for searches on names or codes, although, sadly, many programmers use them. Modeling appropriate situations with qualified associations and using efficient data structures to implement them is crucial to good programming.

For a logical model, there is little point in having a qualified association with a multiplicity of many in the forward direction, because the qualifier does not add any semantic information that an association attribute could not show. In a model intended for the design of algorithms and data structures, however, a qualifier carries an additional connotation—namely, the intent that the selection be efficient. In other words, a qualified association denotes an indexed data structure optimized for lookup on the qualifier value. In this case, a multiplicity of many can be useful to represent a set of values that must be accessible together under a common index value, without having to search other values.

A qualifier attribute should, generally, not be included as an attribute of the target class, as its presence in the association is sufficient. In case of an index value, however, it may be necessary to take a value that is inherently an attribute of the target class and make it a redundant qualifier value. Index values are inherently redundant.

Constraints

Some complicated situations are not straightforward to model with any set of nonredundant relationships. They are best modeled using qualified associations to capture the basic access paths with additional constraints stated explicitly. Because

Figure 13-149. *Simple qualifier*

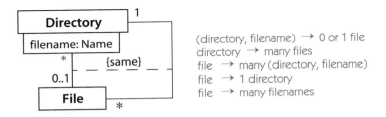

Figure 13-150. *File with multiple names in one directory*

these situations are uncommon, we felt that trying to include them in a notation that could capture all possible multiplicity constraints directly was not worth the added complexity.

For example, consider a directory in which each filename identifies a unique file. A file may correspond to multiple directory-filename pairs. This is the basic model we have seen before. This model is shown in Figure 13-149.

Now, however, we wish to add additional constraints. Suppose that each file must be in just one directory, but within that directory it could have many names—that is, there is more than one way to name the same file. This can be modeled with a redundant association between **File** and **Directory**, with multiplicity one on **Directory** (Figure 13-150). The redundancy of the two associations is indicated by the constraint {**same**}, which implies that the two elements are the same but at different levels of detail. Because these associations are redundant, only the qualified association would be implemented; the other would be treated as a run-time constraint on its contents.

A similar constraint is that each file may appear in multiple directories, but it always has the same name wherever it appears. Other files can have the same name, but they must be in different directories. This can be modeled by making **filename** an attribute of **File** but constraining the class attribute and the qualifier to be the

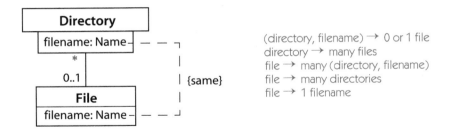

Figure 13-151. *File with same name in all directories*

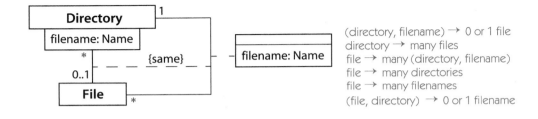

Figure 13-152. *File with at most one name in any directory*

same (Figure 13-151). This pattern occurs frequently as a search index, although in a general index the multiplicity of the qualified target would be many. This situation, therefore, has more semantic content than an index, which is an implementation device.

A third case would allow a file to appear in multiple directories under various names, but the file could appear only once within a single directory. This could be modeled with redundant qualified association and association class that share the same attribute **filename** (Figure 13-152).

These examples have been shown with redundant relations to illustrate the nature of the constraints. In practice, however, it is usually satisfactory to state the constraint textually, with the qualified association shown graphically.

query

An operation that returns a value but does not alter the state of the system; an operation without side effects.

realization

The relationship between a specification and its implementation; an indication of the inheritance of behavior without the inheritance of structure.

See also interface.

Semantics

A specification describes the behavior or structure of something without determining how the behavior will be implemented. An implementation provides the details about how to implement behavior in an effectively computable way. The relationship between an element that specifies behavior and one that provides an implementation is called realization. In general, there are many ways to realize a specification. Similarly, an element can realize more than one specification. Realization is therefore a many-to-many relationship among elements.

The meaning of realization is that the client element must support all the behavior of the supplier element but need not match its structure or implementation. A client classifier, for example, must support the operations of the supplier classifier, and it must support all state machines that specify external behavior of the supplier. But any attributes, associations, methods, or state machines of the supplier that specify implementation are irrelevant to the client. Note that the client does not actually inherit the operations from the supplier. It must declare them itself or inherit them from an ancestor so that all the operations of the supplier are covered. In other words, the supplier in a realization indicates which operations must be present in the client, but the client is responsible for providing them.

Certain kinds of elements, such as interfaces and use cases, are intended for specifying behavior, and they contain no implementation information. Other kinds of elements, such as classes, are intended for implementing behavior. They contain implementation information, but they can also be used in a more abstract way as specifiers. Usually, realization relates a specification element, such as a use case or an interface, to an implementation element, such as a collaboration or a class. It is possible to use an implementation element, such as a class, for specification. It can be placed on the specification side of a realization relationship. In this case, only the specification parts of the supplier class affect the client. The implementation parts are irrelevant for the realization relationship. More precisely, then, realization is a relationship between two elements in which the external behavior specification parts of one constrain the implementation of the other. It might be thought of as inheritance of behavior specification without inheritance of structure or implementation (and with the need to actually declare the operations by the client).

If the specification element is an abstract class with no attributes, no associations, and only abstract operations, any specialization of the abstract class realizes the abstract class, as there is nothing to inherit but specification.

The implementing element must support all of the behavior included in the specifying element. For example, a class must contain all the operations of the interfaces that it realizes, with semantics that are consistent with all the specifications required by the interfaces. The class can implement additional operations, and the implementation of the operations can do additional things, provided the operation specifications of the interfaces are not violated.

Notation

The realization relationship is shown by a dashed path with a closed triangular arrowhead on the end adjacent to the element supplying the specification and with its tail on the element supplying the implementation (Figure 13-153).

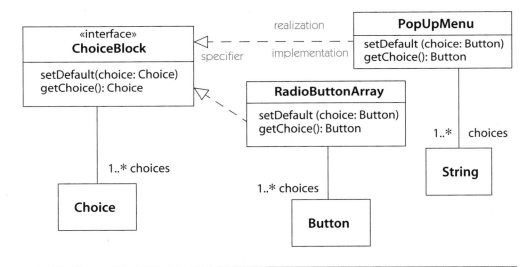

Figure 13-153. *Realization relationship*

Discussion

Another important case is the realization of a use case by a collaboration (Figure 13-154). A use case specifies externally visible functionality and behavioral sequences, but it does not supply an implementation. A collaboration describes the objects that implement the use case behavior and the way that they interact to do it. Usually, one collaboration implements one use case, but a collaboration can be implemented using subordinate collaborations, each of which does part of the job. The objects and classes used to implement a collaboration usually appear in

Figure 13-154. *Realization of use case by collaboration*

other collaborations as well. Each class in the collaboration devotes part of its functionality to the use case being implemented. Therefore, a use case is eventually implemented by slices through several classes.

realize

To provide the implementation for a specification element.
See realization.

receive

To handle a message instance passed from a sender object.
See sender, receiver.

receiver

The object that handles a message instance passed from a sender object.

reception

A declaration that a classifier is prepared to react to the receipt of a signal. It is a member of a classifier.

Semantics

A reception is a declaration that a classifier is prepared to accept and react to an instance of a signal. A reception is similar to an operation. It declares the signature of a message that the classifier supports and specifies its meaning.

Structure

A reception has the following properties.

polymorphism   Whether the response of the classifier to the signal is always the same. Coded by the property isPolymorphic with the following values.

true   The response is polymorphic: It may depend on state, and it can also be overridden by a descendant.

false	The response must be the same, regardless of state, and may not be overridden by a descendant. The net effect is that there must be a single transition on the entire state machine that handles the event.
signal	Designates the signal that the classifier is prepared to respond to.
specification	An expression stating the effects that reception of the signal causes.

Notation

A reception may be shown in the operation list of a class or interface using the syntax for an operation with the keyword «signal» in front of the signal name.

Alternately, a list of signal signatures may be placed in its own compartment; the compartment has the name **Signals**. Both ways are shown in Figure 13-155.

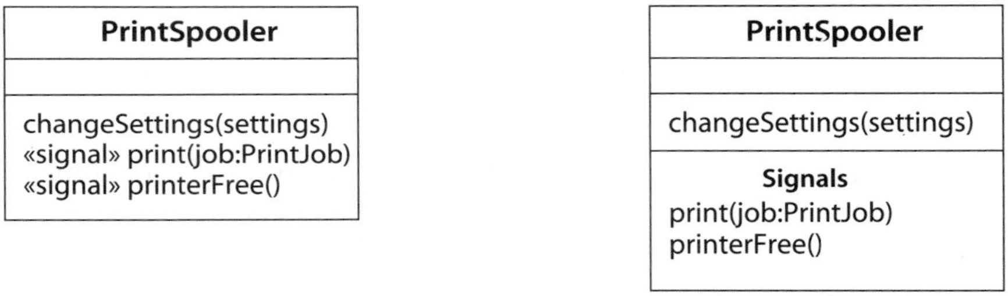

Figure 13-155. *Two ways to notate signal reception*

reference

A denotation of a model element; commonly called a *pointer*.

Semantics

Model elements are connected by two metarelationships: ownership and reference. Ownership is the relationship between an element and its constituent parts, the parts that are defined within it and owned by it. The ownership relationship forms a strict tree. The contained elements are subordinate to the container element. Ownership, configuration control, and storage of models are based on the containment hierarchy.

Reference is a relationship between elements at the same level of detail or between elements in different containers. For example, reference is the relationship between an association and its participant classes, between an attribute and the class or data type that is its type property, between a bound template and its argument values. For a reference to be possible, the element performing the reference must have visibility to the element being referenced. Generally this means that the package containing the source of the reference must have visibility to the package containing the target of the reference. This requires an appropriate access or import relationship between the packages. It also requires that the element being referenced have a visibility setting that allows it to be seen outside its package, unless the source of the reference is in the same package.

Note that reference is an internal metamodel relationship, not a user-visible relationship; it is used to construct the other relationships.

refine

Keyword for a refinement dependency in the notation.

refinement

A relationship that represents a fuller specification of something that has already been specified at a certain level of detail or at a different semantic level.

See also abstraction.

Semantics

A refinement is a historical or computable connection between two elements with a mapping (not necessarily complete) between them. Often, the two elements are in different models. For example, a design class may be a refinement of an analysis class; it has the same logical attributes, but their classes may come from a specific class library. An element can refine an element in the same model, however. For example, an optimized version of a class is a refinement of the simple but inefficient version of the class. The refinement relationship may contain a description of the mapping, which may be written in a formal language (such as OCL or a programming or logic language). Or it may be informal text (which, obviously, precludes any automatic computation but may be useful in early stages of development). Refinement may be used to model stepwise development, optimization, transformation, and framework elaboration.

Structure

Refinement is a kind of dependency. It relates a client (the element that is more developed) to a supplier (the element that is the base for the refinement).

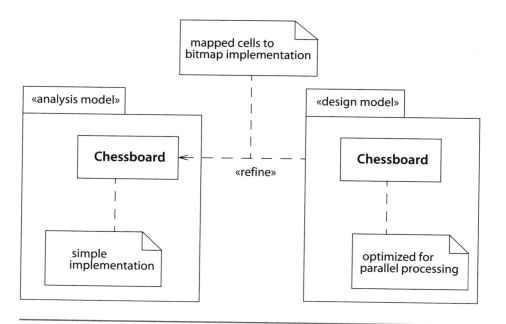

Figure 13-156. *Refinement*

Notation

A refinement is indicated by a dependency arrow (a dashed arrow with its head on the more general element and tail on the more specific element) with the keyword «refine». The mapping may be attached to the dependency path by a dashed line connected to a note. Various kinds of refinement have been proposed and can be indicated by further stereotyping. In many cases, refinement connects elements in different models and will therefore not be visible graphically. Often, it is only implicit.

Example

Optimization is a typical kind of refinement. Figure 13-156 shows a chessboard that has a simple representation in the analysis model, but it has a much more elaborate and obscure representation in the design model. The design class is not a specialization of the analysis class, because it has a totally different form. The class in the analysis model and the one in the design model have the same name, because they represent the same concept at two different semantic levels.

reification

The act of reifying something.
  See reify.

reify

To treat as an object something that is not usually regarded as an object.

Discussion

Reification has a long-standing philosophical and literary meaning. It is used to describe the characterization of abstract concepts as things or persons in mythology and poetry. For example, the god Thor was a reification of thunder. Plato's theory of ideals turned things around from the prevalent perception. He regarded pure concepts, such as Beauty, Good, and Courage, as the true eternal reality, and regarded the physical instantiations as imperfect copies—reification carried to its ultimate limit.

Reification is one of the most useful ideas for object orientation, and it underlies almost every aspect of modeling. Building a model in the first place requires the imposition of objects onto a continuous world. Humans do this naturally in every sentence they speak—a noun is a reification of a thing and a verb is a reification of an action. Reification is particularly useful when applied to things in models or programs that do not start out treated as objects, such as dynamic behavior. Most persons think of an operation as an object, but what about the execution (the word itself is a reification) of an operation? Generally people think of that as a process. But reify it and give it a name—call it an activation—and you can suddenly give it properties, form relationships to other objects, manipulate it, and store it. Reification of behavior transforms dynamic processes into data structures that can be stored and manipulated. This is a powerful concept for modeling and programming.

relationship

A reified semantic connection among model elements. Kinds of relationships include association, generalization, metarelationship, flow, and several kinds grouped under dependency.

Semantics

Table 13-2 shows the various kinds of UML relationships. The first column (kind) shows the groupings under which they are arranged in the metamodel. The second column (variety) shows the different kinds of relationships. The third column (notation) shows the base notation for each relationship: Association is a solid path, dependency is a dashed arrow, and generalization is a solid path with triangular arrowhead. The fourth column (keyword) shows the text keywords and additional syntax for those relationships that require it.

Table 13-2: *UML Relationships*

Kind	Variety	Notation	- - - → Keyword or Symbol
abstraction	derivation	dependency	«derive»
	realization	realization	- - - - ▷
	refinement	dependency	«refine»
	trace	dependency	«trace»
association		association	———
binding		dependency	«bind» (parameter$_{list,}$)
extend		dependency	«extend» (extension point$_{list,}$)
flow	become	dependency	sequence-number: «become»
	copy	dependency	sequence-number: «copy»
generalization		generalization	———▷
include		dependency	«include»
metarelationship	instance	dependency	«instanceOf»
	powertype	dependency	«powertype»
permission	access	dependency	«access»
	friend	dependency	«friend»
	import	dependency	«import»
usage	call	dependency	«call»
	instantiation	dependency	«instantiate»
	parameter	dependency	«parameter»
	send	dependency	«send»

repository

A storage place for models, interfaces, and implementations, part of an environment for manipulating development artifacts.

request

The specification of a stimulus sent to instances. It can be the call of an operation or the sending of a signal.

requirement

A desired feature, property, or behavior of a system.

Semantics

A text requirement may be modeled as a comment with the stereotype «requirement».

Discussion

The term *requirement* is a natural language word that corresponds to a variety of UML constructs that are intended to specify the desired characteristics of a system. Most commonly, requirements corresponding to user-visible transactions will be captured as use cases. Nonfunctional requirements, such as performance and quality metrics, may be captured as text statements that eventually trace to elements of the final design. UML comments and constraints may be used to represent nonfunctional requirements.

responsibility

A contract or obligation of a class or other element.

Semantics

A responsibility can be represented as a stereotype on a comment. The comment is attached to a class or other element that has the responsibility. The responsibility is expressed as a text string.

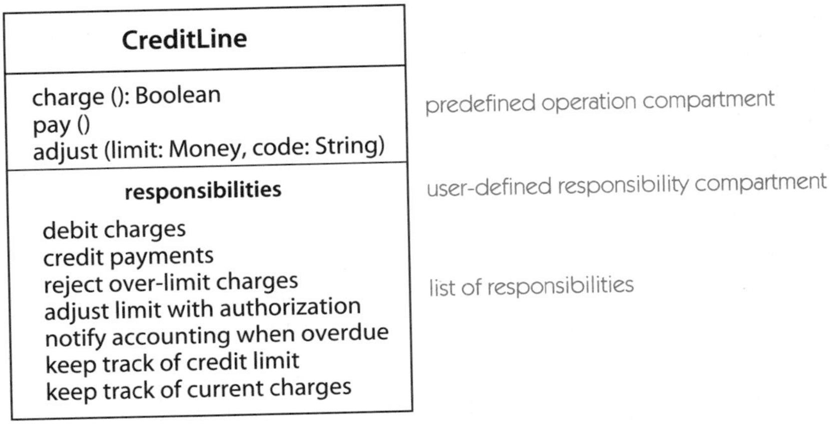

CreditLine

charge (): Boolean
pay ()
adjust (limit: Money, code: String)   predefined operation compartment

responsibilities   user-defined responsibility compartment

debit charges
credit payments
reject over-limit charges   list of responsibilities
adjust limit with authorization
notify accounting when overdue
keep track of credit limit
keep track of current charges

Figure 13-157. *Compartment for responsibilities*

Notation

Responsibilities can be shown in a named compartment within a classifier symbol rectangle (Figure 13-157).

reuse

The use of a pre-existing artifact.

role

A named slot within an object structure that represents behavior of an element that participates in a context (as opposed to the inherent qualities of the element across all usages). A role may be static (such as an association end) or dynamic (such as a collaboration role). Collaboration roles include classifier roles and association roles.

See collaboration.

rolename

A name for a particular association end within an association.

See also pseudoattribute.

Semantics

A rolename provides a name to identify an association end within an association, as well as to navigate from one object to another using the association. Because a rolename can be used in these two complementary ways, the name must be unique in two namespaces simultaneously.

All the rolenames in an association must be different. Within a self-association (an association involving the same class more than once), rolenames are necessary to disambiguate the ends attached to the same class. Otherwise, rolenames are optional, because the class names can be used to disambiguate the ends.

A rolename is also used to navigate from an object to neighboring related objects. Each class "sees" the associations attached to it and can use them to find objects related to one of its instances. By convention, the rolename on the association end attached to a neighboring class is used to form a navigation expression to access the object or set of objects related by that association. In Figure 13-158, consider class B that is associated to class A by a one-to-many association and to class C by a one-to-one association. Given an object bb of class B, the expression bb.theA yields a set of objects of class A, and the expression bb.theC yields an object of class C. In effect, the rolename on the far side of the association is like a

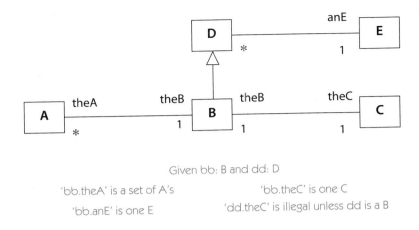

Given bb: B and dd: D

'bb.theA' is a set of A's   'bb.theC' is one C

'bb.anE' is one E   'dd.theC' is illegal unless dd is a B

Figure 13-158. *Navigation over associations*

pseudoattribute of a class—that is, it may be used as a term in an access expression to traverse the association.

Because a rolename can be used like an attribute name to extract values, a rolename enters the namespace of the class on the far side of the association. It goes in the same namespace as attribute names. Both attributes names and rolenames must be unique within that namespace. Attributes and association rolenames are inherited, and the attribute names and pseudoattribute names must be unique among inherited names also. A rolename attached to an ancestor class can be used for navigation in a descendant. In Figure 13-158, the expression **bb.anE** is legitimate, because class **B** inherits the rolename **anE** from class **D**.

Rolenames and association names are optional if each association can be uniquely identified. Either an association name or the rolenames on its ends can identify an association. It is not necessary to have both, although it is permitted to do so. If it is the only association between two classes, both the association name and the rolenames may be omitted. In principle a rolename is required for a navigation expression. In practice, a tool may provide a default rule for creating implicit rolenames from the names of the associated classes.

Notation

A rolename is shown by a graphic string placed near the end of an association path, at which it meets a class box. If it exists, the rolename may not be suppressed.

The rolename may bear a visibility marker—an arrowhead—that indicates whether the element at the far end of the association can see the element attached to the rolename.

run time

The period of time during which a computer program executes. Contrast: modeling time.

run to completion

A transition or series of actions that must be completed in its entirety.
See also action, atomic, state machine, transition.

Semantics

In a state machine, certain actions or series of actions are atomic—that is, they may not be terminated, aborted, or interrupted by other actions. When a transition fires, all the actions attached to it or invoked by it must be completed as a group, including entry actions and exit actions on states that it enters or leaves. The execution of a transition is said to run to completion, because it does not wait to accept other events.

Run-to-completion semantics may be contrasted with the wait semantics of normal states. When a state is active, an event may cause a transition to another state. Any activity in the state is aborted by the transition.

A transition may be composed of multiple segments arranged as a chain and separated by pseudostates. Several chains may merge together or branch apart, so the overall model may contain a graph of segments separated by pseudostates. Only the first segment in a chain may have a trigger event. The transition is triggered when the trigger event is handled by the state machine. If the guard conditions on all the segments are satisfied, the transition is enabled, and it fires, provided no other transition fires. The actions on the successive segments are executed. Once execution begins, the actions on all of the segments in the chain must be executed before the run-to-completion step is complete.

During execution of a run-to-completion transition, the trigger event that initiated the transition is available to actions as the current event. Entry and exit actions can therefore obtain the arguments of the trigger event. Various events may cause execution of an entry or exit action, but an action can discriminate the type of the current event in a case statement.

Because of the run-to-completion semantics of actions, they should be used to model assignments, testing flags, simple arithmetic, and other kinds of bookkeeping operations. Long computations should be modeled as interruptible activities.

scenario

A sequence of actions that illustrates behavior. A scenario may be used to illustrate an interaction or the execution of a use case instance.

scope

The extent of a classifier member, such as an attribute, operation, or rolename—that is, whether it represents a value in each instance or a value shared by all instances of the classifier. When used by itself without qualification, indicates owner scope.

See creation, owner scope, target scope.

Semantics

Scope is either owner scope or target scope.

Owner scope. An indication of whether there is a distinct attribute slot for each instance of a class or if there is one slot of the given name for the entire class.

instance	Each classifier instance has its own distinct copy of an attribute slot or its own set of associated objects. Values in one slot are independent of values in other slots. This is the default situation.
	For an operation, the operation applies to an individual object (a normal operation).
class	The classifier itself has one copy of the attribute slot or set of associated objects. All instances of the classifier share access to the one slot.
	For an operation, the operation applies to the entire class, such as a creation operation or an operation that returns statistics about the entire set of instances. Such an operation may not be applied to an instance.

Target scope. A choice indicating whether the values of an attribute or the target values in an association are instances (the default) or classifiers.

instance	Each attribute slot or each link of the association contains a reference to an instance of the target classifier. The number of links is constrained by the multiplicity. This is the default situation.
class	Each attribute slot or each link of the association contains a reference to the target class itself. The information in the association is therefore fixed at modeling time and does not change at run time, and it need not be stored in each object. In effect, the links involve the class itself, not its instances. This may be useful for some implementation information, but for most modeling purposes, this capability can be ignored.

Discussion

Class-scope attributes or associations provide global values for an entire class and should be used with care or avoided entirely, even though they are provided by most object-oriented programming languages. The problem is that they imply global information, which violates the spirit of object-oriented design. Moreover, global information becomes problematic in a distributed system, as it forces central accesses in a situation in which objects of a class may be distributed over many machines. Rather than use a class as an object with state, it is better to introduce explicit objects to hold any shared information that is needed. Both the model and costs are more apparent.

Constructors (creation operations, factory operations) necessarily have class-level source scope because there is no instance (yet) on which they may operate. This is a necessary and proper use of class scope. Other kinds of class-level source scope operations have the same difficulties as attributes—namely, they imply centralized global information about the instances of a class, which is impractical in a distributed system.

Target scope has a limited usefulness and should be used only in special circumstances—generally, only for detailed programming purposes.

self-transition

A transition in which the source state and the target state are the same. It is considered a state change. When it fires, the source state is exited and reentered so exit actions and entry actions are invoked. It is not equivalent to an internal transition, in which no change of state occurs.

semantic variation point

A point of variation in the semantics of a metamodel. It provides an intentional degree of freedom for the interpretation of the metamodel semantics.

Discussion

The same execution semantics is not suitable for all possible applications. Different programming languages and different purposes require variations in semantics, some subtle, some gross. A semantic variation point is an issue on which various modelers or various execution environments disagree about the specific semantics, often for good reasons. By simply identifying and naming semantic variation points, arguments about the "right" semantics of a system can be avoided.

For example, the choice of whether to permit multiple classification or dynamic classification is a semantic variation point. Each choice is a semantic variation.

Other examples of semantic variation points include whether a call can return more than one value and whether classes exist at run time as actual objects.

semantics

The formal specification of the meaning and behavior of something.

send

To create a signal instance by a sender object and to transfer it to a receiver object in order to convey information.

A send usage dependency relates an operation or method sending a signal or a class containing such an operation or method and the class receiving the signal.

See also signal.

Semantics

A send is a special operation that an object can perform. It specifies a signal to send, a list of arguments for the signal, and a set of target objects to receive the signal.

An object sends a signal to a set of objects—frequently, a set containing only a single object. A "broadcast" can be regarded as sending a message to the set of all objects, although, in practice, it might be implemented as a special case for efficiency. If the set of target objects contains more than one object, one copy of the signal is sent to each object in the set concurrently. If the set is empty, no signal is sent. This is not an error.

Creating a new object may be regarded as sending a message to a factory object, such as a class, which creates the new instance and then passes the message to it as its "birth event." This provides a mechanism for a creator to communicate with its creation—the birth event may be regarded as going from the creator to the new object, with the side-effect of instantiating the new object along the way. Figure 13-159 shows creation of an object using both text syntax and graphical syntax.

This model can be used even if the target language, such as C++, does not support classes as run-time objects. In that case, the creation action is compiled (which imposes some restrictions on its generality—for example, the name of the class must be a literal value) but the underlying intent is the same.

A send dependency is a stereotype of a usage dependency from the sender of the signal to the class receiving the signal.

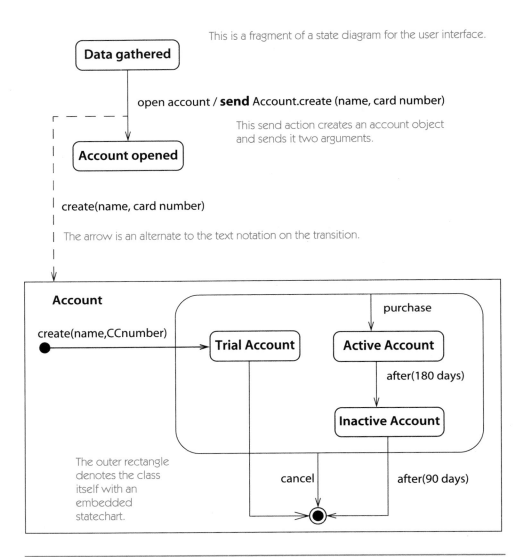

Figure 13-159. *Creation of new object by sending a message*

Text notation

Within a transition, sending a signal has its own syntax, although it is really just a special case of an action. Within the action sequence, the send expression has the syntax

send destination-expression .destination-message-name (argument$_{\text{list,}}$)

The keyword **send** is optional. A call and a send can be distinguished by the declaration of the message name. Sometimes, however, an explicit distinction is helpful.

The destination-expression must evaluate to a set of objects. A set with a single object is legal. The message is sent to each object in the set.

The destination-message-name is the name of a signal or an operation accepted by the target objects. The arguments are expressions that evaluate to values that must be compatible with the declared parameters of the event or operation. The distinction between a signal and an operation is based on the declarations of signals in the package and operations in the target class. There is no ambiguity in the internal model.

Example

This internal transition selects an object within a window using the cursor location, and then it sends a **highlight** signal to it.

right-mouse-down (location) [location **in** window]
/ object := pick-object (location) ; **send** object.highlight ()

Diagram notation

Sending a message can also be shown by diagram symbols.

Sending a message between state machines may be shown by drawing a dashed arrow from the sender to the receiver. The arrow is labeled with the signal name and argument expressions of the message. A state diagram must be contained within a rectangle that represents an object or class within the system. Graphically, state diagrams may be nested physically within an object symbol, or they may be implicit and shown elsewhere. State diagrams represent the control of the collaborating objects. The interactors may be roles of a collaboration, or they may be classes indicating the general ways in which objects of the classes communicate. Figure 13-160 contains state diagrams showing the sending of signals between three objects.

Note that this notation may also be used on other kinds of diagrams to show the sending of events between classes or objects.

The sender symbol (at the tail of the arrow) may be a

class	The message is sent by an object of the class at some point in its life, but the details are unspecified.
transition	The message is sent as part of the action of firing the transition (Figure 13-159 and Figure 13-160). This is an alternate presentation to the text syntax for sending messages.

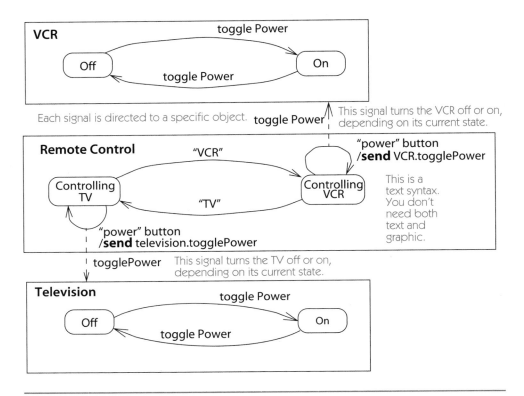

Figure 13-160. *Sending signals between objects*

The receiver symbol (at the arrowhead) may be a

class
: The message is received by the object and may trigger a transition within the object. The class symbol may contain a statechart diagram (Figure 13-160). The receiver object may have multiple transitions that use the same event as a trigger. This notation is not possible when the target object is computed dynamically. In that case, a text expression must be used.

metaclass
: This notation would be used to model the invocation of class-scope operations, such as the creation of a new instance. The receipt of such a message causes the instantiation of a new object in its default initial state. The event seen by the receiver may be used to trigger a transition from its default initial state and therefore represents a way to pass information from the creator to the new object.

transition   The transition must be the only transition in the class
                 using the event, or at least the only transition that could
                 be triggered by the particular sending of the message
                 (Figure 13-159). This notation is not possible when the
                 triggered transition depends on the state of the receiving
                 object. In that case, the arrow must be drawn to the class.

Send dependency. A send dependency is shown as a dashed arrow from the operation or class sending a signal to the class receiving the signal; the stereotype «send»
is attached to the arrow.

sender

The object passing a message instance to a receiver object.
See call, send.

sequence diagram

A diagram that shows object interactions arranged in time sequence. In particular,
it shows the objects participating in an interaction and the sequence of messages
exchanged.
See also activation, collaboration, lifeline, message.

Semantics

A sequence diagram represents an interaction—a set of communications among
objects arranged visually in time order. Unlike a collaboration diagram, a sequence diagram does include time sequences but does not include object relationships. It can exist in a descriptor form (describing all possible scenarios) and in an
instance form (describing one actual scenario). Sequence diagrams and collaboration diagrams express similar information, but they show it in different ways.

Notation

A sequence diagram has two dimensions: the vertical dimension represents time;
the horizontal dimension represents objects participating in the interaction
(Figure 13-161 and Figure 13-162). Generally, time proceeds down the page (the
axes may be reversed if desired). Often, only the sequences of messages are important, but in real-time applications, the time axis can be an actual metric. There is
no significance to the horizontal ordering of the objects.

Each object is shown in a separate column. An object symbol (a rectangle with
the underlined name of the object) is placed at the end of an arrow representing
the message that created the object, at the vertical point that indicates the time at
which the object is first created. If an object exists before the first operation of the

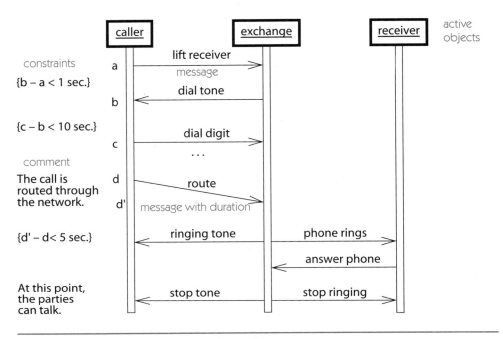

constraints

$\{b - a < 1\ sec.\}$

$\{c - b < 10\ sec.\}$

comment

The call is
routed through
the network.

$\{d' - d < 5\ sec.\}$

At this point,
the parties
can talk.

Figure 13-161. *Sequence diagram with asynchronous control*

diagram, the object symbol is drawn at the top of the diagram before any message. A dashed line is drawn from the object symbol to the point at which the object is destroyed (if that happens during the time shown by the diagram). This line is called the lifeline. A large *X* is placed at the point at which the object ceases to exist, either at the head of the arrow for the message that destroys the object or at the point at which the object destroys itself. For any period during which the object is active, the lifeline is broadened to a double solid line. This includes the entire life of an active object or an activation of a passive object—a period during which an operation of the object is in execution, including the time during which the operation waits for the return of an operation that it called. If the object calls itself recursively, directly or indirectly, then another copy of the double solid line is overlapped on it to show the double activation (potentially it could be more than two copies). The relative ordering of objects has no significance, although it is helpful to arrange them to minimize the distance that message arrows must cover. A comment about the activation may be placed in the margin near it.

Each message is shown as a horizontal arrow from the lifeline of the object that sent the message to the lifeline of the object that received the message. A label may be placed in the margin opposite an arrow to denote the time at which the message is sent. In many models, messages are assumed to be instantaneous, or at least atomic. If a message requires some time to reach its destination, then the message

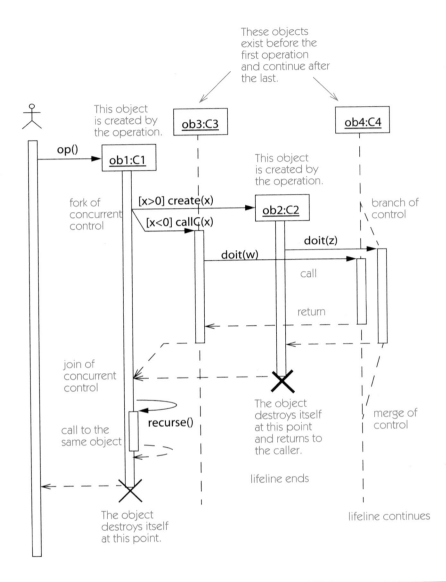

Figure 13-162. *Sequence diagram with procedural flow of control*

arrow is drawn diagonally downward so that the receiving time is later than the sending time. Both ends can have labels to denote the time the message was sent or received.

For asynchronous flow of control among active objects, the objects are represented by double solid lines and the messages are shown as arrows. Two messages

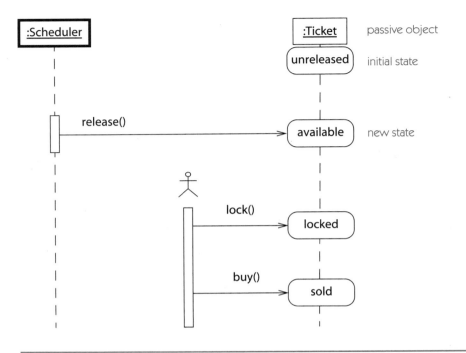

Figure 13-163. *Object states on a sequence diagram*

can be sent simultaneously, but two messages cannot be received simultaneously—there is no way to guarantee simultaneous reception. Figure 13-161 shows an asynchronous sequence diagram.

Figure 13-162 shows procedural flow of control on a sequence diagram. When modeling procedural flow of control, an object yields control on a call until a subsequent return. A call is shown with a solid filled arrowhead. The head of a call arrow may start an activation or a new object. A return is shown with a dashed line. The tail of a return arrow may finish an activation or an object.

Branching is shown by splitting the lifeline of an object. Each branch may send and receive messages. Usually, each branch sends different messages. Eventually, the lifelines for one object must merge again.

Figure 13-163 shows the states during the life of a theater ticket. A lifeline may be interrupted by a state symbol to show a change of state. This corresponds to a become transition within a collaboration diagram. An arrow may be drawn to the state symbol to indicate the message that caused the change of state.

Note that much of this notation is drawn directly from the Object Message Sequence Chart notation of Buschmann, Meunier, Rohnert, Sommerlad, and Stal [Buschmann-96], which is itself derived with modifications from Message Sequence Chart notation.

A sequence diagram can also be shown in a descriptor form, in which the constituents are roles rather than objects. Such a diagram shows the general case, not a single execution of it. Descriptor-level diagrams are drawn without underlines, as the symbols represent roles and not individual objects.

sequence number

A text part of a message label on a collaboration diagram that indicates the relative execution order of the messages in an interaction. A sequence number may show the location of the message within a nested calling sequence, the name of a thread of control, and a specification of conditional and iterative execution.

See collaboration, message.

signal

The specification of an asynchronous communication between objects. Signals may have parameters expressed as attributes.

See also event, message, send.

Semantics

A signal is an explicit named classifier intended for explicit communication between objects. It has an explicit list of parameters, represented as its attributes. It is explicitly sent by an object to another object or set of objects. A general broadcast of a signal can be regarded as the sending of a signal to the set of all objects—although, in practice, it would be implemented differently for efficiency. The sender specifies the arguments of the signal at the time it is sent. Sending a signal is equivalent to instantiating a signal object and transmitting it to the set of target objects. The receipt of a signal is an event that is intended to trigger transitions in the receiver's state machine. A signal sent to a set of objects may trigger zero or one transition in each object independently. Signals are explicit means by which objects may communicate with each other asynchronously. To perform synchronous communication, two signals must be used, one in each direction.

Signals are generalizable elements. A child signal is derived from a parent signal. It inherits the attributes of the parent and may add additional attributes of its own. A child signal triggers a transition declared to use one of its ancestor signals.

A signal declaration has scope within the package in which it is declared. It is not restricted to a single class.

A class or interface may declare the signals it is prepared to handle. Such a declaration is a reception, which may include a specification of the results expected when the signal is received. The declaration has a property stating whether it is polymorphic. If it is polymorphic, then a descendant class can handle the signal, perhaps preventing the signal from reaching the current class. If it is not polymorphic, then no descendant may intercept handling of the signal.

A signal is a classifier and may have operations that may access and modify its attributes. All signals also share the implicit operation **send**.

> **send** (targetSet)

The signal is sent to each object in the target set.

Notation

The stereotype keyword «signal» is placed in front of an operation declaration that has the name of a signal to indicate that a class or interface accepts the signal. The parameters of the signal are included in the declaration. The declaration may not have a return type.

The declaration of a signal may be expressed as a stereotype of a class symbol. The keyword «signal» appears in a rectangle above the name of the signal. The signal's parameters appear as attributes within the attribute compartment. The operation compartment may contain access operations.

Figure 13-164 shows the use of generalization notation to relate a child signal to its parent. The child inherits the parameters of its ancestors and may add additional parameters of its own. For example, the **MouseButtonDown** signal has the attributes **time**, **device**, and **location**.

To use a signal as a trigger of a transition, use the syntax

> event-name (parameter$_{list,}$)

A parameter has the syntax

> parameter-name : type-expression

A signal parameter is declared as an attribute that may have an initial value, which can be overridden during initialization or sending. The initial value is used if a signal instance is created, initialized, and then sent to an object. If a signal is sent using operation-calling syntax, the initial values are default values of the signal's parameters.

Discussion

A signal is the most fundamental communication among objects, having simpler and cleaner semantics than do procedure calls. A signal is inherently a one-way asynchronous communication from one object to another in which all information is passed by value. It is a suitable model for communication in distributed, concurrent systems.

To build synchronous communication, use pairs of signals, one in each direction. A call may be viewed as a signal with an implicit return pointer parameter.

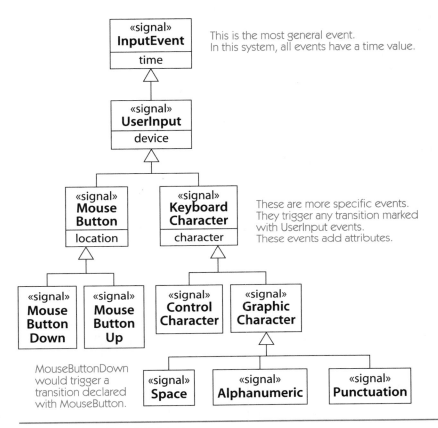

Figure 13-164. *Signal declarations*

signal event

An event that is the receipt by an object of a signal sent to it, which may trigger a transition in its state machine.

signature

The name and parameter properties of a behavioral feature, such as an operation or signal. A signature may include optional return types (for operations, not for signals).

Semantics

The signature of an operation is part of its declaration. Some (but not all) of the signature is used for matching operations and methods to check for conflict or overriding. For this purpose, we include the name of the operation and the ordered list of types of the parameters, but not their names or directions, and return parameters are excluded. If two signatures match but the remaining properties are inconsistent (for example, an in parameter corresponds to an out parameter), then the declarations conflict and the model is ill formed.

simple state

A state that has no nested states within it. A set of nested states forms a tree and the simple states are the leaves. A simple state has no substructure. It may have internal transitions, entry actions, and exit actions. Contrast: composite state.

simple transition

A transition with one source state and one target state. It represents a response to an event with a change of state within a region of mutually exclusive states. The amount of concurrency does not change as a result of executing it.

single classification

An execution regime in which each object has exactly one direct class. The is the execution model in most object-oriented programming languages. Whether to allow single classification or multiple classification is a semantic variation point.

single inheritance

A semantic variation of generalization in which an element may have only one parent. Whether to allow single inheritance or multiple inheritance is a semantic variation point.

singleton

A class that has (by declaration) exactly one instance. A singleton is a way to represent global knowledge in an application, yet keep it within an object-oriented framework.

Semantics

Every application must have at least one singleton class (often implicitly) to establish the context for the application. Often, the singleton class equates to the application itself and is implemented by the control stack and address space on a computer.

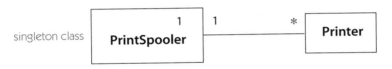

The application has a unique print spooler,
but many printers are controlled by it.

Figure 13-165. *Singleton class*

Notation

A singleton is shown as a class symbol with a small '1' in the upper right corner (Figure 13-165). This value represents the multiplicity of the class within the system.

snapshot

A collection of objects, links, and values that forms the configuration of a system at an instant during its execution.

source scope

An indicator of whether a slot is owned by an instance or by a class.
    See scope.

source state

The state within a state machine from which a transition departs. The transition applies to the source state. If an object is in the state or a state nested within it, then the transition is a candidate for firing.

specialization

To produce a more specific description of a model element by adding children. The opposite relationship is generalization, which is also used as the name of the relationship between the more specific element and the more general element, as there is no good term for the relationship that is undirected. A child element is the specialization of a parent element. Conversely, the parent is the generalization of the child.
    See generalization.

specification

> A declarative description of what something is or does. For example, a use case or an interface is a specification. Contrast: implementation.

stages of modeling

> Development states an element or a model goes through during the process of designing and building a system.
>
> *See also* development process.

Discussion

The overall development effort can be divided into activities focused on different ends. These activities are not performed in sequence; rather, they are performed iteratively during the phases of the development process. Analysis deals with capturing requirements and understanding the needs of a system. Design deals with devising a practical approach to the problem within the constraints of data structures, algorithms, and existing system pieces. Implementation deals with constructing the solution in an executable language or medium (such as a data base or digital hardware). Deployment deals with putting the solution into practice in a specific physical environment. These divisions are somewhat arbitrary and not always clear, but they remain useful guidelines.

These views of development should not be equated with sequential phases of the development process, however. In the traditional Waterfall Process they were indeed treated as distinct phases. In a more modern iterative development process, however, they are not distinct phases. At a given point in time, development activities may exist at various levels, and they may best be understood as different tasks that need to be performed on each element of the system, not all at the same time.

Think of a group of buildings, each with a foundation, walls, and roof; all of them must be completed for all of the buildings, but not all at the same time. Usually, the parts of each building are completed more or less in order. Sometimes, however, the roof can be started before all the walls are complete. Occasionally, the distinction between walls and roof is lost—consider a dome set on the ground.

Some UML elements are intended for all stages of development. Others are intended for design or implementation purposes and would appear only when a model is sufficiently complete. For example, visibility specifications on attributes and operations would tend to appear during the design stage. During the analysis stage mainly public members are included.

Discussion

A waterfall development process is divided into stages, each of which is carried out on the whole system at once. Traditional stages include analysis, design, implementation, and deployment. In an iterative process, however, development of the entire system does not proceed in lock step. Elements may be developed at different paces. Nevertheless, each individual element passes through the same stages during development, but different elements proceed at different rates, so the system as a whole is not in any one stage.

Each modeling stage characterizes an area of concern that must understood and modeled. The earlier stages capture more logical and more abstract properties. The later stages are more focused on implementation and performance. Analysis captures the requirements and the expert vocabulary of a system. Design captures the algorithms and data structures of the abstracted implementation under idealized, but physically plausible, conditions. It is also concerned with efficiency, computational complexity, and software-engineering considerations necessary to build a supportable system. Implementation creates an operational description of a system under real conditions in a real programming language, including the imperfections of real languages and the partitioning of the system artifacts into parts that can be separately developed and stored. Run-time deals with issues of concurrency of resources, the computational environment, and large-scale performance.

UML contains a range of constructs suitable for various stages of development. Some constructs (such as association and state) are meaningful at all stages. Some constructs (such as navigability and visibility) are meaningful during design but represent unnecessary implementation detail during analysis. This does not preclude their definition at an early stage of work. Some constructs (such as specific programming-language syntax) are meaningful only during implementation and impair the development process if introduced prematurely.

Models change during development. A UML model takes a different form at each stage of development, with an emphasis on various UML constructs. Modeling should be performed with the understanding that all constructs are not useful at all stages.

See development process for a discussion of the relationship of modeling stages and development phases.

state

A condition or situation during the life of an object during which it satisfies some condition, performs some activity, or waits for some event.

See also activity, activity graph, composite state, entry action, exit action, final state, internal transition, pseudostate, state machine, submachine, synch state, transition.

Semantics

An object holds a series of states during its lifetime. An object remains in a state for a finite (noninstantaneous) time. Dummy states may be introduced for convenience, which perform trivial actions and exit. But these are not the main purpose of states, and dummy states can, in principle, be eliminated, although they are useful for avoiding duplication.

States are contained in a state machine that describes how the history of an object evolves over time in response to events. Each state machine describes the behavior of the objects of a class. Each class may have a state machine. A transition describes the response of an object in a state to the reception of a an event: The object executes an optional action attached to the transition and changes to a new state. Each state has its own set of transitions.

An action is atomic and noninterruptible. An action is attached to a transition—a change of state, which is also atomic and noninterruptible. Ongoing activity may be associated with a state. Such activity is stated as a nested state machine or a **do** expression. Alternately, ongoing activity may be represented by a pair of actions, an entry action that starts the activity on entry to the state and an exit action that terminates the activity on exit from the state.

States may be grouped together into composite states. Any transition on a composite state affects all of the states within it, so events that affect many substates in the same way can be handled by a single transition. A composite state can be sequential or concurrent. Only one substate of a sequential composite state is active at a time. All substates of a concurrent composite state are active simultaneously.

To promote encapsulation, a composite state may contain initial states and final states. These are pseudostates, the purpose of which is to help structure the state machine. A transition to the composite state represents a transition to its initial state. It is equivalent to making a transition directly to the initial state, but the state can be used externally without knowledge of its internal structure.

A transition to a final state within the composite state represents the completion of activity in the enclosing state. Completion of activity in an enclosing state triggers a completion of activity event on the enclosing state and causes a completion transition on the enclosing state to fire. A completion transition is a transition with no explicit trigger event (or, more precisely, one with the completion event as its implicit trigger, although it is not explicitly modeled). Completion of the outermost state of an object corresponds to its death.

If a state is a concurrent composite state, then all its concurrent subregions must complete before the completion event on the composite state occurs. In other words, a completion transition from a composite concurrent state represents a join of control from all its concurrent subthreads. It waits for all of them to complete before proceeding.

Structure

A state has the following parts.

Name. The name of the state, which must be unique within the enclosing state. The name can be omitted, producing an anonymous state. Any number of distinct anonymous states can coexist. A nested state can be identified by its pathname (if all the enclosing states have names).

Substates. If a state machine has nested substructure, it is called a composite state. A composite state is either a network of disjoint substates (that is, substates that are sequentially active) or a set of concurrent substates (that is, substates that are all active concurrently). A state with no substructure (except possible internal actions) is a simple state.

Entry and exit actions. A state may have an entry action and an exit action. The purpose of these actions is to encapsulate the state so that it can be used externally without knowledge of its internal structure. An entry action is executed when the state is entered, after any action attached to the incoming transition and before any other internal activity. An exit action is executed when the state is exited, after the completion of any internal activity and before any action attached to the outgoing transition. On a transition that crosses several state boundaries, several exit and entry actions may be executed in a nested fashion. First, exit actions are executed, starting with the innermost state and progressing to outermost state, then the action on the transition is executed, then entry actions are executed, starting with the outermost and finishing with the innermost. Figure 13-166 shows the result of firing a transition across state boundaries. Entry and exit actions may not be evaded by any means, including the occurrence of exceptions. They provide an encapsulation mechanism for the specification of state machine behavior, with a guarantee that necessary actions will be performed under all circumstances.

Internal activity. A state may contain internal activity described as an expression. When the state is entered, the activity begins after the entry action is complete. If the activity terminates, the state is complete. A completion transition that departs

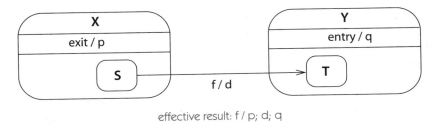

effective result: f / p; d; q

Figure 13-166. *Transition across state boundaries, with exit and entry actions*

the state is then triggered. Otherwise, the state waits for a triggered transition to cause a change of state. If a transition fires while the activity is being performed, the activity is terminated and the exit action on the state is executed.

Internal transitions. A state may have a list of internal transitions, which are like normal transitions except that they do not have target states and do not cause a change of state. If its event occurs while an object is in the state owning the transition, then the action on the internal transition is executed, but no change of state occurs nor are entry or exit actions executed, even if the internal transition is *declared* in an enclosing state (because the current state has not changed). This differentiates it from a self-transition, in which an external transition from a state to the same state occurs, resulting in execution of the exit actions of all states nested within the state with the self-transition, the execution of its exit action, and the execution of its entry action. The actions are executed even on a self-transition to the current state, which is exited and then reentered. If a self-transition on an enclosing state of the current state fires, then the final state is the enclosing state itself, not the current state. In other words, a self-transition may force an exit from a nested state, but an internal transition does not.

Submachine. The body of a state may represent a copy of a separate state machine referenced by name. The referenced state machine is called a submachine because it is nested within the larger state machine, and the state making the reference is called a submachine state. A submachine may be attached to a class that provides the context for actions within it, such as attributes that may be read and written. A submachine is intended to be reused in many state machines to avoid repetition of the same state machine fragment. A submachine is a kind of state machine subroutine.

Within the submachine reference state, the submachine is referenced by name with a possible argument list. The name must be the name of a state machine that has an initial and final state. If the submachine has parameters on its initial transition, then the argument list must have matching arguments. When the submachine state is entered, its entry action is performed first, then execution of the submachine begins with its initial state. When the submachine reaches its final state, any exit action in the submachine state is performed. The submachine state is then considered completed and may take a transition based on implicit completion of activity.

A transition to a submachine reference state activates the initial state of the target submachine. But sometimes a transition to a different state in the submachine is desired. A stub state is a pseudostate placed within a submachine reference state that identifies a state within the submachine. Transitions can be connected to the stub state from other states in the main state machine. If a transition to a stub state fires, the referenced state in the copy of the submachine becomes active.

A submachine represents nested, interruptible activity within a state. It is equivalent to replacing the submachine state with a unique copy of the submachine. Instead of supplying a state machine, a procedural expression can be attached to the submachine (this is an activity). An activity can be regarded as defining a series of states, one per primitive expression, that is interruptible between any two steps. It is not the same as an action, which is atomic and noninterruptible.

Dynamic concurrency. An activity state or submachine state may have a multiplicity and a concurrency expression. The multiplicity specifies how many copies of the state may execute concurrently. The normal case is a multiplicity of exactly one, meaning that the state represents a normal thread of control. If the multiplicity value is not fixed, it means that the number of execution tokens is determined dynamically at run time. For example, the value 1..5 means that from one to five copies of the activity are executed concurrently. If the concurrency expression exists (it is required if the concurrency is not exactly one), then at run time it must evaluate to a set of argument lists. The cardinality of the set indicates the number of concurrent activations of the state. Each state receives a distinct list of argument values as its value of the implicit current event. Actions in the activity can access the values of the current event. When all the executions have completed, the dynamically concurrent state is considered to have completed and execution passes to the next state.

This capability is intended for activity diagrams.

Deferrable events. A list of events whose occurrence in the state is postponed, if they do not trigger a transition, until they trigger a transition or the system makes a transition to a state in which they are not deferred, at which time they are consumed. The implementation of such deferred events would involve an internal queue of events.

Notation

A state is shown as a rectangle with rounded corners. It may have one or more compartments. The compartments are optional. The following compartments may be included.

Name compartment. Holds the (optional) name of the state as a string. States without names are anonymous and are all distinct. It is undesirable to repeat the same named state symbol twice in the same diagram, however, as it is confusing.

Nested state. Shows a state diagram of a composite state itself as composed of subordinate nested states. The state diagram is drawn within the boundary of the outer state. Transitions may connect directly to nested states, as well as to the boundary of the outer state. In a disjoint region, the substates are drawn directly inside the composite state. In a concurrent region, the concurrent state symbol is divided into subregions by dashed lines (that is, it is tiled).

See composite state for details and examples.

Internal transition compartment. Holds a list of internal actions or activities performed in response to events received while the object is in the state, without changing state. An internal transition has the format

event-name$_{opt}$(argument$_{list,}$)$_{opt}$[guard-condition]$_{opt}$/action-expression$_{opt}$

Action expressions may use attributes and links of the owning object and parameters of incoming transitions (if they appear on all incoming transitions).

The argument list (including parentheses) may be omitted if there are no parameters. The guard condition (including brackets) and the action expression (including slash) are optional.

Entry and exit actions have the same form but use reserved words **entry** and **exit** that cannot be used for event names.

entry / action-expression

exit / action-expression

Entry and exit actions may not have arguments or guard conditions (because they are invoked implicitly, not explicitly). To obtain parameters on an entry action, the current event may be accessed by the action. This is particularly useful for obtaining the creation parameters by a new object.

The reserved action name **defer** indicates an event that is deferrable in a state and its substates. The internal transition must not have a guard condition or actions.

event-name / defer

The reserved word **do** represents an expression for a nonatomic activity.

do / activity-expression

Submachine reference state. The invocation of a nested submachine is shown by a string of the following form in the body of the state symbol:

include machine-name(argument$_{list,}$)$_{opt}$

Both do-activities and submachines describe nonatomic computations that usually run until they are complete but that can be aborted by an event that triggers a transition.

Example

Figure 13-167 shows a state with internal transitions. Figure 13-168 shows the declaration and use of a submachine.

Dynamic concurrency. Dynamic concurrency with a value other than exactly one is shown by a multiplicity string in the upper-right part of the state symbol. The string should not be included for normal sequential execution. This notation is mainly intended for activity diagrams and should generally be avoided in statechart diagrams.

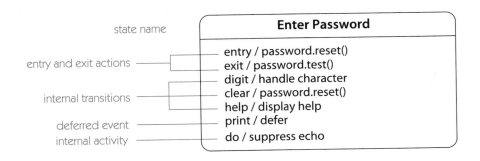

Figure 13-167. *Internal transitions, with entry and exit actions and deferred event*

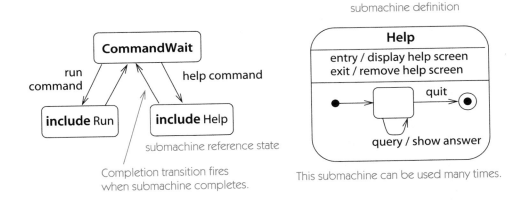

Figure 13-168. *Submachine*

state machine

A specification of the sequences of states that an object or an interaction goes through in response to events during its life, together with its responsive actions. A state machine is attached to a source class, collaboration, or method and specifies the behavior of the instances of the source element.

See also activity graph, composite state, event, pseudostate, state, transition.

Semantics

A state machine is a graph of states and transitions that describes the response of an instance of a classifier to the receipt of events. State machines may be attached to classifiers, such as classes and use cases, as well as to collaborations and methods. The element that the state machine is attached to is called the *master* of the state machine.

An entire state machine is a composite state that has been decomposed recursively into substates. The innermost simple states have no substates.

State machine execution semantics

The semantics of state machine execution are discussed in the remainder of this article. Note that the following section describes the semantic effects of state machine execution and should not be taken as an implementation approach. There are many ways to implement these semantics, many of which compile away some of the explicit steps described here. Most of these semantics are described in other articles, but they are gathered here for convenience.

At any moment, one or more states are active in the active state configuration of the state machine of an object or other instance. If a state is active, then a transition leaving the state may fire, causing the execution of an action and the activation of another state or states in place of the original state. More than one active leaf state indicates internal concurrency. There are constraints on the states that can be active concurrently, imposed by the structure of the state machine and its transitions. Briefly, if a sequential composite state is active, exactly one direct disjoint substate must be active; if a concurrent composite state is active, each direct concurrent substate must be active.

Transition firing and actions

The basic assumption is that a state machine processes one event at a time and finishes all the consequences of that event before processing another event. In other words, events do not interact with other events during event processing. This is known as "run to completion" processing. It does not mean that all computation is noninterruptible. An ordinary extended computation can be broken into a series of atomic steps, and the computation can be interrupted by an outside event between any steps. This is very close to the physical situation within a computer, where interrupts can occur at discrete, but small, steps.

A corollary assumption is that events are asynchronous. Two events never occur at exactly the same time—or, more precisely, if two events occur at the exact same time, it is a coincidence and they can be processed as if they had occurred in either order, with no loss of generality. The results of the different orders of execution may be different—race conditions are an essential property of concurrent systems—but you may not assume simultaneity in a distributed world. Any computation making such an assumption is logically and physically flawed. Concurrent execution requires independence in a distributed world.

Conceptually, actions are instantaneous and events are never simultaneous. In an implementation, execution of actions requires some time, but the important thing is that actions are (conceptually) atomic and noninterruptible. If an object receives an event while it is executing an action, the event is placed on a queue until the execution is complete. Events are handled only when no actions are being executed. If an action sends a signal to another object, then the reception of the signal is not synchronous. It is handled like any other event, after the completion of the action and the transition that it is part of. A call to an operation suspends the caller until the operation has been executed. It may be implemented, at the choice of the receiver, as a method or as a call event that triggers the state machine of the receiver. To avoid problems with long periods during which events cannot be processed, actions should be brief. Actions are not intended for modeling protected regions or long interruptible computations, which should be modeled as submachines or nested activity states. This permits event processing and permits nested computations to be interrupted. If long actions are included in real systems, events may not be processed in a timely manner. This is a consequence of a bad model. Actions must be short, compared to the required response time to events that might occur.

When an object is not performing an action, it will immediately handle an event that it receives. Conceptually, actions are instantaneous, but in practice they take some time; therefore, new events must be stored on a queue for an object. If there are no events in the queue, the object waits until it receives an event and then handles it. Conceptually, an object handles a single event at a time. This is not a limitation, because the actions are assumed to be atomic and brief. In an actual implementation, events may be queued in a definite order. UML semantics, however, do not specify an order of processing concurrent events, and a modeler should not assume one. If events must be processed in a certain order, the state machine should be constructed to enforce the order. A physical implementation would probably select some simple ordering rule.

At the time that an object handles an event, its active state configuration may contain one or more concurrent states. Each state receives a separate copy of the event and acts on it independently. Transitions in concurrent states fire independently. One substate can change without affecting the others, except in the case of a complex transition, such as a fork or join (described later).

For each active state of an object, the outgoing transitions of the state are candidates to fire. A candidate transition is triggered if an event is handled whose type is the same or a descendant of the trigger event on the transition. A transition is not triggered by an ancestor event. When an event is handled and triggers a transition, the guard condition of the transition is evaluated. If the value of the guard condition is true, then the transition is enabled. The guard condition Boolean expression may involve arguments of the trigger event, as well as attributes of the object. Note that guard expressions may not produce side effects. That is, they may not alter the state of the object or the rest of the system. Therefore, the order in which they are evaluated is irrelevant to the outcome. A guard condition is evaluated only when an event is handled. If it evaluates to false, it is not reevaluated if some of its variables change value later.

To structure complex conditions, a transition may be modeled with multiple segments. The first segment has a trigger event and is followed by a branching tree of segments with guard conditions. The intermediate nodes in the tree are pseudostates, dummy states that are present for structuring the transitions but that may not remain active at the end of a run-to-completion step. Each possible path through the tree of segments is regarded as a separate transition and is independently eligible for execution. An individual segment may not fire alone. All the guard conditions along a series of segments must be true or the transition (including any of its segments) does not fire at all. In practice, guard conditions at a branch point often partition the possible outcomes. Therefore, an implementation could process the multisegment transition one step at a time, but not always.

If no transition is enabled, an event is simply ignored. This is not an error. If exactly one transition is enabled, it fires. If more than one transition from a single state is enabled, then only one of them fires. If no constraint is specified, then the choice is nondeterministic. No assumptions should be made that the choice will be fair, predictable, or random. An actual implementation may provide rules for resolving conflicts, but modelers are advised to make their intent explicit rather than rely on such rules. Whether or not any transition fires, the event is consumed.

The transitions leaving an active state are eligible for firing. In addition, transitions on any composite state containing an active state are candidates for firing. This may be regarded as the inheritance of transitions by nested states, similar to the inheritance of operations by subclasses. A transition on an outer state is eligible to fire only if no transition on an inner state fires. Otherwise, it is masked by the inner transition.

When a transition fires, any action attached to it is executed. An action expression may use the arguments of the triggering event, as well as attributes of the owning object or values reachable from it. An action is atomic and is completed before any additional events are processed. If a transition has multiple segments, the parameters of the trigger event are available as the implicit current event.

If an object has concurrent states, then they should not interact through shared memory. Concurrent states are meant to be independent and should act on different sets of values. Any interactions should be explicit by sending signals. If two concurrent states must access a shared resource, they should explicitly send signals to the resource, which can then act as an arbiter. An implementation may compile away such explicit communication, but care must then be taken to ensure that meaningless or dangerous conflicts do not ensue. If concurrent actions do access shared values, the result is nondeterministic.

If a transition that crosses the boundary of a composite state fires, entry actions or exit actions may be executed. A boundary crossing may occur because the source state and target state on the transition itself are in different composite states. It may also occur because the transition that fires is inherited from an outer composite state, thereby forcing the object to exit one or more inner states. Note that an internal transition does not cause a change of state and so never invokes entry or exit actions.

To determine the exit and entry actions that are executed, find the current active state of the object (this might be nested within the composite state that has the transition) and the target state of the transition. Then find the innermost composite state that encloses both the current state and the target state. Call this the *common ancestor*. The exit actions of the current state and any enclosing states up to, but not including, the common ancestor are executed, innermost first. Then the action on the transition is executed. After that, the entry actions of the target state and any enclosing states up to, but not including, the common ancestor are executed, outermost first. In other words, states are exited one at a time until the common ancestor is reached and then states are entered until the target state is reached. The exit and entry actions on the common ancestor are not executed, because it has not changed. This procedure ensures that each state is strongly encapsulated.

The action on the transition is executed after any exit actions have been executed and before any entry actions are performed.

Note that the firing of a self-transition (a transition from a state to itself) will cause the exit of any nested states within the source state that may be active (the transition may have been inherited from an enclosing composite state). It also causes the execution of the exit action of the source state followed by the execution of its entry action. In other words, the state is exited and then reentered. If this effect is not desired, then an internal transition in the state should be used instead. This will not cause a change of state, even if the active state is nested within the state with the transition.

During the execution of a run-to-completion step, all actions have access to an implicit current event, which is the event that triggered the first transition in the run-to-completion sequence. Because there may be more than one event that could result in the execution of an action, the action may discriminate on the type of the current event (as in Ada or by a polymorphic operation) to execute alternate code branches.

After all the actions are performed, the original current state is inactive (unless it is the target state), the target state of the transition is active, and additional events can then be processed.

A transition may be structured with several segments whose intermediate nodes are junction states. Each segment may have its own action. The actions may be interleaved with entry and exit actions for the overall transition. With respect to entry and exit actions, each action on a transition segment occurs where it would occur if the segment were a complete transition. See Figure 13-117 for an example.

Internal transitions

An internal transition has a source state but no target state. Its firing does not cause a change of state, even if the transition that fires is inherited from an enclosing state. Because the state does not change, no exit or entry actions are performed. The only effect of an internal transition is the execution of its action. The conditions for firing an internal transition are exactly the same as for an external transition.

Note that the firing of an internal transition may mask an external transition using the same event. Therefore, there can be a purpose for defining an internal transition with no action. As stated above, only one transition fires per event within a sequential region, and an inner transition has priority over an outer transition.

Internal transitions are useful for processing events without changing state.

Initial and final states

For encapsulation of states, it is often desirable to separate the inside of a state from the outside. It is also desirable to connect transitions to a composite state, without knowing about the internal structure of the state. This can be accomplished using initial states and final states within a composite state.

A state may have an initial and a final state. An initial state is a pseudostate—a dummy state with the connectivity of normal states—and an object may not remain in an initial state. An object may remain in a final state, but a final state may not have any explicit triggered transitions; its purpose is to invoke a completion transition on an enclosing state. An initial state must have an outgoing completion transition. If there is more than one outgoing transition, then they must all lack triggers and their guard conditions must partition the possible values. In other words, exactly one outgoing transition must fire when the initial state is invoked. An object may never remain in the initial state, therefore, but will immediately transition to a normal state.

If a composite state has an initial state, then transitions may be connected directly to the composite state as target. Any transition to the composite state is implicitly a transition to the initial state within the composite state. If a composite state lacks an initial state, then transitions may not be targeted at the composite state; they must be connected directly to substates. A state with an initial state may also have transitions connected directly to inner states, as well as to the composite state.

If a composite state has a final state, then it may be the source of one or more outgoing completion transitions, that is, transitions that lack explicit event triggers. A completion transition is really a transition that is implicitly enabled by the completion of activity within the state. A transition to a final state is therefore a statement that execution of the composite state is complete. When an object transitions to a final state, then the completion transitions leaving its enclosing composite state are enabled to fire if their guard conditions are satisfied.

A composite state may also have labeled outgoing transitions—that is, transitions with explicit event triggers. If an event occurs that causes such a transition to fire, then any ongoing activity within the state (at any nesting depth) is terminated, the exit actions of the terminated nested states are executed, and the transition is processed. Such transitions are often used to model exceptions and error conditions.

Complex transitions

A transition into a concurrent composite state implies a transition into all its concurrent substates. This can happen in two ways.

A transition may have multiple target states, one within each concurrent substate. Note that such a forking transition still has a single trigger event, guard condition, and action. This is an explicit transition into a composite state that specifies each target directly. This represents an explicit fork of control into concurrent subthreads.

Alternately, a transition may omit targets within one or more concurrent substates, or it may have the composite state itself as the target. In this case, each omitted concurrent substate must have an initial state within it to indicate its default starting state. Otherwise, the state machine is ill formed. If the complex transition fires, the explicit target concurrent substates become active, as do the initial states of the other concurrent substates. In short, any transition into any concurrent substate implies a transition to the initial states of any other peer concurrent substates not explicitly mentioned. A transition to a composite state itself implies a transition to the initial states of each of its concurrent regions. If a concurrent composite state is active, each of its subregions is also active.

Similarly, a transition from any concurrent substate implies a transition from them all. If the occurrence of an event causes such a transition to fire, the activity in the remaining substates is terminated, they execute their exit actions, the action of the transition itself is executed, and the target state becomes active, thereby reducing the number of active concurrent states.

The transition to the final state of a concurrent substate does not force the termination of other concurrent substates (this is not a transition out of the substate). When all the concurrent substates have reached their final states, the enclosing composite state is deemed to have completed its activity and any completion transitions leaving the composite state are enabled to fire.

A complex transition may have multiple source states and multiple target states. In that case, its behavior is the combination of the fork and join described above.

History state

A composite state may contain a history state, which is a pseudostate. If an inherited transition causes an automatic exit from the composite state, the state "remembers" the substate that was active when the forced exit occurred. A transition to the history pseudostate within the composite state indicates that the remembered substate is to be reestablished. An explicit transition to another state or to the enclosing state itself does not enable the history mechanism, and the usual transition rules apply. However, the initial state of the composite state can be connected to the history state. In that case, a transition to the composite state does (indirectly) invoke the history mechanism. The history state may have a single outgoing completion transition without guard condition; the target of this transition is the default history state. If the state region has never been entered or if it was exited normally, then a transition to the history state goes to the default history state.

There are two kinds of history state: a *shallow history state* and a *deep history state*. The shallow history state restores states contained directly (depth one) in the same composite state as the history state. The deep history state restores the state or states that were active prior to the last explicit transition that caused the enclosing composite state to be exited. It may include states nested within the composite state to any depth. A composite state can have at most one of each kind of history state. Each may have its own default history state.

The history mechanism should be avoided if the situation can be modeled more directly, as it is complicated and not necessarily a good match to implementation mechanisms. The deep history mechanism is particularly problematical and should be avoided in favor of more explicit (and more implementable) mechanisms.

Notation

A statechart diagram shows a state machine or a nested portion of a state machine. The states are represented by state symbols, and the transitions are represented by arrows connecting the state symbols. States may also contain subdiagrams by physical containment and tiling. Figure 13-169 shows an example.

The statechart notation was invented by David Harel and incorporates aspects of Moore machines (actions on entry) and Mealy machines (actions on transitions), as well as adding the concepts of nested states and concurrent states.

For more details, *see* state, composite state, submachine, pseudostate, entry action, exit action, transition, internal transition, and activity. For a variant form of notation suitable for flow of activity, *see* activity graph. *See also* control icons for

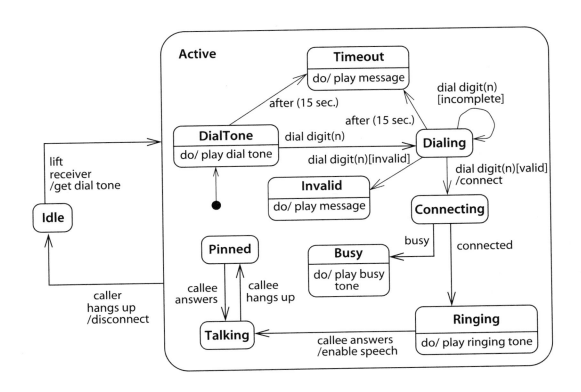

Figure 13-169. *State diagram*

some optional symbols intended for use within activity diagrams but that may be used in statechart diagrams.

Discussion

State machines can be used in two ways. Therefore, their meaning can be understood in either way. In one case, the state machine may specify executable behavior of its master element—typically, a class. In that case, the state machine describes the response of the master as it receives events from the rest of the universe. The response is described by transitions, each of which indicates what happens when the master receives an event while in a given state. The effect is expressed as an action and a change of state. Actions can include sending signals to other objects, which trigger their state machines. State machines provide a reductionist specification of the behavior of a system.

In the second case, the state machine may be used as a protocol specification, showing the legal order in which operations may be invoked on a class or interface.

In such a state machine, transitions are triggered by call events and their actions invoke the desired operation. This means that a caller is allowed to invoke the operation at that point. The protocol state machine does not include actions to specify the behavior of the operation itself. It shows which operations can be invoked in a particular order. Such a state machine specifies valid operation sequences. This is a use of a state machine as a generator of sequences in a language (from computer science language theory). Such a machine is meant as a constraint on the design of the system. It is not directly executable and does not indicate what happens if an illegal sequence occurs—because it is not supposed to occur. It is the responsibility of the system designer to ensure that only legal sequences occur. This second usage is more abstract than the first form, which specifies, in an executable form, what happens in all cases. But it is often convenient, especially at a high level and with procedural coding.

state machine view

That aspect of the system dealing with the specification of the behavior of individual elements over their lifetimes. This view contains state machines. It is loosely grouped with other behavioral views in the dynamic view.

statechart diagram

A diagram that shows a state machine, including simple states, transitions, and nested composite states. The original concept was invented by David Harel.
See state machine.

static classification

A semantic variation of generalization in which an object may not change type or may not change role. The choice of static classification or dynamic classification is a semantic variation point.

static view

A view of the overall model that characterizes the things in a system and their static relationships to each other. It includes classifiers and their relationships: association, generalization, dependency, and realization. Sometimes called *class view*.

Semantics

The static view shows the static structure of a system, in particular, the kinds of things that exist (such as classes and types), their internal structure, and their relationships to other things. Static views do not show temporal information, although they may contain reified occurrences of things that have or describe temporal behavior, such as specifications of operations or events.

The top-level constituents of a static view include classifiers (class, interface, data type), relationships (association, generalization, dependency, realization), constraints, and comments. It also contains packages and subsystems as organizational units. Other constituents are subordinate to and contained within the top-level elements.

Related to the static view and often combined with it on diagrams are the implementation view, deployment view, and model management view.

The static view may be contrasted with the dynamic view, which complements it and builds upon it.

stereotype

A new kind of model element defined within the model based on an existing kind of model element. Stereotypes may extend the semantics but not the structure of pre-existing metamodel classes.

See also constraint, tagged value.

See Chapter 14, Standard Elements, for a list of predefined stereotypes.

Semantics

A stereotype represents a variation of an existing model element with the same form (such as attributes and relationships) but with a different intent. Generally, a stereotype represents a usage distinction. A stereotyped element may have additional constraints, beyond those of the base element, as well as a distinct visual image. It is expected that code generators and other tools will treat stereotyped elements specially, by generating different code, for example. The intent is that a generic modeling tool, such as a model editor or a repository, should treat a stereotyped element for most purposes as an ordinary element with some additional text information, while differentiating the element for certain semantic operations, such as well-formedness checking, code generation, and report writing. Stereotypes represent one of the built-in extensibility mechanisms of UML.

Each stereotype is derived from a base model element class. All elements bearing the stereotype have the properties of the base model element class.

A stereotype can also be specialized from another stereotype. Stereotype definitions are generalizable elements. The child stereotype has the properties of the parent stereotype. Ultimately, each stereotype is based on some model element class.

A stereotype may have a list of required tags and some of them may have default values that are used if no explicit tagged value is supplied. The permitted range of values for each tag may also be specified. Each element bearing the stereotype must have tagged values with the listed tags. Tags with default values are automatically implied if they are not explicit on a stereotyped element.

A stereotype may have a list of constraints that add conditions beyond those implied by the base element. Each constraint applies to each model element bearing the stereotype. Each model element is also subject to the constraints applicable to the base element.

A stereotype is a kind of virtual metamodel class (that is, it is not manifest in the metamodel) that is added within a model rather than by modifying the predefined UML metamodel. For that reason, the names of new stereotypes must differ from existing UML metaclass names or other stereotypes or keywords.

Any model element can have at most one stereotype. This rule may not be logically essential, but it simplifies the semantics and the notation for stereotypes without any real loss in power, as multiple inheritance of stereotypes themselves is permitted. Stereotypes may be children of other stereotypes. Any situation in which an element has multiple stereotypes can therefore be recast as having a single stereotype that is a child of the others. Occasionally this may force the modeler to create an extra dummy stereotype to combine other stereotypes, but we feel that the greater simplicity in the average case compensates for this inconvenience.

Certain stereotypes are predefined in UML; others may be user defined. Stereotypes are one of three extensibility mechanisms in UML.

See Chapter 14, Encyclopedia of Terms, for a list of predefined stereotypes,

See constraint, tagged value.

Notation

The general notation for the use of a stereotype is to use the symbol for the base element but to place a keyword string above the name of the element (if any). The keyword string is the name of the stereotype within matched guillemets, which are the quotation mark symbols used in French and some other languages—for example: «foo». (Note that a guillemet looks like a double angle-bracket, but it is a single character in most extended fonts. Most computers have a character map utility in which special symbols can be found. Double angle-brackets may be used as a substitute by the typographically challenged.) The keyword string is generally placed above or in front of the name of the model element being described. The keyword string may also be used as an element in a list. In that case, it applies to subsequent list elements until another stereotype string replaces it, or until an empty stereotype string («») nullifies it. Note that a stereotype name should not be identical to a predefined keyword applicable to the same element type. (To avoid confusion, a predefined keyword name should be avoided for any stereotype even if it applies to separate elements and is distinguishable in principle.)

To permit limited graphical extension of the UML notation, a graphic icon or a graphic marker (such as texture or color) can be associated with a stereotype.

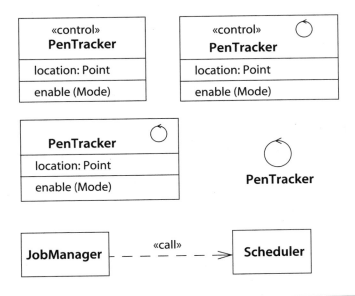

Figure 13-170. *Varieties of stereotype notation*

UML does not specify the form of the graphic specification, but many bitmap and stroked formats exist and might be used by a graphical editor (although their portability is a difficult problem). An icon can be used in two ways. In one case, it may be used instead of or in addition to the stereotype keyword string within the symbol for the base model element on which the stereotype is based. For example, in a class rectangle it is placed in the upper-right corner of the name compartment. In this form, the normal contents of the item can be seen in its symbol. Alternately, the entire element symbol may be "collapsed" into an icon that contains the element name or has the name above or below the icon. Other information contained by the base model element symbol is suppressed.

Figure 13-170 shows various ways of drawing a stereotyped class.

UML avoids the use of graphic markers, such as color, that present challenges for certain persons (the color blind) and for important kinds of equipment (such as printers, copiers, and fax machines). None of the UML symbols *require* the use of such graphic markers. Users *may* use graphic markers freely for their own purposes (such as for highlighting within a tool) but should be aware of their limitations for interchange, and they should be prepared to use the canonical forms when necessary.

Stereotype declaration. The classification hierarchy of the stereotypes themselves can be displayed on a class diagram. However, this is a metamodel diagram and must be distinguished (by user and tool) from an ordinary model diagram. In such a diagram, each stereotype is shown as a class symbol (rectangle) with the

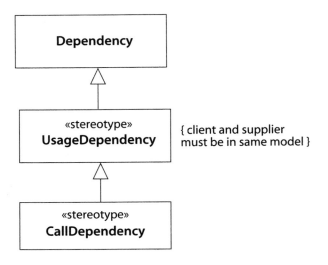

Figure 13-171. *Stereotype declaration*

keyword «**stereotype**». Generalization relationships may show the extended meta-model hierarchy (Figure 13-171). Because of the danger of extending the internal metamodel hierarchy, a tool may, but need not, expose this capability on class diagrams. Declaration of stereotype names is not a capability required by ordinary modelers, but it might be performed as a support task.

string

A sequence of text characters. The details of string representation depend on implementation and may include character sets that support international characters and graphics.

Semantics

Many semantic properties, especially names, have strings as their values. A string is a sequence of characters in some suitable character set used to display information about the model. Character sets may include non-Roman alphabets and characters. UML does not specify the encoding of a string, but it assumes that the encoding is sufficiently general to permit any reasonable usage. In principle, the length of a string should be unlimited; any practical limit should be large enough to be nonrestrictive. Strings should also include the possibility of characters in various human languages. Identifiers (names) should consist entirely of characters in a finite character set. Comments and similar kinds of descriptive strings without direct semantic content might contain other kinds of media elements, such as diagrams, graphs, pictures or video clips, and other kinds of embedded documents.

Notation

A graphic string is a primitive notation element with some implementation flexibility. It is assumed to be a linear sequence of characters in some language, with the possible inclusion of embedded documents of various kinds. It is desirable to support the use of various human languages, but the details are left to editing tools to implement. Graphic strings can be one to a line, in lists, or they can be labels attached to other symbols.

Strings are used to display semantic properties that have string values and also to encode the values of other semantic properties for display. Mapping from semantic strings to notational strings is direct. Mapping of other properties to notational strings is governed by grammars, described in the articles for various elements. For example, the display notation for an attribute encodes the name, type, initial value, visibility, and scope into a single display string.

Noncanonical extensions to the encodings are possible—for example, an attribute might be displayed using C++ notation. Some of these encodings may lose some model information, however, so a tool should support them as user-selectable options while maintaining support for the canonical UML notation.

Typeface and font size are graphic markers that are normally independent of the string itself. They may code for various model properties, some of which are suggested in this document and some of which are left open for the tool or the user. For example, italics show abstract classes and abstract operations, and underlining shows class-scope features.

Tools may treat long strings in various ways, such as truncation to a fixed size, automatic wrapping, and insertion of scroll bars. It is assumed that there is a way to obtain the full string when desired.

structural feature

A static feature of a model element, such as an attribute or an operation.

structural view

A view of an overall model that emphasizes the structure of the objects in a system, including their types, classes, relationships, attributes, and operations.

stub state

A pseudostate within a submachine reference state that identifies a state in the referenced submachine.

See also stubbed transition, submachine, submachine reference state.

Semantics

A transition to a submachine reference state activates the initial state of the target submachine. But sometimes a transition to a different state in the submachine is desired. A stub state is placed within a submachine reference state and identifies a state within the submachine. Transitions can be connected between the stub state and states in the containing state machine. If a transition to a stub state fires, the identified state in the submachine becomes active. If a state in the submachine is active, then a transition from a stub state that identifies it is a candidate for triggering. Connections among stub states in the same submachine reference state are not permitted.

Notation

A transition to or from a stub state is drawn as a stubbed transition into or from the submachine reference state—that is, as an arrow that finishes or begins on a short bar inside the state symbol for the submachine reference state. The bar is labeled with a name, which must match the name of a state in the referenced submachine.

Figure 13-173 shows a stub within a subroutine reference state. Figure 13-174 shows the corresponding submachine definition.

stubbed transition

A notation indicating that a transition explicitly transfers into a composite state, but the details are suppressed.

See also stub state.

Notation

A *stub* is shown as a small vertical line drawn inside the boundary of the enclosing state (Figure 13-172). The stub may be labeled with the name of the state, but it is often omitted when details are being suppressed. It indicates that a transition is connected to a suppressed internal state. Stubs are not used for transitions to initial states or leaving final states. A stub shows that additional substates are present in the model but are missing from the diagram.

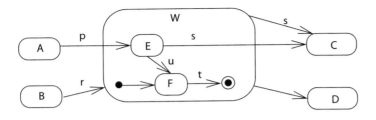

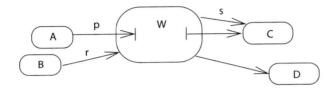

Figure 13-172. *Stubbed transition*

A stub state in a submachine reference state (Figure 13-173) references a state within the corresponding submachine definition (Figure 13-174). This is not a case of suppressed detail and the stub name must be included.

subclass

The child of another class in a generalization relationship—that is, the more specific description. The child class is called the subclass. The parent class is called the superclass.

See generalization, inheritance.

Semantics

A subclass inherits the structure, relationships, and behavior of its superclass and may add to it.

submachine

A state machine that may be invoked as part of another state machine. It is not attached to a class but instead is a kind of state machine subroutine. It has semantics as if its contents were duplicated and inserted at the state that references it.

See state, state machine, submachine reference state.

submachine reference state

A state that references a submachine, a copy of which is implicitly part of the enclosing state machine in place of the submachine reference state. It may contain stub states, which identify states in the submachine.

See also state, state machine, stub state.

Semantics

A submachine reference state is equivalent to inserting a copy of the submachine in place of the reference state.

Notation

A submachine reference state is drawn as a state symbol with a label of the form

include submachine-name

Transition arrows may be drawn to stub states in the submachine reference state. They are drawn as stubbed transitions—that is, arrows that terminate on a crossbar. The crossbar is labeled with the name of a state in the referenced submachine.

Example

Figure 13-173 shows part of a state machine containing a submachine reference state. The containing state machine sells tickets to customers with accounts. It must identify the customer as part of its job. Identifying the customer is a requirement of other state machines so it has been made into a separate state machine. Figure 13-174 shows the definition of state machine **Identify,** which is used as a submachine by other state machines. The normal entry to the submachine provides for reading the customer's card, but there is an explicit entry state that provides for manual entry of the customer's name by the box office clerk. If the identification process is successful, the submachine terminates at its final state. Otherwise, it goes to state **Failure.**

In Figure 13-173, the submachine reference is shown by a state icon with the **include** keyword and the name of the submachine. Normal entry to the submachine is shown by an arrow to its boundary. This transition activates the initial state of the submachine. Normal exit is shown by a completion transition from the boundary. This transition fires if the submachine terminates normally.

Entry to explicit state **ManualEntry** is shown by a transition to a stub inside the submachine reference symbol. The stub is labeled with the name of the target state in the submachine. Similarly, exit from explicit state **Failure** is shown by a completion transition from a stub. Transitions to stubs may be triggered or triggerless.

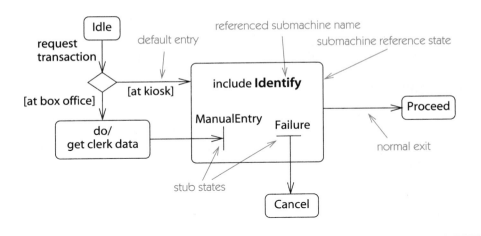

Figure 13-173. *Submachine reference state*

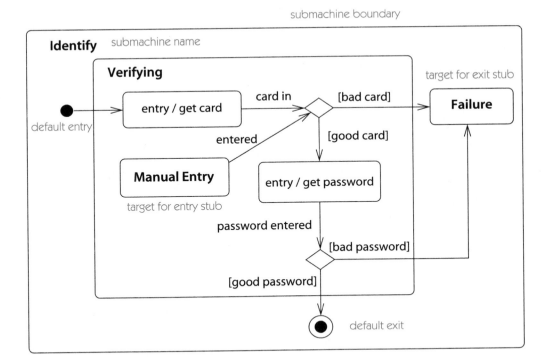

Figure 13-174. *Submachine definition*

substate

A state that is part of a composite state.

See composite state, concurrent substate, disjoint substate.

substitutability principle

The principle that, given a declaration of a variable or parameter whose type is declared as X, any instance of an element that is a descendant of X may be used as the actual value without violating the semantics of the declaration and its use. In other words, an instance of a descendant element may be substituted for an instance of an ancestor element. (Attributed to Barbara Liskov.)

See also generalization, implementation inheritance, inheritance, interface inheritance, polymorphic, private inheritance.

Discussion

The purpose is to ensure that polymorphic operations work freely. This is not a principle of logic but rather a pragmatic rule of programming that provides a degree of encapsulation. The generalization relationship supports substitutability.

The consequence of the substitutability principle is that a child may not remove or renounce properties of its parent. Otherwise, the child will not be substitutable in a situation in which a use of the parent is declared.

subsystem

A package of elements treated as a unit, including a specification of the behavior of the entire package contents treated as a coherent unit. A subsystem is modeled both as a package and as a class. A subsystem has a set of interfaces that describe its relationship to the rest of the system and the circumstances under which it can be used.

See also interface, package, realization.

Semantics

A subsystem is a coherent piece of a system that can be treated as an abstract single unit. It represents emergent behavior of a piece of the system. As a unit, it has its own behavior specification and implementation portion. The behavior specification defines its emergent behavior as a unit that can interact with other subsystems. The behavior specification is given in terms of use cases and other behavioral elements. The implementation portion describes the implementation of the behavior in terms of the subordinate elements that comprise its contents and is given as a set of collaborations among the contained elements.

The system itself constitutes the top-level subsystem. The implementation of one subsystem may be written as a collaboration of lower-level subsystems. In this way, the entire system may be expanded as a hierarchy of subsystems until the bottom-level subsystems are defined in terms of ordinary classes.

A subsystem may include structural elements and specification elements, such as use cases and operations exported by the subsystem. Subsystem specifications are implemented by structural elements. The behavior of the subsystem is the behavior of the elements in it.

Structure

The specification on a subsystem comprises elements designated as specification elements, together with operations and interfaces defined on the subsystem as a whole. Specification elements include use cases, constraints, relationships between use cases, and so on. These elements and operations define the behavior performed by the subsystem as an emergent entity, the net result of its parts working together. Use cases specify complete sequences of interactions of the subsystem with outside actors. Interfaces specify operations that the subsystem or its use cases must supply. The specification does not reveal what the parts are or how the parts interact to accomplish the necessary behavior.

The remainder of the elements in the subsystem realize its behavior. These may include various kinds of classifiers and their relationships. A set of collaborations among realization elements of the subsystem realize the specifications. In general, one or more collaborations realize each use case. Each collaboration describes how instances of the implementation elements cooperate to jointly perform the behavior specified by a use case or operation. All messages to and from the subsystem at the specification level must be mapped onto messages between its implementation elements and those of other subsystems.

A subsystem is a package and has package properties. In particular, the importation of subsystems works as described for packages, and generalization among subsystems has the same consequences for visibility of its contents.

Notation

A subsystem is notated as a package symbol (rectangle with small tab) containing the keyword «subsystem» above the subsystem name (Figure 13-175).

Discussion

A subsystem in an emergent grouping of design elements, such as logical classes. A component is an emergent grouping of implementation elements, such as implementation-level classes. In many cases, subsystems are implemented as components. This simplifies the mapping from design to implementation; therefore, it is

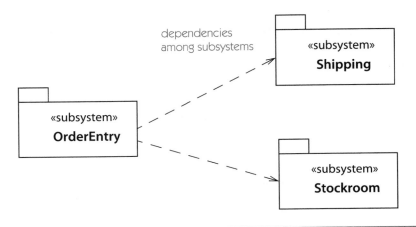

Figure 13-175. *Subsystems*

a common architectural approach. Furthermore, many components are implemented as dominant classes that directly implement the component interfaces. In this case, a subsystem, component, and class may all have the same interface.

subtype

A type that is a child of another type. The more neutral term child may be used for any generalizable element.

See generalization.

summarization

To filter, combine, and abstract the properties of a set of elements onto their container in order to give a higher level, more abstract view of a system.

See package.

Semantics

Containers, such as packages and classes, can have derived properties and relationships that summarize the properties and relationships of their contents. This permits the modeler to get a better understanding of a system at a higher, less detailed level that is easier to understand. For example, a dependency between two packages indicates that the dependency exists between at least one pair of elements from the two packages. The summary has less detail than the original information. There may be one or many pairs of individual dependencies represented by package-level dependencies. In any case, the modeler knows that a change to one package *may* affect the other. If more details are needed, the modeler can always examine the contents in detail once the high-level summary has been noticed.

Similarly, a usage dependency between two classes usually indicates a dependency between their operations, such as a method on one class calling an operation (not a method!) on another class. Many dependencies at the class level derive from dependencies among operations or attributes.

In general, relationships that are summarized on a container indicate the existence of at least one occurrence of the relationship among the contents. They do not usually indicate that all the contained elements participate in the relationship.

superclass

The parent of another class in a generalization relationship—that is, the more general element specification. The child class is classed the subclass. The parent class is called the superclass.

See generalization.

Semantics

A subclass inherits the structure, relationships, and behavior of its superclass and may add to it.

supertype

Synonym for superclass. The more neutral term parent may be used for any generalizable element.

See generalization.

supplier

An element that provides services that can be invoked by others. Contrast: client. In the notation, the supplier appears at the arrowhead of a dashed dependency arrow.

See dependency.

swimlane

A partition on activity graphs for organizing responsibilities for activities. Swimlanes do not have a fixed meaning, but they often correspond to organizational units in a business model.

See also activity graph.

Semantics

The activity states within an activity graph may be organized into partitions called swimlanes because of their notation. Swimlanes are groupings of states for organizing an activity graph. Each swimlane represents some meaningful partition of

the responsibilities for the states—for example, the business organization responsible for a workflow step. They may be used in any way that suits the modeler. If
swimlanes are present, they divide the states of the activity graph among them.

Each swimlane has a name that is distinct from other swimlanes. It has no additional semantics within UML but it may carry some real-world implications.

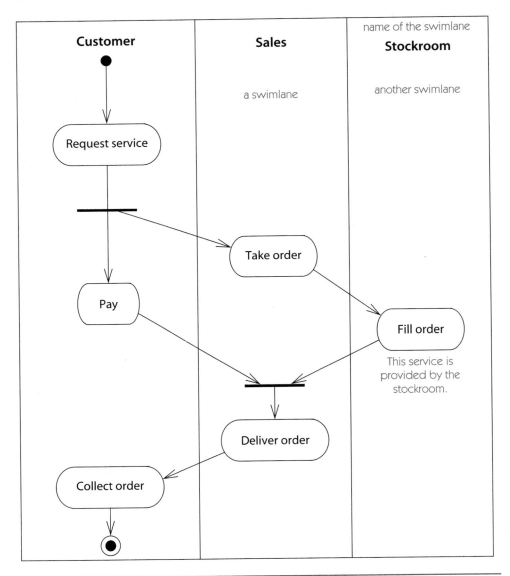

Figure 13-176. *Swimlanes on an activity diagram*

Notation

An activity diagram may be divided visually into swimlanes, each separated from its neighboring swimlanes by vertical solid lines (Figure 13-176). Each swimlane represents high-level responsibility for part of the overall activity, which may eventually be implemented by one or more objects. The relative ordering of the swimlanes has no semantic significance but might indicate some real-world affinity. Each activity state is assigned to one swimlane and placed within it visually. Transitions may cross lanes; there is no significance to the routing of a transition path.

Because swimlanes are just partitions into arbitrary categories, they may be indicated by other means if a geometrical arrangement into regions is impractical. Possibilities include the use of color or simply the use of tagged values to show the partition.

synch state

A special state that enables synchronization of control between two concurrent regions in a state machine.

See also complex transition, composite state, fork, join, state machine, transition.

Semantics

A composite state can consist of several concurrent regions, each with its own sequential set of states. When a concurrent composite state is entered, each concurrent region becomes active. There is one thread of control in each concurrent region, and each executes independently of the others (the meaning of concurrency). Occasionally, however, control must be synchronized among concurrent regions. One approach is for a transition in one region to have a guard condition that depends on the state of another region. This can be useful for mutual exclusion, including shared resources, but it does not capture situations in which an activity in one region has subsequent consequences in another region (even though the first region may then move on). To capture the latter situation, synch states can be used.

A synch state is a special state that connects two concurrent regions. The regions may be peers—that is, two concurrent regions that belong to the same composite state—or they may be nested within peers at any depth. The regions may not be sequentially related.

One transition connects the output of a fork in one region to the input of the synch state, and another transition connects the output of the synch state to the input of a join in the other region. In other words, a synch state is a buffer that indirectly connects a fork in one region to a join in another region. The fork and the join must each have one input state and one output state within their own regions.

The firing of a transition in the first region is remembered by the synch state until the join transition fires in the second region. If the conditions on the join transition are satisfied before the synch state is active, then the join must wait until the transition in the first region fires. In other words, it represents a transition in the second region that cannot fire until a transition in the first region has fired. Otherwise, it blocks until the first transition fires. Note that because each fork and join must have one input and one output within its own region, synch states do not change the fundamental sequential behavior of each concurrent region, nor do they alter the nesting rules for forming composite states (except that a synch state and its arcs do not belong to either concurrent region, but rather to their composite superstate).

A producer-consumer situation is a typical example of a synch state. The producer fires a transition that activates the synch state; the consumer has a transition that requires the synch state before it can fire.

If the input transition to the synch state is part of a loop, it is possible that the first region can get ahead of the second region. In other words, the synch state might have more than one *token* on it (to use the Petri net term). Therefore, a synch state, unlike a normal state, represents a counter or a queue (the latter if information flows between the regions—if the synch state is an object flow state, for example). By default, a synch state can hold an unlimited number of tokens, but the modeler may specify an upper bound on the number a synch state may hold. If the capacity of the synch state is exceeded, it represents a run-time error. Most often, the bound is unlimited or 1, the latter representing a simple latch. A bound of 1 would generally be used only if it can be guaranteed than overrun will not occur. This is the modeler's responsibility.

If there are tokens on a synch state when the enclosing composite state exits, they are destroyed. Each time the composite region is entered, the synch state is empty.

There may be more than one input arc entering a synch state, but all of them must come from forks in the same sequential region. Similarly, there may be more than one output arc leaving a synch state to merges in the sequential region. Because each region is sequential, there is no danger of conflict from multiple arcs.

A synch state can be an object flow state. In that case, it represents a queue of values that pass from one region to the other.

Notation

A synch state is displayed as a small circle with a single upper bound inside it, either an integer or a star (*) indicating unlimited. There is a transition arrow from

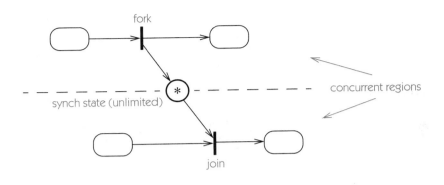

Figure 13-177. *Synch state configuration*

a synch bar symbol (a heavy bar) into the synch state, and another transition arrow from the synch state to a synch bar symbol in another region (Figure 13-177).

The synch state is preferably drawn on the boundary between two regions, but this is not always possible (the regions may not be adjacent), and the topology of the connection is unambiguous, in any case.

Within an activity diagram, each transition arc implicitly represents a state. Therefore, an arrow can be drawn from the output of a fork to the input of a join without explicitly showing the synch state (but the synch state is needed to show an explicit bound).

Example

Figure 13-178 shows a state diagram of a ticket-purchasing situation. Ticketing and charging proceed concurrently, except the seats must be selected before the changes can be computed and posted. This synchronization is shown by inserting a synch state between **Pick seats** and **Post charges**. There is a fork after **Pick seats**, because it is followed by both **Print tickets** and the synch state. **Print charges** does not have to wait for the synchronization. There is a join before **Post charges**, because it must wait for both **Validate account** and the synch state. When both **Print tickets** and **Post charges** are complete, the composite state terminates and **Mail tickets** is performed.

The synch state has a bound of one. A larger bound is unnecessary, because there is only one synchronization per execution of the composite state.

Figure 13-179 shows a batch-processing version of the order-filling process. In this variation, many orders are filled off line. The orders are filled by one server and the changes are made by another server. A change cannot be made before its order is filled, but orders can get ahead of charges so the synch state has an unlimited bound. This is a classic producer-consumer situation.

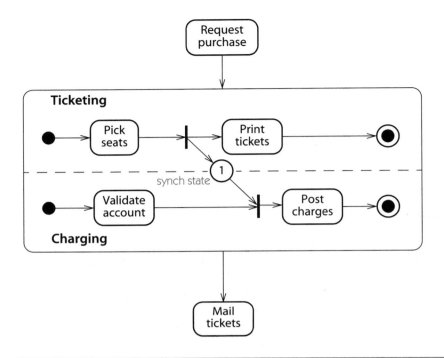

Figure 13-178. *Synch state for single order*

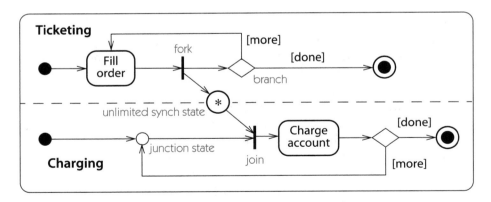

Figure 13-179. *Producer-consumer situation with unlimited synch state*

Discussion

Synch states provide the ability to model producer-consumer situations with minimal overhead and with greater safety than more general concurrency constructs, because each concurrent region maintains a single thread of control at all times.

There is no danger of overrun (if the synch state bound is unlimited), because the synch state is emptied whenever the concurrent superstate is exited. If synch states are used within loops that contain branches, there is a danger of hang-up, however, in which one region has terminated but the other region is waiting for a synch token that will never arrive. Deadlock is also a possibility if each region is in a branch that waits for a token from the other region. There is no way to entirely avoid such situations in concurrent systems that permit decisions. Even without synch states, termination cannot be guaranteed because of the *halting problem*.

synchronous action

A request in which the sending object pauses to wait for a response; a call. Contrast: asynchronous action.

system

A collection of connected units organized to accomplish a purpose. A system can be described by one or more models, possibly from different viewpoints. The system is the "complete model."

Semantics

The system is modeled by a top-level subsystem that indirectly contains the entire set of model elements that work together to accomplish a complete real-world purpose.

Notation

A system can be shown as a package with the stereotype «system». It is rarely necessary to show a system as a unit, however.

tag

The selector value in a tagged value pair. It represents the name of a property defined at modeling time.

tagged value

A tag-value pair attached to an element to hold some piece of information.
See also constraint, stereotype.
See Chapter 14, Standard Elements, for a list of predefined tags.

Semantics

A tagged value is a selector-value pair that may be attached to any element (including model elements and presentation elements) to carry various kinds of information, generally secondary to the element semantics but possibly important to the modeling enterprise. The selector is called a tag; it is a string value. Each tag represents a property that may be applicable to one kind of element or to many kinds. On any element in a model, a tag name may appear at most once. The value may be of various types, but it is encoded as a string. The interpretation of the value is a convention between the modeler and the modeling tool. It is expected that tagged values will be implemented as lookup tables indexed by tags for efficient access.

Tagged values represent arbitrary information expressed in text form and are commonly use to store project management information, such as the author of an element, the testing status, or the importance of the element to a final system (the tags might be **author**, **status**, and **importance**).

Tagged values represent a modest extension to the meta-attributes of UML metaclasses. This is not a fully general extension mechanism but can be used to add information to existing metamodel classes for the benefit of back-end tools, such as code generators, report writers, and simulators. To avoid confusion, tags should differ from existing meta-attributes of model elements to which they are applied. This check can be facilitated by a modeling tool.

Certain tags are predefined in the UML; others may be user defined. Tagged values are an extensibility mechanism permitting arbitrary information to be attached to models.

Notation

Each tagged value is shown in the form

    tag = value

where tag is the name of a tag and value is a literal value. Tagged values may be included with other property keywords in a comma-separated property list enclosed in braces.

A keyword may be declared to stand for a tag with a particular value. In that case the keyword can be used alone. The absence of the tag is treated as equivalent to one of the other legal values for the tag.

    tag

Example

    { author=Joe, status=tested, requirement=3.563.2a, suppress }

Discussion

Most model editor programs provide basic facilities for defining, displaying, and searching tagged values as strings, but they do not use them to extend the UML semantics. However, back-end tools, such as code generators, report writers, and the like, can read tagged values to alter their semantics in flexible ways. Note that tagged value lists are an old idea—for example, property lists in the Lisp language.

Tagged values are a means of attaching nonsemantic project management and tracking information to models. For example, tag **author** might hold the author of an element and tag **status** might hold the development status, such as **incomplete, tested, buggy,** and **complete.**

Tagged values are also a way to attach implementation-language-dependent controls to a UML model without building the details of the language into UML. Code generator flags, hints, and pragmas can be encoded as tagged values without affecting the underlying model. Multiple sets of tags are possible for various languages on the same model. Neither a model editor nor a semantic analyzer need understand the tags—they can be manipulated as strings. A back-end tool, such as a code generator, can understand and process the tagged values. For example, a tagged value might name the container class used to override the default implementation of an association with multiplicity many.

Tagged values accommodate the need for many kinds of information that must be attached to models, but they are not intended as a full metamodel extensibility mechanism. Tags form a flat namespace that must be managed by adopting conventions to avoid naming conflicts. They do not include a provision for specifying the types of values in them. Neither are they intended for serious semantic extensions to the modeling language itself. Tags are *somewhat* similar to metamodel attributes, but they are *not* metamodel attributes and have not been formalized as such.

The use of tags, like the use of procedures in programming language libraries, may require a period of evolution during which there may be conflict among developers. Over time, some standard uses will develop. UML does not include a "registry" of tags nor does it offer the expectation that early users of tags may "reserve" them to prevent other uses in the future.

target scope

A specification of whether a value is an instance or a classifier.

See scope.

Discussion

Target scope is used mainly for storing classes as attribute values or association targets. Its usefulness is limited. The word scope by itself means owner scope.

target state

The state machine state that results from the firing of the transition. After an object handles an event that causes a transition to fire, the object is in the target state of the transition (or target states if it is a complex transition with multiple target states). Not applicable to an internal transition, which does not cause a change of state.

See transition.

template

A parameterized model element. To use it, the parameters must be bound (at model time) to actual values. Synonym: parameterized element.

See also binding, bound element.

Semantics

A template is the descriptor for an element with one or more unbound formal parameters. It therefore defines a family of potential elements, each element specified by binding the parameters to actual values. Typically, the parameters are classifiers that represent attribute types, but they can also represent integers or even operations. Subordinate elements within the template are defined in terms of the formal parameters, so they too become bound when the template itself is bound to actual values.

A template class is the descriptor for a parameterized class. The body of a template may contain occurrences of the formal parameters, as well as a default element that represents the template itself. An actual class is produced by binding the parameters to values. Attributes and operations within the template class can be defined in terms of the formal parameters. The template class can also have relationships, such as associations and generalization, between itself and one of its parameters. When the template is bound, the result is a relationship between the bound template class and the classes bound to the relationship parameters.

A template class is not a directly usable class because it has unbound parameters. Its parameters must be bound to actual values to create a real class. Only a real class can be the parent or the target of an association (a one-way association *from* the template *to* another class is permissible, however). A template class may be a subclass of an ordinary class, which implies that all classes formed by binding the template are subclasses of the given class. It can also be a child of one of the template parameters; this implies that the bound template class is a child of the class passed as the argument.

Parameterization can be applied to other model elements, such as collaborations and even entire packages. The description given here for classes applies to other modeling elements in the obvious way.

The contents of a template are not directly subject to the well-formedness rules of models. That is because they include parameters that do not have full semantics until they are bound. A template is a kind of second-level model element—not one that models systems directly, but one that models other model elements. The contents of a template are therefore outside the semantics of the system. The results of binding a template are ordinary model elements that are subject to well-formedness rules and are normal elements in the target system. Certain well-formedness rules for templates could be derived from the considerations that their bound results must be well formed, but we will not attempt to list them. In a sense, when a template is bound, its contents are duplicated and the parameters are replaced by the arguments. The result becomes part of the effective model as if it had been included directly.

Other kinds of classifiers, such as use cases and signals, can be parameterized. Collaborations can also be parameterized; they are then patterns.

Notation

A small dashed rectangle is superimposed on the upper-right corner of the class rectangle or another modeling element. The dashed rectangle contains a list of formal parameters for the class. Each parameter has a name and a classifier. The list must not be empty (otherwise, there is no template), although it might be suppressed in the presentation. The name, attributes, and operations of the parameterized class appear as normal in the class rectangle, but occurrences of the formal parameters may also be included. Other kinds of parameterized elements are treated similarly. Occurrences of the formal parameters can occur inside the template body, for example, to show a related class identified by one of the parameters.

Parameters have the syntax

name:type

> where name is an identifier for the parameter, with scope inside the template; and

> where type is a string designating a *type expression* for the parameter.

If the type name is omitted, it is assumed to be a type expression that resolves to a classifier, such as a class name or a data type. Other parameter types (such as Integer) must be shown explicitly and must resolve to valid type expressions.

Figure 13-180 shows a template with an integer parameter and a class parameter. The template has an association to one of its parameters.

Discussion

The *effective model* is the implicit model resulting from binding all templates; it is the implicit model that describes a system. Template parameters have no meaning within the effective model itself, because they will have been bound. They may be

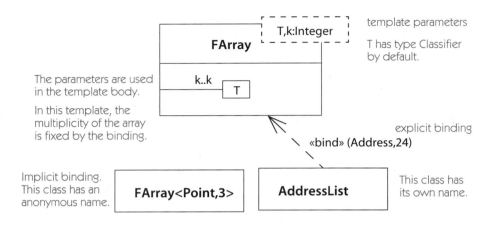

Figure 13-180. *Template notation with use of parameter as a reference*

used only within the scope of the template body itself. This is adequate to handle constituent elements contained within the parameterized element, for example, for attributes or operations within a parameterized class.

There is more difficulty with elements that are usually external to the parameterized element. For example, a class may have associations or generalizations to other classes. If those classes are parameters of the template, they cannot be part of the effective model, yet they are not part of an ordinary class either. Therefore, a parameterized element includes a *body* that represents a model fragment. The model fragment is not part of the effective model. It is part of the template itself, and it may include template parameters, such as a parameter that represents a (as yet unspecified) class. When the template is bound, the body is implicitly copied, the parameters are replaced by arguments, and the copy becomes part of the effective model. Each instantiation of the template produces an addition to the effective model. Figure 13-181 shows an example.

The body of the template implicitly contains an element that represents the instantiated template element itself—for example, the class produced by binding a template. This implicit element may be used to construct relationships, such as associations and generalizations, to template parameters. In the notation, the parameters are drawn inside the template boundary, and a connection to the inside of the template boundary denotes a relationship to the implicit instantiated template element. When the template is instantiated, these become relationships in the effective model between the (newly instantiated) bound template element and the (previously existing) elements that are template arguments.

A template can be a child of another element. This means that each bound element generated from it is a child of the given element. For example, in Figure 13-181, every variable array (**VArray**) is an array (**Array**). Therefore, **VArray<Point>** is a child of **Array**, **VArray<Address>** is a child of **Array**, and so on.

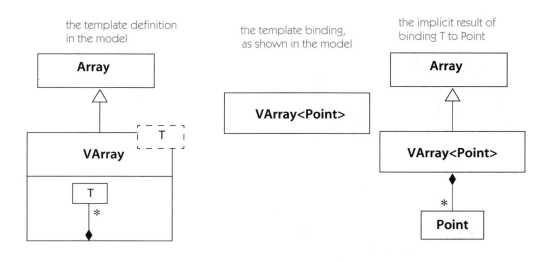

Figure 13-181. *Template with relationship to one of its parameters*

A template usually cannot be a parent of another element. This would mean that each element generated by binding the template is the parent of the other element. Although someone could perhaps assign a meaning to such a situation, it is implausible.

Two templates do not have associations to each other simply because they share the same parameter name. (Trying to do this would mean that every instantiation of the first template is related to every instantiation of the second template, which is not what is usually desired. This point has been misunderstood frequently by authors in the past.) A parameter has scope only inside its own template. Using the same name for a parameter in two templates does not make it the same parameter. Generally, if two templates have parameterized elements that must be related, one of the templates must be instantiated inside the body of the other. (Recall that a template is implicitly instantiated inside its own body. Therefore, both templates are effectively instantiated inside the body, and relationships are therefore between the instantiated elements.) Figure 13-182 shows an incorrect and a correct attempt to define such a relationship—in this case, with a parameterized "pointer" class that points to a parameterized array of the same kind.

A similar approach can be used to declare a parameterized class that is a child of another template class bound with the same parameter. Another approach is to instantiate both templates inside a third template that has a parameter. The parameter is used to bind a copy of each of the other templates. An association may then be constructed between the instantiated copies of the templates. In most practical cases, this is not needed because the relationship can be declared in the body of one of the templates.

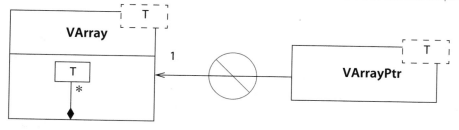

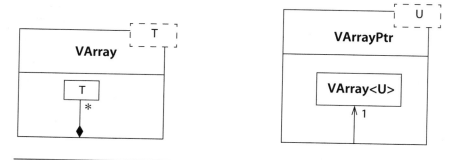

Figure 13-182. *Associations between templates*

thread

(from *thread of control*) A single path of execution through a program, dynamic model, or other representation of control flow. Also a stereotype for the implementation of an active object as a lightweight process.

See active object, complex transition, composite state, state machine, synch state.

time

A value representing an absolute or relative moment in time.

See time expression.

time event

An event that denotes the satisfaction of a time expression, such as the occurrence of an absolute time or the passage of a given amount of time after an object enters a state.

Semantics

A time event is an event that depends on the passage of time and therefore on the existence of a clock. In the real world, the clock is implicit. In a computer, it is a physical entity, and there may be different clocks in different computers. The time event is a message from the clock to the system. Note that both absolute time and elapsed time may be defined with respect to a real-world clock or to a virtual internal clock (in the latter case, it may differ for various objects).

Time events may be based on absolute time (the time of day or a clock setting within a system) or relative time (the elapsed time since the entry to a certain state or the occurrence of an event).

Notation

Time events are not declared as named events the way signals are. Instead, a time expression is simply used as the trigger of a transition.

Discussion

In any real implementation, time events do not come from the universe—they come from some clock object inside or outside the system. As such, they become almost indistinguishable from signals, especially in real-time and distributed systems. In such systems, the issue of which clock is used must also be determined—there is no such thing as the "real time." (It doesn't exist in the real universe either—just ask Einstein.)

time expression

An expression that resolves to an absolute or relative value of time. Used in defining a time event.

Semantics

Most time expressions are either elapsed time after the entry to a state or the occurrence of a particular absolute time. Other time expressions must be defined in an ad hoc way.

Notation

Elapsed time. An event denoting the passage of some amount of time after entry to the state containing the transition is notated with the keyword **after** followed by an expression that evaluates (at modeling time) to an amount of time.

    after (10 seconds)

    after (10 seconds since exit from state A)

If no starting point is specified, then it is the elapsed time since entry to the state containing the transition.

Absolute time. An event denoting the occurrence of an absolute time is notated with the keyword **when**, followed by a parenthetical Boolean expression involving time.

> **when** (date = Jan. 1, 2000)

timing mark

A denotation for the time at which an event or message occurs. Timing marks may be used in constraints.

Semantics

A timing mark is formed as an expression from the name of a message. A message may be given a name in an interaction so that timing mark expressions can be formed from it. In the following expressions, message is the name of a message.

> message.**sendTime** ()   Time that message is sent
>
> message.**receiveTime** ()   Time that message is received

Notation

Timing mark expressions are shown as text.

Example

The following constraint limits the time required to produce a dial tone.

> { dialtone.sendTime () – offhook.sendTime () < 1 second }

trace

A dependency that indicates a historical development process or other extra-model relationship between two elements that represent the same concept without specific rules for deriving one from the other. This is the least specific kind of dependency, and it has minimal semantics. It is mostly of use as a reminder for human thought during development.

See dependency, model.

Semantics

A trace is a variety of dependency that indicates a connection between two elements that represent the same concept at different levels of meaning. It does not represent semantics within a model. Rather, it represents connections between elements with different semantics—that is, between elements from different models on different planes of meaning. There is no explicit mapping between the elements. Often, it represents a connection between two ways of capturing a concept at different stages of development. For example, two elements that are variations of the same theme might be related by a trace. A trace does not represent a relationship between run-time instances. Rather, it is a dependency between model elements themselves.

A major use of trace is for tracking requirements that have been changed throughout the development of a system. The trace dependencies may relate elements in two kinds of models (such as a use case model and a design model) or in two versions of the same kind of model.

Notation

A trace is indicated by a dependency arrow (a dashed arrow with its tail on the newer element and its head on the older element) with the keyword «**trace**». Usually, however, the elements are in different models that are not displayed simultaneously, so in practice, the relationship would most often be implemented in a tool as a hyperlink.

transient link

A link that exists for a limited duration, such as for the execution of an operation.
See also association, collaboration, usage.

Semantics

During execution, some links exist for a limited duration. Of course, almost any object or link has a limited lifespan, if the time period is great enough. Some links, however, exist only in certain limited contexts, such as during the execution of a method. Procedure arguments and local variables can be represented by transient links. It is possible to model all such links as associations, but then the conditions on the associations must be stated very broadly, and they lose much of their precision in constraining combinations of objects. Such situations can instead be modeled using collaborations, which are configurations of objects and links that exist within special contexts.

An association role from a collaboration can be regarded as a transient link that exists only within the execution of a behavioral entity, such as a procedure. It appears within a class model as a usage dependency. For full details it is necessary to consult the behavioral model.

Notation

A transient link is shown as an association with a stereotype attached to the link role to indicate various kinds of implementation. The following stereotypes may be used:

«parameter»	Procedure parameter
«local»	Local variable of a procedure
«global»	Global variable (something visible within an entire model or package); avoid, if possible, as it violates the spirit of object-orientation
«self»	Self-link (the ability of an object to send a message to itself, implicit in objects and useful to show only in dynamic situations with message flows)
«association»	Association (default, unnecessary to specify except for emphasis); not a transient link but listed for completeness

transient object

An object that exists only during the execution of the thread that created it.

transition (phase)

The fourth phase of a software development process, during which the implemented system is configured for execution in a real-world context. During this phase, the deployment view is completed, together with any of the remaining views that were not completed in previous phases.

See development process.

transition

A relationship within a state machine between two states indicating that an object in the first state will perform specified actions and enter the second state when a specified event occurs and specified guard conditions are satisfied. On such a change of state, the transition is said to fire. A simple transition has a single source state and a single target state. A complex transition has more than one source state and/or more than one target state. It represents a change in the number of concurrently active states, or a fork or join of control. An internal transition has a source state but no target state. It represents a response to an event without a change of state. States and transitions are the vertices and nodes of state machines.

See also state machine.

Semantics

Transitions represent the potential paths among the states in the life history of an object, as well as the actions performed in changing state. A transition indicates the way an object in a state responds to the occurrence of an event. States and transitions are the vertices and arcs of a state machine that describes the possible life histories of the instances of a classifier.

Structure

A transition has a source state, an event trigger, a guard condition, an action, and a target state. Some of these may be absent in a transition.

Source state. The source state is the state that is affected by the transition. If an object is in the source state, an outgoing transition of the state may fire if the object receives the trigger event of the transition and if the guard condition (if any) is satisfied.

Target state. The target state is the state that is active after the completion of the transition. It is the state to which the master object changes. The target state is not used in an internal transition, which does not perform a change of state.

Event trigger. The event trigger is the event whose reception by the object in the source state makes the transition eligible to fire, provided its guard condition is satisfied. If the event has parameters, their values are available to the transition and may be used in expressions for the guard condition and actions. The event triggering a transition becomes the current event and may be accessed by subsequent actions that are part of the run to completion step initiated by the event.

A transition without an explicit trigger event is called a completion transition (or a triggerless transition) and is implicitly triggered on the completion of any internal activity in the state. A composite state indicates its completion by reaching its final state. If a state has no internal activity or nested states, then a completion transition is triggered immediately when the state is entered after any entry action is executed. Note that a completion transition must satisfy its guard condition to fire. If the guard condition is false when the completion occurs, then the implicit completion event is consumed and the transition will not fire later even if the guard condition becomes true. (This kind of behavior can be modeled instead with a change event.)

Note that all appearances of an event within a state machine must have the same signature.

Guard condition. The guard condition is a Boolean expression that is evaluated when a transition is triggered by the handling of an event, including an implicit completion event on a completion transition. If the state machine is performing a run-to-completion step when an event occurs, the event is saved until the step is complete and the state machine is quiescent. Otherwise the event is handled immediately. If the expression evaluates to true, the transition is eligible to fire. If the expression evaluates to false, then the transition does not fire. If no transition becomes eligible to fire, the event is ignored. This is not an error. Multiple transitions having different guard conditions may be triggered by the same event. If the event occurs, all the guard conditions are tested. If more than one guard condition is true, only one transition will fire. The choice of transition to fire is nondeterministic if no priority rule is given.

Note that the guard condition is evaluated only once, at the time when the event is handled. If the condition evaluates to false and later becomes true, the transition will not fire unless another event occurs and the condition is true at that time. Note that a guard condition is not the appropriate way to continuously monitor a value. A change event should be used for such a situation.

If a transition has no guard condition, then the guard condition is treated as true and the transition is enabled if its trigger event occurs. If several transitions are enabled, only one will fire. The choice may be nondeterministic.

For convenience, a guard condition can be broken into a series of simpler guard conditions. In fact, several guard conditions may branch from a single trigger event or guard condition. Each path through the tree represents a single transition triggered by the (single) trigger event with a different effective guard condition that is the conjunction ("and") of the guard conditions along its path. All the expressions along such a path are evaluated before a transition is chosen to fire. A transition cannot partially fire. In effect, a set of independent transitions may share part of their description. Figure 13-183 shows an example.

Note that trees of guard conditions and the ability to order transitions for eligibility are merely conveniences, as the same effect could be achieved by a set of independent transitions, each with its own disjoint guard condition.

Action. A transition may contain an action expression that describes an action. This is an expression for procedural computation that may affect the object that owns the state machine (and, indirectly, other objects that it can reach). This expression may use parameters of the trigger event, as well as attributes and associations of the owning object. The trigger event is available as the current event during the entire run-to-completion step initiated by the event, including later triggerless segments and entry and exit actions.

An action may be an action sequence. An action is atomic—that is, it may not be externally terminated and must be executed completely before any other actions or events may be handled. Actions should be of minimal duration to avoid hanging the state machine. Any events received during execution of an action are saved until the action is completed, at which time they are evaluated.

Branches. For convenience, several transitions that share the same trigger event but have different guard conditions can be grouped together in the model and notation to avoid duplication of the trigger or the common part of the guard condition. This is merely a representational convenience and does not affect the semantics of transitions.

See branch for details of representation and notation.

Notation

A transition is shown as a solid arrow from one state (the *source* state) to another state (the *target* state), labeled by a transition string. Figure 13-184 shows a transition between two states and one split into segments.

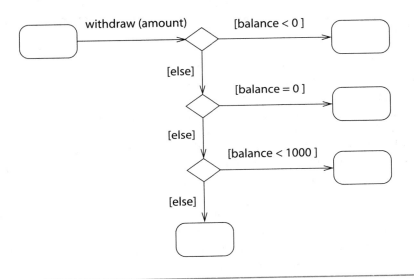

Figure 13-183. *Tree of guard conditions*

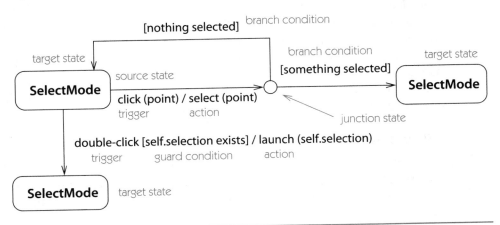

Figure 13-184. *Transitions*

An internal transition is shown as a transition string inside a state symbol. A transition string has the following format:

$$\overline{\text{name :}}_{\text{opt}} \text{ event-name}_{\text{opt}} \overline{(\text{ parameter-list})}_{\text{opt}} \overline{[\text{ guard-condition }]}_{\text{opt}}$$
$$\overline{/\text{ action-list}}_{\text{opt}}$$

The *name* may be used to reference the transition in expressions, particularly for forming timing marks. It is followed by a colon.

The *event-name* names an event and is followed by its parameters. The parameter list may be omitted if there are no parameters. The event name and parameter list are omitted for a completion transition. The parameter-list has the format:

$$\overline{\text{name :type}}_{\text{list,}}$$

The *guard-condition* is a Boolean expression written in terms of parameters of the triggering event and attributes and links of the object described by the state machine. The guard condition may also involve tests of the status of concurrent states of the current machine or explicitly designated states of some reachable object—[**in** State1] and [**not in** State2] are examples. State names may be fully qualified by the nested states that contain them, yielding pathnames of the form State1::State2::State3. This may be used if the same state name occurs in different composite state regions of the overall machine.

The *action-list* is a procedural expression that is executed if and when the transition fires. It may be written in terms of operations, attributes, and links of the owning object and the parameters of the triggering event. Actions may include call, send, and other kinds of actions. The action-list may contain more than one action clause separated by semicolon delimiters:

$$\text{action}_{\text{list;}}$$

Branches. A transition may include a segment with a trigger event followed by a tree of junction states, drawn as small circles. This is equivalent to a set of individual transitions, one for each path through the tree, whose guard condition is the "and" of all the conditions along the path. Only the final segment of any path may have an action.

A junction state may alternately be drawn as a diamond if it represents a branch or a merge. There is no difference in meaning.

Discussion

A transition represents an atomic change from one state to another, possibly accompanied by an atomic action. A transition is noninterruptible. The actions on a transition should be short, usually trivial, computations, such as assignment statements and simple arithmetic calculations.

transition time

See timing mark.

trigger

An event whose occurrence makes a transition eligible to fire. The word may be used as a noun (for the event itself) or as a verb (for the occurrence of the event).

See also completion transition, transition.

Semantics

Each transition (except a completion transition that fires on the completion of internal activity) has a reference to an event as part of its structure. If the event occurs when an object is in a state containing an outgoing transition whose trigger is the event or an ancestor of the event, then the guard condition on the transition is tested. If the condition is satisfied, then the transition is enabled to fire. If the guard condition is absent, then it is deemed to be satisfied. If more than one transition is eligible to fire, only one will actually fire. The choice may be nondeterministic. (If the object has more than one concurrent state, one transition from each state may fire. But at most one transition from each state may fire.)

Note that the guard condition is tested once, at the moment when the triggering event occurs (including an implicit completion event). If no transition is enabled to fire by the occurrence of an event, the event is simply ignored. This is not an error.

The parameters of the trigger event are available for use in a guard condition or an action attached to the transition or to an entry action on the target state.

Throughout the execution of a run-to-completion step after a transition, the trigger event remains available to the actions of the substeps of the transition as the current event. The exact type of this event may be unknown in an entry action or in a later segment in a multiple-segment transition. Therefore, the type of event may be discriminated in an action using a polymorphic operation or a case statement. Once the exact event type is known, its parameters can be used.

Notation

The name and signature of the trigger event are part of the label on a transition.

See transition.

The trigger event may be accessed in an expression by the reserved word **currentEvent**. This keyword references the trigger event on the first segment of a multiple-segment transition.

triggerless transition

A transition without an explicit event trigger. When it leaves a normal state, it represents a completion transition, that is, a transition that is triggered by the completion of activity rather than by an explicit event. When it leaves a pseudostate, it represents a transition segment that is automatically traversed when the preceding segment has completed its action. Triggerless transitions are used to connect initial states and history states to their target states.

tuple

An ordered list of values. Generally, the term implies that there is a set of such lists of similar form. (This is a standard mathematical term.)

type

As an adjective: The declared classifier that the value of an attribute, parameter, or variable must hold. The actual value must be an instance of the type or one of its descendants.

As a noun: A stereotype of class used to specify a set of instances (such as objects) together with the operations applicable to the objects. A type may not contain any method. Contrast: interface, implementation class.

Type and implementation class

Classes can be stereotyped as types or implementation classes (although they can be left undifferentiated as well). A type is used to specify a domain of objects, together with operations applicable to the objects, without defining the physical implementation of the objects or operations. A type may not include methods, but it may provide behavioral specifications for its operations. It may also include attributes and associations in order to specify the behavior of operations. A type's attributes and associations do not determine the implementation of its objects.

An implementation class defines the physical data structure and methods of objects, as implemented in traditional languages, such as C++ and Smalltalk. An implementation class is said to realize a type if the implementation class includes all the operations as the type with the same behavior. An implementation class may realize multiple types, and multiple implementation classes may realize the same type. The attributes and associations of an implementation class do not have to be the same as those of a type it realizes. The implementation class may provide methods for its operations in terms of its physical attributes and associations, and may declare additional operations not found in any types.

An object must be an instance of no more than one implementation class, which specifies the physical implementation of the object. However, an object be an instance of multiple types. If the object is an instance of an implementation class, then the implementation class must realize the types of which the object is an instance. If dynamic classification is available, then an object may gain and lose types over its lifetime. A type used in this way characterizes a changeable role that an object may adopt and later abandon.

Although the use of types and implementation classes differs, their internal structure is the same, so they are modeled as class stereotypes. They fully support generalization; the substitutability principle; and the inheritance of attributes, associations and operations. Types may only specialize types, however, and implementation classes may only specialize implementation classes. Types may be related to implementation classes only by realization.

Notation

An undifferentiated class is shown with no keyword. A type is shown with the keyword «type», and an implementation class is shown with «implementation class». Figure 13-185 shows an example.

The implementation of a type by an implementation class is modeled using the realization relationship, shown as a dashed line with a solid triangular arrowhead (a "dashed generalization arrow" or a "dependency with solid arrowhead"). This symbol implies inheritance of operations but not of structure (attributes or associations). Realization may be used between any two classifiers for which one supports the operations of the other, but implementation of a type by an implementation class is a common use of it.

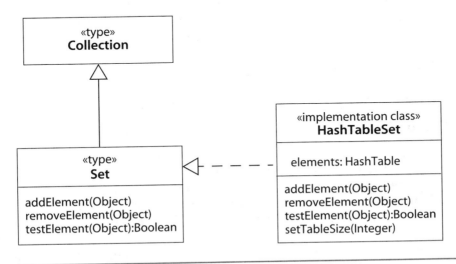

Figure 13-185. *Notation for types and implementation classes*

Discussion

Type and implementation class are somewhat limited concepts aimed at conventional programming languages, such as C++ and Smalltalk. The UML concept of class can be used directly in a more general way. UML supports both multiple classification and dynamic classification, which remove the need for distinctions between types and implementation classes. The distinctions are useful, however, for designing code for conventional languages.

type expression

An expression that evaluates to a reference to one or more data types. For example, an attribute type declaration in a typical programming language is a type expression.

Example

In C++ the following are type expressions:

Person*

Order[24]

Boolean (*) (String, int)

uninterpreted

A placeholder for a type or types whose implementation is not specified by the UML. Every uninterpreted value has a corresponding string representation. In any physical implementation, such as a model editor, the implementation would have to be complete, so there would be no uninterpreted values.

unspecified value

A value that has not yet been specified by the modeler.

Discussion

An unspecified value is not a value at all in the proper sense and cannot appear within a complete model except for properties whose value is unnecessary or irrelevant. For example, multiplicity cannot be unknown; it must have some value. A lack of any knowledge is tantamount to a multiplicity of many. The semantics of UML therefore do not allow or deal with the absence of values or unspecified values.

There is another sense in which "unspecified" is a useful part of an unfinished model. It has the meaning: "I have not yet thought about this value, and I have made a note of it so that I will remember to give it a value later." It is an explicit statement that the model is incomplete. This is a useful capability and one that tools may support. By its very nature, such a value cannot appear in a finished model, and it makes no sense to define its semantics. A tool can automatically supply a default value for an unspecified value when a value is needed—for example, during code generation—but this is simply a convenience and not part of the semantics. Unspecified values are outside the semantics of UML.

Similarly, there is no semantic meaning to a default value for a property. A property in the model simply has a value. A tool may automatically supply values for properties of newly created elements. But again, this is just an operational convenience within the tool, not part of UML semantics. Semantically-complete UML models do not have default or unspecified values; they simply have values.

usage

A dependency in which one element (the client) requires the presence of another element (the supplier) for its correct functioning or implementation—generally, for implementation reasons.

See also collaboration, dependency, transient link.

Semantics

A usage dependency is a situation in which one element requires the presence of another element for its correct implementation or functioning. All the elements must exist at the same level of meaning—that is, they do not involve a shift in the level of abstraction or realization (such as a mapping between an analysis-level class and an implementation-level class). Frequently, a usage dependency involves implementation-level elements, such as a C++ include file, for which it implies compiler consequences. A usage may be stereotyped further to indicate the exact nature of the dependency, such as calling an operation of another class or instantiating an object of another class.

Notation

A usage is indicated by a dashed arrow (dependency) with the keyword «use». The arrowhead is on the supplier (independent) element, and the tail is on the client (dependent) element.

Discussion

A usage usually corresponds to a transient link—that is, a connection between instances of classes that is not meaningful or present all the time, but only in some context, such as the execution of a subroutine procedure. The dependency construct does not model the full information in this situation, only the fact of its existence. The collaboration construct provides the capability to model such relationships in full detail.

Standard elements

call, create, instantiate, send

use

Keyword for the usage dependency in the notation.

use case

The specification of sequences of actions, including variant sequences and error sequences, that a system, subsystem, or class can perform by interacting with outside actors.

See also actor, classifier.

Semantics

A use case is a coherent unit of functionality provided by a classifier (a system, subsystem, or class) as manifested by sequences of messages exchanged among the system and one or more outside users (represented as actors), together with actions performed by the system.

The purpose of a use case is to define a piece of behavior of a classifier (including a subsystem or the entire system), without revealing the internal structure of the classifier. Each use case specifies a service the classifier provides to its users—that is, a specific way of using the classifier that is visible from the outside. It describes a complete sequence initiated by a user (as modeled by an actor) in terms of the interaction between users and classifier, as well as the responses performed by the classifier. The interaction includes only the communications between the system and the actors. The internal behavior or implementation is hidden. The entire set of use cases of a classifier or system partition and cover its behavior. Each use case represents a meaningful quantized piece of functionality available to users. Note that *user* includes humans, as well as computers and other objects. An actor is an idealization of the purpose of a user, not a representation of a physical user. One physical user can map to many actors, and an actor can represent the same aspect of multiple physical users.

See actor.

A use case includes normal mainline behavior in response to a user request, as well as possible variants of the normal sequence, such as alternate sequences, exceptional behavior, and error handling. The goal is to describe a piece of coherent functionality in all its variations, including all the error conditions. The complete set of use cases for a classifier specifies all the different ways to use the classifier. Use cases can be grouped into packages for convenience.

A use case is a descriptor; it describes potential behavior. An execution of a use case is a use case instance. The behavior of a use case can be specified by an attached state machine or by text code (which is equivalent to a state machine). It can also be described by an informal text description. Behavior can be illustrated, but not formally specified, by a set of scenarios. But at early stages of development, this may be sufficient.

A use case instance is an execution of a use case, initiated by a message from an instance of an actor. As a response to the message, the use case instance executes a sequence of actions specified by the use case, such as sending messages to actor instances, not necessarily only to the initiating actor. The actor instances may send messages to the use case instance, and the interaction continues until the instance has responded to all input. When it does not expect any more input, it ends.

A use case is a specification of the behavior of a system (or other classifier) as a whole in its interactions with outside actors. The internal interactions among internal objects in a system that implements the behavior is described by a collaboration that realizes a use case.

Structure

A use case may have classifier features and relationships.

Features. A use case is a classifier and therefore has attributes and operations. The attributes are used to represent the state of the use case—that is, the progress of executing it. An operation represents a piece of work the use case can perform. It is not directly callable from the outside, but may be used to describe the effect of the use case on the system. The execution of an operation may be associated with the receipt of a message from an actor. The operations act on the attributes of the use case, and indirectly on the system or class that the use case is attached to.

Associations to actors. An association between an actor and a use case indicates that the actor instance communicates with the system instance or classifier instance to effect some result that is of interest to the actor. Actors model external users of a classifier. Thus, if the classifier is a system, its actors are the external users of the system. Actors of lower-level subsystems may be other classes within the overall system.

One actor may communicate with several use cases—that is, the actor may request several different services of the system—and one use case may communicate with one or more actors when providing its service. Note that two use cases that specify the same system cannot communicate with each other because each of them individually describes a complete usage of the system. They may interact indirectly through shared actors.

The interaction between actors and use cases can be defined with interfaces. An interface defines the operations an actor or a use case may support or use. Different interfaces offered by the same use case need not be disjoint.

Use cases are related to other use cases by generalization, extend, and include relationships.

Generalization. A generalization relationship relates a specialized use case to the more general use case. The child inherits the attributes, operations, and behavior sequences of the parent and may add additional attributes and operations of its own. The child use case adds incremental behavior to the parent use case by inserting additional action sequences into the parent sequence at arbitrary points. It may also modify some inherited operations and sequences, but this must be done with the same care as any overriding so that the intent of the parent is preserved. Any include or extend relationships to the child use case also effectively modify the behavior inherited from the parent use case.

Extend. An extend relationship is a kind of dependency. The client use case adds incremental behavior to the base use case by inserting additional action sequences into the base sequence. The client use case contains one or more separate behavior sequence segments. The extend relationship contains a list of extension point names from the base use case, equal in number to the number of segments in the client use case. An extension point represents a location or set of locations in the base use case at which the extension could be inserted. An extend relationship may also have a condition on it, which may use attributes from the parent use case. When an instance of the parent use case reaches a location referenced by an extension point in an extend relationship, the condition is evaluated; if the condition is true, the corresponding behavior segment of the child use case is performed. If there is no condition, it is deemed to be always true. If the extend relationship has more than one extension point, the condition is evaluated only at the first extension point prior to execution of the first segment.

An extend relationship does not create a new instantiable use case. Instead, it implicitly adds behavior to the original base use case. The base use case implicitly includes the extended behavior. The nonextended original base use case is not available in its unaltered form. In other words, if you extend a use case, you cannot explicitly instantiate the base use case without the possibility of extensions. A use case may have multiple extensions which all apply to the same base use case and can be inserted into one use case instance, if their separate conditions are satisfied. On the other hand, an extension use case may extend several base use cases (or the same one at different extension points), each at its own proper extension point (or list of extension points). If there are several extensions at the same extension point, their relative execution order is nondeterministic.

Note that the extension use case is not to be instantiated, the base use case must be instantiated to obtain the combined base-plus-extensions behavior. The extension use case may or may not be instantiable, but in any case it does not include the base use case behavior.

Include. An include relationship denotes the inclusion of the behavior sequence of the supplier use case into the interaction sequence of a client use case, under the control of the client use case at a location the client specifies in its description. This is a dependency, not a generalization, because the supplier use case cannot be substituted in places at which the client use case appears. The client may access the attributes of the base to obtain values and communicate results. The use case instance is executing the client use case. When it reaches the inclusion point, it begins executing the supplier use case until it is complete. Then it resumes executing the client use case beyond the inclusion location. The attributes of the supplier use case do not have values that persist between executions.

A use case may be abstract, which means that it cannot be directly instantiated in a system execution. It defines a fragment of behavior that is specialized by or included in concrete use cases, or it may be an extension of a base use case. It may also be concrete if it can be instantiated by itself.

Behavior. The behavior sequence of a use case can be described using a state machine, activity graph, or text code in some executable language. The actions of the state machine or the statements of the code may call on the internal operations of the use case to specify the effects of execution. The actions may also indicate sending messages to actors.

A use case may be described informally using scenarios or plain text, but such descriptions are imprecise and meant for human interpretation only.

The actions of a use case may be specified in terms of calls to operations of the classifier that the use case describes. One operation may be called by more than one use case.

Realization. The realization of a use case may be specified by a set of collaborations. A collaboration describes the implementation of the use case by objects in the classifier the use case describes. Each collaboration describes the context among the constituents of the system within which one or more interaction sequences occur. Collaborations and their interactions define how objects within the system interact to achieve the specified external behavior of the use case.

A system can be specified with use cases at various levels of abstraction. A use case specifying a system, for example, may be refined into a set of subordinate use cases, each specifying a service of a subsystem. The functionality specified by the superordinate (higher-level) use case is completely traceable to the functionality of the subordinate (lower-level) use cases. A superordinate use case and a set of subordinate use cases specify the same behavior at two levels of abstraction. The subordinate use cases cooperate to provide the behavior of the superordinate use case. The cooperation of the subordinate use cases is specified by collaborations of the

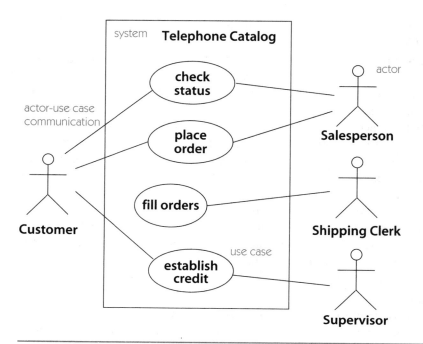

Figure 13-186. *Use cases and actors*

superordinate use case and may be presented in collaboration diagrams. The actors of a superordinate use case appear as actors of the subordinate use cases. Moreover, the subordinate use cases are actors of each other. This layered realization results in a nested set of use cases and collaborations that implement the entire system.

Notation

A use case is shown as an ellipse containing the name of the use case. If attributes or operations of the use case must be shown, the use case can be drawn as a classifier rectangle with the keyword «use case». Figure 13-186 shows a use case diagram.

An extension point is a named entity within a use case that describes locations at which action sequences from other use cases may be inserted. It provides a level of indirection between the extensions and the behavior sequence text. An extension point references a location or set of locations within the behavior sequence of the use case. The reference can be changed independently of extend relationships that use the extension point. Each extension point must have a unique name within a use case. Extension points may be listed in a compartment of the use case with the heading **extension points** (Figure 13-187).

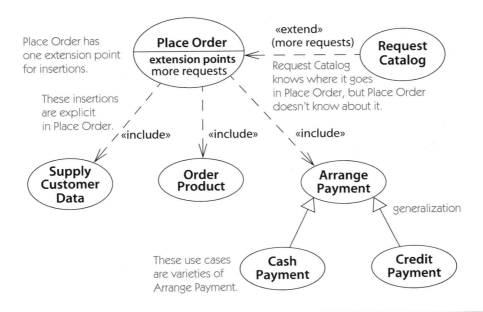

Figure 13-187. *Use case relationships*

A communication relationship between a use case and an actor is shown using an association symbol—a solid path between the use case and the actor symbols. The «communication» keyword can usually be omitted, because this is the only kind of association between actors and use cases. Generally, no name or role names are placed on the line, as the actor and the use case define the relationship uniquely.

A generalization relationship is shown by a generalization arrow—a solid path from the child use case to the parent use case, with a closed triangular arrowhead on the parent use case.

An extend relationship or an include relationship is shown by a dependency arrow with the keyword «extend» or «include»—a dashed line with a stick arrowhead on the client use case. An extend relationship also has a list of extension point names on it (they may be suppressed in the diagram).

Figure 13-187 shows various kinds of use case relationships.

Behavior specification. The relationship between a use case and its external interaction sequences is usually represented by a hyperlink to sequence diagrams. The hyperlink is invisible but it can be traversed in an editor. The behavior may also be specified by a state machine or by programming language text attached to the use case. Natural language text may be used as an informal specification.

See extend for a sample of some behavior sequences.

The relationship between a use case and its implementation may be shown as a realization relationship from a use case to a collaboration. But because these are often in separate models, it is usually represented as an invisible hyperlink. The expectation is that a tool will support the ability to "zoom into" a use case to see its scenarios and/or implementation as a collaboration.

use case diagram

A diagram that shows the relationships among actors and use cases within a system.

See actor, use case.

Notation

A use case diagram is a graph of actors, a set of use cases enclosed by a system boundary (a rectangle), associations between the actors and the use cases, relationships among the use cases, and generalization among the actors. Use case diagrams show elements from the use case model (use cases, actors).

use case generalization

A taxonomic relationship between a use case (the child) and the use case (the parent) that describes the characteristics the child shares with other use cases that have the same parent. This is generalization as applicable to use cases.

Semantics

A parent use case may be specialized into one or more child use cases that represent more specific forms of the parent (Figure 13-188). A child inherits all the attributes, operations, and relationships of its parent, because a use case is a classifier. The implementation of an inherited operation may be overridden by a collaboration that realizes a child use case.

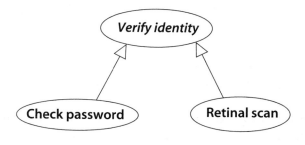

Figure 13-188. *Use case generalization*

Use case behavior for parent **Verify Identity:**

> The parent is abstract, there is no behavior sequence.
> A concrete descendant must supply the behavior as shown below.

Use case behavior for child **Check Password:**

Obtain password from master database
Ask use for password
User supplies password
Check password against user entry

Use case behavior for child **Retinal Scan**

Obtain retinal signature from master database
Scan user's retina and obtain signature
Compare master signature against scanned signature

Figure 13-189. *Behavior sequences for parent and child use cases*

The child inherits the behavior sequence of the parent and may insert additional behavior into it (Figure 13-189). The parent and the child are potentially instantiable (if they are not abstract), and different specializations of the same parent are independent, unlike an extend relationship, in which multiple extends all implicitly modify the same base use case. Behavior may be added to the child use case by adding steps into the behavior sequence inherited from the parent, as well as by declaring extend and include relationships to the child. If the parent is abstract, its behavior sequence may have sections that are explicitly incomplete in the parent and must be provided by the child. The child may modify steps inherited from the parent, but as with the overriding of methods, this capability must be used with care because the intent of the parent must be preserved.

The generalization relationship connects a child use case to a parent use case. A child use case may access and modify attributes defined by the parent use case.

Substitutability for use cases means that the behavior sequence of a child use case must include the behavior sequence of its parent. The steps in the parent's sequence need not be contiguous, however; the child can interleave additional steps among the steps of the behavior sequence inherited from the parent.

The use of multiple inheritance with use cases requires an explicit specification of how the behavior sequences of the parents are interleaved to make the sequence for the child.

Use case generalization may use private inheritance to share the implementation of a base use case without full substitutability, but this capability should be used sparingly.

Notation

The normal generalization symbol is used—a solid line from the child to the parent with a hollow triangular arrowhead on the line touching the parent symbol.

Example

Figure 13-188 shows abstract use case **Verify identity** and its specialization as two concrete use cases, whose behavior is shown in Figure 13-189.

use case instance

The execution of a sequence of actions specified in a use case. An instance of a use case.
    See use case.

use case model

A model that describes the functional requirements of a system or other classifier in terms of use cases.
    See actor, use case.

Semantics

The use case model represents functionality of a system or other classifier as manifested to external interactors with the system. A use case model is shown on a use case diagram.

use case view

That aspect of the system concerned with specifying behavior in terms of use cases. A use case model is a model focused on this view. The use case view is part of the set of modeling concepts loosely grouped together as the dynamic view.

utility

A stereotype of **Class** that groups global variables and procedures in the form of a class declaration. The attributes and operations of the utility become global variables and global procedures, respectively. A utility is not a fundamental modeling construct, but a programming convenience. It has no instances.

Semantics

The attributes of the utility are global variables, and the operations of the utility are global operations. Utilities are unnecessary for object-oriented programming, as global attributes and operations can be better modeled as class-scope members.

The construct is provided for compatibility with non-object-oriented languages, such as C.

Notation

A utility is shown as a class symbol with the stereotype keyword «utility» above the class-name string. The attributes and operations represent global members. No class-scope members may be declared in the symbol.

value

See data value.

vertex

A source or a target for a transition in a state machine. A vertex can be either a state or a pseudostate.

view

A projection of a model, which is seen from one perspective or vantage point and omits entities that are not relevant to this perspective. The word is not used here to denote a presentation element. Instead, it includes projections in both the semantic model and the visual notation.

visibility

An enumeration whose value (**public, protected,** or **private**) denotes whether the model element to which it refers may be seen outside its enclosing namespace.

See also access for a discussion of visibility rules applied to interpackage references.

Semantics

Visibility declares the ability of a modeling element to reference an element that is in a different namespace from the referencing element. Visibility is part of the relationship between an element and the container that holds it. The container may be a package, class, or some other namespace. There are three predefined visibilities.

public	Any element that can see the container can also see the indicated element.
protected	Only an element within the container or a descendant of the container can see the indicated element. Other elements may not reference it or otherwise use it.

private   Only an element within the container can see the element. Other elements, including elements in descendants of the container, may not reference it or otherwise use it.

Additional kinds of visibility might be defined for some programming languages, such as C++ *implementation* visibility (actually, all forms of nonpublic visibility are language-dependent). The use of additional choices must be by convention between the user and any modeling tools and code generators.

Notation

Visibility can be shown by a property keyword or by a punctuation mark placed in front of the name of a model element.

public	+
protected	#
private	−

The visibility marker may be suppressed. The absence of a visibility marker indicates that the visibility is not shown, not that it is undefined or public. A tool should assign visibilities to new elements even if the visibility is not shown. The visibility marker is a shorthand for a full visibility property specification string.

Visibility may also be specified by keywords (public, protected, private). This form is often used as an inline list element that applies to an entire block of attributes or other list elements.

Any language-specific or user-defined visibility choices must be specified by a property string or by a tool-specific convention.

Classes. In a class, the visibility marker is placed on list elements, such as attributes and operations. It shows whether another class can access the elements.

Associations. In an association, the visibility marker is placed on the rolename of the target class (the end that would be accessed using the visibility setting). It shows whether the class at the far end can traverse the association toward the end with the visibility marker.

Packages. In a package, the visibility marker is placed on elements contained directly within the package, such as classes, associations, and nested packages. It shows whether another package that accesses or imports the first package can see the elements.

well formed

Designates a model that is correctly constructed, one that satisfies all the predefined and model-specified rules and constraints. Such a model has meaningful semantics. A model that is not well formed is called ill formed.

14

Standard Elements

Standard elements are predefined keywords for constraints, stereotypes, and tags. They represent concepts of general utility that are not significant enough or not different enough from core concepts to include as UML core concepts. They have the same relation to UML core concepts as a built-in subroutine library has to a programming language. They are not part of the core language itself, but they are part of the environment a user can count on when using the language. The list also includes notation keywords—keywords that appear on the symbol for another model element but that denote built-in model elements, not stereotypes. For keywords, the notation symbol is listed.

The cross-references are to articles in Chapter 13, Encyclopedia of Terms.

access

(stereotype of Permission dependency)

A stereotyped dependency between two packages, denoting that the public contents of the target package are accessible to the namespace of the source package.

See access.

association

(stereotype of AssociationEnd)

A constraint applied to an association end (including a link end or an end of an association role), specifying that the corresponding instance is visible via an actual association, rather than via a transient link, such as a parameter or local variable.

See association, association end, association role.

become

(stereotype of Flow relationship)

A stereotyped dependency the source and target of which represent the same instance at different points in time, but each with potentially different values, state instance, and roles. A become dependency from **A** to **B** means that instance **A** becomes **B** with possibly new values, state instance, and roles at a different moment in time/space. Become notation is a dashed arrow from the source to the target with the «**become**» keyword.

See become.

bind

(keyword on Dependency symbol)

A keyword on dependency that denotes a binding relationship. It is followed by a comma-separated argument list in parentheses.

See binding, bound element, template.

call

(stereotype of Usage dependency)

A stereotyped dependency the source of which is an operation and the target of which is an operation. A call dependency specifies that the source invokes the target operation. A call dependency may connect a source operation to any target operation that is within scope, including, but not limited to, operations of the enclosing classifier and operations of other visible classifiers.

See call, usage.

complete

(constraint on Generalization)

A constraint applied to a set of generalizations, specifying that all children have been specified (although some may be elided) and additional children are not expected to be declared later.

See generalization.

copy

(stereotype of Flow relationship)

A stereotyped flow relationship the source and target of which are different instances, but each with the same values, state instance, and roles (but a distinct identity). A copy dependency from A to B means that B is an exact copy of A. Future changes in A are not necessarily reflected in B. Copy notation is a dashed arrow from the source to the target with the «**copy**» keyword.

See access, copy.

create

(stereotype of BehavioralFeature)

A stereotyped behavioral feature denoting that the designated feature creates an instance of the classifier to which the feature is attached.

(stereotype of Event)

A stereotyped event denoting that the instance enclosing the state machine to which the event type applies is created. Create may be applied only to an initial transition at the top-most level of this state machine. In fact, this is the only kind of trigger that may be applied to an initial transition.

(stereotype of usage Dependency)

Create is a stereotyped dependency denoting that the client classifier creates instances of the supplier classifier.

See creation, usage.

derive

(stereotype of Abstraction dependency)

A stereotyped dependency the source and target of which are elements, usually, but not necessarily, of the same type. A derive dependency specifies that the source may be computed from the target. The source may be implemented for design reasons, such as efficiency, even though it is logically redundant.

See derivation, derived element.

destroy

(stereotype of BehavioralFeature)

A stereotyped behavioral feature denoting that the designated feature destroys an instance of the classifier to which the feature is attached.

(stereotype of Event)

A stereotyped event denoting that the instance enclosing the state machine to which the event type applies is destroyed.

See destruction.

destroyed

(constraint on ClassifierRole and AssociationRole)

Denotes that an instance of the role exists at the beginning of execution of the enclosing interaction but is destroyed prior to completion of execution.
  See association role, classifier role, collaboration, destruction.

disjoint

(constraint on Generalization)

A constraint applied to a set of generalizations, specifying that one object may not be an instance of more than one child in the set of generalizations. This situation would arise only with multiple inheritance.
  See generalization.

document

(stereotype of Component)

A stereotyped component representing a document.
  See component.

documentation

(tag on Element)

A comment, description, or explanation of the element to which it is attached.
  See comment, string.

enumeration

(keyword on Classifier symbol)

A keyword for an enumeration data type, the details of which specify a domain consisting of a set of identifiers that are the possible values of an instance of the data type.
  See enumeration.

executable

(stereotype of Component)

A stereotyped component denoting a program that may be run on a node.
  See component.

extend

(keyword on Dependency symbol)

A keyword on dependency symbol denoting an extend relationship among use cases.

See extend.

facade

(stereotype of Package)

A stereotyped package containing nothing but references to model elements owned by another package. It is used to provide a public view of some of the contents of a package. A facade does not contain any model elements of its own.

See package.

file

(stereotype of Component)

File is a stereotyped component representing a document containing source code or data.

See component.

framework

(stereotype of Package)

A stereotyped package consisting mainly of patterns.

See package.

friend

(stereotype of Permission dependency)

A stereotyped dependency the source of which is a model element, such as an operation, class, or package, and the target of which is a different package model element, such as a class or package. A friend relationship grants the source access to the target, regardless of the declared visibility. It extends the visibility of the source so that the target can see into the source.

See access, friend, visibility.

global

(stereotype of AssociationEnd)

A constraint applied to an association end (including link ends and ends of association roles), specifying that the attached object is visible because it is in a global scope relative to the object at the other end of the link.

See association, association end, collaboration.

implementation

(stereotype of Generalization)

A stereotyped generalization denoting that the client inherits the implementation of the supplier (its attributes, operations, and methods) but does not make public the supplier's interfaces nor guarantee to support them, thereby violating substitutability. This is private inheritance.

See generalization, private inheritance.

implementationClass

(stereotype of Class)

A stereotyped class that is not a type and that represents the implementation of a class in some programming language. An object may be an instance of, at most, one implementation class. By contrast, an object be an instance of multiple ordinary classes at one time and may gain or lose classes over time. An instance of an implementationClass may also be an instance of zero or more types.

See implementation class, type.

implicit

(stereotype of Association)

A stereotype of an association, specifying that the association is not manifest (implemented), only conceptual.

See association.

import

(stereotype of Permission dependency)

A stereotyped dependency between two packages, denoting that the public contents of the target package are added to the namespace of the source package.

See access, import.

include

(keyword on Dependency symbol)

A keyword on dependency symbols denoting an include relationship among use cases.
See include.

incomplete

(constraint on Generalization)

Incomplete is a constraint applied to a set of generalizations, specifying that not all children have been specified and that additional children are expected to be added.
See generalization.

instanceOf

(keyword on Dependency symbol)

A metarelationship the client of which is an instance and the supplier of which is a classifier. An instanceOf dependency from **A** to **B** means that **A** is an instance of **B**. The notation for instanceOf is a dashed arrow with the keyword «instanceOf».
See descriptor, instance, instance of.

instantiate

(stereotype of Usage dependency)

A stereotyped dependency among classifiers indicating that operations on the client create instances of the supplier.
See instantiation, usage.

invariant

(stereotype of Constraint)

A stereotyped constraint that must be attached to a set of classifiers or relationships. It denotes that the conditions of the constraint must hold for the classifiers or relationships and their instances.
See invariant.

leaf

(keyword on GeneralizableElement and BehavioralFeature)

Indicates an element that may not have descendants or may not be overridden—that is, one that is not polymorphic.
See leaf, polymorphic.

library

(stereotype of Component)

A stereotyped component representing a static or dynamic library.
See component.

local

(stereotype of AssociationEnd)

A stereotype of an association end, link end, or association role end, specifying that the attached object is in a local scope of the object on the other end.
See association, association end, collaboration, transient link.

location

(tag on Classifier symbol)

The component that supports the classifier.

(keyword on Component instance symbol)

The node instance on which the component instance resides.
See component, location, node.

metaclass

(stereotype of Classifier)

A stereotyped classifier denoting that the class is a metaclass of some other class.
See metaclass.

new

(constraint on ClassifierRole and AssociationRole)

Denotes that an instance of the role is created during execution of the enclosing interaction and still exists at the completion of execution.
See association role, classifier role, collaboration, creation.

overlapping

(constraint on Generalization)

A constraint applied to a set of generalizations, specifying that an object may be an instance of more than one child in the set of generalizations. The situation can arise only with multiple inheritance or multiple classification.

See generalization.

parameter

(stereotype of AssociationEnd)

A stereotype of association end (including link end and the end of an association role), specifying that an attached object is an argument of a call to an operation on the object on the other end.

See association role, classifier role, collaboration, parameter, transient link.

persistence

(tag on Classifier, Association, and Attribute)

Denotes whether an instance value should outlive the process that created it. Values are persistent and transient. If used on attributes, allows a finer discrimination about which attribute values should be preserved within a classifier.

See persistent object.

postcondition

(stereotype of Constraint)

A stereotyped constraint that must be attached to an operation. It denotes the conditions that must hold after the invocation of the operation.

See postcondition.

powertype

(stereotype of Classifier)

A stereotyped classifier denoting that the classifier is a metaclass whose instances are subclasses of another class.

(keyword on Dependency symbol)

A relationship whose client is a set of generalizations and whose supplier is a powertype. The supplier is the powertype of the client.

See powertype.

precondition

(stereotype of Constraint)

A stereotyped constraint that must be attached to an operation. It denotes the conditions that must hold at the time of invocation of the operation.
See precondition.

process

(stereotype of Classifier)

A stereotyped classifier that is an active class representing a heavyweight process.
See active class, process, thread.

refine

(stereotype on Abstraction dependency)

A stereotype on dependency that denotes a refinement relationship.
See refinement.

requirement

(stereotype of Comment)

A stereotyped comment that states a responsibility or obligation.
See requirement, responsibility.

responsibility

(stereotype on Comment)

A contract by or an obligation of the classifier. It is expressed as a text string.
See responsibility.

self

(stereotype of AssociationEnd)

A stereotype of an association end (including link end and the end of an association role), specifying a pseudolink from an object to itself for the purpose of calling an operation on the same object within an interaction. It does not imply an actual data structure.
See association role, classifier role, collaboration, parameter, transient link.

semantics

(tag on Classifier)

The specification of the meaning of the classifier.

(tag on Operation)

The specification of the meaning of the operation.
  See semantics.

send

(stereotype of Usage dependency)

A stereotyped dependency the client of which is an operation or a classifier and the supplier of which is a signal, specifying that the client sends the signal to some unspecified target.
  See send, signal.

stereotype

(keyword on Classifier symbol)

A keyword for the definition of a stereotype. The name may be used as a stereotype name on other model elements.
  See stereotype.

stub

(stereotype of Package)

A stereotyped package representing a package that provides the public parts of another package, but nothing more.
  Note that the word is also used in UML to describe stubbed transitions.
  See package.

system

(stereotype of Package)

A stereotyped package containing a set of models of a system, describing it from different viewpoints, not necessarily disjoint—the top-most construct in the specification of the system. It also contains relationships and constraints among model elements from different models. These relationships and constraints add no semantic information to the models. Instead they describe the relationships of the models themselves, for instance, requirements tracking and development history.

A system may be realized by a set of subordinate systems, each described by its own set of models collected in a separate system package. A system package can only be contained in a system package.

See package, model, system.

table

(stereotype of Component)

A stereotyped component representing a database table.

See component.

thread

(stereotype of Classifier)

A stereotyped classifier that is an active class, representing a lightweight flow of control.

Note that the word is used in a broader sense in this book to mean any independent, concurrent locus of execution.

See active class, thread.

trace

(keyword on Abstraction dependency)

A keyword on a dependency symbol that denotes a trace relationship.

See trace.

transient

(constraint on ClassifierRole and AssociationRole)

States that an instance of the role is created during execution of the enclosing interaction but is destroyed before completion of execution.

See association role, classifier role, collaboration, creation, destruction, transient link.

type

(stereotype of Class)

A stereotyped class used for specification of a domain of instances (objects), together with the operations applicable to the objects. A type may not contain any methods, but it may have attributes and associations.

See implementation class, type.

use

(keyword on Dependency symbol)

A keyword on dependency that denotes a usage relationship.
See usage.

utility

(stereotype of Classifier)

A stereotyped classifier that has no instances. It describes a named collection of nonmember attributes and operations, all of which are class scope.
See utility.

xor

(constraint on Association)

A constraint applied to a set of associations that share a connection to one class, specifying that any object of the shared class will have links from only one of the associations. It is an exclusive-or (not inclusive-or) constraint.
See association.

Part 4: Appendices ———————

Appendix A
UML Metamodel

UML Definition Documents

The UML is defined by a set of documents published by the Object Management Group [UML-98]. These documents are included on the companion CD to this book. This chapter explains the structure of the UML semantic model described in the documents.

The UML is formally defined using a metamodel—that is, a model of the constructs in UML. The metamodel itself is expressed in UML. This is an example of a metacircular interpreter—that is, a language defined in terms of itself. Things are not completely circular. Only a small subset of UML is used to define the metamodel. In principle, this fixed point of the definition could be bootstrapped from a more basic definition. In practice, going to such lengths is unnecessary.

Each section of the semantic document contains a class diagram showing a portion of the metamodel; a text description of the metamodel classes defined in that section, with their attributes and relationships; a list of constraints on elements expressed in natural language and in OCL; and a text description of the dynamic semantics of the UML constructs defined in the section. The dynamic semantics are therefore informal, but a fully formal description would be both impractical and unreadable by most.

Notation is described in a separate chapter that references the semantics chapter and maps symbols to metamodel classes.

Metamodel Structure

The metamodel is divided into three main packages (Figure A-1).

- The foundation package defines the static structure of the UML.
- The behavioral elements package defines the dynamic structure of the UML.
- The model management package defines the organizational structure of UML models.

Foundation Package

The foundation package contains four subpackages.

Core

The core package describes the main static constructs of the UML. These include classifiers, their contents, and their relationships. Their contents include attribute, operation, method, and parameter. Their relationships include generalization, association, and dependency. Several abstract metaclasses are also defined, such as generalizable element, namespace, and model element. The package also defines template and various kinds of dependency subclasses, as well as component, node, and comment.

Data types

The data types package describes the data type classes used in the metamodel.

Extension mechanisms

The extension mechanisms package describes the constraint, stereotype, and tagged value mechanisms.

Behavioral Elements Package

The behavioral package has a subpackage for each major view plus a package for behavior constructs that are shared by the three major views.

Common behavior

The common behavior package describes signal, operation, and action. It also describes instance classes corresponding to various descriptors.

Collaborations

The collaborations package describes collaboration, interaction, message, classifier role, and association.

Use cases

The use cases package describes actor and use case.

State machines

The state machines package describes state machine structure, including state and various kinds of pseudostate, event, signal, transition, and guard condition. It also describes additional constructs for activity models, such as action state, activity state, and object flow state.

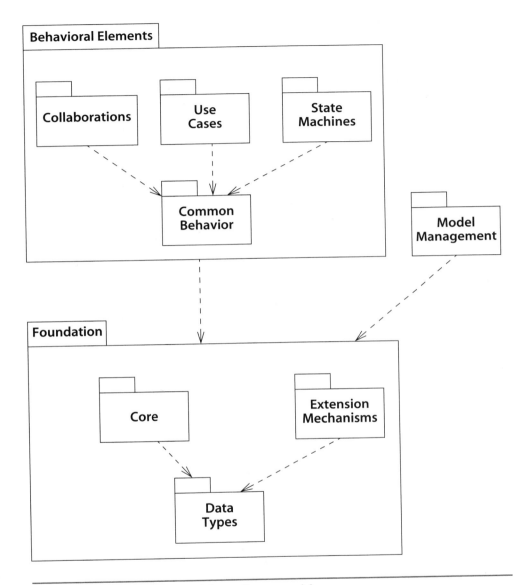

Figure A-1. *Package structure of the UML metamodel*

Model Management Package

The model management package describes package, model, and subsystem. It also describes the ownership and visibility properties of namespaces and packages. It has no subpackages.

Appendix B

Notation Summary

This chapter contains a brief visual summary of notation. The major notational elements are included, but not every variation or option is shown. For full details, see the encyclopedia entry for each element.

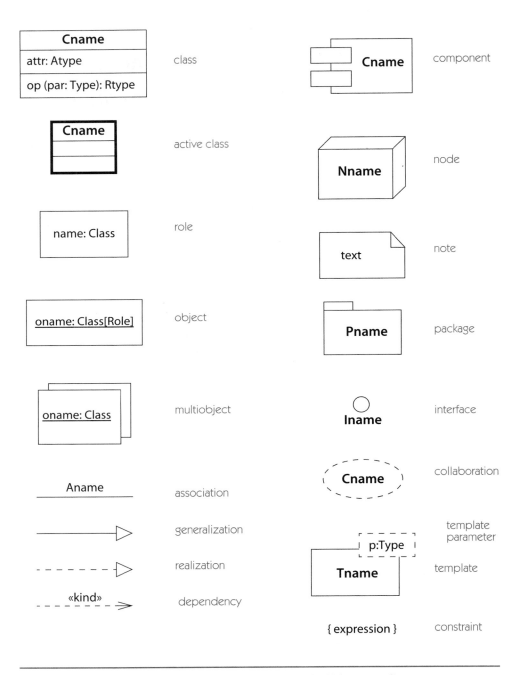

Figure B-1. *Icons on class, component, deployment, and collaboration diagrams*

class

public attribute with initial value

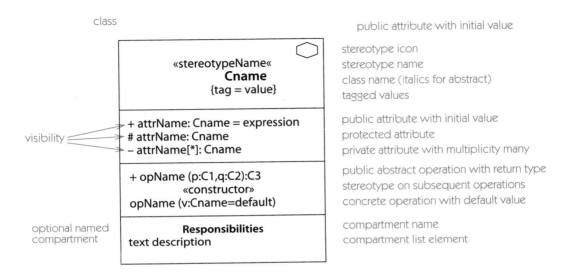

stereotype icon
stereotype name
class name (italics for abstract)
tagged values

public attribute with initial value
protected attribute
private attribute with multiplicity many

public abstract operation with return type
stereotype on subsequent operations
concrete operation with default value

compartment name
compartment list element

Figure B-2. *Class contents*

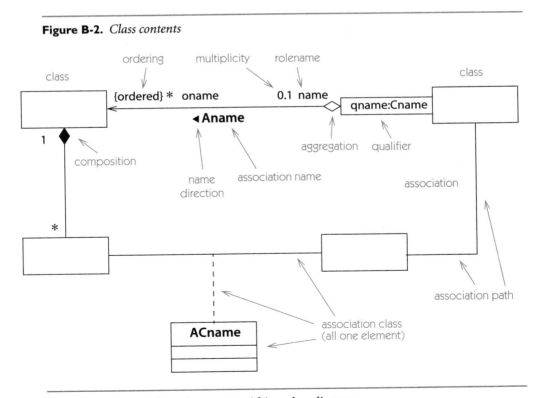

Figure B-3. *Association adornments within a class diagram*

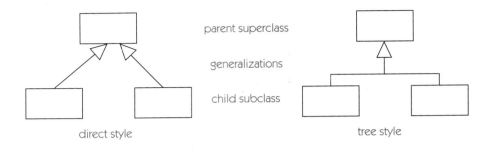

Figure B-4. *Generalization*

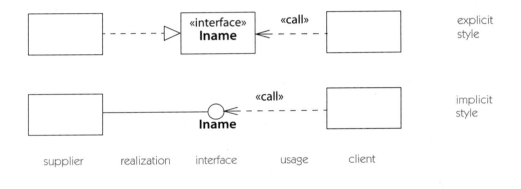

Figure B-5. *Realization of an interface*

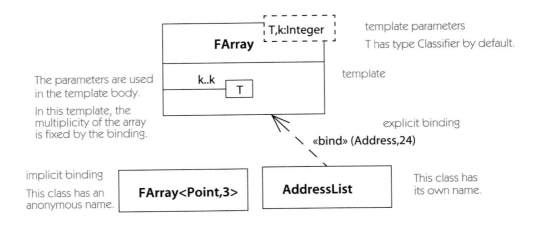

Figure B-6. *Template*

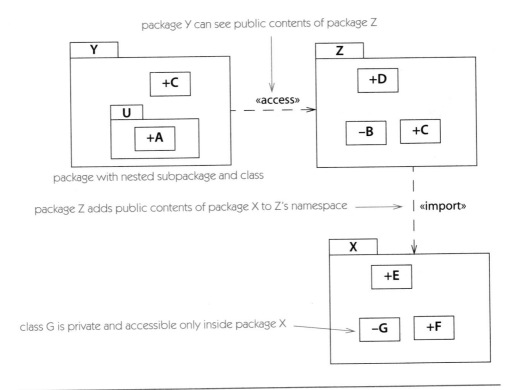

Figure B-7. *Package notation*

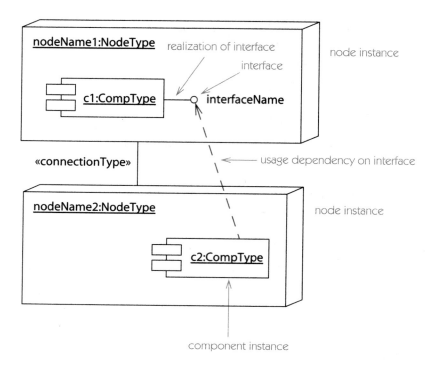

Figure B-8. *Component and node notation*

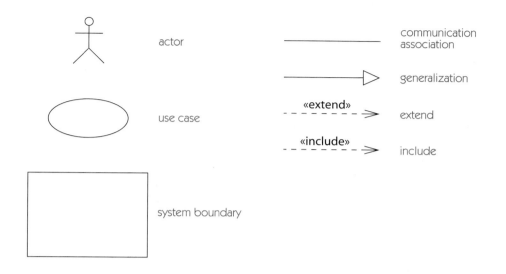

Figure B-9. *Icons on use case diagrams*

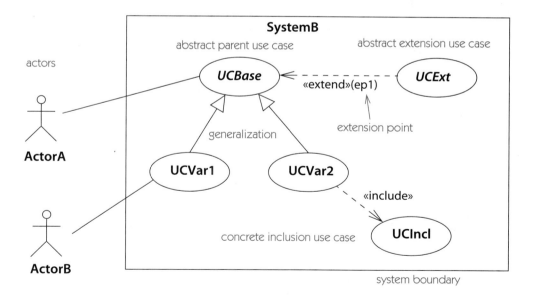

Figure B-10. *Use case diagram notation*

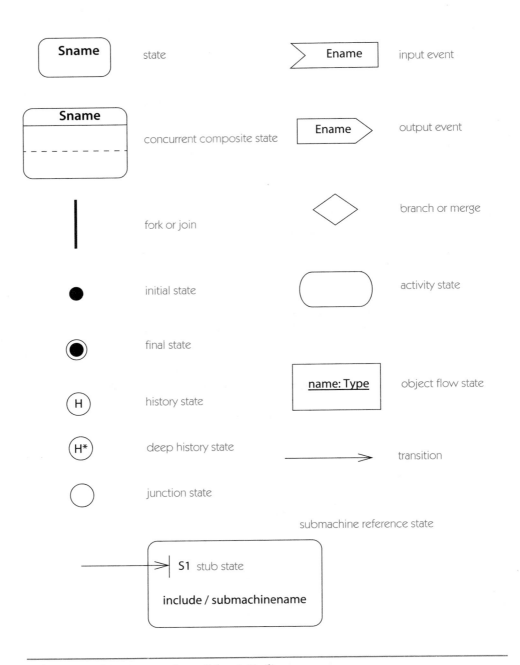

Figure B-11. *Icons on statechart and activity diagrams*

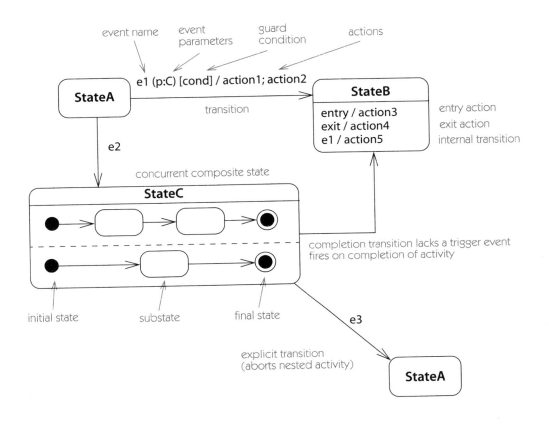

Figure B-12. *Statechart notation*

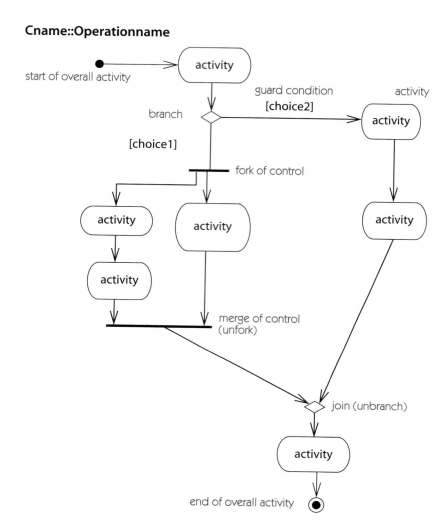

Figure B-13. *Activity diagram notation*

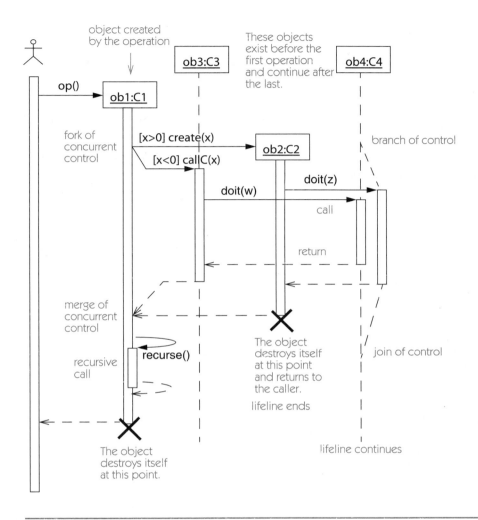

Figure B-14. *Sequence diagram notation*

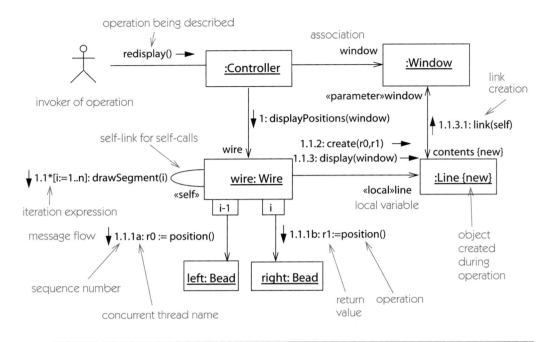

Figure B-15. *Collaboration diagram notation*

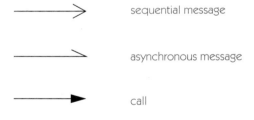

sequential message

asynchronous message

call

Figure B-16. *Message notation*

Appendix C
Process Extensions

Tailoring the UML

The UML is intended to be usable for many purposes. Although UML is a universal language that can express a large number of fundamental modeling properties, there are times when a language tailored to a particular domain area is desirable. In natural languages, cant, jargon, and specialized vocabularies often facilitate communication within a specialized craft or discipline, but impede it with outsiders. The UML can be tailored in a similar way, using various mechanisms, such as naming conventions, style rules, predefined classes, and implicit mappings to software. In particular, a UML extension can be defined using predefined stereotypes, constraints, and tagged values.

The UML has many expressive constructs, so a specialized extension should be avoided unless absolutely necessary. By definition, an extension serves a limited community and can lead to misunderstanding and confusion by those outside. Nevertheless, if a target community is tightly focused, the expressive power of an extension can sometimes outweigh the loss of uniformity. Over time, some extensions may be useful enough to add to standard UML; others may fall into disuse.

This chapter describes two extensions packaged with the UML documents themselves. Their use is not mandatory or even recommended necessarily, but they indicate how an extension can be defined for a development process. A number of similar extensions have been defined in the literature.

Software Development Process Extensions

These extensions are based on the Objectory development process, a precursor to the Unified Process. They are intended for use during a software development process that consists of four stages: use case capture, analysis, design, and implementation.

These extensions include stereotypes on packaging units, classes, and associations, as well as some constraints on connecting elements. There are no new tags.

Table C-1: *Organizational Stereotypes for Software Development Process*

Base Class	Stereotypes by Process Stage			
	Use Case	*Analysis*	*Design*	*Implementation*
model	use case model	analysis model	design model	implementation model
package	use case system use case package			implementation system implementation subsystem
subsystem		analysis system analysis subsystem analysis service package	design system design subsystem design service package	

Organizational Stereotypes

Table C-1 shows the organizational stereotypes—that is, the stereotypes on model, package, and subsystem. There are various stereotypes applicable to each stage of development. In the Objectory process, each stage has a distinct model, with trace relationships among elements in different models. From top to bottom, the terms system, subsystem, and service package describe layers of packaging.

The organizational stereotypes do not have special icons. They are shown as folder icons, with the stereotype name in guillemets, as shown in Figure C-1.

Class stereotypes

Three stereotypes are defined on class: control, boundary, and entity. They are shown in Figure C-2.

A *control class* describes objects that manage interactions, such as a transaction manager, a device controller, or an operating system monitor. It has behavior specific to a use case. A control class usually does not outlive the use case that it supports. A control class is displayed as a circle with an arrowhead on it.

A *boundary class* describes objects that mediate between a system and outside actors, such as an order entry form or a sensor. It is displayed as a circle with a T-bar attached to it. Boundary objects often exist for the life of a system.

An *entity class* describes objects that are passive. They do not initiate interactions. Entity objects may participate in many use cases and usually outlive single interactions. It is displayed as a circle with a line under it.

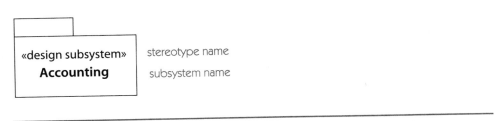

Figure C-1. *Organizational stereotype notation for software development process*

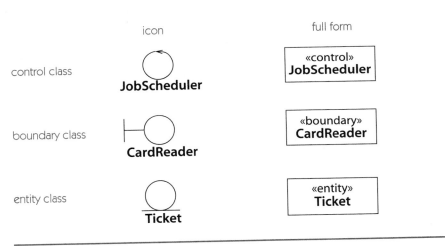

Figure C-2. *Class stereotypes for software development process*

Association stereotypes

There are two stereotypes on association: communicate and subscribe. The notation is an association path with the stereotype name in guillemets.

A *communicate association* connects an actor to a use case with which it communicates. This is the only association between actors and use cases, so the keyword may be omitted.

A *subscribe association* connects a client class (the subscriber) to a supplier class (the publisher). The subscriber specifies a set of events the publisher may produce. The subscriber is notified when one of the events occurs.

Business Modeling Extensions

These extensions are intended for modeling real-world business organizations and for understanding real-world situations, rather than the implementation of software. These stereotypes are not necessary for business modeling, but they cover some common situations.

These extensions include stereotypes on packaging units, classes, and associations, as well as some constraints on connecting elements. There are no new tags.

Organizational stereotypes

Table C-2 shows the organizational stereotypes for business process modeling.

The use case model is a model of the use case view. The use case system and use case package are two layers of organization of its content.

The object model is a model of the internal structure of the business system. The object system is its top-level subsystem that contains organizational units and work units as lower layers. An organizational unit corresponds to an organizational unit of the actual business, and a work unit is a smaller, but meaningful, grouping.

Table C-2: *Organizational Stereotypes for Business Modeling*

Base Class	Use Case Capture	Object Model
model	use case model	object model
package	use case system use case package	
subsystem		object system organization unit work unit

There are no special icons for business modeling organizational units; they use the folder symbol with a stereotype in guillemets.

Class stereotypes

In addition to actors (defined in standard UML), business objects have several stereotypes on class—worker, case worker, internal worker, entity. They are shown in Figure C-3.

A worker represents a human who acts within the system. A case worker is a worker who interacts directly with outside actors. An internal worker is a worker who interacts with workers and entities within the system.

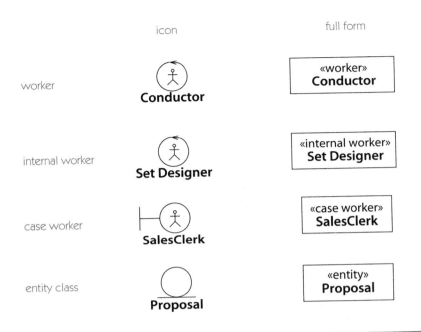

Figure C-3. *Class stereotypes for business modeling*

An entity class describes objects that are passive. They do not initiate interactions. Entity objects may participate in many use cases and usually outlive single interactions. In a work situation, entities usually represent work products.

Association stereotypes

There are two stereotypes on association: communicate and subscribe. These are the same as for the software development process. The notation is an association path with the stereotype keyword in guillemets.

A communicate association connects an actor to a use case with which it communicates. This is the only association between actors and use cases, so the keyword may be omitted.

A subscribe association connects a client class (the subscriber) to a supplier class (the publisher). The subscriber specifies a set of events that the publisher may produce. The subscriber is notified when one of the events occurs.

Bibliography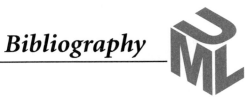

[**Blaha-98**] Michael Blaha, William Premerlani. *Object-Oriented Modeling and Design for Database Applications*. Prentice Hall, Upper Saddle River, N.J., 1998.

[**Booch-91**] Grady Booch. *Object-Oriented Analysis and Design with Applications, 1st ed.* Benjamin/Cummings, Redwood City, Calif., 1991.

[**Booch-94**] Grady Booch. *Object-Oriented Analysis and Design with Applications, 2nd ed.* Benjamin/Cummings, Redwood City, Calif., 1994.

[**Booch-96a**] Grady Booch. *Object Solutions: Managing the Object-Oriented Project*. Addison-Wesley, Menlo Park, Calif., 1996.

[**Booch-96b**] Grady Booch. *Best of Booch: Designing Strategies for Object Technology*. SIGS Books, New York, N.Y., 1996.

[**Booch-99**] Grady Booch, James Rumbaugh, Ivar Jacobson. *The Unified Modeling Language User Guide*. Addison-Wesley, Reading, Mass., 1999.

[**Buschmann-96**] Frank Buschmann, Regine Meunier, Hans Rohnert, Peter Sommerlad, Michael Stal. *Pattern-Oriented Software Architecture: A System of Patterns*. Wiley, Chichester, U.K., 1996.

[**Coad-91**] Peter Coad, Edward Yourdon. *Object-Oriented Analysis, 2nd ed.* Yourdon Press, Englewood Cliffs, N.J., 1991.

[**Coleman-94**] Derek Coleman, Patrick Arnold, Stephanie Bodoff, Chris Dollin, Helena Gilchrist, Fiona Hayes, Paul Jeremaes. *Object-Oriented Development: The Fusion Method*. Prentice Hall, Englewood Cliffs, N.J., 1994.

[**Cox-86**] Brad J. Cox. *Object-Oriented Programming: An Evolutionary Approach*. Addison-Wesley, Reading, Mass., 1986.

[**Embley-92**] Brian W. Embley, Barry D. Kurtz, Scott N. Woodfield. *Object-Oriented Systems Analysis: A Model-Driven Approach*. Yourdon Press, Englewood Cliffs, N.J., 1992.

[**Gamma-95**] Erich Gamma, Richard Helm, Ralph Johnson, John Vlissides. *Design Patterns: Elements of Reusable Object-Oriented Software*. Addison-Wesley, Reading, Mass., 1995.

[Goldberg-83] Adele Goldberg, David Robson. *Smalltalk-80: The Language and Its Implementation.* Addison-Wesley, Reading, Mass., 1983.

[Harel-98] David Harel, Michal Politi. *Modeling Reactive Systems With Statecharts: The STATEMATE Approach.* McGraw-Hill, New York, N.Y., 1998.

[Jacobson-92] Ivar Jacobson, Magnus Christerson, Patrik Jonsson, Gunnar Övergaard. *Object-Oriented Software Engineering: A Use Case Driven Approach.* Addison-Wesley, Wokingham, England, 1992.

[Jacobson-95] Ivar Jacobson, Maria Ericsson, Agneta Jacobson. *The Object Advantage: Business Process Reengineering with Object Technology.* Addison-Wesley, Wokingham, England, 1995.

[Jacobson-97] Ivar Jacobson, Martin Griss, Patrik Jonsson. *Software Reuse: Architecture, Process and Organization for Business Success.* Addison-Wesley, Harlow, England, 1997.

[Jacobson-99] Ivar Jacobson, Grady Booch, James Rumbaugh. *The Unified Software Development Process.* Addison-Wesley, Reading, Mass., 1999.

[Martin-92] James Martin, James Odell. *Object-Oriented Analysis and Design.* Prentice Hall, Englewood Cliffs, N.J., 1992.

[Meyer-88] Bertrand Meyer. *Object-Oriented Software Construction.* Prentice Hall, New York, N.Y., 1988.

[Rumbaugh-91] James Rumbaugh, Michael Blaha, William Premerlani, Frederick Eddy, William Lorensen. *Object-Oriented Modeling and Design.* Prentice Hall, Englewood Cliffs, N.J., 1991.

[Rumbaugh-96] James Rumbaugh. *OMT Insights: Perspectives on Modeling from the Journal of Object-Oriented Technology.* SIGS Books, New York, N.Y., 1996.

[Rumbaugh-99] James Rumbaugh, Ivar Jacobson, Grady Booch. *The Unified Modeling Language Reference Manual.* Addison-Wesley, Reading, Mass., 1999.

[Selic-94] Bran Selic, Garth Gullekson, Paul T. Ward. *Real-Time Object-Oriented Modeling.* Wiley, New York, N.Y., 1994.

[Shlaer-88] Sally Shlaer, Stephen J. Mellor. *Object-Oriented Systems Analysis: Modeling the World in Data.* Yourdon Press, Englewood Cliffs, N.J., 1988.

[Shlaer-92] Sally Shlaer, Stephen J. Mellor. *Object Lifecycles: Modeling the World in States.* Yourdon Press, Englewood Cliffs, N.J., 1992.

[UML-98] *Unified Modeling Language Specification.* Object Management Group, Framingham, Mass., 1998. Internet: www.omg.org.

[Ward-85] Paul Ward, Stephen J. Mellor. *Structured Development for Real-Time Systems: Introduction and Tools.* Yourdon Press, Englewood Cliffs, N.J., 1985.

[Warmer-99] Jos B. Warmer, Anneke G. Kleppe. *The Object Constraint Language: Precise Modeling with UML.* Addison-Wesley, Reading, Mass., 1999.

[Wirfs-Brock-90] Rebecca Wirfs-Brock, Brian Wilkerson, Lauren Wiener. *Designing Object-Oriented Software.* Prentice Hall, Englewood Cliffs, N.J., 1990.

[Yourdon-79] Edward Yourdon, Larry L. Constantine. *Structured Design: Fundamentals of a Discipline of Computer Program and Systems Design.* Yourdon Press, Englewood Cliffs, N.J., 1979.

Index

Main entries are in boldface; references to figures are in italics.

Addison-Wesley Computer and Engineering Publishing Group

How to Interact with Us

1. Visit our Web site

http://www.awl.com/cseng

When you think you've read enough, there's always more content for you at Addison-Wesley's web site. Our web site contains a directory of complete product information including:

- Chapters
- Exclusive author interviews
- Links to authors' pages
- Tables of contents
- Source code

You can also discover what tradeshows and conferences Addison-Wesley will be attending, read what others are saying about our titles, and find out where and when you can meet our authors and have them sign your book.

2. Subscribe to Our Email Mailing Lists

Subscribe to our electronic mailing lists and be the first to know when new books are publishing. Here's how it works: Sign up for our electronic mailing at **http://www.awl.com/cseng/mailinglists.html**. Just select the subject areas that interest you and you will receive notification via email when we publish a book in that area.

3. Contact Us via Email

cepubprof@awl.com

Ask general questions about our books.
Sign up for our electronic mailing lists.
Submit corrections for our web site.

bexpress@awl.com

Request an Addison-Wesley catalog.
Get answers to questions regarding your order or our products.

innovations@awl.com

Request a current Innovations Newsletter.

webmaster@awl.com

Send comments about our web site.

jcs@awl.com

Submit a book proposal.
Send errata for an Addison-Wesley book.

cepubpublicity@awl.com

Request a review copy for a member of the media interested in reviewing new Addison-Wesley titles.

We encourage you to patronize the many fine retailers who stock Addison-Wesley titles. Visit our online directory to find stores near you or visit our online store: **http://store.awl.com/** or call **800-824-7799**.

Addison Wesley Longman
Computer and Engineering Publishing Group
One Jacob Way, Reading, Massachusetts 01867 USA
TEL 781-944-3700 • FAX 781-942-3076